HESTER

ALSO BY IAN MCINTYRE

The Proud Doers: Israel after Twenty Years

Words: Reflections on the Use of Language
(editor and contributor)

Dogfight: The Transatlantic Battle over Airbus

The Expense of Glory: A Life of John Reith

Robert Burns: A Life

Garrick

*Joshua Reynolds: The Life and Times of the
First President of the Royal Academy*

❧ HESTER ❧

*The Remarkable Life of Dr Johnson's
'Dear Mistress'*

IAN McINTYRE

CONSTABLE
London

Constable & Robinson Ltd
3 The Lanchesters
162 Fulham Palace Road
London W6 9ER
www.constablerobinson.com

First published in the UK by Constable,
an imprint of Constable & Robinson, 2008

A copy of the British Library Cataloguing in Publication
Data is available from the British Library

ISBN: 978-1-84529-449-6

Set in Monotype Fournier by Ewan Smith, London
Printed and bound in the EU

1 3 5 7 9 10 8 6 4 2

HLM
1925–92
Best of brothers

Contents

Illustrations

1. *Hester Lynch Thrale* by Richard Cosway. Reproduced by courtesy of the Harry Ransom Humanities Research Center, the University of Texas at Austin.

2. *Henry Thrale* after Sir Joshua Reynolds. Reproduced by courtesy of the Houghton Library, Harvard College Library [MS Hyde 74 (2.135)].

3. *Mrs Thrale and Her Daughter Hester* by Sir Joshua Reynolds. © Bridgeman Art Library/Beaverbrook Art Gallery, Fredericton, N.B., Canada.

4. *Thrale Place* by William Ellis. Reproduced by courtesy of Guildhall Library, City of London.

5. *The Southwark Macaroni* by M. Darly. © Trustees of the British Museum.

6. *Sophia Streatfeild*. Miniature by an unknown artist. Reproduced by courtesy of the Houghton Library, Harvard College Library [MS Hyde 75 (3.339)].

7. *Barclay's Brewery, 1829*, after William Henry Prior, reproduced by courtesy of Ash Rare Books.

8. *The Family Book*. Reproduced by courtesy of the Houghton Library, Harvard College Library [MS Hyde 35 (3)].

9. *Samuel Johnson* by James Barry. © National Portrait Gallery, London.

10. *Giuseppe Baretti* after Sir Joshua Reynolds. © National Portrait Gallery, London.

11. *Fanny Burney* by Edward Francisco Burney. © National Portrait Gallery, London.

12. *Gabriel Piozzi*. Artist unknown. Reproduced by courtesy of the Houghton Library, Harvard College Library [*2003JM-9].

13. *Hester Lynch Thrale* by Robert Edge Pine. Reproduced by courtesy of Scottish & Newcastle UK.

14. *Mrs Montagu*. Print by John Raphael Smith after Sir Joshua Reynolds. © Trustees of the British Museum.

15. *Sarah Siddons* by John Downman. © National Portrait Gallery, London.

16. *James Boswell* after Sir Thomas Lawrence. © National Portrait Gallery, London.

17. *'Signor Piozzi ravishing M*ˢ *Thrale.'* Caricature by Samuel Collings. Print Collection, Miriam and Ira D. Wallach Division of Art, Prints and Photographs, New York Public Library, Astar, Lenox and Tilden Foundation.

18. *'Bozzy Madame Piozzi.'* Caricature by Thomas Rowlandson. © Trustees of the British Museum.

19. *Hester Lynch Piozzi* by George Dance. © National Portrait Gallery, London.

20. *William Augustus Conway* by George Henry Harlow. Courtesy of the Royal Shakespeare Company.

21. *John Piozzi Salusbury Piozzi* by John Jackson. Reproduced by courtesy of the Houghton Library, Harvard College Library [*2003JM-6].

22. *Brynbella*. Watercolour by Harriet Salusbury. Reproduced by courtesy of the Houghton Library, Harvard College Library [*2003JM-23].

23. *Mrs Hester Lynch Piozzi*. Engraving published in *The Ladies' Monthly Museum*, February 1820. Reproduced by courtesy of the London Library.

Preface

Hester Salusbury – Hester Thrale – Hester Piozzi. Diminutive, witty, impulsive, warm-hearted. The only child of impoverished Welsh gentry. Born in the reign of George II, she outlived John Keats. A precocious child, she grew into a remarkable woman – a good deal more remarkable than tabloid labels like 'Dr Johnson's Mrs Thrale' suggest.

It is of course true that for sixteen years she frequently sat into the small hours brewing countless cups of tea for the 'Great Insatiable' – and keeping her end up in strenuous bouts of verbal pugilism. But that is only part of the story. She also endured more than a dozen pregnancies – and after her first husband's death, married her daughters' Italian music master.

We know as much as we do about this semi-detached bluestocking because throughout her long life she was a compulsive scribbler. Shortly before her thirteenth wedding anniversary, her first husband – rich brewer, philanderer, rider to foxhounds, Member of Parliament – presented her with six handsome blank volumes. Over the next thirty years she filled their pages with her bold masculine hand – poetry, gossip, cameo portraits of friends and enemies, religious speculation, her views on domestic politics and the French Revolution. It is a goldmine for anyone writing about her or her acquaintances. Its range of reference is unequalled. 'From Cato to Cuzzona, & from Cuzzona to Cumberland,' she wrote. It is that and much more – from Johnson to Napoleon, from Streatham to Milan, from Latin epigrams to the price of a shirt in 1801.

Thraliana, as this glorious ragbag is called, is lodged in the Huntington Library in California and was edited more than sixty years ago by Katharine Balderston. Nobody writing about Georgian and Regency England gets any distance without incurring substantial debts to American academic scholarship. That to Professor Balderston is one of many. The 1940s also saw the publication of the first modern biography of Hester; it was the work of the distinguished Johnson scholar James L.

Clifford, and it remains an outstanding monument of Thrale/Piozzi scholarship.

There has in recent years been a good deal more interest in women's writing than there was in Clifford's day, and I have sought to reflect this in telling again the story of Hester's eventful life. Many more of her letters have also come to light in the intervening years. I have been greatly helped in my research by the splendid six-volume edition of her later correspondence edited by Edward and Lillian Bloom for the University of Carolina Press – sparkling, witty, vivid letters to her children, to her friends, to actors, servants, lawyers and business acquaintances.

Our understanding of her has also been enriched by the American scholar William McCarthy's *Hester Thrale Piozzi, Portrait of a Literary Woman*, a sensitive study of the formidable range of her output – her *Anecdotes of Johnson*, her *Observations and Reflections*, the entertaining travel book that grew out of her extended honeymoon with her second husband, and *Retrospection*, an ambitious attempt at a world history. Yet another stone was added to the cairn by Margaret Anne Doody, who contributed a perceptive new introduction when a second edition of Clifford's book was published in 1987.

Quotations from the Thrale/Piozzi material held by the University of Manchester are reproduced courtesy of the University Librarian and Director, the John Rylands University Library; I am grateful to Dr Dorothy Clayton for granting the necessary permission. Quotations from a manuscript in the Donald and Mary Hyde Collection of Dr Samuel Johnson are made courtesy of the Houghton Library, Harvard College Library, and I am grateful to John Overholt, the Assistant Curator of the Collection, for agreeing to their use and for much valuable advice about the Library's holdings.

Spelling was still in a fluid state in the eighteenth century, and the oddities and inconsistencies of Hester's in her letters and *Thraliana* have been preserved – she could, for instance, never quite decide whether *i* came before or after *e* in writing the name of Sophy Streatfeild, her sometime rival for the affections of her first husband.

Although it would be tedious to do so on every occasion, an indication of comparative money values is sometimes given in the text. In the year of Hester's birth, £100, using the retail price index, would today be worth approximately £13,000. By the time she died in 1821, the equivalent figure would be just under £7,000.

No book is solely the work of the author. As so often in the past, my wife patiently read each chapter as it was written and had a view about it. So did Louise Greenberg, who brings to literary agency the energy and qualities of mind that shaped so many outstanding programmes during her years as a producer and editor at the BBC.

I was greatly helped in the hunt for illustrations by Melissa Atkinson of the National Portrait Gallery; Kathryn Charles-Wilson of British Museum Images; Sarah Dick of the Beaverbrook Art Gallery, Fredericton, New Brunswick; Andrea Felder and Stephan Saks of the New York Public Library; Tina Gostling of Scottish & Newcastle UK Ltd; Mary Haegert of the Houghton Library at Harvard; Seamus McKenna of COLLAGE (London Metropolitan Archives); Lindsay Nutbrown of Thomas Ross Ltd; Helen O'Neill of the London Library; Caroline Ray and David Howells of the Royal Shakespeare Company; Rick Watson of the Harry Ransom Center, the University of Texas at Austin and Laurence Worms of Ash Rare Books.

The elegant design of the book is the work of Ewan Smith, who hit on the imaginative idea of setting it in a font by the celebrated eighteenth-century French typographer Pierre-Simon Fournier. The jacket was the responsibility of Max Burnell, the copy-editor was Jacqueline Jackson, the index was compiled by Ed Emery; publicity was the province of Sam Evans. Andreas Campomar took a kindly interest in the manuscript when it was first delivered, and Eli Dryden, Constable & Robinson's Managing Editor, kept a watchful eye on the various stages of the production process. To all of them I offer my warmest thanks – as I also do most specially to Becky Hardie, whom it was my great good fortune to have as my editor.

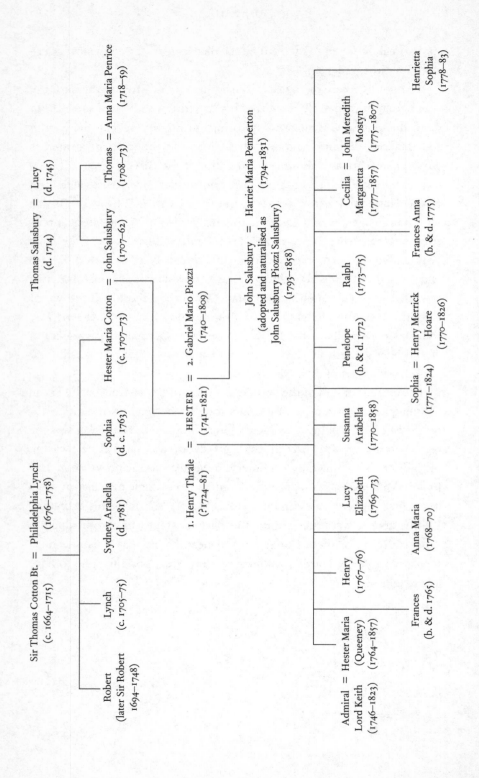

1741–63
Hester Salusbury

Daughter of Wales

SHE COULD be a bit of a bore about her family. Her various accounts of the origins of the Salusburys call to mind the chapter in Genesis that rehearses the generations of the sons of Noah. Was there an Adam of Salzburg who came over in 1070 in the train of the Conqueror? Almost certainly not. Was there a crusader called Henry Salusbury, knighted on the field of battle by Richard Cœur de Lion? Possibly. What is not in dispute is that the girl born to Hester and John Salusbury near Pwllheli in Caernarvonshire in 1741 was descended on both sides from Catrin of Berain, granddaughter of an illegitimate son of Henry VII, and known, because of the prodigious number of her descendants, as *Mam Cymru* – Mother of Wales.

Throughout her life, Hester was inordinately proud of her Welsh ancestry – of Mam Cymru and her four husbands and many lovers, of Sir John the Strong ('he had two Thumbs on each Hand, and was eminent for performing singular Feats') and of her pious paternal grandmother, Lucy, who had 'been educated herself to Literature, being an Eleve of the famous Doctor Halley the Astronomer'.

She had less reason to be proud of her father. John Salusbury's mother had been widowed when he was four and the family estate in Flintshire, Bach-y-Graig, with its striking six-storey mansion built of Dutch bricks, was heavily mortgaged. The redoubtable Lucy nevertheless resolved that her sons 'should not be bred in Ignorance'; she sent them first to Whitchurch School and subsequently contrived to have John and his brother Thomas entered at Trinity Hall, Cambridge.[1] After taking his MA, John Salusbury had gravitated to London – 'a wild young Fellow with Spirit to spend Money', although that was a commodity of which he was in chronically short supply. After his death, his daughter would paint a highly coloured but circumstantial picture of his bachelor days in London, where she asserts he rubbed along for a time as a gigolo, initially to 'a very famous Woman' called Harriott Edwards: 'She was a Young Person of large & independent Fortune, who set Reputation at Nought, & Scandal at Defiance; resolved to avoid Marriage, yet have a Son on whom to settle her Estate. She took as I have been told a fancy to my Father; whom She supplied with Money as long as her Taste to his Company subsisted ...'

Salusbury subsequently toured the continent as travelling companion to his cousin Sir Robert Cotton. There, we are told — the sequence would not be out of place in a novel by Henry Fielding — he formed an attachment to a French marquise, who died in his arms after a six-month dalliance at Lyons, '& left him the little he had not spent of hers before'.

Robert Cotton had succeeded to the baronetcy at the age of twenty-one. His mother, Philadelphia Lynch, daughter of a governor of Jamaica, had been married at thirteen and widowed at thirty-four; she had in that time borne her husband seventeen children. Our interest is in Hester Maria, the eleventh of the brood, eight years old at the time of her father's death, and, after her mother's remarriage to an Irish officer, neglected and half-starved. When she was eighteen, she ran away and put herself under the protection of her brother Robert and his wife. At first she was treated as a Cinderella; although Sir Robert successfully pursued their mother at law over their inheritance, it was several years before Hester Maria and her sisters received their due.

Gradually, however, this 'untaught Gawkee Girl' acquired some education; more importantly, 'She became so lovely a Creature both in Body & Mind, that her Bro^r Sir Robert grew proud of her, and she was always about with him & Lady Betty, who introduced her into gay Life.' Her wit and her beauty brought her many tempting proposals of marriage: 'She, however, declined accepting any, having secretly set her Heart upon her flashy Cousin John.'

. The end of 1738 found flashy 'Cousin John' back in England. He was now thirty-one — the same age as Hester Maria — with his finances in a worse state than ever. The nature of his feelings for his cousin is unclear, although it is known that they had been in correspondence. Years later, their daughter wrote of her mother's 'Mad Attachment'. Matters moved swiftly. Early in 1739, Hester Maria commissioned Thomas

Salusbury, now making his way as a lawyer in Doctors' Commons,[2] to travel to Wales on her behalf and settle the most pressing of his brother's debts.

From Bach-y-Graig he sent her a detailed account of how her money had been spent. The letter is postmarked 12 February. The following day a marriage settlement was signed in London. Hester Maria's liquid capital amounted to £2,500 – about £320,000 today. Of this, £1,200 was to be employed for the immediate settlement of encumbrances on her cousin's estate. She also had an annuity of £125 a year for as long as her mother should live. Her trustees were adamant that John Salusbury should place a number of his properties in trust for Hester Maria as her marriage portion.[3]

'I return you my best thanks for make poor Jack yors,' old Lucy wrote to her new daughter-in-law.[4] The bride's brother was less pleased. Sir Robert Cotton, who was Lord Lieutenant of Denbigh, had previously thought well enough of his erstwhile travelling companion to appoint him his Deputy and Captain of the local Militia.[5] The idea of acquiring him as a brother-in-law did not appeal, however, and he declared, 'he would never see either of them more'.

A house in London was out of the question. With Hester Maria's capital heavily depleted there remained only her annuity of £125. Salusbury himself had an income of £80–£100 a year from a small estate in Caernarvonshire, and there, in the Lleyn peninsula, they found a farmhouse to rent. It was known as Bodvel Hall. Old Lucy sent furniture from Bach-y-Graig. The newly-weds moved in in the spring of 1739, and it was there that their only child was born on 16 January 1741.[6]

Years later, accompanied by her husband and Dr Johnson, Hester Thrale revisited her birthplace. She did not warm to what she saw: 'It is a truly wild & solitary Place; the whole circumjacent Country varying only from Bog to Mountain, from Mountain to Bog; 115 Miles from the nearest English Ground …'

Life in this remote backwater was not good for John Salusbury's temper. He and his wife were both, in their daughter's phrase, 'People of strong Parts', and his irascibility soon turned to violence. Hester's account of relations between her parents in those early years of their marriage makes chilling reading:

Now for a Woman to quarrel with her Husband under the Eye of the
World may sometimes perhaps answer a trifling Purpose, but for a
Woman to contend with a Man She is shut up with at a Distance from
Society, where the natural Roughness of the Sex is not restrained ...
is so dangerous, that I wonder almost how She escaped with her Life,
which was as I have been credibly informed, not seldom in actual
Danger.

Hester Maria worked hard at her marriage, teaching her infant daughter 'to play a thousand pretty Tricks, & tell a Thousand pretty Stories
and repeat a Thousand pretty verses to divert Papa'. The strategy had
some success:

Rakish men seldom make tender Fathers, but a Man must fondle something ... I therefore grew a great favourite it seems, in spite of his long
continued Efforts to dislike me, and now they had a Centre of Unity in
their Offspring for which both were equally interested, they began to
agree a little better I believe, & bear with patience their Irrevocable Lot.

Salusbury's lot, it seemed, was to sink beneath an ever-heavier burden
of debt. His outrageous treatment of his wife was attributable partly to
a gnawing anxiety over the tangled skein of the broader family finances.
His mother's inept management of Bach-y-Graig and her extravagant
determination to keep up appearances had swelled the mortgage on the
estate. And then there was brother Thomas, whose visits 'were always
for Money'. Years later, his niece dipped her pen in acid to describe his
single-minded pursuit of legal preferment. He lived, she wrote:

from Lord to Duke, & from Bishop to Baronet, making himself agreeable by a pliant disposition, high Health and Sweet Temper, & expecting daily the Reward of his Diligence in some lucrative Place; must be
maintained in Clothes Horses etc. to carry on his Schemes, which my
Father fully believ'd would answer sometime, so cheerfully paid all
Expences, for old Lucy had always inculcated it strongly, that whatever
my Father possessed, my Uncle was always to share.

The only part of the Salusbury family properties not now mortgaged
to the hilt were those farms cleared of debt through Hester Maria's

generosity at the time of the marriage. After five years of marriage, Salusbury bullied his wife into agreeing that her portion should be attached; he and Thomas travelled to London carrying a letter written under duress to her trustees, arranged for the jointure to be remortgaged and apportioned the lion's share of the receipts to Thomas. More than thirty years later Hester wrote bitterly about the transaction as 'The Mortgage laid by fraud & Violence on my poor Mother's Joynture for Sir Thomas Salusbury's emolument.'

Lucy Salusbury died the following year, enjoining John and Thomas on her deathbed to care for their handicapped brother and, somewhat superfluously, one might think, 'never to possess an undivided Guinea'. Her granddaughter closed the chapter of the old lady's life with a sardonic passage in *Thraliana*: 'My Uncle returned to his Quality Friends with the marks of honest Sorrow on his Face, for which everybody honor'd pitied and esteemed him; and my Father came home to his Wife swearing that *no virtuous* Woman *now* was *left in being.*'

Such boorishness from her husband made the poverty and deprivation of her early married life all the more difficult for Hester Maria to bear. In all their years at Bodvel Hall she only ever bought one new gown, and that cost a guinea from a pedlar at the door. And yet for all the brittleness and misery of their existence together, the Salusburys found it possible to encourage and indulge the precocity of their small daughter: 'I was their Joynt Play Thing, & although Education was a Word then unknown, as applied to females; They had taught me to read, & speak, & think; & translate from the French, till I was half a Prodigy.'[7] When she was four, she was given the translation of Homer by the Scottish author John Ogilby; before she was seven the books in her little library included translations of Plutarch and Livy.

Six months after Old Lucy died there was a death on the other side of the family and Hester Maria's estranged brother, Robert, found himself a widower at fifty-one.[8] There had been no children of the marriage. Sir Robert heartily disliked the wife of his brother Lynch, who now became his heir. Bereft of his wife, he had also recently lost his seat in Parliament. Lonely, and with little to occupy the empty hours, his thoughts turned wistfully to the estranged sister of whom he had been so fond; he invited the Salusburys to come and live with him at Lleweney Hall.

Thirty years later Hester set down an account of Sir Robert's reception of his poor relations: 'My *Father* was received *civilly*, my Mother kindly, and myself Affectionately: so that it seems I told Sir Robert the next Day – why Sir said I "how good & kind you are at last? And there my Papa & Mama have been puzz'ling what *they* should say, and what I should say to the *old Baronet* as they call you to one another ..."' The doting parents presumably wished that the earth would swallow them; the 'old Baronet', it seems, responded with 'Astonishment & Delight': 'Sir Robert, after mentioning my Superiority to the Children of his next Brother ... protested that if I would live always with him, I should be his Housekeeper, & he would give me ten Thousand Pounds.'

The Salusburys remained under Sir Robert's roof for several months. He became greatly attached to his niece – Fiddle, as he called her – and she to him: 'I always was in his Sight, reading the Roman History, or marking on the Maps the Places where Battles had been Fought, and such like fancies.'

Her uncle's keen interest in all she did extended to her handwriting, which was formed early and would remain clear and firm to her dying day. For a small child, her hands were unusually large and muscular. When she was an old lady one of her admirers complimented her on the 'exquisite beauty' of her writing. Spreading out her fingers, she offered him an explanation: 'I owe what you are pleased to call my good writing, to the shape of this hand, for my uncle, Sir Robert Cotton, thought it was too manly to be employed in writing like a boarding-school girl; and so I came by my vigorous, black manuscript.'[9]

It was all too good to last. Before long Sir Robert suggested to his brother-in-law that while his wife and daughter were welcome to remain, it was time for him to find a way of earning his own living. 'My Father was a Man of quick Parts,' Hester later wrote. 'His Sensibility – quickened by Vanity & Idleness was *keen* beyond the *Affectation* of any other Mortal.' It certainly was; and on this occasion it found expression in a rejoinder that blew away his daughter's expectations: 'Great as you think yourself, Sir Robert, I think as well of myself and Family, and when I go to get *my* Living as a Cobler, *Your Sister* shall keep the Stall clean; and when I go for a Soldier, She shall carry the Knapsack.'

'This degree of odly exerted Spirit struck Sir Robert of a Heap,'

Hester recorded. It also prompted him to show his guests the door. 'The good Baronet fairly cried over me at parting,' she wrote, 'and I remember I was like to break my foolish little heart.'

Towards the end of 1747 they travelled to London and took lodgings at a staymaker's in Soho. Hester's father 'ran about among his Friends who had not wholly forgotten him'. She and her mother took comfort from a stream of kind letters from her uncle, who presently suggested they should move into his house in Albemarle Street – 't'would save us a Lodging he said; & air the Place for him'. Sir Robert planned to come to London in the spring to make his will. He had assured his sister that in spite of everything, and although the estate must pass by law to his brother Lynch, he intended that £10,000 should be set aside for Hester. She herself would have an annuity of £200 – this for her 'sole and separate use, not amænable to my Father's Power nor subject to his debts'.

For a time the sun shone a little more brightly. While Hester's father went off to Flintshire to bring some order to his affairs, her mother was introduced to the family of Lord Halifax, 'and as Sir Robert dressed both her & me in the finest Silks and Linnens, we set off in great State & great Comfort for this first Winter'. The pert six-year-old made a great impression on her parents' fashionable new acquaintances:

> I became a Favourite with the Duke & Duchess of Leeds, where I
> recollect often meeting the famous Actor Mr Quin, who taught me to
> speak Satan's Speech to the sun in Paradise lost; and when they took
> me to see him act Cato – I remember making him a formal Courtsy,
> much to the Dutchess' amusement ... The Fire Works for the Peace of
> Aix la Chapelle were the next sights my Fancy was Impress'd with, We
> sate on a Terrace belonging to the Hills of Tern – now Lord Berwick's
> Family;– & David Garrick was there & made me sit in his Lap feeding
> me with Cates &c.[10]

What had seemed like spring turned quickly to winter. Sir Robert, on the eve of his departure for London, suffered a stroke; a second followed and carried him off. Sir Lynch, the new baronet, agreed that the Salusburys might stay in Albemarle Street until he and his wife came to town, but on the night they arrived Hester went down with what was thought to be smallpox, and they were hustled out into lodgings in the house of a mantua maker in Lincoln's Inn Fields.

Hester made a speedy recovery and quickly made new friends:

> I was as familiar at Grosvenor Square with Lord Halifax's daughters as if I had been at home ... Lady Anne Montagu too used to fondle me shamefully; She had Apartments at court as Lady of the Bed-Chamber, and I well remember I used to meet this present Prime Minister there – my Lord North, for he was a longlegged Lad about fifteen, and I was a thing of six or seven at most; so that he used to pinch me, & pull me by the Hair till I squealed ...

Salusbury's visit to Wales had brought no improvement to his finances. Although Thomas had by now secured a number of lucrative sinecures[11] and was worth some £700 a year, he never seemed to have any money to lend – 'the doctrine of the *un*divided Guinea, not having impressed *him* perhaps equally with my Father'. Hester recalled drily:

> My Father, like other Men of desperate Fortunes, flew to improbable Schemes for his Relief; & our little Lodging was now every Sunday a Place appointed for the meeting of rascally Projectors, who pretended to find Mines on our Estate at Bachygraig: upon these Wretches the small portion of ready Money wch we possessed was soon expended.

Just when things seemed at their blackest, the Salusburys' acquaintance with the Halifax family came to their rescue. Although the wars between France and Britain in the eighteenth century were triggered by European dynastic issues, they were fought in the New World as well as the Old. Little Hester may have thrilled at the display of fireworks marking the peace of Aix-la-Chapelle, but the balance of power established by the treaty was fragile. The War of the Austrian Succession had in truth gone badly for Great Britain. Its sole important conquest had been Louisbourg, the French naval base on Cape Breton Island that commanded the Gulf of St Lawrence; but at the end of what the Anglo-Americans called King George's War, all conquests were restored to their pre-war owners. The return of Louisbourg went down particularly badly with the New Englanders, who saw it as a betrayal.

The Privy Council remained convinced that France remained the greatest threat to British interests, and the activities of the French in the Ohio Country gave particular cause for concern. George Montagu Dunk, second earl of Halifax, had been placed at the head of the Lords Commissioners of Trade and Plantations in the autumn of 1748. From the moment of his appointment he had been alert to French attempts to encroach on the American colonies, and sought to counter possible French aggression by increasing the efficiency of colonial administration.

The French colony of Acadia had been ceded to Britain in the Treaty of Utrecht in 1713 and became known once again as Nova Scotia.[12] The Jesuits, however, had kept up a determined propaganda among the population, overwhelmingly French-speaking and Catholic, to maintain their allegiance to France; Halifax decided to strengthen the British position by a renewed attempt at colonization and the establishment of a base for the increasingly important presence of the Royal Navy in the North Atlantic.

By the spring of 1749 the scheme had received parliamentary approval and a rash of advertisements appeared offering grants of land to 'such of the officers and private men lately dismissed His Majesty's land and sea service, as shall be willing to settle in the said Province'. Private soldiers or seamen qualified for fifty acres, free of rent or taxes for ten years; at the other end of the scale officers above the rank of captain could expect 600 acres.

The conditions proposed for private soldiers were also offered to carpenters, shipwrights, smiths, masons, joiners, bricklayers 'and all other artificers necessary in building or husbandry'. To men abruptly thrown out of military employment by the peace of 1748 it must have seemed like an offer of free passage to the Land of Cockayne. Grub Street, always suspicious of euphoria, thought that a little satirical deflation was called for:

> Let's away to New Scotland, where Plenty sits queen
> O'er as happy a country as ever was seen;
> And blesses her subjects, both little and great,
> With each a good house, and a pretty estate ...
> ...They've no duties on candles, no taxes on malt,

Nor do they, as we do, pay sauce for their salt;
But all is as free as in those times of old,
When poets assure us the age was of gold.[13]

It was felt that a military man was required at the head of the enter-prise. The Hon. Edward Cornwallis, sixth son of the fourth Baron Cornwallis, was appointed Governor.[14] Halifax offered John Salusbury the post of Register and Receiver of Rents – 'the next Place to the Governor's for Honour, & the Salary a Guinea a Day'. The New World beckoned: 'My Father now was happy in the hope of getting his Living.'

~2~
Great Expectations

JOHN SALUSBURY was not cast in the pioneering mould of a Ralegh or a William Penn. By the time he had raised the money to fit himself out and travelled down to Portsmouth, he was already getting cold feet. A somewhat snivelling letter, which he wrote to his wife on the eve of his departure, survives:

> To Live an individual – Not thought of by any body – Is of all Others the Most Forelorne State; and, Except Thy Dear Self, Life, I am the Very Man.
>
> I think, perhaps, I could have laid Aside My Own Honour, Ambition, call it what you will For the Happyness, the Joy of being always with thee: but then, not to be able to Live up to Thy Rank, without this Prostitution of That Joy, Determined Me ...[1]

He sailed at the end of May 1749 on the *Sphinx* – 'leaving my Mother & myself to scrattle on how we could', as Hester later wrote. They found cheaper lodgings with a Methodist milliner in Charles Street, St James's, and were invited to spend holidays with various relatives. Hester Maria's mother, Lady Cotton, was still alive and had a fine house at East Hyde in Bedfordshire. It was here that Hester acquired her love of horses: 'When my Mother hoped I was gaining Health by the Fresh air, I was kicking my heels on a Corn Binn, & learning to drive of the old Coachman, who like every body else small & Great, delighted in taking me for a Pupil.'[2]

The *Sphinx*, a fast sloop of war with twenty guns, made landfall on 21 June, and Cornwallis and his companions got their first sight of Chebookt, the name given to the magnificent natural harbour by the Mi'kmaq Indians. The first of the thirteen transports that had left Plymouth with the *Sphinx* arrived six days later, and by 1 July they were all safely in. They had carried the largest contingent of settlers ever to leave England – English for the most part, but there were also Swiss, Irish, Jews and Germans. The 'principal settlers' included a surgeon, a schoolmaster, a brewer and an attorney; there were merchants and tradesmen – and a sprinkling of gentlemen eager, like Salusbury, to make the fortune that had eluded them at home.

Early reports were encouraging. 'The coasts are as rich as ever they have been represented; we caught fish every day since we came,' Cornwallis wrote in his first dispatch. Initially, at least, Salusbury seems to have had thoughts of carving out a new life there. 'In time it is to be Hop'd we shall get a little further into the Country,' he wrote to his wife, 'and then a snug farm will be comfortable enough, for the Climate is certainly Healthy and not too warm …'[3]

Within a matter of weeks, however, it became plain to the Governor that the human material at his disposal was not up to the task in hand:

Of soldiers there is only 100 – of Tradesmen Sailors & others able & willing to work not above 200 more – the rest are poor idle worthless vagabonds that embraced the opportunity to get provisions for one Year without labour … Many have come as into a Hospital, to be cured, Some of Venereal Disorders, some even incurables –[4]

Within a few months, almost 700 of the original settlers had melted away, almost all of them listed as 'likely gone to New England'. And almost at once, there was trouble with the Indians. A sawmill had been established to supply materials for new houses. At the end of September it was attacked by a party of Mi'kmaq, who scalped two of the workers and decapitated two more.[5]

Although Salusbury was a member of the Governor's Council, he felt that his voice was disregarded and that Cornwallis listened too readily to those enterprising New England merchants attracted to the fledgling colony by the prospect of commercial opportunities. His journal and his letters are full of complaints about real or imagined slights and disobliging remarks about his colleagues. Early in October the Governor's house on shore was ready for him. 'I am left in my old hole on board the Beaufort,' Salusbury wrote, adding sourly, 'Davidson takes possession of the Cabbin. I care not. The Doctor His lick spittle.'[6]

By the early months of 1750 he was thoroughly homesick. 'Valentines

Day Dear Hetty,' he wrote in his journal, '– and I am all but Broken hearted – please God If I live I will never pass another without thee.' It is clear from the same entry that he was already hoping that Halifax could be persuaded to intervene to have him recalled.[7]

Although her annuity was only £125, Hester Maria contrived by dint of scrimping and scraping to set aside a small sum – 'half of which She laid out in finery for my Father to cut a figure at the King's Birthday in Nova Scotia, which she sent by a Ship that was lost'. The other half, which she put in Thomas's hands, might equally well have been consigned to the deep. When news of Salusbury's departure to America reached the ears of his creditors there was a threat of foreclosure on two of the farms at Bach-y-Graig. Thomas, who had been given power of attorney in Salusbury's absence, was so dilatory that the land was lost.[8]

In the late spring Salusbury joined an expedition to put down a rumoured Indian uprising fomented by the French, but it was compelled to beat a retreat when it came upon a strongly entrenched French force. By July, it was plain from his letters home that he was heartily sick of the whole undertaking.

Unsurprisingly, Hester Maria's health began to suffer – something her daughter would later attribute to 'her Fancy of living almost wholly on Vegetables & Water, for She never would touch a Glass of wine on any Acct'. She felt that she could not support another winter in London, and resolved to go out to Hampstead, where she and Hester spent a winter and a summer in lodgings in Church Row.

Hester's reading while they were there included Paul de Rapin's *History of England*. There was an English translation, but she devoured it in the original French, an exhaustive eight-volume affair which chronicled the history of Britain from the time of the Romans to the reign of Charles I. She also laboured over translations from French to English and English to French.

Thomas turned up one day in a state of high excitement. Bursting into tears, he gathered his sister-in-law into his arms and announced that he had news which would make them all happy for ever – he had won the heart of an heiress. He confessed that his neglect of his brother's affairs over the mortgage had been occasioned only 'by his Mind being wholly taken up in this much greater Concern'. A letter was immediately dispatched to Salusbury, urging him to get leave to attend the wedding. As it happened he was already on his way home, Cornwallis having at last agreed to his repeated requests to be allowed to carry dispatches to England. 'And now came over my Father from America,' Hester wrote, 'and all was Gayety, Transport, & Frenzy of Enjoyment.'

The bride-to-be was a neighbour of Hester's grandmother's in Hertfordshire, the only daughter of Sir Henry Penrice of Offley Court – 'Judge of the Admiralty a famous Miser, tho' a literary Man', as Hester later described him. She and her mother had been frequent visitors, and her lively precocity had made two more conquests: 'This Lady & her Father took a liking to me forsooth; the old Gentleman called me his little Spright on account I guess of my Activity and Paleness, and I used to read & talk with them very much & be familiar in the Family.'

At thirty-three, Anna Maria Penrice was ten years younger than Thomas. She had been given a good education. Hester described her as plump and fair, with a fine complexion, although she later rounded out the picture with her customary candour: 'She had a strong and cultivated Mind, a good Person but coarse Manners, bad Health, and an Appetite for Meat & Drink She never tried to restrain.'

For Thomas, her severe stammer and her epilepsy mattered less than the substantial fortune she stood to inherit. Sir Henry was in his early seventies. He declared himself quite prepared to plead illness or advancing years and resign his place in the Court of Admiralty – but only if Thomas could be shoehorned in to succeed him. Did his prospective son-in-law have enough interest with friends in high places to be sure that matters could be so arranged? Until Sir Henry knew the answer to that question, his consent to the marriage would be withheld. Thomas rose to the challenge: 'And now the Quality Friends came in play again; & oh how they were solicited & tormented to get him this post, wch in a few Months however he had the good Fortune to obtain.'

Thomas's cup was full almost to the brim. He had his seat on the bench; he had the knighthood that went with it; he had his bride, with her stammer and her fits and her expectations. And within the year her father was dead, and Sir Thomas was master of Offley Park.[9]

While Thomas's good fortune clearly improved the family's prospects, it did nothing immediately to ease his brother's chronic need for cash, and Salusbury was plunged into yet another round of unpleasant meetings with restive creditors. Edward Bridge, his Welsh agent, declared that the credit of the Salusbury family had 'sunk down to the Lowest Ebb'. No doubt it had, although that was partly Bridge's doing; the family later became convinced that he was a scoundrel and had been cheating them for many years.

In the summer of 1752, at the urging of Lord Halifax, Salusbury reluctantly agreed to return to Nova Scotia, leaving his wife and daughter to resume their former routine of lengthy visits in the role of poor relations. 'I was never a Moment from her Side,' Hester wrote of her mother, 'yet I never saw her lowspirited, tho' her Health was always bad, & her Circumstances always low.'

That Mrs Salusbury refused to be cast down was the more remarkable given the flow of dispiriting letters that reached her from Halifax. Salusbury was homesick; he hated the new Governor (Cornwallis had been replaced by Peregrine Hopson); had indeed fought a duel at Madeira on the outward voyage with Captain Young of the *Sphinx* for showing more civilities to the new Governor than to him; his estate was being frittered away through the mismanagement of that miserable dog his brother ...

The 'miserable dog', however, had his uses. Thomas knew his way about in government circles, and it was he who eventually made a case for his brother's recall. Salusbury returned home for good in the summer of 1753 – 'gloriously out of humour' and with scarcely a penny to his name.

Hester's life now assumed a more even tenor. When she reviewed this part of her childhood in *Thraliana* she conceded that the doctrine of the undivided Guinea now seemed to make a stronger impression on her uncle than hitherto: 'I fancy Sir Thos coaxed his Lady out of Money for us, or fed us with it privately, for we now lived much smarter than ever.'

Thomas's newfound prosperity also made it possible for matters to be tidied up at Bach-y-Graig. In the event of John having no son, the estate was entailed on his brother, who therefore had every interest in seeing that it remained in the family. John was now in his late forties and seemed unlikely to produce a male heir. In the summer of 1755 he accordingly made over Bach-y-Graig to Thomas; Thomas paid off the mortgage, and John formally acknowledged indebtedness to him for the whole amount. It was an arrangement that suited everyone very well at the time; thirty years later, John's daughter would have cause to regret it most bitterly.

The Salusburys now moved to Soho, to a house in Dean Street, where they were able to rise to a manservant and two maids – 'and might have been very happy, if my Father's violent Temper had not put peace & Quietness out of the Question'. For all that, they were made welcome both at Offley Park and at Thomas's chambers in Doctors' Commons.

Anna Maria Salusbury was greatly taken with her little niece: 'She was extremely kind and indulgent to me, gave me fine Silks, Pearls and a thousand Things. In short She loved my Uncle passionately & me tenderly as his favourite plaything: my Mother She rather fear'd as her Superior in Knowledge & elegance; and my Father she hated heartily as who can wonder?'

Many years later Hester would name one of her daughters after her aunt, but a chilling marginal comment in *Thraliana* indicates that although Lady Salusbury's affection was appreciated, it was not fully reciprocated: 'The kind & constant Partiality she shew'd me claim'd all my Gratitude, but as I always lov'd & hated after my Mother – I never did *much love her.*'

Whatever the equivocal nature of their feelings towards their sister-in-law, Hester's parents now decided that it would be politic to flatter her by setting their daughter to learn Italian, a language of which Anna Maria had a good knowledge. Her aunt's interest in Romance languages also extended to Spanish. The Lisbon earthquake of 1755 had focused attention on the Iberian peninsula, and some months later a notary public called Isaac Netto had preached a sermon on it in Spanish in a London synagogue. Hester's mother urged her to translate it and dedicate it to her aunt. Lady Salusbury was delighted. 'As your uncle will be in Town next Week, I desire you will tell him what Books in any Language you shou'd like, or Ornaments for your Person,' she wrote. 'I beg you will not be sparing in your Demands.'[10] Hester chose a set of pearl and garnet ornaments.

Her father set her a more ambitious exercise. In 1737 John Carteret, 1st Earl Granville, had sponsored the publication of a luxurious new edition, in Spanish, of *Don Quixote*. Granville felt that it should be accompanied by a Life of Cervantes, and this was commissioned from Gregorio Mayans y Siscar, then Librarian to the King of Spain. 'I had not the sense to enquire slyly for other Translations to help me out,' Hester wrote in *Thraliana*, 'so I plodded and blundered on, & translated the Verses into Rhymes of my own.' More eccentrically, she tried her hand at an obscure Spanish dissertation on the Celtic deity Endovellicus.[11] Years later, coming across the notebook containing her translation, she wrote on the cover, 'This was a strange thing for a Child to do.'

❧

Hester's father was on friendly terms with Hogarth, and the painter quite often came to dine. One day when Hester was taken to his house in Leicester Fields Hogarth was at his easel, and bade her sit to him:

> And now look here said he I am doing this for *you* – you are not 14 Years old yet I think, but you will be 24; and this Portrait will then be like you. 'Tis the Lady's last Stake – See how She hesitates between her Money and her Honour, Take you care; I see an Ardour for Play in your Eyes and in Your heart – don't indulge it, I shall give you this Picture as a Warning, because I love you now, you are so good A Girl. – In a fortnight's Time after that Visit we went out of Town – *he* died somewhat suddenly I believe – and I never saw my poor Portrait again – till going to Fonthill many, *many* Years afterward I met it there, and *Mr Piozzi* observed the Likeness –[12]

It's a charming story, and one that would vary in the telling over the years. Hogarth was certainly at work by the autumn of 1758 on the picture now known as *The Lady's Last Stake*, but he was painting it for the Anglo-Irish connoisseur and politician Lord Charlemont. The terms of the commission were 'the most agreeable that can be wish'd for', he told a friend: 'I am desir'd to choose my subject, am allow'd my own time, and what mony I shall think proper to ask.'[13]

The picture could well have brought him 400 guineas – that was what he asked for the *Sigismunda* commission he was working on at the same time for Sir Richard Grosvenor. It is therefore highly unlikely, volatile and capricious as he could be, that Hogarth would have decided on the whim of a moment to make a present of it to the daughter of a friend.[14] Hester, to the end of her days, would think differently: 'I wonder who got dear Hogarth's Picture of the Lady's last Stake? which he intended as a present for me,' she wrote many years later. 'I lost what now would have been invaluable.'[15]

Sometime in the late 1750s the Salusburys decided that Hester should have a tutor. Their choice fell on Dr Arthur Collier, a bachelor in his early fifties who had chambers near those of Thomas Salusbury's in Doctors' Commons and was a frequent guest at Offley. Collier's father had been a country parson who took a keen interest in metaphysics and was convinced of the non-existence of an external world;[16] his son was characterized in a contemporary sketch as 'ingenious, but unsteady and eccentric',[17] a judgement borne out by an assessment which Hester wrote in later life: 'To many, nay to most people the Doctor was no agreable Companion; he loved to talk better than to hear, & to dispute better than to please; his Conversation too was always upon such Subjects as the rest of Mankind seem by one Consent to avoid.'

If his choice of subjects was of narrow appeal, Collier's conversational style could be downright rebarbative:

> To perplex and disappoint was indeed so much his Disposition that he seemed to converse for scarcely any other Purpose; so that if a Man had expressed a desire of talking with him on some Critical or metaphysical subject, he would that day purposely expatiate on the Skill of curing Hams, or making Minced Pyes, or say what pains he had taken to invent an universal Pickle.

In his professional capacity he had as one of his clients the colourful Elizabeth Chudleigh, Countess of Bristol, later to be arraigned before the House of Lords for bigamy.[18] His prime merit in the eyes of the Salusbury family was that he was a good classical scholar; an earlier pupil had been Sarah, one of Henry Fielding's sisters, and like her more famous brother a novelist.[19]

Collier was not immediately over-impressed by his new pupil. 'My Dear Child You are enough to make a parson Swear,' he wrote: 'I wont write a word of Latin more to you till you learn your Accidence at lest, and know what ought to be nominative and what accusative case before and after verbs. What can be the matter? there must be something strangely wrong in your Head that so plain and simple a doctrine will not make its way into your understanding ...'[20]

Although he was a demanding teacher, Hester quickly became very attached to him – 'a Man who engrossed my whole Heart, & deserved it', she later wrote. '*Love* (as it is falsely called,) had no Share in the Connection: but nobody ever did feel more fond & true affection for another, than I did for my dear Dr Collier, & he for his *sweetest Angel* as he call'd me.'

The comparison that has been drawn with Swift and Vanessa is an apt one. She found him kind, and gentle in his manners. Fastidious in his dress, he invariably wore black ('but with Ruffles – to distinguish him from a Clergyman'). She remembered appreciatively a certain cheerful toughness – he 'made less Bustle about real Calamities, than the people I have since lived amongst, do with imaginary ones'. It was something that would emerge as one of her own salient characteristics. 'My first friend formed my mind to resemble his,' she said in old age. 'It never did resemble that of either of my husbands, and in that of Doctor Johnson's mine was swallowed up and lost.'[21]

When they were not together they wrote letters. Hester's have disappeared, but a hundred or more of Collier's survive. Although many of them are in Latin, they are by no means all concerned with Cicero or the ablative absolute. For a few short years, Collier rivalled her mother as the most important person in Hester's life – 'My Friend D^r. Collier from whom I concealed nothing'. Part father confessor, part favourite uncle, part good companion, he clearly admired his 'sweetest Angel' greatly; it is not certain that love had no share in the connection.

Collier not only taught her Latin and logic and rhetoric; at times he assumed the role of moral tutor, at times that of a somewhat eccentric guide to the ways of the world. In later life Hester quite often dipped into her tenacious memory and dredged up assorted sayings of his to illustrate a point or reinforce an argument: 'Doctor Collier used to caution me always against any Tendency towards secrecy or Clandestine Conduct; never said he be mysterious about Trifles; it is the first advance towards Evil, particularly in the Female Sex; who if they begin by concealing innocent Intentions, will soon have corrupted ones to conceal ...' and 'Doctor Collier used to say that one might discern generosity or Avarice merely by observing the manner of a Man who was counting out his Money; it sticks says he even literally to the Fingers of a Fellow truly covetous.'

He took her about, introduced her to his wide circle of friends, of which one was the great 'Hermes' Harris, Member of Parliament for Christchurch, celebrated as the author of *Hermes, or a Philosophical Enquiry Concerning Universal Grammar*:

> James Harris gave me his 'Hermes' interleaved, that I might write my remarks on it, proving my attention to philosophical grammar, for which study I had shown him signs of capacity, I trust; but Collier would not suffer him to talk metaphysics in my hearing, unless he himself was the respondent. Oh, what conversations! What correspondences were these![22]

Another of Collier's friends was Dr William Oliver, physician to the Bath Mineral Water Hospital, author of a *Practical Essay on Use and Abuse of Warm Bathing in Gouty Cases* and the inventor of the Bath Oliver biscuit. He was so taken with some of her verse that he sent her eight highly complimentary four-line stanzas in return.

Collier's efforts were supplemented by those of Dr William Parker, a close friend of Hester's father, who was the rector of St James's, Piccadilly and a chaplain-in-ordinary to George II and later to George III. From Parker she received some instruction in French; he was warm in his praise of her translation of the first of Louis Racine's two *Epîtres sur l'homme*: 'The Performance upon careful Perusal greatly exceeds my Expectation; though my Expectation was very high, and always will be, of every thing wch comes from dear Miss Salusbury.'[23]

The warmth was not reciprocated. There was no room for Parker on the pedestal occupied by Collier. His fame as a pulpit orator counted for little with Hester: 'Doctor Parker has some pleasant Stories,' she wrote 'but he tells them so tediously, they give more disgust than Pleasure.'

She did, however, in a much later entry, include him in a list of 'my very earliest Friends, Admirers & Sweethearts'.

The Racine translation is interesting for several reasons. Hester's earliest verses – she had been trying her hand at poetry since she was sixteen – were predictably derivative, with obvious echoes of Milton and Pope and Gray, but this was rather more than a routine schoolroom exercise; she was beginning to find her own voice. A draft of an introduction survives which suggests that she intended to seek publication; she imagines how it might be received by the critics, and strikes at them pre-emptively in a manner at once aggressive and defensive: 'Another sort ... cries Heav'n protect me! A paltry Imitation! & ye best Lines in it palpably stole from Racine. However let 'em 1st try y^m selves, next consider my Sex, want of School Learning, my manifest Disadvantages, in attempting a Translation never tho^t of before, I shall then appeal to their Candour, & boldly give it ye Name of a free Translation.'[24]

Throughout her life, Hester's attitude to her poetry would remain ambivalent. She thought well enough of it in her teens to seek a wider audience than that afforded by the family circle: 'I took a fancy to write in the "St James's Chronicle", unknown to my parents and my tutor too: it was my sport to see them reading, studying, blaming or praising their own little whimsical girl's performances ...'[25]

Later she was more critical of her early work. 'Now will I write out a miserable Performance of my own,' reads an early entry in *Thraliana*: 'It is an Ode written when I was between sixteen and seventeen Years old, in which I fancied – God help me – I had imitated the eminent English Poets as well as Addison himself ... I see 'tis too bad to mend – so here it is – with all its Imperfections on its Head!'

Written on New Year's Day 1759 her 'Irregular Ode on the English Poets' is an ambitious salute to the diversity of the English poetic tradition; her imitations of Spenser, Shakespeare, Milton, Dryden and the rest are in need of less mending than she supposes.

꧁ ꧂

Lady Salusbury's health remained indifferent. 'After Seven Years Marriage She had never been pregnant,' Hester later wrote, 'nor ever had desired to bring Children; they would have been distempered Creatures like herself she said.' She died in 1759, at the age of forty-one – 'of dropsy of the breast', by her niece's account.[26] Thomas went to stay briefly with Hester and her parents in Dean Street, before taking them back with him to Offley – 'where We were now no longer Visitors Sir Thomas said – but at home'.

The next two or three years were among the most carefree of Hester's life. 'Oh how happily and comfortably I did live,' she wrote:

> I used to be my Father's Favourite, my Mother's Comforter and
> Companion, & my Uncle's Darling. I was next Heir both to the Welch
> Estate and the Hertfordshire one; & Sir Tho⁵ having No Joy except in
> his Dogs, his Horses and myself, I was looked up to – as the principal
> Person of the Family – my Influence was courted by every one, and
> I never in my Life did ask a Favour of Sir Thomas which he refused:
> all this made me love him very tenderly, & if he fell from his Horse or
> had any Accident befall him I was his true & affectionate Attendant: if
> I wrote verses it was about his Park, or his Possessions; and to my dear
> Offley I did rivet my poor foolish Heart.

She kept pet dogs and pet deer and she was allowed to follow the hunt in a post chaise. Sir Thomas entertained lavishly, and it fell to Hester to write the invitations and menu cards. The poor of the village came to the house twice a week for milk and twice for broth: 'Every week we killed an Ox; the Sir Loyn was roasted on the Sunday for our Table, and the cuttings were on Saturday all thrown into a Pye Dish of immense Magnitude, over which a Pudding was poured & baked in the Oven for Saturdays Dinner at the Servants Table.'

She continued under Collier's tutelage and she continued to write; several months after the death of her aunt she composed some lines in which she imagines an old ash of which Lady Salusbury had been particularly fond pining away at the loss of its mistress:

> Then shrunk her favrite Plant, his Leaves grew pale,
> Bow'd to each Blast, and sigh'd to ev'ry Gale;
> For his fair Patroness ten Months he pin'd,
> His faithful Heart consum'd, his head declin'd
> Then feebly fell, faint yielding to the Wind.

The rather more prosaic fact of the matter was that the tree had come down in a storm. No matter: 'This trifling Performance brought tears into my Uncle's Eyes, and Money into my Pocket for having celebrated so artfully I will own the virtues of a Woman he remembered with Gratitude and Esteem.' More significantly, her doting uncle frequently declared – 'ten times a Day I believe' – that he had ten thousand pounds ready for her 'whenever a proper Match might be offer'd'.

In an era when everybody knew a great deal about how much everybody else was worth, the heiress of Offley Park did not lack admirers. After her aunt's death, she later wrote, the house was haunted by young men who paid court to the niece and expressed admiration of the horses: 'Every suitor was made to understand my extraordinary value. Those who could read, were shown my verses; those who could not, were judges of my prowess in the field. It was my sport to mimic some, and drive others back, in order to make Dr Collier laugh, who did not perhaps *wish* to see me give a heart away which he held completely in his hands ...'[27]

There was a further complication, which was that at the faintest whisper of a proposal to his darling daughter, John Salusbury, like a stock character in a thousand old comedies, flew into a violent passion. 'As his Ill humour generally fell heavy on my poor dear Mother,' Hester wrote, 'I used to keep clear of Solicitations to Marriage with more assiduity than other Girls use to procure them.'

There was a Doctor Owen, but he was deemed too old, although he made 'most liberal Offers'. Mr Maurice of Lloran was regarded as 'not an eligible Husband on account of his Character'. A young man called Chaworth Levinz was the nephew of the Receiver-General of the Customs, who offered to settle the whole of his considerable fortune on the boy if Hester would have him – 'to which no Objection but my Father's Oddity could have been made'. In this instance, her father's oddity may have saved her from early widowhood; early in 1765 young Levinz was dining at the Star and Garter tavern in Pall Mall with his second cousin, Lord Byron, brother of the poet's grandfather. A violent dispute over the game laws led to a duel, and Levinz was killed.

George Clifford, a wealthy young merchant in the Dutch trade, was in the frame for a time, and so was a young lawyer called James

Marriott, who not only shared Hester's passion for poetry but had actually published some – 'Dr. Marriott wrote the prettiest verses in French
of any Englishman I know,' she recalled in *Thraliana* many years later.
Inexplicably, she allowed her father to see one of Marriott's letters, and
this provoked an explosion:

Sir

My daughter shewed me an extraordinary letter from you; she
resents the ill treatment as conscious that she never gave any pretence
to take such Liberties with her. I think it hard that insolence and
Impudence should be suffered to interrupt the tranquil state of Youth
and innocence.

I therefore insist on no altercations – no more trash on the subject:
But should you continue to insult my poor child, I so assume the Father,
I shall take the Insult to myself; – be then most certainly Assured that I
will be avenged on you – much to the detriment of your Person and –
So Help me God.

John Salusbury[28]

Marriott survived this verbal assault to become Master of his Cambridge
college and vice-chancellor. He followed Sir Thomas as a judge of the
High Court of Admiralty, and subsequently entered Parliament. Many
years later Hester considered turning to him for legal advice, remember-
ing him fondly as 'another old *Loveyer true*'.

She would have less fond memories of another would-be suitor who
entered her life at that juncture. Thelwall Salusbury – 'my Cousin, my
Pretendant – & my Enemy' as she would later describe him (he was
in fact a second cousin) came to Offley at this time as the curate. His
arrival 'fretted' her uncle and put her father in a fury. Their father's half-
brother had married beneath him – 'a Welch Wench whose Character
was so bad that She contracted a *Disorder* wch in her *Children* appeared
to be the *King's Evil*'. Here now on the doorstep at Offley was one of
those very children, and although there had been bad blood between
the two branches of the family for many years, some show of civility
seemed called for.

It achieved little. Thelwall Salusbury, with his clerical garb and his scrofulous face, emerges from the pages of *Thraliana* as a cross between Shakespeare's Iago and Trollope's Obadiah Slope:

> No Civilities could conquer his internal hate to the Family, which he concealed under the most obsequious carriage towards both my Father & Uncle; but particularly towards my Father, who he meant to make his principal Dupe.
>
> *Me*, he considered as grossly in his way; for I believe he even then had hope of the Estate, tho' then I little suspected it, & he resolved to try by distant Looks & Assiduities whether I was not to be had – This Scheme – from my Contempt of the Fellow – proving abortive; he certainly did not like to see anyone else offer … He therefore flattered my Father's Humour in making him jealous of every Gentleman who came to the house …

The disdain with which his 'distant Looks and Assiduities' were received by his diminutive cousin rankled deeply. The Reverend Thelwall Salusbury nursed his resentment and would have his revenge.

⇜ 3 ⇝
The Bartered Bride

EARLY IN 1761 Lord Halifax was appointed Lord Lieutenant of Ireland. As summer came on he embarked on a leisurely progress to Dublin. His route lay through Wales, and John and Thomas Salusbury felt it appropriate to accompany their patron on part of his journey. Sir Thomas was not away for many weeks, but Hester's father was detained by business in Flintshire. He would return late in the summer to discover that two new characters had joined the cast at Offley. Their impact on the storyline would be dramatic.

The Hon. Mrs King was a new neighbour of Sir Thomas's – 'a young & blooming Widow', Hester later wrote, 'whose Character was that of rapacious Avarice'. (She was, in fact, already forty, which would not have been considered particularly young at the time.) The daughter of a Master in Chancery, she had been married to a brother of the Earl of Kingston. She was plainly setting her cap at Sir Thomas. Hester and her mother viewed his growing susceptibility with jealous apprehension, concerned at the threat it posed to Hester's prospects: 'She cast her Eyes upon my poor Sir Thomas ... pretending the most tender Affection for his Person, wch tho' once eminently handsome, was now at the Age of threescore – loaded with fat, & bloated with hard Drinking no Object as I believe of any Passion but Disgust.'

Sir Thomas's infatuation with the widow King did not blunt his interest in finding a suitable husband for Hester. He returned from London one day in high excitement: 'What an excellent, what an incomparable young Man he had seen – who was in short a Model of Perfection: ending his Panegyric by saying that he was a *real Sportsman*. Seeing me disposed to laugh, he looked very grave, said he expected us to like him – & that seriously.'[1]

This paragon made a first appearance at Offley the very next day – a visit arranged, as Hester later learned, with careful regard to her father's absence. She was not exactly bowled over, although she conceded that he was 'a very handsome and well accomplished Gentleman'; indeed the account she later wrote of her first impressions is tinged with irritation: 'Mr Thrale . . . applied himself so diligently to gain my Mother's attention – ay & her heart too: that there was little doubt of her approving the pretensions of so very shewy a suitor – if Suitor he was to me; who certainly had not a common share in the Compliments he paid to my Mother's Wit, Beauty, & Elegance.'[2]

Sir Thomas had met Henry Thrale, a wealthy young brewer in his early thirties, at the house of the Receiver-General of Customs, that same William Levinz who had been so eager for Hester to marry his nephew. The talk had turned to Hertfordshire, and it emerged that Thrale had a family connection – not just with the county but with Offley itself. His father was the son of a cottager in the village; the house in which he was born now served as kennels for Sir Thomas's pack of hounds.

Mrs Salusbury was captivated: 'She had no Notion She told me that very night, of a Man so handsome, so well educated, and so well bred, being thus totally insensible to the apparent Shame of acknowledging an old Cottager in our Village for his Grandfather, and our *Dog Kennel* for his *Family Seat*.'

Thrale had brought with him his aunt – 'a very ordinary old Woman indeed' sniffed Hester – and Mrs Salusbury made it her business to draw the old lady out on the family's history. Shades of Dick Whittington. Thrale had a great-uncle, Edmund Halsey, the son of a miller at St Albans. Quarrelling with his father, he took himself off to London with only a few shillings in his pocket and found employment at Child's Old Anchor Brewery in Southwark as a broomstick clerk, charged with such menial tasks as sweeping the yard.

Within two years he had married one of Child's daughters and been taken into partnership. Less than ten years after his first appearance in the firm's accounts he was lending £1,000 to the King, and on Child's death the brewery was his. He amassed a great fortune, represented Southwark in Parliament, became a Director of the South Sea Company; he also married his daughter off to the soldier and politician Lord Cobham, the friend of Pope and creator of the great gardens at Stowe.

Halsey also had two sons, but both had died young. With public affairs

absorbing so much of his time he followed Child's example and brought
new blood into the business – his nephew Ralph Thrale, Henry's father.
Relations between them were not always smooth – partly, as Hester put
it, 'because the poor young Fellow had married a Wench that Halsey
wanted to have for his own Pleasure'. Certainly, when Halsey died there
was no mention of Ralph Thrale in his will, and the brewery passed
to Cobham. The idea of a peer of the realm soiling his hands in trade
was unthinkable, however. A price of £30,000 was agreed – equivalent
to about £4 million today – and at the age of thirty-one Ralph Thrale
found himself the owner of the Anchor Brewhouse.

The business expanded and Thrale grew rich. He acquired the
100-acre estate of Streatham Park in Surrey and built a villa there. He
had his portrait painted by Hudson, the master of Joshua Reynolds and,
like Halsey before him, sat for Southwark in Parliament. One of his
daughters married a prosperous sugar refiner who became Lord Mayor of
London; another became the wife of John Lade, who sat in the Commons
for Camelford and became a baronet.[3]

Ralph Thrale remained on good terms with his cousin's husband, and
this connection with the Cobhams and their circle – Grenvilles, Lytteltons
and Pitts – proved of great value, particularly to his only son, Henry,
who as Hester put it, 'was bred up at Stowe & Stoke, and Oxford, and
every genteel Place'. Henry matriculated at University College, Oxford,
in June 1744. He came down, as was not uncommon, without taking
a degree, at the end of the following year and went off on the Grand
Tour with William Henry Lyttelton, later Lord Westcote, who became
a life-long friend.[4] After he left Oxford his father allowed him £1,000 a
year – worth £140,000 or so today. 'If this young dog does not find so
much after I am gone as he expects,' Boswell records Ralph as saying,
'let him remember that he had a great deal in my own time.'[5]

The years that separate Henry Thrale's return from the Grand Tour
and his appearance at Offley in the summer of 1761 are largely blank.
His father took him into the business in 1748, but his interest in the
brewery in those early years was slight. He was much in the company
of Arthur Murphy, a witty and quarrelsome Irishman who had been
educated by the Jesuits at St Omer and subsequently flitted from commerce to journalism, from journalism to the theatre and from the theatre

to the law. Thrale and Murphy – 'Atty', as Thrale called him – were familiar figures in the gaming houses and green rooms of the capital. There were liaisons with actresses and women of the town – the line between the two professions was often blurred. Murphy lived for some years with the actress Ann Field, who later became the mistress of the Duke of Cumberland. Thrale's name was linked with the courtesan Polly Hart, who later drifted into the theatre and figured in Edward Thompson's *Meretriciad* in 1761:

> With regal grace H——t fills the fretting Stage,
> And would do honour to the train, and page,
> But now she's changed the operative plan,
> To sleep in peace, with an endearing man.

As he approached his thirties, Thrale's mind turned to weightier matters. In 1754 he made an unsuccessful bid to enter Parliament for Abingdon.[6] When his father died in 1758 he became the sole owner of the brewery. He applied himself vigorously to the expansion and modernization of the business, and by 1760 its annual production had risen to 30,000 barrels. In the same year one of the Southwark Members announced that he would not be standing again, and Thrale decided to throw his hat into the ring. He wrote to the Duke of Newcastle, then at the Treasury, to solicit his support, but eventually withdrew when he realized the strength of the opposition.

Easy manners, eyes of the deepest blue, the owner of a famous pack of foxhounds in Surrey – such was Sir Thomas's candidate for the hand of his niece. Hester herself remained unpersuaded; her father, she was convinced, would never hear of a match with someone of such 'mean birth':

> Besides he was of late grown so Jealous lest I should ever marry at
> all that there was no hope of My Mother's and Sir Thomas' Scheme
> succeeding – add to this that Mr Thrale had himself taken less Notice
> of me than any other Man I had ever seen come to the House almost.
> My Friend Dr Collier from whom I concealed nothing, seemed likewise
> rather to dislike the Business, & I apprehended nothing but Mischief
> could come of their unlucky Partiality.

Mischief there was, and the odious Thelwall Salusbury obligingly took a hand in the making of it:

> He artfully represented to my Father at his return, that I was to be
> sold to a Man I did not like for a Barrel of Porter; at once inflaming
> his Jealousy, & exciting his Abhorrence of a Man whose Family was
> so far beneath our own. My Father's Passions were ready to be played
> upon; he inveigh'd against their new Friend, said he was a Beau Brewer,
> would soon be a Bankrupt &c. told me what Mistresses he kept, & what
> Enormities he committed, and charged me never to have him.

Hester realized she was unlikely to inherit Offley unless she married the man her uncle had set his heart on. But she was equally clear about where her duty as an eighteenth-century daughter lay: 'I durst not commit a positive Offence against God by disobliging my Father who had the sole Right to dispose of me,' she wrote: 'With this promise he grew more content; insulted my Uncle upon it, and half harassed my Mother to Death: diverted himself by ridiculing Sir Thomas' Taste of new Acquaintance, & I think contrived to alienate his Affection from us all as fast as he could. – So well did Parson Thelwall's Schemes succeed.'

Those schemes clearly succeeded only because they had John Salusbury's character defects to work on. With a little help from his kinsman and Mrs King, he now, for the second time, succeeded in blighting his daughter's prospects: 'My Uncle grown weary of our Company – sought Relief from the Widow, & shewed us that our Absence would no longer – as formerly – be a Concern to him.'

John Salusbury's temper flared. Impetuous as always, he carried his wife and daughter off to London. Hester presented her uncle with a long, romantic poem in heroic couplets called *Offley Park*. Offley would remain for her throughout her life the scene of her golden years; she would only ever see it once again.

Back in Dean Street, she resumed her studies with Collier and continued to write – September of that year saw the marriage of George III to the formidably ugly Charlotte of Mecklenburg-Strelitz, and Hester celebrated the occasion with a *Song on his Majesty's Nuptials*:

... She, fair, unaffected could conquer each Heart
And wise without Cunning could please without Art;
In private Life cheerful, in Publick – serene;
How sweet a Companion! How gracious a Queen!

Two weeks later she was a guest in the Duke of Devonshire's box in Westminster Hall to witness the traditional banquet that followed the coronation. Tradition also required that the King's Champion ride into the Hall in armour and throw down the gauntlet to anyone who denied that the sovereign was rightfully heir to the crown. At this point a hush fell over the assembly. The buzz had been that the Young Pretender had made his way to England and intended to take up the challenge. A piece of nonsense, of course – Charles Edward Stuart, bonnie no more, was roaming aimlessly round Europe, bloated now with drink. A poor match for the Champion. The feasting and chatter resumed.

The following year, 1762, saw the publication of *Fingal*, James Macpherson's bogus epic which he claimed to have translated from the Gaelic. Hester was 'frantic with admiration' (she was in distinguished company; Goethe was taken in, too) and composed 'An American Eclogue – imitating the Style of Fingal'. It appeared in the *St James's Chronicle* – her first identified publication. The same paper also accepted from her a much more substantial piece in prose. 'Albion Manor' was occasioned by the dismissal of the Duke of Newcastle in May 1762, when he lost his place to the King's mentor and favourite, Lord Bute. Newcastle is portrayed as a faithful old retainer, ungratefully cast off by his new master in favour of 'a dirty Scotch Boy Steward'. Collier, who quite often wrote to Hester in Latin, dubbed her 'vilissima Whiggula'.[7]

Towards the end of the year she attempted something on a grander scale. As the Seven Years' War drew to a close she composed an 'Ode on the Blessings of Peace', and submitted it to the composer Dr Arne, hoping that it might be set for the stage at Ranelagh. It was an ambitious essay in the heroic pastoral, but it was never performed. In the closing weeks of 1762 it was withdrawn – the Salusbury family had been engulfed in crisis.

Thrale had come visiting from time to time since their return to London. Hester insisted he came to call on her mother – visits 'render'd

more terrifying to *me* every Day from Papa's Violence of Temper'.[8] In
the middle of December Collier, whose ear was usually close to the
ground, wrote privately to Hester to say that her uncle was to marry
Mrs King the following Sunday. He begged her to say nothing; he
would come himself to break the news to her father the following day.
Salusbury somehow sensed that something was amiss, and the fat was in
the fire: 'My Father charged me violently that I carried on a clandestine
Correspondence with M[r] Thrale, a Charge I could not bear, as I had
suffered so much, & was like to suffer so much more by discouraging his
Addresses – that I answered very warmly ... & so high ran our Contest,
that I fainted that Night from the Effects of this Dispute.'

Hester eventually showed her father the letter, and he apologized.
The angry confrontation had gone on into the small hours. Salusbury
resolved the next morning to set out for Offley. When she was old,
Hester recalled the events of the day with bleak economy:

> At 9 we rose – He to go cross the Park in search of my Maternal Uncle
> Sir Lynch Salusbury Cotton, from whom, & from Dr Crane Preb-
> endary of Westmr. he meant to seek Counsel & Comfort; Me, to the
> Employment of calling our Medical Friend Herbert Lawrence to dinner
> by a Billet of earnest Request – *All of us* were *Ill* – but by the Time he
> came, my Father died – & was brought us home a Corpse – before the
> Dining hour.[9]

Hester's feelings about her father were complex. Miserable as he had
made her with his jealous rages, his 'easy his elegant Gaiety' was still
something she would remember in later life with some pride: 'His Affections and Aversions were proportionably violent – he adored his Wife,
he doated on his Brother, and his anxious Tenderness for me would
often pass the Bounds of common or of *un*common Attention. Yet so
he contrived that though we could not help being sorry, yet I think we
all three felt as if relieved by his Death ...'

His death left Hester and her mother extremely exposed financially.
Bach-y-Graig now passed to Sir Thomas, although it would become
Hester's if he left no heir. The only charge on the estate was an annuity
of £200 for Mrs Salusbury and a sum of £2,000 to be settled on Hester
in the event of her marriage.

Within days of his brother's death Sir Thomas promised that Hester should have a marriage bond of £10,000,[10] but persuading him to deliver proved difficult, and Lord Halifax and other family friends were enlisted to bring pressure to bear. Collier, in particular, exerted himself, going so far as to draw up a draft bond, but was roused to a pitch of frustration with his old friend. 'I am now convinced this same Sr. Honesty's a very dirty, base, ungenerous, low-designing man,' he told Hester: 'He kept me awake the greatest part of last night, for I find that after all his filthy protestations of affection, His Puffy promises and Declarations, He will allow – He'll give if – He'll do most wondrous things – But nothing certain ... and so I have done with Him.'[11]

Collier's efforts earned him little gratitude from Mrs Salusbury. Jealous of his influence over Hester, she suspected – rightly – that he would rather she did not marry anyone. 'Well!' Hester wrote, 'She knew her power, & resolved to exert it; fomented a trifling Quarrel between the Dr & me, so as to keep us at a Distance a while; and in the mean Time encouraging Mr Thrale's Visits ...'

The 'trifling Quarrel' was patched up, but Mrs Salusbury watched her moment, and it was not long before Collier obligingly overstepped the mark. In one of his letters to Hester, having spoken of her father, he continued: 'Doubtless his Daughter will be *doubly carefull* not to *encourage* or *cultivate* any *acquaintance* or *connection* that she must know Her father Held in full as much abhorrence for herself.'[12] No names were mentioned, but he was clearly suggesting it should be a matter of conscience – and of filial piety – not to marry Thrale. The letter is endorsed in Hester's hand: 'the last I ever recd. from Dr. Collier, as my Mother would not permit me to answer it or see the Dr. any more'.

Years later, in *Thraliana*, she would write warmly and perceptively about him – 'my earliest and most disinterested friend', as she called him: 'Ill used by everyone, I also used him ill; and repaid the long and diligent Care he paid to my Improvement, with Slights & Coldness: It was not however easy for me to do better; my Mother, who did not approve of some of his Doctrines, nor delight in the Confidence I shewed for him, parted us with Assiduity & Pleasure.'

Thrale, meanwhile, continued his bizarre dual courtship of mother and daughter. His intentions remained as obscure as his feelings. On his visits to Dean Street, Hester was largely ignored. As a wooing strategy it was decidedly original – Jane Austen's Mr Darcy appears downright importunate by comparison. Towards the end of June, however, Thrale put pen to paper: 'Mr Thrale presents his most respectful compliments to Mrs and Miss Salusbury & wishes to God he could have communicated His Sentiments to them last night, which is absolutely impossible for Him to do to any other Person breathing; He therefore most ardently begs to see Them at any Hour this afternoon ...'[13]

The audience was granted, the question put. Hester felt obliged to point out that she 'was not now the Fortune he once thought me'. She received an extremely handsome reply: 'Mr Thrale . . . said he knew I had an independent ten Thousand Pounds . . . & that for the rest he was willing to take his Chance either for Offley, or Bachŷgraig, or both or neither; for that if I had been 10,000£ in Debt, he would have been happy to have paid the Debt & then married me.'

Thrale made short work of negotiating the marriage contract with Sir Thomas, who confirmed that Hester would have her £10,000. In return Thrale agreed to place an estate he owned in Oxfordshire in trust and Hester was to be allowed from it an annual income of £200. In the event of her husband's death that would be doubled, and she would receive in addition a lump sum of £13,400.[14]

What was Hester's state of mind in those summer months of 1763? She wrote to a maiden aunt in Bath to tell of her engagement, and a discarded draft of the letter survives: 'With what Spirits I us'd to sit down to write to my Dear Aunt Sydney, & how slowly my Pen moves this Even,' she wrote. And later: 'Our mutual Preference of each other to all the rest of the World, that Preference not founded on Passion but on Reason, gives us some Right to expect some Happiness.'[15] Hardly the letter of a young woman eagerly counting the days on her calendar.

She was married in St Anne's Church, Soho, on 11 October. Sir Thomas gave her away and the service was conducted (somewhat oddly, one might think, given all that had passed between them) by her egregious cousin – 'the false parson Thelwall'. He had, she wrote coldly, 'pretended to rejoyce, begged he might tye the Knot as he call'd it, to which Mr Thrale of course made no Objection, as he knew nothing of my Affairs'.

Afterwards the wedding party drove out into the Surrey countryside to Streatham Park: 'And what a House it was then! A little squeezed miserable Place with a wretched Court before it, & all those noble Elm Trees out upon the Common. Such Furniture too! I can but laugh when it crosses my Recollection.'

All rather different from her dear Offley Place – 'where I pass'd my Youth – *and hoped to pass my Age*'. But that was a dream that was fading fast. Less than a month after her own wedding came the news that her uncle had finally married the widow King.

~❧ 1763–84 ❧~
Hester Thrale

~❧ 4 ❧~
Mistress of Streatham

'EXCEPT for *one* five minutes only by mere accident,' Hester later wrote, 'I never had had a Teste a Teste with my Husband in my whole Life till quite the Evening of the Wedding Day.' There was clearly work to be done in breathing some warmth into their relationship. 'I was now a married Woman: young enough to be proud of being such,' she recalled:

> – & silly enough to expect that my husband's heart was to be won by the same empty Tricks that had pleased my Father & my Uncle. so I wrote verses in *his* praise instead of *theirs* ... It seemed odd when I observed them repress'd as Impertinent, or rejected as superfluous: but it was Natural to try, & try again: so Instead of Dressing showily, or behaving usefully – I sate at home & wrote Verses.[1]

Thrale was unmoved. The newly installed mistress of Streatham quickly understood that outside the bedroom, her master required little of her. Even the kitchen was off-limits. Thrale, who was fond of his food, claimed that as part of his domain; the domestic skills Hester had acquired at Offley were of no use to her here: 'We kept the finest table possible at Streatham Park; but *his* Wife was not to *stink of the Kitchen* so I never knew what was for Dinner till I saw it.'[2] Thrale also frowned on the idea of her continuing to ride, pronouncing it too masculine a pursuit for a lady.

Mrs Salusbury, for whom Thrale always showed great affection and respect, had stayed on at Streatham. In those first months after Hester's marriage, the two women occupied themselves quietly with reading, needlework and backgammon: 'Mean Time my Husband went every day to London & returned either to dinner or Tea, said he always found two agreeable Women ready to receive him, & thus we lived on Terms of great Civility & Politeness, if not of strong Alliance and Connection.'

That civility and politeness came briefly under strain when a young cousin, one of Sir Lynch Cotton's daughters, came to stay: 'Mr Thrale grew passionately fond of her,' Hester recalled, 'so fond indeed that I was not much pleased with the partiality – from *Female* Motives perhaps ... I apprehended some Mischief to her, and blame to Mr Thrale.'

Thrale had little time for what he termed 'Neighbourhood' – 'My Mother perfectly agreed with him,' Hester wrote, 'so we visited nobody.' Occasionally, however, Thrale brought down friends from his bachelor days to meet his bride – '*les amis du Maison*', as Hester ungrammatically called them.

Georgie Bodens was enormously fat, walked with a limp and spoke with a stammer – 'a Man of much Wit, Archness, & a peculiar Vein of humour'. He had recently left the army after twenty-four years in the Coldstream Guards. Peter King – the sixth Baron King of Ockham – was the grandson of a former Lord Chancellor. Hester would later discover that her low opinion of him was shared by Johnson: 'It is a Mind in which nothing has grown up of itself & where whatever has been transplanted – has degenerated.'

Another of '*les amis*' was a Captain Conway, a hot-tempered naval man; a relative of Hester's said of him that he was 'like a Man who had been drown'd, & then set on his Head; which so displaced all his Ideas that they never could get settled again'. Thrale's circle also included Simon Luttrell, notorious as 'the wicked madman' or 'King of Hell'. His son, Colonel Henry Luttrell, would be the opponent of Wilkes in the famous Middlesex election of 1768. His father once challenged him to a duel, but the younger man refused – not because he was his father, but because he was not a gentleman.

Such was the *galère* which Hester found herself called on to receive in her drawing room in the early months of her marriage: 'I liked none of 'em but Murphy, & my Mother despised them all.' She did, for all that, have a soft spot for an elderly Irish doctor called Fitzpatrick who had spent much of his early life abroad and was, when not in his cups, an agreeable companion.

As he had been a friend of Thrale's father, Hester felt that by quizzing him she might learn something of what she termed '*les tracasseries de famille*'.[3] In due course the old doctor let the cat out of the bag about something that she had puzzled over since her engagement. Why had Thrale chosen her? 'He had, the doctor said, asked several women ... but all except *me* refused to live in the Borough, to which, and to his business, he observed, that Mr Thrale was as unaccountably attached *now* as he had been in his father's time averse from both.'[4]

Borough or Brewery House was where Thrale normally lived during the winter – an austere four-storeyed mansion at the entrance to the cobbled brew yard in Southwark. He had not thought to consult his bride about the alterations he had set in hand there, but by January they were complete, and he no longer had to make the sometimes risky journey from Streatham – only a few months earlier a highwayman had held up his coach and relieved him of his watch, thirteen guineas and his silver shoe buckles.[5]

The house backed on to the nine-acre site of the brewery itself – storehouses, stabling for close on a hundred horses, dung pits, thirty-eight huge vats. It was not the most salubrious part of town: 'London's scrap-heap' was how one writer described it – 'the refuge of its excluded occupations and its rejected residents'. The Globe Theatre had stood here in Shakespeare's day; the address, Dead Man's Place, was a reminder of the pest-houses established during the great plague. Nearby were Dirty Lane and Naked Boy Yard, Potts's vinegar factory and the old decayed Clink Prison.

'Our Society at the Borough House was exceedingly circumscribed,' Hester wrote: 'Few people would come to so strange a Place – few indeed *could* come; but as we kept Two Equipages I had it always in my Power to go out. My mother however thought the closer I kept home the better.'[6]

That was Thrale's view, too, although he himself, having spent the morning in his counting house, felt free to pass his evenings at the opera or the theatre or at Carlisle House. Here Teresa Cornelys, a former mistress of Casanova's, presided over subscription balls and masquerades. Some were attracted by the Bach-Abel concerts held there for some years; others went to gamble; the house, lavishly decorated in the Chinese taste, had a reputation for loose conduct.

Many years later, when she was very old, a young friend told Hester that his mother had once seen her with her husband at the theatre, in the winter of 1764, sparkling in diamonds. She had written it down when she came home, he told her, 'observing how beautiful you were'. Hester was obliged to disabuse him: 'I never possessed a diamond in my life,' was my reply, 'never was in a theatre from my first wedding day, till my daughter born in 1764 went with me; and never was considered through the early periods of my life as even tolerably pretty.'[7]

Was it Polly Hart who sparkled in diamonds that night in the theatre? A piece of gossip in one of Horace Walpole's letters suggests that she had by then passed into others' 'keeping'.[8] Whoever it was, it is clear that on the day he stood in church before Hester's creepy cousin and answered 'I will', Henry Thrale had his fingers firmly crossed.

᠆᠊᠊ᥫ᠊ᥨ᠊᠊

Mrs Salusbury chose not to stay in Southwark and returned to the house in Dean Street – 'and thither I went – oh how willingly!' Hester wrote, 'to visit her every day'.[9] She normally went at noon and stayed until five – '& then most probably went again in the Afternoon when My Master drove out to divert himself'. Her few visitors at Brewery House included Thrale's three sisters, but they were not received with much warmth: 'My Mother charged me not to be free or intimate with 'em, & none of them pleased me enough to make me wish to break her Injunction.'

Early in 1764 Hester discovered she was pregnant. She gave birth to a girl on 17 September. Thrale, who for some reason had got it into his head that they were unlikely to have children, was delighted. 'As for poor me,' Hester wrote plaintively, 'I believe he might visit my Chamber two or Three Times a Week in a sort of formal Way, which my Mother said was *quite right*, – & therefore I appeared to think so too.'

The child was named after Mrs Salusbury – Hester Maria – and christened at St Saviour's Church, Southwark, the present-day Southwark Cathedral. Hester breast-fed the infant – the only time she would ever do so; she became so thin and run-down in consequence that an ass was purchased so that she might regain her strength by drinking quantities of its milk.

To the modern mind, Hester's passivity towards her husband is less remarkable only than her submissiveness to her mother. Mrs Salusbury's new status as a grandmother did nothing to make her less officious:

It was now Time to *teach* the little Girl my Mother said, & bring
her forward as She had done by me; I was reproached with want of
Attention to my Daughter, & told that I had now – *or ought* to have,
something to amuse me without visiting or fooling at Places of publick
Resort, like fashionable Wives & Parents. I therefore did buckle hard to
my Business, taught this poor Infant twenty pretty Tricks, she was no
better for Learning ...

She was soon to discover that time could be employed in a manner that
was rather less stultifying. On 9 January 1765 Arthur Murphy came to
dinner at Dead Man's Place and brought with him his friend Samuel
Johnson.

When she was a girl Hester had heard Johnson's praises sung by Hogarth.
His conversation, he said, 'was to the talk of other men, "like Titian's
painting compared to Hudson's"'.[10] Now she had the opportunity to
judge for herself.

At fifty-five, Johnson was more than thirty years her senior. Widowed
more than a decade previously, he was living in disorderly squalor in
Inner Temple Lane, surrounded by the oddly assorted household which
was the source of such bafflement to his friends: the blind poetess Anna
Williams, the silent and unprepossessing Robert Levet described by
Boswell as 'an obscure practiser in physick among the lower people',
Francis Barber, the young negro from Jamaica whom Johnson had taken
into his service and whom he would later send to the grammar school
at Bishop's Stortford to learn Latin and Greek.[11]

The *Dictionary*, *The Vanity of Human Wishes* and the *Rambler* were all
behind him. For several years now he had written almost nothing. The
contract he had signed in 1756 to complete an eight-volume edition of
Shakespeare remained unfulfilled, something which had attracted the hostile attention of Charles Churchill in his digressive satire *The Ghosts*:

He for *subscribers* baits his hook
And takes their cash – but where's the Book?[12]

Although he contrived in the main to conceal it from his friends,

Johnson had for some years been teetering on the verge of mental break-down. 'A kind of strange oblivion has overspread me,' he wrote in his journal in the spring of 1764, 'so that I know not what has become of the last year.'[13] And in the small hours of Easter morning, he penned an entry which is part supplication, part cry of anguish: 'Almighty and most merciful Father, who hast created and preserved me ... deliver me from the distresses of vain terrour.'[14]

Murphy had given the Thrales 'general cautions not to be surprised at his figure, dress or behaviour', but the evening was a success: 'We liked each other so well,' Hester wrote, 'that the next Thursday was appointed for the same Company to meet,' and from that time Johnson dined with them regularly through the winter.

Hester showed Johnson some of her poetry. 'Ode to a Robin Red-breast' was one of the pieces written in her early days at Streatham in an attempt to please her husband. The great man liked it better than Thrale had done: 'Mr Johnson says the verses are Very pretty, & much in Lord Lyttelton's Style. A good one says he – for a *Lady*.'

Johnson was sufficiently impressed to suggest a collaboration. He had been contemplating a translation from the Latin of Boethius,[15] and together they set to work on the poems in his *Consolations of Philosophy*. Johnson was also busy at this time soliciting poems from friends to plump up a rather slim collection that Anna Williams was eager to publish. 'Have you any Verses by You which have never been seen?' he asked Hester: 'I show'd him a Tale that I had written the Week before & he liked it so well it was seized on Instantly, & called *The Three Warnings*.'[16]

The tale is of old Farmer Dobson, to whom Death has promised three warnings before coming to claim him. When the Grim Reaper finally appears, Dobson vehemently denies that he has received any warnings at all, but Death is implacable:

> ... If you are lame, and deaf, and blind,
> You've had your three sufficient Warnings.
> So come along, no more we'll part,
> He said, and touch'd him with his dart.

In 1770 the piece would find its way into Dodsley's *Collection of Poems by Several Hands*, the most widely read anthology of the day – the first time anything had appeared under her own name. It was reprinted many times, figured frequently in public recitations and would remain the best known of all her poems.

In the summer the Thrales travelled down to Brighthelmstone, the modern Brighton, where Thrale had a house in West Street. Hester was expecting her second child, and the pregnancy was proving troublesome. They invited Johnson to join them. 'I am afraid to make promises even to myself,' he replied in the middle of August, 'but I hope that the week after next, will be the end of my present business.'[17]

He had finally buckled down to finishing the Shakespeare edition, and was at work on the Preface. By early September the work was done; Adam Smith, who did not much like Johnson, would describe it as 'the most *manly* piece of criticism that was ever published in any country'.

'Where should pleasure be sought but under Mrs Thrale's influence?' he had written. But he arrived in Brighton to discover that the Thrales had left suddenly for London; news had come of the death of one of the two members of Parliament for Southwark, and Thrale had hurried back to press his candidature. Johnson, unable to contain his disappointment, fired off an angry letter. Murphy was called in to pour oil on the waters, and Johnson, suitably mollified, was soon lending a hand with Thrale's election literature.

The campaign was only a few days old when Hester gave birth to her second daughter. 'I had never had a Day's Health during the whole Gestation,' she wrote, '– the Labour was however particularly short and easy.'[18] The child was baptized Frances on 3 October, but died three days later of what Hester called 'the watery gripes' – infantile diarrhoea, presumably, brought on by an infection.

It was a century noted for its tough-mindedness, a quality which Hester would exhibit throughout her life. Mastering her grief, she threw herself into the campaign: 'I grew useful now, *almost* necessary; wrote the advertisements, looked to the treats, and people to whom I was till then unknown, admired how happy Mr Thrale must be in such a *wonder* of a wife.'[19]

Thrale's opponent eventually withdrew. Two days before Christmas he was officially returned and embarked on his fifteen-year career in the Commons.

❧ ❦

While he was at work on his Shakespeare Preface, Johnson had moved yet again. He was now installed at 7 Johnson's Court, just off Fleet Street together with his increasingly dysfunctional household. 'At home we do not much quarrel,' he would write sardonically, 'but perhaps the less we quarrel the more we hate. There is as much malignity amongst us, as can well subsist, without any thoughts of daggers or poisons.'[20]

He was plagued by insomnia and increasingly convinced that he was going mad. His visits to Southwark became less frequent. The Thrales, concerned, took to calling on him, and were treated to alarming talk about 'the horrible condition of his mind, which he said was nearly distracted'. One morning in June they found him on his knees before John Delap, an Anglican clergyman and minor playwright, 'beseeching God to continue him the use of his understanding'; as Delap took his leave, Johnson cried out after him, asking to be remembered in his prayers. 'I felt excessively affected with grief, and well remember my husband involuntarily lifted up one hand to shut his mouth,' Hester wrote: 'Mr Thrale went away soon after, leaving me with him, and bidding me prevail on him to quit his close habitation in the court and come with us to Streatham, where I undertook the care of his health, and had the honour and happiness of contributing to its restoration.'[21]

Johnson stayed at Streatham until October. Not since his boyhood had he known what it was like to live as a member of a family. For the first time in his life, he was indulged. Never before had he had a coach at his disposal. Now, if he wished – he quite often did – he could gorge himself on peaches before breakfast. Slowly, he began to mend.

5

Enter James Boswell

THE THRALES' virtual adoption of Johnson made for difficulties with Mrs Salusbury: 'My Mother and he did not like one another much the first two or three years of their Acquaintance.' Mrs Salusbury was affronted when Johnson declared bluntly to Hester in her presence that she lived like her husband's kept mistress – 'shut from the world, its Pleasures, or its Cares'.[1] Johnson, for his part, was not best pleased when Mrs Salusbury's pet spaniel, Belle, gobbled up the buttered muffin that had been placed near the fire to keep warm for his breakfast.[2]

On her daughter's second birthday, Hester began to keep a journal. She called it *The Children's Book* and the first entry was a progress report on little Hester Maria's 'Corporeal & Mental Powers':

> She is neither remarkably big nor tall, being just 34 Inches high, but eminently pretty. She can speak most Words & speak them plain enough too, but is no great Talker: She repeats the Pater Noster, the three Christian Virtues & the Signs of the Zodiac in Watts's Verses … She can tell all her Letters great & small & spell little Words as D,o,g, Dog, C,a,t, Cat &c . . . She knows all the heathen Deities by their Attributes & counts 20 without missing one.[3]

Hester had now entered into the cycle of almost permanent pregnancy which was to characterize the years of her marriage to Thrale, and early the following year she presented her husband with a son and heir: 'Henry Salusbury Thrale was born the 15: Feby 1767. strong & lively at Southwark,' she wrote in the *Family Book*, '– he appears likely to live thank God.' A wet-nurse was quickly found but for the time being it was the accomplishments of her clever little daughter that commanded Hester's attention. Except in one particular, the child was every bit as precocious as she herself had been: 'She cannot read at all, but knows the Compass as perfectly as any Mariner upon the Seas; is mistress of the Solar System can trace the Orbits & tell the arbitrary Marks of the planets as readily as Dr Bradley.'[4]

As Dr Bradley was the Astronomer Royal we must perhaps aim off slightly here for maternal pride, but even in the eighteenth century it was not every two-year-old who knew the names of all the capital cities in Europe, could recite the first page of Lilly's Latin Grammar and also 'tell a little Story with some Grace & Emphasis, as the Story of the Fall of Man, of Perseus & Andromeda of the Judgment of Paris ...'[5]

The hand of Johnson is discernible here. 'The remembrance of what had passed in his own childhood,' Hester later wrote, 'made Mr Johnson very solicitous to preserve the felicity of children.' He interested himself in the welfare and education of all her offspring, and they were devoted to him, viewing him, in Walter Jackson Bate's happy phrase, 'as a combination of friend and a sort of toy elephant'.[6] The bond with 'Miss Hetty' was particularly strong. It was Johnson who started calling her 'Queen Hester', and 'Queeney' she remained.

Later he would teach her Latin and urge the importance of studying arithmetic. His letters as she grew to womanhood are full of endearments – 'My dear Sweeting', 'my lovely dear', 'my charming Queeney' – although that did not prevent him from reading her gentle lessons in moral philosophy – 'before you mingle in the crowd of life I wish you to exterminate Captiousness from your mind, as a very powerful and active cause of discontent'.[7] In lighter mode, he issues a warning against idleness: 'If ever therefore you catch yourself contentedly and placidly doing nothing, *sors de l'enchantement*, break away from the snare, find your book or your needle, or snatch the broom from the Maid.'[8]

Attendance at Westminster meant that Thrale was even less at home than before. As her acquaintance with Johnson ripened into friendship, Hester occasionally felt able to talk to him about her relations with her husband:

One Day that I mentioned Mr Thrale's cold Carriage to me, tho' with no Resentment, for it occasioned in me no Dislike; He said in Reply – Why How for Heaven's Sake Dearest Madam should any Man delight in a Wife that is to him neither Use nor Ornament? He cannot talk to you about his Business, which you do not understand; nor about his

Pleasures which you do not partake … You divide your Time between your Mamma & your Babies, & wonder you do not by that means become agreeable to your Husband.

This was an outrageous rejoinder, even by Johnson's robust standards, and he could not reasonably have complained if she had turned him out of the house there and then. Not a bit of it: 'This was so plain I could not fail to comprehend it, & gently hinted to my Mother that I had some Curiosity about the Trade, which I would may be one day get Mr Thrale to inform *me* about …'

Mrs Salusbury was totally unsympathetic – and almost as brutal as Johnson:

I had my Children to nurse and to teach, & that She thought that was better Employment than turning into *My Lady Mashtub* … so I went on in the old Way, brought a Baby once a Year, lost some of them & grew so anxious about the rest, that I now fairly cared for nothing else, but them and her; & not a little for Johnson, who I felt to be my true Friend, though I could not break thro' my Chains to take his Advice …

By the summer of 1767 Johnson was writing of Streatham as 'that place which your kindness and Mr Thrale's allows me to call *my home*'.[9] But he was also what Hester described as 'something like a regular inmate' at Southwark: 'Mr Thrale fitted him up an Apartment over the Counting House Two Pairs of Stairs high – & called it the *Round Tower*.'[10]

Johnson had quickly developed a healthy respect for Thrale. 'I know no man,' he later told Boswell, 'who is more master of his wife and family than Thrale. If he holds up a finger, he is obeyed.'[11] And he was quite ready to hold up a finger to Johnson: 'There, there,' he would say coldly, 'now we have had enough for one lecture, Dr Johnson; we will not be upon education any more till after dinner, if you please.'[12]

The Thrales also exerted themselves to improve Johnson's appearance. It was not just a matter of getting him to change his shirt more often or enliven the dark clothes he invariably wore with metal buttons. 'It was a perpetual miracle that he did not set himself on fire reading a-bed,' Hester wrote:

The fore-top of all his wigs were burned by the candle down to the very net-work. Mr Thrale's valet-de-chambre, for that reason, kept one always in his own hands, with which he met him at the parlour-door when the bell had called him down to dinner, and as he went up stairs to sleep in the afternoon, the same man constantly followed him with another.[13]

The early months of 1768 were an exhausting and stressful time for Hester. Parliament had been dissolved and Thrale was campaigning to retain his seat. Across the river, in Middlesex, the outlawed John Wilkes, enemy of the established order, was a candidate. He had no particular programme, but he had the support of 6,000 Spitalfields weavers, and the streets echoed to drunken shouts of 'Wilkes and Liberty'. Hester's fourth pregnancy was far advanced; anxious about the result in South-wark, she appealed for help to Johnson, who was on an extended visit to Oxford. Johnson, busy helping his young friend Robert Chambers with his Vinerian lectures, clearly did not believe Thrale faced defeat: 'Though I do not perceive that there is any need of help, I shall yet write another advertisement, lest you might suspect that my complaisance had more of idleness than sincerity.'[14]

On the reverse of the letter he had written an election address, which appeared in the London papers under Thrale's name. Thrale himself wrote three more, and on 23 March was returned top of the poll, 89 votes ahead of Sir Joseph Mawbey, a Vauxhall vinegar distiller. Hester, utterly drained, returned immediately to Streatham, and a week later gave birth to a daughter.

Mrs Salusbury stood godmother for the fourth time, and the Thrales' choice as godfather fell on a young man called Jeremiah Crutchley. Thrale was his guardian; his father – the family had been dyers in Clink Street, Southwark – had been a close friend of Ralph Thrale's. Crutchley would impinge on Hester's life more than once; it is not clear when a rumour which she recorded in *Thraliana* some years later first came to her ears: 'He is supposed by those that knew his Mother & her Connec-tions to be Mr Thrale's natural son, & in many Things he resembles him, but not in Person; as he is both ugly & aukward. Mr Thrale certainly believed he was his Son, & once told me as much ...'

Thrale would have been seventeen when Crutchley was born, and the boy's mother twenty-two. Why would Thrale acknowledge paternity if it were not the case? The question hangs in the air, like so many others about this strange man. Katharine Balderston, the editor of *Thraliana*, disposed of the matter in a brief deadly footnote: 'No confirmation of this scandal survives, except the known libertinism of Mr Thrale.'[15]

The choice of names for the Thrales' fourth child was not particularly happy – 'Anna Maria Thrale so named after my Dear Aunt & friend the first Wife of Sir Thos Salusbury my Uncle'.[16] Hester had not seen her uncle since her marriage. Mrs Salusbury had made no effort to conceal her bitter resentment of her brother-in-law's new wife, and Sir Thomas had repaid her hostility by reneging on his promise to pay her an annuity. Hester remained fond of her uncle, but her mother grimly opposed any idea of trying to build bridges: 'If I offered to think of paying him a Visit or a Compliment of any Sort, She would be out of humour & cry for whole Days ...'

Hester still nursed a hope that she might one day inherit Offley. The dread widow had now, after all, been married to Sir Thomas for four years; there had been no children, and she was already well into her forties. It was obtuse of Hester not to see how much better her interest might have been served if she had flattered the second Lady Salusbury by naming the child after her – just how obtuse would become painfully clear before many more years had passed.

❧

James Boswell was in town in the spring and early summer of 1768 – his first visit for two years. His *Account of Corsica*, part travelogue, part biography, had just appeared, and a first edition of 3,500 copies sold out in six weeks. Gratified by his newfound celebrity and eager to renew his acquaintance with Johnson and Garrick and Goldsmith, he took lodgings in Half Moon Street and promptly 'sallied forth like a roaring lion after girls'. He quickly found his prey: 'I had a neat little lass *in armour*, at a tavern in the Strand.' He soon became careless, however, and was confined to his lodgings with a severe bout of gonorrhoea. The cure – his ninth – lasted six weeks, but his sociability was unblunted. Johnson called to see him, and so did Garrick and David Hume and Benjamin Franklin.

Johnson had not previously told him anything of his friendship with

the Thrales and the change it had made to his life. Now Boswell's antennae quivered. Calling at Johnson Court shortly before his return to
Scotland, he encountered Mrs Thrale who had come to take Johnson
to Streatham in her coach. Never slow to seize an opportunity, Boswell
jumped in unbidden. He recalled their brief conversation in a letter to
Hester the following year: 'I told you, Madam, that you and I were
rivals for that great man. You would take him to the country, when I was
anxious to keep him in town.'[17] It was the beginning of an acquaintance
that could never ripen into friendship; what began as polite rivalry would
eventually make them bitter enemies.

Boswell travelled north to gamble at cards and continue his search for
a wife and Hester carried Johnson off to Streatham. He was still far from
well, and in September, hoping to improve his health, the Thrales took
him on what Hester called 'a little Tour into Kent'. Shortly after their
return, when Johnson had gone up to London for a few days, she went
into his apartment 'to see that all was left as it should be'. In a drawer
that had not been closed she caught sight of his journal. It lay open at
an entry made on the night of 18 September – his birthday – which they
had spent in Town Malling, a small market town near Maidstone. She
found what she read there so remarkable that she made a copy: 'I have
now begun the sixtieth year of my life,' it began. 'How the last year has
past I am unwilling to terrify myself with thinking …'[18]

It was more than a decade before Hester made any mention in writing
of what passed between them in the following weeks – a veiled reference
in *Thraliana* to his having entrusted her 'with a Secret far dearer to him
than his Life':

> Such however is his nobleness, & such his partiality, that I sincerely
> believe he has never since that Day regretted his Confidence, or ever
> looked with less kind Affection on her who had him in her Power …
> Well does he contradict the maxim of Rochefoucault, that no Man is a
> Hero to his Valet de Chambre. – Johnson is more a Hero to me than to
> any one – & I have been more to him for Intimacy, than ever was any
> Man's Valet de Chambre.

What was that secret? Many have assumed it related to an earlier attachment to some woman other than his wife, but it was more complicated

and more painful than that. Johnson was gripped for much of his life by powerful sexual urges and by even stronger fears of insanity. Freud would not have detained him long in his consulting room. Johnson's 'vile melancholy' was triggered by feelings of guilt at the lustful fantasies which took possession of him from time to time and by the recurring belief that he was going out of his mind.

'Poor Johnson!' Hester would write shortly after his death. 'I see they will leave *nothing untold* that I laboured so long to keep secret; & I was so very delicate in trying to conceal his fancied Insanity, that I retained no Proofs of it – or hardly any –'

Many years later, one of those proofs came to light. After her death, the contents of her library and other belongings were dispersed in a sale at Manchester. One item in the catalogue was identified by a note in Hester's own hand: '*Johnson's padlock, committed to my care in the year 1768.*' Walter Jackson Bate has noted how frequently expressions of dread on Johnson's part employ imagery of fetters or shackles – it was, after all, an age in which the insane were still often kept in chains. The padlock which he gave into Hester's keeping was a weapon in the fight he believed he was waging against madness. That he could entrust it to her and talk to her about the fantasies produced by his diseased imagination is a measure of the trust that had grown up between them. It was not the last time that he would surrender himself to her in this way.

It was by no means all intense communing about Johnson's anguished imaginings. The easy, relaxed nature of their relations in these early years shines out from the pages of *Thraliana*. Johnson once told Hester that of all animals she most resembled the rattlesnake – 'for many have felt your Venom, few have escap'd your Attractions, and all the world knows you have the Rattle'. Hester's powers of repartee were well developed: 'In return I observed to him that he most resembled an Elephant whose Weight could crush the Crocodile, & whose Proboscis could from its Force and Ductility either lift up the Buffalo, or pick up the Pin.'

Johnson's domestication at Streatham and Southwark enlarged and enriched Hester's social circle. Several of Thrale's *louche* cronies from bachelor days fell away and Hester was able to enjoy the more congenial and stimulating company of some of Johnson's friends and acquaintances – Joshua Reynolds, newly appointed the first President of the infant Royal Academy, David Garrick, Edmund Burke, Oliver Goldsmith. Some of them made a better first impression than others: 'Doctor Goldsmith was certainly a Man extremely odd: the first Time he dined with us, he gravely asked Mʳ Thrale how much a Year he got by his Business? Who answered with singular propriety, we don't talk of those things much in Company Doctor – but I hope to have the honour of knowing you so well that I shall wonder less at the Question.'

Thrale himself was a good listener, but not noted as a conversationalist – the waspish A. M. Broadley wrote that he had acquired at Oxford 'a laborious tincture of scholarship which he improved by silence'.[19] Johnson formed a higher opinion of the man to whom he owed so much – his 'Master', as he called him. 'Is Mr Thrale a man of conversation, or is he only wise and silent?' someone once asked him. 'Why, Sir,' Johnson replied, 'his conversation does not show the minute hand; but he strikes the hour very correctly.'[20] He also insisted to Boswell that it was a mistake to suppose that Hester's literary attainments were superior to those of her husband: 'He is a regular scholar; but her learning is that of a school-boy in one of the lower forms.'[21]

❧ ❦

'Hester Maria Thrale is this Day four Years & a Quarter old.' Hester continued to record the progress of her young in the *Children's Book*. 'She has this day repeated her Catechism quite thro', her Latin Grammar to the end of the 5 Declensions, a Fable in Phædrus, an Epigram in Martial, the Revolutions Diameters & Distance of the Planets ...' But there were limits to her pride in this infant prodigy: 'Her Temper is not so good; reserved to all, insolent where She is free, & sullen to those who teach or dress or do anything towards her. Never in a Passion, but obstinate to that uncommon Degree that no Punishment except severe Smart can prevail on her to beg Pardon if She has offended.'[22] Queeney, that is to say, was no stranger to the rod that lay on the mantelpiece in the nursery.

In the early summer of 1769 Hester gave birth to her fifth child, who was 'large strong and handsome', she wrote and, 'likely to live'.[23] She was named Lucy after her Welsh great-grandmother, and the Thrales indulged Johnson in his wish that she might be called Elizabeth after his beloved 'Tetty'. They also asked him to be the child's godfather and he made hurried preparations to return 'home' from Oxford. 'Mr Thrale tells me that my furlough is shortened,' he wrote to Hester: 'I have not yet found any place from which I shall not willingly depart, to come back to you.'[24]

Later in the summer, the Thrales went down to Brighton, and prevailed on Johnson to join them. Hester, in the *Anecdotes* she published after his death, recalled his reluctance to leave the metropolis. 'There is in this world no real delight (excepting those of sensuality), but exchange of ideas in conversation,' he declared: 'Whoever has once experienced the full flow of London talk, when he retires to country friendship and rural sports, must either be contented to turn baby again and play with the rattle, or he will pine away like a great fish in a little pond, and die for want of his usual food.'[25]

He shared Hester's pleasure in sea-bathing, however; she recorded the admiring remark of one of the men whose job it was to dip people in the sea: 'Why Sir (says the dipper), you must have been a stout-hearted gentleman forty years ago.'[26]

Thrale, determined that Queeney should feel at home in the water, used to teach her with a frog in a large basin – 'and be so rough with her if she alleged terror', Hester recalled, 'that we swam in our own defence, for he swore he would follow us with a horsewhip if we dug a hole in the water, as he justly called it'.[27] Hester herself remained an enthusiastic swimmer into old age.

Before the end of their Brighton holiday, Hester received a letter from Boswell. 'After much inconstancy I am fixed in my choice of a wife,' he wrote, 'and am to be married when I return to Scotland. Before entering on that important state to happiness or misery, I am anxious to hear the Oracle ...'[28] The Oracle was soon back in town and before long presented him with what Boswell described as his 'first ticket to a great deal of most agreeable society' – an invitation from Hester to dine at Streatham. Johnson, he recorded, 'though quite at home, was yet looked up to with an awe, tempered by affection'. There was some banter about Scotland and the Scots, and then Hester and Johnson engaged in a spirited dispute over the merits of Prior. Johnson maintained that he wrote of love like a man who had never experienced it: 'Mrs. Thrale stood to her gun with great courage, in defence of amorous ditties, which Johnson despised, till he at last silenced her by saying, "My dear Lady, talk no more of this. Nonsense can be defended but by nonsense."'[29]

Hester was never silenced for long – that was one of the reasons Johnson valued her company so highly. For him, conversation was a compulsively competitive business. He always talked for victory. 'There's no chance in arguing with such a man,' Goldsmith once said, 'for, like the Tartar horse, if he does not conquer you in front, his kick from behind is sure to be fatal.' For Johnson the 'full flow of London talk' involved knocking his interlocutor to the ground as frequently as possible. Hester might be less than five feet tall and plump with it, but she always got up again, eager for the next round.

6

Thrale's Annus Horribilis

HESTER'S younger children now began to challenge Queeney for space in the *Children's Book*:

> Henry Salusbury Thrale went into Breeches at the age of two Years & 3 Months: he was not quite two, when he carried a Bag containing 27:^{s} in Copper from the Compting House to the Breakfast parlour in the Borough. He is remarkably strong made, course & bony: – not handsome at all, but of perfect Proportion; & has a surly look with the honestest & sweetest Temper in the World.[1]

Little Anna Maria was much more delicate, and as the winter of 1769–70 came on, Hester's mother took her to live with her in Dean Street, which was considered more salubrious than Southwark. She was a high-spirited child – and clearly something of a madam: 'She could kiss her hand at 9 Months old, & understand all one said to her: could walk to perfection, and even with an Air at a Year old, & seems to intend being Queen of us all if She lives which I do not expect She is so very lean – I think she is consumptive –'[2]

Anna Maria became ill early in the New Year. Purging, blistering, bleeding with leeches all proved ineffective; 'a Dropsy of the Brain', pronounced one of the doctors called in for consultation. Mrs Salusbury, who was constantly at the child's bedside, revived her briefly by the application of a feather dipped in wine, but hope was short-lived. 'She fell into a violently imflammatory fever & died Yesterday, 20: March 1770.' Hester wrote in the *Children's Book*: 'I am now myself near five Months gone with Child, and I fear the Shock and anxiety of this last fortnight has done irreparable injury to my little Companion – if so I have lost two Children this Spring – how dreadful!'[3]

Life expectancy in England was then little higher than in the poorest countries of Africa today. Fewer than half the children born in grimy, disease-ridden London survived until their tenth birthday. Our eighteenth-century ancestors looked death more squarely in the face than we do. So it is perhaps not entirely surprising to read that on the day after Anna Maria died Hester went to the theatre – 'the first Theatre I have set foot in, since my eldest Daughter was born'.[4] She took the five-year-old Queeney with her to Drury Lane, to a command performance of *Judas Maccabeus*:

> When She came home She swaggered poor Harry with telling him the Wonders She had seen. I saw the King said She, do you know what a King is? Yes replies Harry, a Picture of a Man, a Sign of a Man's head – no, no, cried the Girl impatiently the King that wears the Crown: do you know what a Crown is – Yes I do, says Harry very well, it is 3ˢ and 6ᵈ ...[5]

Big sisters have not changed much over the years.

The child that Hester was carrying was born more than two months prematurely – 'miserably lean and feeble indeed, quite a mournful Object', she wrote. The 'mournful Object' was christened Susanna Arabella. She grew to be quite a beauty, had what her mother described as 'the unenviable distinction' of attracting the Prince of Wales's attention at Brighton – and lived to be eighty-eight.

❧

News came later that year that Sir Thomas was dying and Hester resolved to go to him: 'It had now been nine Years since I had seen Offley, and seven since I saw him; yet my Affection for him suddenly renewed at the thoughts of his Danger, & besides I had a large Stake depending, and supposed myself interested in his Welfare in a pecuniary Sense.'

It was the first time she had ever gone against the wishes either of Thrale or her mother: 'My Mother try'd all *her* Power, & when that failed, my Husband's had little Chance; nor did he trouble himself much either to encourage or contradict me, but laughed at the project as a wild one, & said Lady Salusbury would shut me out of Doors he suppos'd ...'

On her arrival she found that her uncle was out of danger. He made a great fuss of her, enquired after her children, spoke of her in front of the servants as his heiress – at which Lady Salusbury 'sate like one

Thunderstruck – yet swelling with rage'. The next morning Sir Thomas's manner was notably cooler, and the mistress of the house did not come down to breakfast; words had clearly been exchanged. Hester took her leave, her uncle insisting on sending her twenty miles on the road in his own carriage:

> Well! I returned to Streatham jocund enough, & highly pleased with my Expedition; I found my Mother & My Master well pleased too, & chearfully resumed my usual Employments and Amusements. I was grown fond of my Poultry my Dairy &c. and had now no other Desire than that of sitting down safely and quietly at Streatham to which of late I had rather begun to attach myself.

But she added – perhaps on rereading what she a had written – a bleak footnote: 'The agitation of my Mind added to the Journey made me miscarry, but as I had now Children enough, nobody much cared about that: my Health indeed never was much the Cause of their Concern.'

❧ ❧

It was at the Thrales' in 1770 that Johnson wrote *The False Alarm*,[6] the first of his four political pamphlets and the one of which he himself thought most highly. Wilkes had not taken his seat after the 1768 election as he had been committed to prison before Parliament met. Although he was subsequently returned on four successive occasions, the government contrived to have his election declared void. Thrale had voted consistently with the government, and Johnson shared his view of Wilkes's radicalism – and of the London mob from which he drew his support. *The False Alarm* has often been ignorantly represented as a case of the Tory Johnson prostituting his talent to show that he was worth his pension, but this overlooks the inconvenient fact that he was defending the policy of a Whig administration. One of the best things in it is the celebrated passage in which he mocks the ease with which signatures can be gathered for petitions: 'One man signs because he hates the papists; another because he has vowed destruction to the turnpikes; one because it will vex the parson; another because he owes his landlord nothing; one because he is rich; another because he is poor; one to shew that he is not afraid, and another to show that he can write.'

Hester herself was now scribbling busily in a number of different notebooks, including one devoted exclusively to the sayings of Johnson. 'I mean one day or another to digest and place them in some order,' she wrote.[7] The scope of the *Children's Book* had gradually expanded, and at some point she amplified the title on the cover to read *The Children's Book or rather Family Book*. Further instances of Queeney's precocity are regularly recorded but there were aspects of her daughter's character which she continued to view with a colder eye: 'Her Temper continues the same too; reserved and shy with a considerable Share of Obstinacy, & I think a Heart void of all Affection for any Person in the World ...'[8]

Hester had all her children inoculated against smallpox by Daniel Sutton, who until recently had been the inoculator of first choice for the wealthy.[9] Although it was half a century since Lady Mary Wortley Montagu had introduced the practice from Constantinople, it remained controversial. Sutton had made a fortune since setting up in independent practice in 1763 – he earned 2,000 guineas in his first year – but a year before inoculating Queeney in 1767, he had appeared at Chelmsford summer assizes charged with causing the epidemic then raging in the town.

One evening in the spring of 1771 Hester persuaded Johnson to go with her to a performance of *Messiah* at Covent Garden. She knew she was taking a risk – 'he was for the most part an exceedingly bad playhouse companion, as his person drew people's eyes upon the box, and the loudness of his voice made it difficult for me to hear any body but himself'.[10] On this occasion he sat surprisingly quiet, although it emerged when they got home that his mind had not been entirely on the music. He recited some Latin verses he had composed during the performance; sixteen lines on the inability of theatrical performance to fill the heart and mind. He invited Hester to produce an English version by breakfast time – a challenge to which she rose with some spirit.[11]

Thrale had ambitions to improve the house at Streatham, and in 1771 work began on the addition of a library and several other rooms. In time the library would be hung with thirteen portraits by Reynolds, a gallery devoted to her 'Streatham worthies' as Hester called them. Johnson and Goldsmith and old friends of Thrale's like Murphy and Lyttelton were among the earliest to be painted and over the next decade they would be joined by Burke and Garrick and Chambers and Reynolds himself – the well-known self-portrait now in the Tate in which he holds his left hand up to his ear in a clear allusion to his deafness. Johnson was not flattered by his own likeness. Reynolds, he told Hester, could paint himself as deaf as he chose, but 'I will not be blinking Sam'.

Johnson had a passion for chemical experiments – 'chymist', as he spelt it, was defined in the *Dictionary* as 'a philosopher by fire'. It was an interest which Hester shared: 'When we come together to practice chymistry,' he wrote to her from Derbyshire in the summer of 1771, 'I believe we shall find our furnaces sufficient for most operations.'[12] A fortnight later he wrote again to request a favour: 'Be pleased to make my compliments to Mr Thrale and desire that his builders will leave about a hundred loose bricks. I can at present think of no better place for Chimistry in fair weather, than the pump side of the kitchen garden.'[13]

They amused themselves for some time with 'drawing essences and colouring liquors' but their attempts to extend the frontiers of science were short-lived:

> The danger Mr Thrale found his friend in one day when I was driven to London, and he had got the children and servants round him to see some experiments performed, put an end to all our entertainment; so well was the master of the house persuaded that his short sight would have been his destruction in a moment, by bringing him close to a fierce and violent flame.[14]

Towards the end of July, Hester gave birth for the seventh time. 'Sophia Thrale born,' she wrote in the *Children's Book*: she was 'large and likely to live'. The child had been a month overdue. 'This naughty Baby stays so long that I am afraid it will be a Giant like King Richard,' Johnson had written.[15] Thrale conveyed the news to him in a brief note. 'Our Mistress,' he wrote matter-of-factly, 'gives us good expectations of her recovery, considering how much more she suffer'd, than usual.'[16] Johnson dashed off a letter to Queeney – 'My sweet, dear, pretty, little Miss', as he called her: 'Please to tell little Mama, that I am glad to hear, that she is well ... desire her to make haste and be quite well, for, You know, that You and I are to tye her to the tree, but we will not do it while she is weak.'[17]

~ぺ ぽ~

Rickets, anaemia, mastoids, umbilical rupture, worms – Hester continued to catalogue in the *Children's Book* the grim succession of ailments that afflicted her ever-growing brood and which the best efforts of physicians, surgeons and apothecaries seemed powerless to alleviate. She appeared at times to view her children with a detachment verging on the unnatural: 'Susanna Arabella Thrale is now two years old: small, ugly & lean as ever; her Colour like that of an ill painted Wall grown dirty.'[18]

The doctors the Thrales summoned were all prominent in their profession. Robert Bromfield, physician to the British Lying-In Hospital, believed Susanna was suffering from scurvy, and purged her accordingly. Herbert Lawrence was an old family friend. It was he who had been summoned to Dean Street ten years earlier when Hester's father suffered his fatal attack. He recommended cold bathing and the administration of bark, a powder from the cinchona tree given to reduce fever. A third consultant, Fleming Pinkstan, recommended fumigation. 'She has gone through all the rest, and shall now begin to be smoked,' Hester wrote – the two-year-old was to be subjected, that is to say, to a tobacco smoke enema. 'I will send her to my Mother at Streatham,' she resolved; 'perhaps country air may do something.'[19]

There was little country air could do for Mrs Salusbury. 'My Mother's Disorder – a Cancer – admitting of no Cure,' Hester wrote, 'I bore it, as one always does bear real Evils I think, with a sort of sullen Resignation.' Her mother and Johnson had long made up their differences, and he was full of solicitude. 'Tell dear Grandmama that I am very sorry for her pain,' he wrote to Queeney.[20] He also drew to Hester's attention a pamphlet by a Worcester physician called John Wall, who recommended the waters at Malvern for a variety of ailments, including cancer. 'The water can, I think, do no harm,' he wrote: 'If Mrs Salusbury should think fit to go before you can go with her I will attend her, if She will accept of my company, with great readiness at my own expence, and if I am in the Country will come back.'[21]

Cancer had not robbed Mrs Salusbury of her robust good sense. She remained at Streatham.

·❧ ❦·

Hester's anxieties were not all domestic:

> Mr Thrale had for some Time appeared pensive and gloomy – when I
> asked the Cause, he told me it was something relative to his Business:
> I grew more inquisitive & he told me that it was the bad Hops he had
> bought the year before which had spoyl'd all his Beer: I would have
> laughed at this, but found the Business too serious, and indeed he lost
> all Sleep & Appetite so fast that it alarmed me.

Her alarm was compounded by her condition ('I was big with Child –
as I almost always am') but more generally by the jittery state of the
markets. The most prominent victim of the recession of 1772 was the
Scottish banker Alexander Fordyce. He had lost heavily in the market
fluctuations caused by the dispute with Spain over the Falklands, and
had absconded. The ripples of the crash spread wide, and the Bank of
England had to step in to prop up some of the shakiest firms.

It took Thrale a week after Hester had first quizzed him to come clean
about the full extent of his difficulties, and he then did so not only to
her but also to her mother and to Johnson – '& begged for Counsel &
Comfort'. Always eager to steal a march on his rivals Whitbread and
Calvert, he had been talked into a project that had brought his business
to the verge of ruin. For Hester and for her mother, for the employees
of the brewery and for everyone who has ever written about the Thrales,
there was no question about who the villain of the piece was. Hester had
long been curious over whom her husband mainly turned to for advice
about his business: 'I wondered all the while where his heart lay; but it
was found at last ... A vulgar fellow, by name Humphrey Jackson, had,
as the clerks informed me, all in a breath, complete possession of it.'[22]

Jackson had been a friend since Thrale's bachelor days. Born in
Yorkshire, he had come to London and set up as a chemist in Upper
East Smithfield at the age of twenty-two. His inventive mind had previously won him a whole slew of patents – one for a highly commercial
medicinal compound called 'Cordial Bitter Tincture for the Stomach',
another for a method of producing isinglass from the air bladders of
certain fish. He was also the author of what is today regarded as the
first reliable book on the chemical detection of food adulteration. Now,

by Hester's account, he had persuaded Thrale of the viability of a novel method of brewing beer – 'without the *beggarly elements* of malt and hops', as she drily put it.[23]

The traditional charge sheet against Jackson contains a second item, to which Hester, in old age, gave vivid expression in an autobiographical note written for a friend:

> He had persuaded him to build a copper somewhere in East Smithfield, the very metal of which cost 2000*l.*, wherein this Jackson was to make experiments and conjure some curious stuff, which should preserve ships' bottoms from the worm; gaining from Government money to defray these mad expenses. Twenty enormous vats, holding 1000 hogsheads each – costly contents! – Then more holding 1000 Barrels each, were constructed to stew in this pernicious mess; and afterwards erected, on I forget how much ground bought for the ruinous purpose.[24]

Hester clearly believed that Jackson exercised a Svengali-like hold over Thrale, and her resentment was heightened by a certain snobbish disdain. She characterized him at one point as 'that wicked *Haman!*' – the Persian official in the Old Testament who sought the destruction of the Jews but was hanged from his own gallows when Esther exposed his scheming to King Ahasuerus.[25]

Modern research into Jackson's writings and activities[26] suggest that Hester was both confused and misinformed. In 1768, four years before the crisis at the brewery, Jackson had been granted a patent for a method of hardening and preserving wood; this was approved by the College of Physicians and successfully applied to a number of warships. When Captain Cook returned from his second round-the-world voyage, he had warm praise for a beer concentrate of Jackson's, which had been effective in combating scurvy. And in November 1772, a matter of months after the near-collapse of Thrale's business, Jackson was elected a Fellow of the Royal Society – not an honour conferred all that frequently on someone regarded as an out-and-out charlatan. The certificate recommending him for membership specified that it related to his work on isinglass and 'likewise for his invention of preserving Naval Timber from speedy decay'.

The detail of the advice Jackson offered to Thrale cannot now be known, but there is a clue in the long subtitle of his *Essay on British Isinglass* which he had published in 1765: 'Interspersed with hints for the further improvement of malting, brewing, fermenting and for preventing the wooden apparatus in the brewery from speedy decay'. Jackson argued that 'a much larger Yield of equally good beer can be obtained from a given Quantity of Materials, than in ordinary Practice, and that Barley, by a different Procedure in the art of Malting, will afford a much greater Quantity of genuine fermentable Matter, than what is procurable by the present Practice ...'

Common prudence would have dictated a small-scale trial, but Thrale preferred to go for broke. It was a reckless decision, and it had brought him face to face with the spectre of bankruptcy. A whole year's supply of beer had been ruined. He had very little ready money, and in the prevailing economic climate it was well nigh impossible to obtain the sort of credit that would have been required to keep the brewery going.

Mrs Salusbury was the first to respond: 'My Mother said She had 2 or 3 Thousand Pounds at his Service – it was her all, but she could live on her Annuity, which if Things came to the worst we should share with her.'

When Hester heard from Thrale that the workforce was about to walk out, she and Johnson immediately drove up from Streatham to Southwark: 'I now tried first to conciliate the necessary People about the Brewhouse, who declared they would not live *with Mr Thrale*, but they would do *anything* for *me*; only says They Madam get rid of that Fiend! He will entirely ruin your whole Family else. I did so, and we soon began to understand each other.'

It was not easy. Hester recorded a long conversation she had with the chief clerk, Perkins, from which it emerges that Thrale's skills in man management were non-existent: 'Why 'tis a hard Thing Mrs Thrale (those were his words) to live always in Servitude, a Servitude never made light by kind or even civil Treatment.'[27]

Hester then drove down to Brighton, where she begged £6,000 from Charles Scrase, 'an old gouty solicitor' who had been a friend of Thrale's father. Another family friend called Rush also came up with £6,000 and Lady Lade, Hester's sister-in-law, lent £5,000. These four loans – the equivalent of £2 million or so today – made it possible to maintain operations at the brewery, although it would take nine years for outstanding debts of £130,000 to be repaid.

It is unclear how widely it became known that Thrale was in financial straits, but he found himself in the public eye at this time for a different but equally unwelcome reason when he was lampooned in the print shops as 'The Southwark Macaroni'. The word had originally been applied to those who affected extreme manners and styles of dress picked up on the Grand Tour – Horace Walpole writes about 'travelled young men who wear long curls and spying-glasses'. Extravagance has always excited ambivalence among the English – to some the macaronis were merely ridiculous; others viewed them disapprovingly as foppish or effeminate. A writer in the *Oxford Magazine* in 1770 had been severe: 'There is indeed a kind of animal, neither male nor female, a thing of the neuter gender, lately started up amongst us. It is called Macaroni. It talks without meaning, it smiles without pleasantry, it eats without appetite, it rides without exercise, it wenches without passion.'[28]

The animal had not, in fact, started up all that recently – David Garrick had written a play in the 1750s called *The Male-Coquette* with a character called the Marchese di Macaroni. Now, in 1772, the climate was rather different. Throughout the summer the town buzzed with stories of homosexual scandal. Garrick himself was forced to initiate proceedings for libel to rebut allegations of a homosexual relationship with a dramatist called Bickerstaffe who had fled to France after an incident in the park with a guardsman, and in July a man called Robert Jones was sentenced to death at the Old Bailey for sodomizing a thirteen-year-old boy.

Jones, a lieutenant in the Royal Regiment of Artillery, was a man of parts. The author of books on fireworks and ice-skating, he was well known in London society, noted for his wit and the elegance of his attire. Like Thrale, he was regularly to be seen at Mrs Cornelys's in Soho Square – one newspaper noted that he had appeared there variously got up as a Bear, a Holland Skater, a Monkey and Punchinello.

His trial, and subsequent royal pardon, excited a wide-ranging public debate. The papers were flooded with Letters to the Printer – 'Censorinus', 'Inquisitor', 'An Admirer of the Fair Sex' and 'Antipederast' all had their say. Sodom and Gomorrah got quite a few mentions. 'Good God, what times do we live in!' exclaimed a correspondent to the *Morning*

Chronicle, who went on to characterize the King's leniency as the act of an 'ideot'.

Several letters to the *Public Ledger* were signed simply A MAN. The country, he wrote, was overrun with Catamites, 'or, to speak in a language which all may understand, with MACCARONIES'. Sodomy, he declared, was a crime 'imported from Italy by our spindle-shanked Gentry, who make the grand Tour but to bring home the vices of our Neighbours'. Jones was 'a MILITARY MACCARONI, too much engaged in every scene of idle Dissipation and wanton Extravagance'; his execution would, he hoped, teach a lesson to 'his CORNELLYAN Brethren'.

It was against this background that Thrale found himself caricatured as the Southwark Macaroni. He was not alone in being lampooned in this way. The flamboyant artist Richard Cosway, for instance, recently elected a Fellow of the Royal Academy and widely but mistakenly believed to be homosexual, figured as 'The Macaroni painter'. It is not clear why Thrale should have attracted this sort of satirical attention – the caricature, as it happens, apart from a slightly odd piece of headgear, does not make him look particularly macaronic. Whatever the reason, it was attention of a sort that a Member of Parliament and a man prominent in business could well have done without – particularly at a time when his business affairs were in such disarray.

He appeared for a time to be totally stunned by the situation in which he found himself. Hester feared that he might follow the example of some of those bankrupted in the crash and take his own life, but Johnson reassured her: 'Such was my charming mother's firmness and such her fond attachment to us both, that our philosophical friend, embracing her, exclaimed, that he was equally charmed by her conduct, and edified by her piety. "Fear not the menaces of suicide," said he; "the man who has two such females to console him, never yet killed himself, and will not *now*."'[29]

Johnson was right, but Thrale was permanently affected by the events of that dreadful summer. Hester later described it as the year when her husband 'seem'd *first* affected with that horrible Stupor which at last quench'd entirely the Spark of Life so far as related to *this World*'. He had lost the respect of those who worked for him; he had been saved by the efforts of two women and an eccentric man of letters; he became morose and withdrawn and never recovered the carefree assurance of his younger days.

Hester would look back on the frantic weeks of the summer with some satisfaction: 'Women have a manifest Advantage over Men in the doing Business,' she later reflected; 'every thing smooths down before them, & to be a Female is commonly sufficient to be successful, if she has a little Spirit & a little common Sense.' She also felt that the crisis had done something for her marriage for 'Mr Thrale saw his Wife capable to be trusted, and I saw that he was not insensible to the Tenderness which it was my Duty to shew him ...'

But the *Children's Book* that autumn records the price she paid for the tireless way she had performed that duty: 'Penelope Thrale was born – liv'd but 10 hours, looked black & could not breathe freely – poor little Maid! One cannot grieve after her much, and I have just now other things to think of ...'[30]

~7~
Siberian Winter

APART FROM her mother's illness it was now principally the affairs of the brewery that weighed on Hester's mind. For a time she, Johnson and Perkins effectively assumed control of the business. Hester spent what time she could with her mother, but drove regularly to Southwark each Tuesday. Mrs Salusbury, clearly believing she did not have long to live, began to distribute some of her most treasured belongings. Johnson was greatly touched by a note he received shortly before setting off on his annual visit to Lichfield and Ashbourne:

> Mrs Salusbury presents her kind Compliments to Mr Johnson; when She considered her *Possessions* again, She reflected that few things were more likely to be found acceptable to him than a Chair of Mrs Thrale's work when She was a good little Girl and minded her Book and her Needle.
>
> Mrs Salusbury wishes Mr Johnson all manner of Pleasure on his little Journey, and above all a safe return to his friends in Surrey.[1]

Whenever Johnson was away, he and Hester corresponded, and their letters now were frequently taken up with business affairs. 'The Brewhouse must be the scene of action, and the subject of speculation,' Johnson wrote from Lichfield: 'The first consequence of our late trouble ought to be, an endeavour to brew at a cheaper rate, an endeavour not violent and transient, but steady and continual, prosecuted with total contempt of censure or wonder, and animated by resolution not to stop while more can be done ...'[2]

Early in November, as a measure of economy, the Thrales moved to Southwark, leaving Mrs Salusbury to be looked after at Streatham. 'She & I parted with a resolution to contend who shall live cheapest,' Hester told Johnson: 'My folks I believe think my head is turned I do so scold & bluster about, and but that *Abdalmelech* the Turk was before hand with me, the name of *Skin Flint* would have been made for me.'[3]

She was clearly impatient to have Johnson back. 'Here we are,' she wrote three days later, 'doing nothing in the World but saving a Candle's end and wishing for you at home; till then there is no chance for me to do anything except by a little ineffectual teizing to keep my tongue in Tune ...' It is plain from the same letter that her Master was proving difficult: 'Mr Thrale will not stir now he is in Town, nor can all the influence I have over him make him speak a kind word to a Customer when he knows it would save him a house. You see this is a *private Letter*.'[4]

Johnson, gratified to think he was missed, nevertheless lingered in the Midlands. 'When I come I entreat I may not be flattered, as your letters flatter me,' he wrote roguishly in late November: 'You have read of heroes and princes ruined by flattery, and I question if any of them had a flatterer so dangerous as you. Pray keep strictly to your character of governess.'[5]

When he did return, he was of no great use to her, as he was almost immediately laid low with gout and catarrh and bronchitis and was housebound. Hester remained heavily dependent on him for comfort and support. One day in January, anxious for his approbation after a series of meetings with customers, she visited him at Johnson's Court: 'He approved of all I had done & all my Master had done.'[6] She again turned to Johnson when she was caught up in a dispute with a chemist called Alexander in Long Acre who accused Thrale of fraud and threatened to sue him. Johnson urged her to take a hard line and was gratified to hear that the tactic had succeeded: 'Your Advice was precisely right, upon my talking in a higher & more fearless Tone my friend Alexander was much disconcerted,' Hester wrote: '... [He] profess'd his Confidence in Mr Thrale's honour & Perkins's Honesty, both which he said I had clear'd to him. He then expatiated in praise of my powers of negotiation ...'[7]

Mrs Salusbury's cancer had spread. Johnson relayed to Hester a conversation with his old schoolfellow Robert James, inventor of the famous Fever Powder, and one of those called in to attend her: 'Dr. James called on me last night, deep, I think, in wine. Our dialogue was this – You find the case hopeless. – Quite hopeless.– But I hope you can procure her an easier dismission out of life. – That, I believe is in our power.'[8]

James visited Streatham late that night, but the sum of his advice was that the patient must be purged 'still more briskly'. Hester was distraught. 'I do not know what to wish,' she wrote to Johnson: 'She is so weak She can hardly totter down Stairs, but will not keep up, tho She fainted yesterday with the Effort ... She mentioned You, and said you would meet together in heaven *She humbly hoped* – that was all. I can write no more ...'[9]

Johnson sent her letters almost daily: 'Mr Hector says, that a poultice of rasped carrots is very powerful to abate any offensive smell. I think the London Chirurgeons use it.'[10] But to such severely practical advice, he does not hesitate to add robust pastoral counselling: 'Fill your mind with hope of her happiness, and turn your thoughts first to Him who gives and takes away in whose presence the Living and Dead are standing together ... Grief is a species of idleness, and the necessity of attention to the present preserves us by the disposition of providence from being lacerated and devoured by sorrow for the past.'[11]

From Thrale there was little help to be had, and Hester had no inhibitions about telling Johnson so:

> My dear cruel Master is more Tyger-hearted than the worst among the Set; you saw the Leave we took, & He has never sent me a scrap since to ask or tell me anything; nor would I firmly believe if I remained *here*, or in *Siberia* six Russian Winters ... Your Letter is like yourself, so wise, so good, so kind: I have read it twenty times I dare say, and resolved to take the Advice when the Event shall require it.[12]

She was now spending much of each day and night in her mother's room – 'Nobody can guess what a Winter this has been to me,' she wrote in the *Children's Book* – '& big with Child too again God help me!'[13] The coming of spring brought no relief. Early in April, the *Westminster Magazine*, under the title 'The Court of Cupid', raked slyly over Thrale's liaison with Polly Hart:

> Miss H–t is the daughter of a dancing-master ... Under the bridge of the fiddle this lady passed her early days; but not content with the graces of *Terpsichorè*, she tripped away to Cytherean joys, and fell into the wide-spreading arms of a Borough Brewer, more famed for his

amours than celebrated for his beer. The honours of this Gentleman's rural seat were conducted by this Nymph of Whim; and the Borough Bucks made her the Goddess of their chace ... Mr. T----- grew enamoured with this conduct: She was the Genius of the Wood and Table; equally sylvan, festive and gay ... but being solicitious to enter into a town life, and such well pleaded solicitations not being in his power to refuse, she entered vigorously on the fashionable sea, and pursued *folly* as fast and as strong as she had done the fox ...[14]

None of this was calculated to improve Thrale's temper, but it was not only Thrale that Grub Street had in its sights. Boswell arrived in London for a brief visit in April, and recorded in his Journal a visit he paid to Goldsmith:

He showed me in some newspaper two paragraphs of scandal about Mr Johnson and Mrs Thrale. How an eminent brewer was very jealous of a certain author in folio, and perceived a strong resemblance to him in his eldest son. 'Now,' said he, 'is not this horrid?' 'Why,' said I, 'no doubt though to us who know the characters it is the most ludicrous nonsense, yet it may gain credit with those who do not. The assertions of a newspaper are taken up insensibly. I long believed Burke to be a Jesuit.'[15]

Despite these vexations, the Thrales continued to entertain. Boswell was a guest at Southwark on three occasions during this visit. He found Johnson, although still far from well, in good declamatory form, and the *Life* contains several briskly entertaining exchanges between him and his hostess:

At Mr Thrale's, in the evening, he repeated his usual paradoxical declamation against action in publick speaking. 'Action can have no effect upon reasonable minds. It may augment noise, but it never can enforce argument. If you speak to a dog, you use action; you hold up your hand thus, because he is a brute; and in proportion as men are removed from brutes, action will have the less influence upon them.' MRS. THRALE. 'What then, Sir, becomes of Demosthenes's saying? "Action, action, action!"' JOHNSON. 'Demosthenes, Madam, spoke to an assembly of brutes; to a barbarous people.'[16]

And Hester still found time to record her chillingly dispassionate impressions of her children's development. 'Her general Health is mended, her Rupture almost well,' she wrote of Susanna on her third birthday:

but her Colour still like that of a Clorotic Virgin at 15, instead [of] a Baby; and her Stature very low: her Temper is so peevish & her Person so displeasing, that I do not love to converse with her: I was saying yesterday to my Mother – sure this Child swallowed something in her Infancy, that makes such a Creature of her: – Ay replies my Mother, a *Wasp* I fancy.[17]

During April and May Johnson applied himself to trying 'to learn the Low Dutch language' but the strain of reading small print caused a severe inflammation of his one good eye. 'I have had a poor darkling week,' he wrote to Hester at the end of May: 'I wish you would fetch me on Wednesday. I long to be in my own room … I hope I shall not add much to your trouble, and will wish at least to give you some little solace or amusement. I long to be under your care.'[18]

It seemed likely that he would add very considerably to Hester's trouble. To concern for her dying mother had been added anxiety about Lucy, Johnson's goddaughter, now approaching her fourth birthday. She had suffered a severe mastoid infection during the winter, and this had been followed by a large swelling in the throat – 'It was as big as a Hen's Egg, I am sure,' Hester wrote.[19] A third invalid, particularly one as demanding as Johnson, was the last thing Hester needed in the house. Her coach was nevertheless dispatched to fetch him.

It did not prove the homecoming he had longed for. Thrale had taken himself off to Southwark. Hester was almost entirely taken up with nursing her mother. Johnson, left alone for long hours of the day, brooded on his own infirmities. Unable to read, he killed time by writing Latin verses. Then, although they were living under the same roof, he took up his pen and composed a letter to Hester.

He chose to write it in French. Possibly he feared it might fall into the hands of a servant. More probably he could not bring himself to clothe what he wished to say in the rolling English periods with which he normally expressed himself. Because this was no normal letter. He begins with an oblique complaint of neglect. As he is obliged to spend several hours of each day *dans une profonde solitude*, he wishes to know whether he is permitted to roam freely, or whether he is required to remain 'within prescribed limits'. If he is still thought worthy, as formerly, of her care and protection, he asks her to write him a note defining what is permitted and what is forbidden to him. If it is her wish that he remain in a particular place, he begs her to spare him 'the necessity of constraining himself'. If her judgement and vigilance are to come to the aid of his weakness, he declares, *il faut agir tout a fait en Maîtresse*.

As he moves towards a conclusion, he sounds an extended note of reproach. Is it too much to ask that she, mistress of others, should also be mistress of herself? He levels accusations of inconstancy, of broken promises. Finally, addressing her as 'my Mistress' – *ma patronne* – he expresses a wish: 'that you should hold me in that bondage which you know so well how to render agreeable' – *que vous me tiennez dans l'esclavage que vou[s] sçavez si bien rendre heureuse*.

Almost a century would pass before the publication of a novel called *Venus im Pelz* (*Venus in Furs*), which tells the story of Severin von Kusiemski, a man so infatuated with a beautiful widow called Wanda that he asks to be treated as her slave, urging her to treat him in increasingly degrading and humiliating ways. It was by a writer called Sacher-Masoch, a native of Austro-Hungary. In all his writing he drew heavily on his own fantasies and fetishes, although he was not best pleased when the psychiatrist Krafft-Ebbing appropriated half of his name to coin the word masochism.[20]

The word was new, but the perversion was not. There are scenes of masochism in Otway's *Venice Preserved*; it informs the character of the Chevalier Des Grieux in Prévost's *Manon Lescaut* and runs like a thread through Rousseau's *Confessions*. Krafft-Ebbing, with Johnson's letter before him, would certainly have thought it worth a footnote. Hester's reply was at once patient, tender, generous and perceptive; she found English quite adequate to her purpose:

What Care can I promise my dear Mr Johnson that I have not already taken? What Tenderness that he has not already experienced? ... If it be possible shake off these uneasy Weights, heavier to the Mind by far than Fetters to the body. Let not your fancy dwell thus upon Confinement and Severity. I am sorry you are obliged to be so much alone; I foresaw some ill Consequences of your being here while my Mother was dying thus; yet could not resist the temptation of having you near me, but if you find this irksome and dangerous Idea fasten upon your fancy, leave me to struggle with the loss of one Friend, and let me not put to hazard what I esteem beyond Kingdoms, and value beyond the possession of them.

She knew of the long-projected Highland jaunt with Boswell, and ended on a shrewdly practical note: 'Dissipation is to you a glorious medicine, and I believe Mr Boswell will be at last your best Physician.' Then this beautifully judged, gently ironical envoi: 'I will detain you no longer, so farewell and be good; and do not quarrell with your Governess for not using the Rod enough —'[21]

Mrs Salusbury died shortly after this remarkable exchange. She had remained calm and lucid to the end — 'and even kept her powers of delighting by her humour', Hester wrote: 'on my enquiring how She did — She replied in allusion to the old Story of the Irishman — "not dead but speechless"'. On the morning of 18 June, Hester saw that life was ebbing away and sent for her husband:

I then called up Mr Johnson, who when he felt her Pulse wonder'd at its Vigor but when he observed the dimness of her Eyes and universal languor, he leaned on the bed, kissed her Cheek, & said in his emphatical Way — May God bless you Dear madam for Jesus Christ's Sake. At these Words She looked up and smiled w:th a sweet Intelligence that expressed Hope, Friendship & Farewell ...[22]

For a brief moment, the great man-child Hester had taken into her care assumed the role of father.

❧ ☙

The death of her mother induced in Hester a sense of desolation: 'To whom now shall I tell the little Foibles of my heart?' she wrote: 'On this day She died, & left me destitute of every *real* and *natural* Friend: for Sir Thos Salusbury has long ago cast me off, & Mr Thrale & Mr Johnson are the mere Acquisitions of Chance; which chance, or change of Behaviour,

or Intervention of new Objects or twenty Things besides Death can rob
me of. One solid Good I had & that is gone – my Mother!'[23]

Mrs Salusbury's death coincided with further salacious gossip in
the *Westminster Magazine* concerning Thrale's alleged philandering, this
time with a young woman whose mother kept a well-known porter house
in the Strand:

> Mr. Th–le did not come in the machine of his occupation, a dray, but in
> a chariot; and That being laid at the feet of the sweet *Susan*, with many
> other promises of love and elegance, she did not long hesitate about
> the indiscretion of elopement, but readily resigned her fair hand to this
> most amorous Brewer ...
>
> The time roll'd on in harmony and rapture, and every moment that
> was passed from her ivory arms was tedious and heavy.

Harmony and rapture were short-lived: 'Mr. Th–le, who was for ever
the dupe of a *Duenna* (who was always springing new game to divert his
fancy, and indulge his passions) had procured him a new favourite, the
celebrated Mrs. R–. His visits, in consequence of this new connexion,
became less frequent, and neglect at last sunk into coolness and indifference ...'[24]

In July Thrale travelled to Oxford. The Prime Minister, Lord North,
had recently become Chancellor of the University. This accorded him the
prerogative of deciding who should receive honorary degrees at the annual commemoration of founders and benefactors. It was a useful – and
inexpensive – way of paying political debts, and Thrale was rewarded
for his support at Westminster with a Doctorate of Civil Laws. Joshua
Reynolds was similarly honoured; he was now a frequent guest of the
Thrales and shortly after his return to London, Thrale took Hester
and Queeney up the river to dine with the painter at the house he had
recently had built on Richmond Hill.

When they returned at night they found that Harry was feverish
and had come out in spots. All five children went down with measles.
Hester had been looking forward to welcoming Johnson back to a new
room at Streatham – there had been extensive building work during the
summer. 'Have you ever had the measles?' she now wrote, 'if not you
must sleep away.'[25] She was concerned not only for Johnson. 'I have had

all the Symptoms of the Disorder myself,' she wrote in the *Children's Book*, '— the truth is I am near 8 Months gone with Child, so perhaps my Baby has catched them too.'[26]

But she was well enough to give a dinner party three days later. The guests included Reynolds and his sister Fanny, and they brought with them the Scottish poet and philosopher James Beattie, Professor of Moral Philosophy at Marischal College, Aberdeen. His *Essay on the Immutability of Truth*, an attack on the 'sceptical philosophy' of David Hume, had brought him great celebrity; it had also, as Hester would later record, excited the envy of Goldsmith: 'Here is much ado about nothing, cries Doctor Goldsmith why the Man has written but one Book, and I have writ several. So you have Doctor replies M[r] Johnson but there go many Halfpence remember — to one Guinea.'

Beattie had come to London earlier in the year hoping for a pension — to which end, wrote the modern editor of his diaries, 'he directed all his energies, determined to leave, if necessary, no official unpestered and no man of influence unplagued'.[27] 'We all love Beattie,' Johnson told Boswell. 'Mrs Thrale says, if ever she has another husband, she'll have Beattie.'[28] The admiration was mutual. Beattie later wrote that he had greatly admired Hester for her vivacity, learning, affability and beauty — 'I thought her indeed one of the most agreeable women I ever saw.'[29]

Johnson himself was not present at this dinner. He had set out the previous week for Edinburgh. A decade earlier, when he had received his pension, he said, 'Had this happened twenty years ago, I should have gone to Constantinople to learn Arabic.' Now, at the age of sixty-three, he was going with Boswell to visit the Hebrides.

~8~
Travelling Hopefully

JOHNSON was away for more than three months. He kept Hester informed of his progress in a stream of discursive, highly entertaining letters – the longest he ever wrote to her. From Edinburgh he described a dinner party where he had met the Duchess of Douglas – 'an old lady who talks broad Scotch with a paralytick voice, and is scarce understood by her own countrymen'.[1] Dundee got short shrift ('a dirty despicable town') but Montrose pleased him better – 'a neat place, with a spacious area for the market, and an elegant townhouse'. Passing through Kincardineshire they dined at Lord Monboddo's – 'the Scotch Judge who has lately written a strange book about the origin of Language, in which he traces Monkeys up to Men, and says that in some countries the human Species have tails like other beasts'.[2]

By early September they had reached Skye. 'Little did I once think of seeing this region of obscurity,' he wrote, 'and little did you once expect a salutation from this verge of European Life.'[3] The Scottish weather did not agree with him: 'I have a cold and am miserably deaf, and am troublesome to Lady Macleod; I force her to speak loud, but she will seldom speak loud enough.'[4] Boswell's account of their stay at Dunvegan suggests that this might well have been because she found Johnson extremely alarming: 'Lady M'Leod asked, if no man was naturally good? – *Johnson*. 'No, madam, no more than a wolf.' – *Boswell*. 'Nor no woman, sir?' *Johnson*. 'No, sir.' Lady M'Leod started at this, saying, in a low voice, 'This is worse than Swift.'[5]

The clan Chief, however, was clearly much taken with his guest. 'Macleod has offered me an Island,' Johnson told Hester in his next letter:

If it were not too far off I should hardly refuse it; my Island would be pleasanter than Brighthelmston, if You and Master could come to it, but I cannot think it pleasant to live quite alone ... That I should be elated by the dominion of an Island to forgetfulness of my friends at Streatham, and I hope never to deserve that they should be willing to forget me.[6]

No fear of that. Johnson found six letters waiting for him on his return to Glasgow and sent a detailed and orderly reply to the points raised in each of them. All but one of Hester's letters to Scotland are now lost. That which survives, written on the last day of October, contained disturbing news:

> My Uncle is dead: he has left all his personal Estate to his Wife, and his real Estate to her likewise for her Life, after which it goes to a distant relation in Wales ... After him & his Heirs Male it goes to Thelwall the parson (who is just married,) & his heirs Male ... It then is to revert to the right heirs. If I should say I was neither angry nor sorry for all this it would be very monstrous, for I am as angry & as sorry as I can be.

She added an alarming postscript: 'To compleat my Vexation poor Lucy is very ill. I think in a Decline.'[7]

Back in Edinburgh, Johnson sent a consoling reply: 'I never had much hope of a will in your favour, but was willing to believe that no will would have been made,' he wrote. 'Surely my dear Lucy will recover,' he added. 'I love her very much: and should love another godchild, if I might have the honour of standing to the next baby.'[8]

The child — a boy — was born early in November and christened Ralph. Johnson's wish to stand as godfather again was not granted, the honour going instead to Thrale's friends Sandys and Lyttelton. The birth of Hester's ninth child merited scarcely a mention in the *Children's Book* — a measure of her anxiety at the time about her daughter. That anxiety was well founded. Before the month was out Lucy was dead.

On the last day of the year Hester passed in sorrowful review the twelve months that were gone: 'I have suffered the Loss of a Parent, a Child, & the almost certain Hopes of an ample Fortune, in the full expectation of which I had been bred up from twelve Years old.' It was the loss of Offley that hurt the most. She wrote bitterly of 'the cutting Mortification of seeing my Estate snatched from me in a manner most base & vile by wretches whom I despise ... I had depended upon ending my Days at dear Offley, where they first began to be agreeable.' Thrale was relaxed about the whole business, but did not show great delicacy in trying to comfort Hester: 'He would rather be without the Estate I believe, than hold it of a *Wife*: He therefore bids me keep up my Spirits, for that we do not want it, & that He would never have lived at Offley if we had had it &c.'[9]

It is doubtful whether Hester ever ceased to fret over her uncle's will – 'dictated by his Wife no doubt & *dear Parson Thelwall*' as she wrote some years later. An anecdote elsewhere in *Thraliana* demonstrates how painful the memory remained:

> Doctor Goldsmith said here one Day, in a merry Humor that every young Person setting out in Life should learn to love Gravy, I have says He known a Man disinherited for not loving Gravy; – I loved Gravy well enough – yet I got myself disinherited – The Wound is still open I perceive for it bleeds again at my writing out a Poem which I wrote to please my Uncle in old Days ...

References to Sir Thomas and to Offley in her later correspondence suggest that the wound remained open even in old age.

❧ ☙

Johnson was no longer the Thrale's sole house-guest. The precocious Queeney – or Niggey, as Hester sometimes called her – was now nine, and it was felt that she would benefit from some tuition in modern languages. The assignment was offered to Giuseppe Baretti, an Italian man of letters long resident in London. Prickly, shortsighted, hot-tempered, Baretti was well known as the author of an Italian–English dictionary and a number of successful travel books.

Four years previously he had stood trial for murder. Walking up the Haymarket one evening he had been accosted by two prostitutes, one of whom grasped him by the genitals. Baretti struck one of the women on the face, and her screams brought three pimps on the scene. In the mêlée that followed Baretti drew a small fruit knife that he carried. Two of his assailants were stabbed; one of them died the next morning and Baretti was taken before the Chief Justice, Lord Mansfield.

He did not lack influential friends. Burke, Reynolds and Garrick all stood surety for him and spoke in his defence when he came to trial, as did Goldsmith and Johnson. 'Never did such a constellation of genius enlighten the aweful sessions-House,' wrote Boswell. Garrick was shown the murder weapon and asked whether he carried such a knife when he travelled abroad. 'Yes,' he replied, 'or we should have no victuals.' Johnson was asked whether Baretti was addicted to picking up women in the street:

Dr Johnson: 'I never knew that he was.'
Question: 'How is he as to his eye-sight?'
Dr Johnson: 'He does not see me now, nor I do not see him.'[10]

Baretti was deemed to have acted in self-defence and acquitted. His knife was returned to him. He was not greatly chastened by his brush with the law. While eating dessert at the Thrales' one day he drew the company's attention to the fact that the knife he was using was the one with which he had killed his assailant.

Hester had admired Baretti's *Journey from London to Genoa* when it appeared in 1770 and it is clear from the *Children's Book* that she thought she had made quite a catch: '17: Octr 1773. This Day, my eldest daughter H: M: Thrale began to study Italian under the instruction of Mr Baretti whose Skill in modern Languages is unrivalled I suppose.'[11] She also found him good value at the dinner table:

Will: Burke was tart upon Mr Baretti for being too dogmatical in his Talk about Politicks: You have says he no Business to be investigating the Characters of Ld Falkland or Mr Hampden – you cannot judge of their Merits, they are no Countrymen of Yours – True replied Baretti, and *you* should learn by the same Rule to speak very cautiously about Brutus & Mark Antony; they are my Countrymen, and I must have their Characters tenderly treated by *Foreigners*.

Every day except Sunday Queeney was set to work with her tutor in the library. Once she had mastered the vocabulary lists he gave her they moved on to what Baretti called his 'dialogues' – the pupil chose a subject, the master dashed off a conversation to illustrate it. It was an imaginative way of engaging the child's attention – a dog accuses a cat of loving liberty as much as the Americans; a peacock discusses with his hens the latest world events reported in the newspapers; Poppet and Ramper, the two coach horses, complain of the coach being overloaded with children. Baretti had also undertaken to read the Italian poets with Hester, but he complained that the mistress of Streatham was so taken up with her geese and turkeys and peafowl that Dante went unexplored.

The Streatham circle was diminished in the spring of 1774 by the death of Goldsmith, carried off at forty-five by a bladder condition and kidney infection. 'A man made up of Contradictions,' Hester later wrote in *Thraliana*. 'Knowledge & Ignorance, Artlessness and design, Delicacy & Grossness. Poor dear little Dr.' But she also wrote of the piety of his sentiments and the elegance of his writings and believed that he would have written Johnson's biography better than anyone.

There was now some discussion of a journey to Italy. Things were looking up at the brewery; Hester, for once, was not pregnant; she and Johnson were both eager to see the antiquities of Rome; in Baretti they would have a willing bear-leader. Eventually, however, the project was shelved. There were pressing problems to do with Mrs Salusbury's Welsh estate, which had now passed to Hester, and Thrale thought it important to inspect the properties and discuss matters with Bridge, the agent.

Queeney was to accompany them, but Hester was in low spirits at leaving the other children. Go she did, however, and the Thrale coach and four set off from Streatham on 5 July. The first stage of their journey took them close to Offley. While Johnson buried his nose in Cicero's *Letters*, Hester drank in the familiar landscape: 'Here I hunted with my Uncle, here I fished or walked with my Father, here my Grandmother reproved my Mother for her too great indulgence of me, here poor dear Lady Salusbury fainted in the coach and charged me not to tell Sir Thomas of the accident lest it should affect him ...'[12]

The next day's stage, to Lichfield, was eighty-three miles. Johnson, who had urged the importance of rising at six so they might get there before dark, did not appear until ten o'clock. This put Hester, concerned about the effect of a heavy day's journey on Queeney, out of sorts – 'tho' I hope I gave nobody reason to perceive it'. The clock struck midnight shortly after they arrived at the old Swan Inn, close to the cathedral: 'Mr

Johnson continued in good spirits, and often said how much pleasanter it was travelling by night than by day.'[13]

The following morning Hester went downstairs in what she described as a morning nightgown and close cap. This did not meet with Johnson's approval: 'He made me alter it entirely before he would stir a step with us about the town, saying most satirical things concerning the appearance I made in a riding-habit.'[14] Three days passed in a round of visits – breakfast with Erasmus Darwin, grandfather of Charles (Hester admired a rose as tall as an apple tree in his garden), supper with Peter Garrick, brother of David: 'the resemblance between him and his brother is so striking that I took the liberty to mention it'.[15]

On to Ashbourne where Johnson's old school-friend John Taylor lived in some style in his lavishly appointed rectory. Hester was impressed: 'He has very fine pictures which he does not understand the beauties of, a glorious Harpsichord which he sends for a young man out of the town to play upon, a waterfall murmuring at the foot of his garden, deer in his paddock, pheasants in his menagerie, the finest coach horse in the County, the largest horned cattle, I believe, in England ...'[16]

Taylor took them to Chatsworth – to which only a few days previously John, the fifth Duke of Devonshire, had brought his new bride, the seventeen-year-old Georgiana Spencer. 'I was pleased with scarcely anything,' Hester wrote: 'The cascade is too artificial to satisfy an eye accustomed as one is in this Country to see water falling with rapidity from real rocks and swallowed up at last by real rivers. The other waterworks are bawbles fit only to amuse Boarding School Misses by wetting their playfellows' clothes.'[17]

Queeney was not standing up well to long hours on the road, but neither Thrale nor Johnson evinced much sympathy: 'I had many feelings for Queeney which I was forced to suppress,' Hester wrote at Lichfield, 'as I was often told how little it signified whether she catch'd cold or no.' Matters had not improved as they moved on to Ashbourne: 'Queeney breaks my heart and my head with her cough. I am scarce able to endure it.' By the time they reached Dovedale, eleven days into the tour, the cough had all but gone; Hester's concern now was with her own loneliness:

'Tis so melancholy a thing to have nobody one can speak to about
one's clothes, or one's child, or one's health, or what comes uppermost.
Nobody but *Gentlemen*, before whom one must suppress everything
except the mere formalities of conversation and by whom every thing is
to be commended or censured. Here my paper is blistered with tears for
the loss of my companion, my fellow traveller, my Mother … I hoped,
and very vainly hoped that wandering about the World would lessen
my longing after her, but who now have I to chat with on the Road?
Who have I to tell my adventures to when I return?[18]

She had a sharp eye for people as well as places. They dined one
evening at Hopton Hall with a former sheriff of Derbyshire called Philip
Gell, a man in his fifties who had recently married a girl in her teens:
'Never did my aversion rise so suddenly and in such high tides,' Hester
wrote in her journal: 'A man visibly impaired by age and particularly
ugly, talking largely and loudly on every subject, understanding none
as I could find, foppish without elegance, confident without knowledge,
sarcastic without wit and old without experience, a man uniting every
hateful quality, a deist, a dunce, and a cotquean.'[19]

Hester's journal makes for livelier reading than the prosaic jottings
that comprise Johnson's account of their journey. Neither of them was
overwhelmed by Kedleston, which Robert Adam had completed for the
Curzon family nine years previously. 'Very costly, but ill contrived',
was Johnson's verdict;[20] Hester found it ostentatious, and saw 'nothing
but what so much money would buy, and what would apparently sell
for so much money again'.[21]

They crossed into Wales, and from Llewenny, at that time the home
of Hester's cousin Robert Cotton, they made an expedition to Bach-
y-Graig. 'I went to see my possessions, which I found far worse than
I had expected,' Hester wrote.[22] 'We found an old house built 1567, in
an uncommon and incommodious form,' wrote Johnson. 'My Mistress
chattered about tiring, but I prevailed on her to go to the top. The floors
have been stolen; the windows are stopped.'[23]

The next day they attended divine service at St Asaph Cathedral – very
much a family affair in which the Dean preached and the Bishop, who
was his father, gave the blessing. Hester was not at her most charitable:

His Lordship invited us all to his Palace ... His wife gave us Cakes and Currants, pressed us to stay to dinner, and was as civil as she knew how, but she is a vulgar woman, and indeed I never saw a Spiritual Lord who had a genteel Wife. The reason is evident. They are commonly mean men raised by Scholarship to the rank of a Bishop, but as they marry in their youth, they marry to their equals, and the woman, who never rises in her behaviour, as the man often contrives to do, grows only more disagreeable as her situation in life gives her more opportunities of displaying herself.[24]

By the middle of August Hester was beginning to feel homesick:

I hear Harry has had a black eye and Ralph cuts his teeth with pain, but I have nobody to tell how it vexes me. Mr Thrale will not be conversed with by *me* on any subject, as a friend, or comforter, or adviser. Every day more and more do I feel the loss of my Mother. My present Companions have too much philosophy for me. One cannot disburthern one's mind to people who are watchful to cavil, or acute to contradict before the sentence is finished.[25]

It pained her that neither Thrale nor Johnson shared the intense pleasure she felt in being in the land of her birth. 'Wales has nothing that can much excite or gratify curiosity,' Johnson wrote to John Taylor on his return. 'The mode of life is entirely English. I am glad I have seen it, though I have seen nothing, because I now know that there is nothing to be seen.'[26] Some years later, at Streatham, Fanny Burney recorded a revealing exchange with Johnson:

Mrs Thrale. I remember, Sir, when we were travelling in Wales, how you called me to account for my civility to the people; 'Madam,' you said, 'let me have no more of this idle commendation of nothing. Why is it, that whatever you see, and whoever you see, you are to be so indiscriminately lavish of praise?' 'Why I'll tell you, Sir,' said I, 'when I am with you, and Mr Thrale, and Queeny, I am obliged to be civil for four!'[27]

But there were also occasions when she was touched by Johnson's consideration: 'We went to the little town of Pwllhey, where Mr. Johnson

would buy something, he said, in memory of his little Mistresses' market
Town; he is on every occasion so very kind, feels friendship so acutely
and expresses it so delicately that it is wonderfully flattering to me to
have his company.'

'He could find nothing to purchase,' she added, 'but a Primmer.'[28]

Thrale and Hester had a number of unsatisfactory interviews with the
agent, Bridge, who showed extreme reluctance to produce any account
of his stewardship: 'Mr Thrale persecutes Bridge every day for this
odious account,' Hester wrote, 'but cannot get it.'[29] When it was at last
wrung out of him, it became plain that the man was a scoundrel: 'My
good Steward Mr Bridge, whom my Mother thought the worthiest of
Mankind, had plundered us for 20 Years most grossly: – still keeping
the whole Family under a Notion that he was doing his best.'

He was immediately dismissed, and Hester's cousin Robert agreed
that the rents should in future be paid to him or his agent.

Early in September the horses' heads were turned for home. Hester
was in the early stages of her eleventh pregnancy, and the daily round
of sightseeing was beginning to pall. 'We walked about, and we did
our best,' she wrote in Shrewsbury, 'but the day went off very heavily
indeed.' In Worcestershire they were the guests at Ombersley Court of
Lord Sandys, Ralph's godfather, who entertained them 'with a liberality
of friendship which cannot be surpassed'. Five years previously Sandys
had married a widow who brought him an immense fortune. 'The Lady's
attention to her friends makes more than amends for her ignorance and
deformity,' Hester wrote in her journal.

They were less well received at Hagley when they called on Ralph's
other godfather, William Henry Lyttelton. In the evening their host,
observing that Johnson had laid down his book to walk about, told him
that if he did not mean to use his candle he should put it out. 'We were
disappointed of the respect and kindness that we expected,' Johnson
noted stiffly in his journal.[30] Hester, although she begged to be excused,
was pressed by the ladies of the company to play at cards. She took a
poor view of their 'ill-bred but irresistible importunity' – although she
had the satisfaction of winning three shillings.[31]

In Birmingham they met Johnson's school-friend Edmund Hector,
established there for many years as a surgeon. 'I hoped to extract some

juvenile anecdotes of Mr. Johnson,' Hester wrote, 'but I was by this time too sick for relation or enquiry, and was forced to go to bed by 9 o'clock.'[32]

They continued by way of Woodstock and Oxford, and stopped briefly to inspect Thrale's 400-acre agricultural property at Crowmarsh. Then in the last days of September they came to Gregories, the estate in Buckinghamshire which Edmund Burke had acquired some years previously for £20,000, most of it borrowed. 'We were received with open arms by our friends at Beaconsfield,' Hester wrote, 'each seemed to contend who should be kindest.' Drink flowed freely in the Burke household:

> There was an old Mr Lowndes dined with us and got drunk talking
> Politics with Will Burke and my Master after dinner. Lord Verney and
> Edmund came home at night much flustered with liquor, and I thought
> how I had spent three months from home among dunces of all ranks
> and sorts, but had never seen a man drunk till I came among the Wits.[33]

The visit remained vividly in Hester's mind. When she came to publish her *Anecdotes* of Johnson she wrote of 'the delightful society in which we had spent some time at Beconsfield', but some years earlier she recorded an unsanitized and much more colourful account of it in *Thraliana*:

> Tis now Time [to] turn over a new leaf for the great Orator Mr Edmund
> Burke – who ... was the first Man I had ever seen drunk, or heard talk
> Obscænely – when I lived with him & his Lady at Beaconsfield among
> Dirt Cobwebs, Pictures and Statues that would not have disgraced the
> City of Paris itself: where Misery & Magnificence reign in all their
> Splendour, & in perfect Amity. That Mrs Burke drinks as well as her
> Husband, & that their Black a moor carries Tea about with a cut finger
> wrapt in Rags ...

Hester was spared further exposure to drunkenness and cobwebs and blackamoors with cut fingers. When she rose the next morning Thrale announced that Parliament had been dissolved, and that 'all the World was to bustle'. The planned return to Streatham must be abandoned; they must go instead to Southwark and make an immediate start on the canvass. Hester was deeply upset. 'So all my hopes of pleasure blow away,' she wrote: 'I thought to have lived at Streatham in quiet and comfort, have kissed my children and cuffed them by turns, and had a place always for them to play in, and here I must be shut up in that odious dungeon, where nobody will come near me, the children are to be sick for want of air, and I am never to see a face but Mr. Johnson's. Oh, what a life that is!'[34]

'*And I am never to see a face but Mr. Johnson's.*' The words stand out from this last page of her Welsh journal. It was no more, possibly, than a fleeting twinge of irritation. It had been a draining three months, physically and emotionally. 'I had been tied to my eldest Girl hard & fast for so long,' she later wrote in *Thraliana*; 'to make, to mend, to comb, & to pack; till I was cruelly tired of my Journey.' Tired of jolting over rough roads, tired of morning sickness that lasted all day, tired of Thrale's chilling inattention, tired of being civil for four ... '*And I am never to see a face but Mr. Johnson's.*' A little cloud out of the sea, like a man's hand, such as the servant of Elijah saw? Maybe not even that. Perhaps just the faintest rumble of distant thunder.

9

'Sure We are Made of Iron'

THRALE relented. He directed that the coach should after all make for Streatham. Hester was relieved and gratified by what she found – 'Ralph is most exceedingly come on; grown vastly handsome, & much more intelligent,' she noted in the *Children's Book*; 'Harry is the very best Boy in the World, has minded his Business as If I had been watching him.' But she was obliged to cram her kissing and cuffing into one short weekend: 'Now for this filthy Election! I must leave Queeney to the Care of Mr Baretti I believe, or him to hers; & she must keep House here at Streatham, while I go fight the Opposition in the Borough: Oh my sweet Mother! How every thing makes your Loss more heavy!'[1]

Lord North had called the election six months sooner than he was obliged to by the terms of the Septennial Act. His easy command of fiscal policy and his skill as a parliamentarian had won him solid support on the backbenches and given him four relatively untroubled years on the domestic front. His handling of the credit crisis in 1772, which had threatened to engulf the East India Company, had been assured, but the ingenious provision devised for disposing of the Company's surplus stocks of tea had led in the following year to the Boston Tea Party. This direct action by the Massachusetts radicals provoked a wave of indignation in England and led to the coercive legislation of 1774. It was widely believed that North's decision to go to the country early was taken to pre-empt any colonial influence on the outcome.

Two days into the campaign in Southwark Hester dashed off a dispatch from the front to Johnson: 'We lead a wild Life, but it will be over tomorrow sevennight; the Election will be carried, but not so triumphantly as I hoped for: some are stupid, and some are sullen. No less than four Candidates beside my Master – the Patriots have the Mob of Course ...'[2]

Two Members would be returned. It was a Wilkes supporter called

Polhill who posed the greatest threat to Thrale; another of the candidates, an American called William Lee who had settled in London some years previously, also formed part of the Wilkes faction. Johnson weighed in with a pamphlet called 'The Patriot', a robust demolition of Wilkes's claim to that title, composed in the course of a single day:

> He is no lover of his country, that unnecessarily disturbs its peace. Few errours, and few faults of government can justify an appeal to the rabble; who ought not to judge of what they cannot understand, and whose opinions are not propagated by reason, but caught by contagion ...
>
> No man can reasonably be thought a lover of his country, for roasting an ox, or burning a boot, or attending the meeting at Mile-End ... He may, among the drunkards, be a hearty fellow, and among sober handicraftsmen, a free-spoken gentleman; but he must have some better distinction before he is a patriot.[3]

The rabble was much in evidence in Southwark during the campaign – 'our constituents', Hester later wrote, 'were run mad with Republican Frenzy'. She asked one of Thrale's electors one day how it was that the Wilkesite opposition could muster so much support: 'Madam says the Man, you have known the Borough twelve Years I have liv'd in it 40. & I know that if Jesus Christ and Saint Paul were to stand Candidates next Election our folks would raise an Opposition in favour of *Barabbas* ...'

Thrale was returned, although it was Polhill who topped the poll, with 1,195 votes to Thrale's 1,026. Hester was jubilant: 'Well we have won the race by a Length or so & that is all. Mr Thrale is once more elected for Southwark, & his best Friends say he may thank his Wife for his Seat – the Truth is I have been indefatigable ...'[4]

Thrale returned to a House of Commons in which Lord North could rely on a majority of about eighty. Hester retired thankfully to Streatham to recover from what she called 'the cruel fatigues I had undergone of getting Votes all day, & settling Books with the Clerks all Night'. One day she rode over to the school in Kensington where the two younger girls had been boarding: 'In Hogmore Lane down fell my Horse, down of course fell I – we were on a smart Gallop – the Pommel struck my Side with great Violence, & my Lip was cut almost through: add to this the two black Eyes I had gained, and an immense Swelling at my Jaw, which tho' not broke was greatly injured …'

Badly shocked, she was carried to the school, where she bade a somewhat theatrical farewell to her terrified daughters, and begged the headmistress to be kind to them – 'telling her that M^r. Thrale would probably send Queeney thither too if I should die, as was most to be expected, being four months gone with Child & so monstrously bruised'.[5]

Thrale displayed a degree of solicitude that both surprised and touched her:

My Master's Behaviour on the Occasion claims all my Gratitude; he was very sorry for me indeed, and very tender of me too, and concerned exceedingly lest I should miscarry, which thank God I escaped: But I was now become much more his Friend and Companion than formerly, had been useful at the Election, and in Short tho' less handsome, was more agreeable to him now than ever.

Her injuries proved less serious than they looked, although she was left with a permanent mark at the right of her mouth. When she sat in old age to the deaf and dumb Irish artist Sampson Towgood Roche, she asked him to paint the scar into the miniature he made of her.

❧ ☙

It was decided that autumn that little Ralph, who was now a year old, should be inoculated against smallpox as the other children had been, and Daniel Sutton was once again called in: 'God knows it is a mighty slight Business, none of 'em yet had ever 50 Pustules,' Hester wrote in the *Children's Book*. This time it proved anything but a mighty slight business. 'Here I am well paid for my Presumption. The Child is vastly ill indeed – dying I think,' she wrote a week later: 'Oh Lord Oh Lord! What shall I do? Johnson & Baretti try to comfort me, they only plague me – Up every Night and all Night long again! – well if this don't kill me & the Child I carry, sure we are made of Iron.'[6]

She and the unborn child both survived, and so did Ralph, although Hester found him much altered by the smallpox. 'He seems all relaxed I think, & has no Strength left to battle with his Teeth which are coming every Day,' she wrote. 'Oh when, when, shall I ever know peace & Happiness again ...'[7]

In late December the household moved in to Southwark for the winter. A week before Christmas she received from Johnson a note that could not fail to flatter her: 'I have sent you a book, which will, I hope, have the honour of your acceptance. Mr Strahan does not publish till after the Holidays, and insists that only the King and you shall have it sooner, and that you shall be engaged not to lend it abroad.'[8]

This was his *Journey to the Western Islands*. A second note a few days later reported how it had been received in the royal household: 'You must not tell any body but Mr. Thrale that the King fell to reading the book as soon as he got it, when anything struck him, he read aloud to the Queen ...'[9] Three months later Hester was also afforded an early sight of Johnson's *Taxation No Tyranny* in which he rebutted the arguments of the American Congress.[10]

The Thrales' social circle continued to widen. Early in March 1775 Joshua Reynolds invited them to dinner to meet the writer and literary hostess Elizabeth Montagu, who was sitting to him at the time. 'Mrs Montagu made many polite advances,' Hester wrote, '& desired my Friendship in a Way that flattered my Vanity. She is a very high bred lady, a very conspicuous Character in the World, and her Conversation flows very freely from a very full Mind.' It was Johnson who dubbed her 'Queen of the Blues'. Rich, ambitious, domineering, she presided at her house in Hill Street over large evening assemblies – the nearest thing in England to the French salons.

In 1769 she had published *An Essay on the Writings and Genius of Shakespear*, in which she defended the bard against foreign critics such as Voltaire; she also argued that Johnson, in his Preface, had undervalued Shakespeare's dramatic genius. Horace Walpole dismissed it as a 'dull essay, which would not do credit to a clever school-girl of seventeen'. Johnson had been equally unimpressed: 'I have indeed not read it all. But when I take up the end of a web, and find it packthread, I do not expect, by looking further, to find embroidery.'[11]

Hester would increasingly find herself thrown together in society with Mrs Montagu, and a certain rivalry would develop between them. Fanny Burney, after her introduction to the Thrale circle in 1778, saw a good deal of both women: 'As to Mrs Montagu, she reasons well, and harangues well, but wit she has none. Mrs Thrale has almost too much; for when she is in spirits, it bursts forth in a torrent almost overwhelming.'[12]

Bluestocking assemblies were not to everybody's taste – 'There was no ceremony, no cards and no supper.'[13] Not to mention Mrs Montagu's practice of arranging her guests in one large, disconcerting half-circle. All rather different from the lavish hospitality offered by the Thrales. A frequent guest at Southwark in the early months of 1775 was the Irish writer and preacher Dr Thomas Campbell, paying his first visit to London. 'She is a very learned lady,' he wrote of Hester in his diary, 'and joyns to the charms of her own sex, the manly understanding of ours.' He was astonished by the immensity of the brewery and full of praise for what was set before him at table:

> The dinner was excellent: first course, soups at head and foot removed by fish and a saddle of mutton; second course, a fowl they call Galena at head and a capon larger than some of our Irish turkeys at foot; third course, four different sorts of Ices, Pineapple, Grape, Raspberry and a fourth; in each remove, there were I think fourteen dishes. The first two courses were served in massy plate.[14]

Boswell was also in London that spring, and within a week of his arrival Thrale extended 'a general invitation to dine when not otherwise engaged'. He was cordially received. When he complimented his host on a particular French liqueur that had been served, Thrale said he had half a dozen bottles of it, and would bring one out only when Boswell was with them.[15] One evening, when Johnson was not present, Thrale told him something which caused Boswell to prick up his ears: 'There is a Book of *Johnsoniana* kept in their Family,' he wrote in his journal, 'in which all Mr. Johnson's sayings and all they can collect about him is put down. I must try to get this *Thralian* Miscellany to assist me in writing Mr. Johnson's Life, if Mrs. Thrale does not intend to do it herself.'[16]

Johnson received pleasing news from Oxford at the beginning of April: 'They have sent me a degree of Doctor of Laws,' he told Hester, 'with such praises in the diploma, as, perhaps ought to make me ashamed; they are very like your praises.'[17] It is possible that the doctorate was partly a reward for the writing of *Taxation No Tyranny*. Hester was delighted. 'I rejoyce in your being made Doctor in due Form,' she wrote, 'and next to praising you myself I love to hear others praise you.'[18]

Thrale had developed a nasal polyp, and in the middle of April the distinguished surgeon Percivall Pott was called in to extract it. Pott, Master of the Company of Surgeons and a Fellow of the Royal Society, numbered Garrick, Johnson and Gainsborough among his patients. While he was in the house Thrale, very much against Hester's wishes, asked him to look at Ralph, and the child was brought down. Pott, one of the outstanding diagnosticians of the day, brushed aside all talk of sickness and teething: 'This Boy is in a State of Fatuity, either by Accident, or more probably from his birth,' he told the parents, 'you may see he labours under some nervous Complaint that has affected his Intellects; for his eyes have not the Look of another Child sick or well.' Hester was distracted: 'Oh how this dreadful Sentence did fill me with Horror! & how dismal are now the thoughts of all future Connection with this unhappy Child! A Thing to hide & be ashamed of whilst we live: Johnson gives me what Comfort he can, and laments he can give no more ... Oh Lord give me patience to bear this heaviest of all my Afflictions!'[19]

Her confinement was now imminent: 'Here I am, returned to Streatham with my little Flock, & here if it please God I shall in a fortnights Time add to them another Child.' Distress over her little son was compounded by irrational feelings of guilt – 'I shall perhaps have only this *one* Misfortune. may that expiate my criminal pride in my own & my eldest Daughter's Superiority of understanding!'[20]

She gave birth to a daughter on 4 May. She was christened Frances, the name given to their second child who had lived for only nine days in 1765 – 'she is a small delicate Child, but bears no visible Marks of my many troubles during gestation'.[21] Johnson and Boswell drove down to visit her, and Boswell left with her his manuscript journal of their Hebridean jaunt. If he had hoped to have her comments on it, he was disappointed; she returned it two days later with a brief note of thanks for his 'entertaining Manuscript' – 'Your Journal has almost blinded me, and I can but just see to tell you how earnestly I wish you a happy meeting with your family.'[22]

Thrale was seldom much in evidence at such times, and Hester grumbled to Johnson about his neglect: 'I could pout myself for a Penny to see my Master never come near me but on those Days that he would come if I had never been born – Saturday, Sunday & Monday.'[23] Johnson himself set off later than usual on what in a letter to Boswell he called 'the annual ramble into the middle counties'. He was away in Oxford, Lichfield and Ashbourne for more than two months, and in that time Hester received some thirty letters from him. Three days without news from Streatham was enough to make him fret. 'Dearest dear Lady,' he wrote from Oxford, 'take care of yourself. You connect us, and rule us, and vex us, and please us. We have all a deep interest in your health and prosperity.'[24]

Before he had been gone a month, Hester began to miss him: 'When will you come home? I shall be wondrous glad to see you – though I write every thing so I shall have nothing to tell: but I shall have you safe in your Bow Window to run to, when any thing comes in my head, and you say that's what you are kept for you know.'[25]

While Johnson was away, she got tickets for the first regatta held in England – 'a novel amusement recently introduced from Venice' as one newspaper called it. It attracted enormous crowds: 'I suppose so many will not meet again till the day of judgment,' Horace Walpole wrote to Lady Ossory.[26] The Thames was crowded with pleasure boats and barges, and the avenues to Westminster Bridge were covered with gaming tables. Twelve boats raced against the tide from Westminster Bridge to London Bridge and back again, although the competitors had a hard time of it threading their way between the barges. A Temple of Neptune was constructed at Ranelagh and supper was followed by a fancy-dress ball, where the company danced minuets and cotillions. So great was the crush when the assembly broke up in the small hours that there were a number of accidents and several people drowned.

Johnson had expressed his satisfaction that Hester was to be there: 'You know how little I love to have you left out of any shining part of life,' he wrote. 'You will see a show with philosophick superiority, and therefore may see it safely.'[27] When she told him that she hadn't enjoyed it, Johnson urged a further exercise in philosophical superiority. 'All pleasure preconceived and preconcerted ends in disappointment,' he informed her:

But disappointment when it involves neither shame not loss is as good as success, for it supplies as many images to the mind, and as many topicks to the tongue. I am glad it failed for another reason … This, I think, is Queeney's first excursion into the regions of pleasure, and I should not wish to have her too much pleased. It is as well for her to find that pleasures have their pains …[28]

Hester was no stranger to pain that summer. Early in July she persuaded Thrale to drive her down to Brighton for a few days to see Ralph, who had been sent there in the care of a nurse to try sea-bathing. He was no better. 'This poor unfortunate Child will dye at last,' she wrote in an anguished letter to Johnson: 'What can I do? Has the flattery of my Friends made me too proud of my own Brains? & must these poor Children suffer for my Crime? I can neither go on with this subject nor quit it … I opened the Ball last Night – tonight I go to the Play: Oh that there was a Play or a Ball for every hour of the four & twenty.'[29]

Ralph died the following week. Hester made a bleak record of the post-mortem findings in the *Children's Book*: 'The Brain was found almost dissolved in Water, & something amiss too in the original Conformation of the Head – so that Reason & Life both might, had we known all been despair'd of from the very first. God preserve my other five! This poor Child is much better dead than alive.'[30]

Ralph would today probably have been diagnosed as suffering from hydrocephalus, in which excess cerebrospinal fluid builds up in the brain, causing abnormal enlargement of the ventricles. It is also possible that he was suffering from hydrancephaly, a condition in which a bag of clear fluid forms between the skull and the brain.

His mother bore this latest bereavement with her customary fortitude. 'Finding these five Children well,' she wrote to Johnson, '[I] have resolved to be thankful to God and chearful among my Friends again till new Vexations arise.' There was little comfort to be had from her husband: 'Mr Thrale has been in Town ever since I was gone, but would not come home to me last Night but went to Ranelagh I hear, however I will not be peevish any more, for it torments nobody but myself … farewell My Dear Sir and let us see you *sometime*; I think you shall never run away so again: I lost a Child the last Time you were at a distance.'[31]

While she was in Brighton Hester had a lengthy discussion about the eventual disposal of her Welsh estate – the Bach-y-Graig home of the Salusburys, which she had inherited from her mother. She sought advice from Charles Scrase, the old lawyer who had been so helpful in the matter of the brewery. Gently, insistently, he directed her attention to every conceivable possibility. What if her children were to die without issue? What if Thrale were to remarry and have children by a second wife? That touched a raw nerve and triggered a hasty response: in that event, Hester declared hotly, she would wish her estate to pass to her cousin Robert Cotton. Scrase then shrewdly changed tack – what if Thrale should die and she herself were to remarry? Might she not then wish any sons of that second marriage to be preferred to the daughters of the first? Hester was outraged:

> This Supposition was however *too* shocking; that I should take advantage of my Husband's Permission to dispose of my Fortune, and so settle with an Eye to a second Marriage! – reserving something for the Offspring of another Connection – no! no! Mr Scrase! Not *so* insensible neither to Tenderness, Gratitude or Duty. One must have been *An Attorney*, not a woman to have such a thought in one's head.

A traditionalist in such matters, Hester's strong preference was for the estate to be entailed according to birth alone; if none of her children had issue, it should then pass 'to Mr Thrale & to his heirs for ever'. Wise old Scrase let the matter rest for a time; then, at the end of July, when she had returned to Streatham, he wrote to Thrale, urging that no entail be set up, and that matters should be so arranged that '*you & Mrs T. during your Joint Lives* may at any time revoke or alter the Limitations proposed'.[32]

A draft was prepared along these lines, and at Hester's insistence, a decision deferred until Johnson's return. He disapproved only of a clause that would oblige her daughters and their husbands to assume the name 'Salusbury'. The husbands, he argued, might 'justly object to such insolent Conditions'. It was agreed that Johnson and Thrale's friend John Cator, a prosperous timber merchant, should be appointed trustees. Cator was an odd choice – 'a purseproud Tradesman', Hester thought, 'coarse in his Expressions, & vulgar in Manners & Pronunciation'. She conceded, however, his intelligence and good sense; and as a timber merchant, he would appreciate the value of something Hester was eager to preserve – Bach-y-Graig's fifteen thousand oak trees 'all number'd and marked'. The settlement put Johnson and Cator technically in control of the estate. Hester, however, as Scrase had urged, retained discretionary powers – a provision for which she would one day have reason to be grateful.

During his absence in 'the middle counties' Johnson had fantasized in one of his letters about what he would do if he were rich: 'Perhaps, if you and master did not hold me, I might go to Cairo, and down the Red Sea to Bengal, and take a ramble to India.'[33] Hester had responded enthusiastically: '*My* great delight like yours would be to see how Life is carried on in other Countries,' she wrote:

> Counting Pictures & describing Ruins seems to have been the sole
> Business of modern Travellers – but when *we* go to *Cairo* one shall
> take one Department, another shall take another, and so a pretty Book
> may be made out amongst us that shall be commended, and censured,
> and cuffed about the Town for a Twelve Month, if no new Tub takes
> the Whale's Attention.[34] Well! Now all this is Nonsense and Fancy and
> Flight you know, for my Master has his great Casks to mind, and I have
> my little Children, but he has really half a mind to cross the Water for
> half a Year's Frisk to Italy or France …[35]

By late August plans were well in hand. 'We talk of going to France for a Couple of months & taking Queeney,' reads an entry in the *Children's Book*; 'I think she will pick up some French in the Country, & as Baretti is to be of the party will lose no Italian.'[36] Lessons had been learned from the journey in Wales; this time the party would include Thrale's manservant Sam Greaves and Hester's maid Molly Flanders. They set out in the middle of September. Hester took with her a quarto notebook, and on 15 September she made a first entry in her French journal: 'Notwithstanding the Disgust my last Journey gave me, I have lately been solicitous to undertake another. So true is Johnson's Observation that any thing is better than Vacuity.'[37]

10

Fair Stood the Wind
for France

BARETTI had gone ahead to Dover to book their passage, and was not best pleased when they turned up late, just missing a fine tide. The crossing to Calais took six hours. 'The Weather was lovely,' Hester wrote, '– the Ship all our own, the Sea smooth.' Not smooth enough for Queeney or the two servants, who were all 'cruel sick', but they were soon installed at the Hôtel d'Angleterre, which Hester thought the most magnificent she had ever seen – 'we slept here in Ease & even Splendour'.[1] Johnson passed the night less happily. It was the eve of his birthday, one of several days in the year during which it was his custom to give over to unsparing self-examination.[2] A prayer printed in his posthumous *Prayers and Meditations* is annotated 'Composed at Calais in a sleepless night'.[3]

Hester, like Johnson, had never been abroad before, and was immediately alive to new impressions: 'I was vastly surprised when I landed at Calais to see the Soldiers with Whiskers and the Women mostly so ugly and deform'd. They however seemed desirous to hide their frightfulness, for all wore long Clokes of Camlet that came down to their Heels.'[4]

All the arrangements had been entrusted to Baretti, and although she grumbled at having to get up 'so very betimes' to meet his exacting schedule, Hester acknowledged his 'useful Pow'rs': 'he bustled for us, he cater'd for us, he took Care of the Child, he secured an Apartment for the Maid, he provided for our Safety, our Amusement, our Repose – without him the Pleasure of the Journey would never have balanced the Pain'.

They had spent the night at Canterbury on the way to Dover, and Hester had never been so struck with the sight of any cathedral – 'it is truly grand & majestic'.[5] Over the next week or so, however, as they bowled through northern France, that verdict underwent frequent revision. 'Oh how stupendous is the Pile' – this at St Omer – 'let us

never more talk of English Churches.'[6] The next day she discovered that
Arras had a cathedral 'which for the first Coup D'Oeil exceeds them
all'.[7] Except, that is to say, the one she found waiting for her at Amiens
– 'the cathedral exceeded everything I have yet seen, for Profusion of
Labour & Expence'.[8]

They travelled in two coaches, and thus far, although the post horses
were poor specimens, they had rattled along in style. After Amiens,
however, they turned off the high road, and the ruts put them in constant
danger of overturning.

Hester studied the landscape with interest:

The Agriculture is I believe eminently good and the Country so fertile
that since I was two Miles on this Side Calais I have not seen a Spot of
Common or neglected Land. There are more Pigs than Sheep upon the
Hills & the Cattle are miserably poor, but where there is no Grass how
should they be fat, they must not eat Wheat I suppose & cannot digest
Tobacco.[9]

Johnson, possibly handicapped by his poor eyesight, showed less
interest in his surroundings. His long friendship with Baretti later came
under strain and after his death, Baretti wrote harshly that he had been
'not fit to travel, as every place was equal to him. He mused as much
on the road to Paris as he did in his garret in London.'[10] Hester noted
in her journal some of the more excruciating fruits of his musing:

Mr Johnson has made a little Distich at every Place we have slept at, for
example

| A Calais | St Omer | Arras | A Amiens |
| Trop de frais. | Tout est cher. | Helas! | On n'a rien.[11] |

At Rouen they were joined by one of Hester's oldest friends, Cecilia
Strickland – Johnson was soon calling her Stricky. Hester had known her
since the time she had stayed at her uncle's house in Albemarle Street
and been pinched by Master North. Widowed five years previously, Mrs
Strickland was in Rouen to visit her daughter, who was at a convent
school there. Tall, elegant, energetic, she had drawn up elaborate plans
for the visitors. On the night of their arrival she whisked Hester off to

the theatre to see Racine's *Phèdre*, and the next morning took her to visit two convents. The first belonged to the Poor Clares:

> They were truly wretched indeed, wore only one Petticoat, and that of the very coarsest Stuff, they were bare legged and bare footed, & had no Linnen about them except a sort of Band, which was very dirty … Their Fingers all seem knotted at the Joynts, their Nails broken & miserably disfigured, they are extremely lean, too … & *so cold* when one touches them; but no matter I will have another Touch with 'em tomorrow …[12]

It was a morning of contrasts: 'Mrs Strickland carried me from this Scene of Misery to a Convent of the highest Order, where there is a Royal Abbess – so they call those whom the King chuses.' They were shown the refectory, where Hester noticed that each nun had a silver fork and a silver cup: 'they change their Linnen every day & are most delicately clean'. The lady abbess then escorted them to her own elegant apartment: 'We talked of Literature, of Politicks, of Fashions … She was particularly curious to have me explain to her the Nature & Cause of the Rebellion in America. Their House is full of Lap Dogs, Cats & Parrots; but the Abbess's Favrite is a great *English* Mastiff, which she recommended to my Friendship as a Countryman.'[13]

Mrs Strickland also introduced Johnson to a number of priests, including l'Abbé Roffette, to whom Johnson took a great fancy and with whom he conducted a spirited conversation about the Jesuits. Pope Clement XIV had suppressed the order two years previously, an action loudly condemned by Johnson as a blow to the general power of the Church. 'The gentleman seemed to wonder and delight in his conversation,' Hester wrote: 'The talk was all in Latin, which both spoke fluently, and Mr. Johnson pronounced a long eulogium upon Milton with so much ardour, eloquence, and ingenuity, that the Abbé rose from his seat and embraced him.'[14]

Hester attended high mass one day, and was shocked at the lack of devotion shown by the congregation:

> Some were counting their Money, some arguing with the Beggars who interrupt you without ceasing, some receiving Messages and dispatching

Answers, some beating Time to the Musick, but scarce any one praying
except for one Moment when the Priest elevates the Host … It is indeed
a fine Religion wholly run to Seed; all Pomp, all External Shew, & no
Intelligence as I can find or any true Devotion. I am more & more
delighted with my own dear Religion & Country.[15]

Mrs Strickland now joined the party, but their progress to Paris was
interrupted by a frightening accident to the carriage carrying Thrale,
Queeney and Baretti: 'Their Postillion fell off his Horse on a strong
Descent, the Traces were broken, one of the Horses run over and the
Chaise carried forward with a most dangerous Rapidity.' Thrale jumped
out to try and stop the horses, but landed in a chalk pit:

> This was therefore a day of Distress, & my Master found himself so ill
> when we arrived at S^r. Germains that the Surgeon he sent for, advised
> him to go on to Paris & get himself bled & take a good deal of rest
> which he hoped would restore him … Dr Johnson's perfect unconcern
> for the Lives of three People, who would all have felt for his, shocked
> and amaz'd me, – but that, as Baretti says, is true Philosophy; M^{rs}
> Strickland did not give it so kind a Name …'[16]

Spirits lifted with their arrival in Paris. Thrale was on the mend, there
was a long reassuring letter from home and Baretti had found them
elegant lodgings in the rue Jacob. October was spent in and around the
capital. Hester was struck by the purity of the air: 'no Sea Coal being
Burned, the Atmosphere of the narrowest part of Paris is more transpar-
ent and nitid than that of Hampstead hill'.[17] She also found Baretti's
remark 'that the Extremes of Magnificence & Meanness meet at Paris'
well observed:

> Yesterday I was shewn a Femme Publique dress'd out in a Theatrical
> Manner for the Purpose of attracting the Men with a *Crucifix* on her
> Bosom; and today I walked among the beautiful Statues of the Tuiller-
> ies, a Place which for Magnificence most resembles the Pictures of
> Solomon's Temple, where the Gravel is loose like the Beach at Bright-
> helmstone, the Water in the Basin Royale cover'd with Duck Weed,
> and some wooden Netting in the Taste of our low Junketting Houses at
> Islington dropping to Pieces with Rottenness & Age.[18]

The days were filled with a round of sightseeing – churches and museums, palaces and libraries, the Ecole Militaire, the Sèvres porcelain works, the Gobelin tapestry manufactory. Their visit coincided with the fair of Saint-Ovide, held each year in what is now the place de la Concorde. Hester was enchanted:

The Shops are temporary, & slight enough of course, but adorned with a sort of Frippery Finery, Ribbons, Looking Glasses, Cutlery, Pastry, every thing one can imagine that is at once brilliant & worthless – but which when illuminated with Numberless Lights gives an Air of Festivity which not even the Philosophy of an Englishman can despise nor the stupidity of a Dutchman neglect.[19]

They went several times to the theatre:

The Actors are really excellent; *better than our own*, but every thing shews how far the French are behind us. They suffer a Repetition of the same Stage Tricks, & those the lowest, in a manner that would not be borne in London, nor even at a strolling Theatre. The Queen of France was at the Play tonight sitting in one of the Balcony Boxes like any other Lady, only that she curtsied to the Audience at going out & they applauded her in Return. She is wonderfully pretty, & I fancy perfectly amiable; for she clapped the Players when they pleased her, – & chatted with her Maids in a Manner most engagingly free & lovely – I wished her a better Theatre & handsomer Box to sit in.[20]

Hester saw Marie Antoinette again the next day at the races: 'The Queen is still handsomer by Day than by Night, tho' dress'd with the utmost Simplicity: she praised the Jockey who won, & stroked the Horse: She & her Ladies clapped their Hands, & almost shouted when the Winner came in.'[21] But she was taken aback by instances of what she regarded as 'intolerable Grossness': 'The Youngest and prettiest Ladies of the Court will hawk and spit straight before them without the least Attention to Delicacy, & today at the Horse Race we were shewn a Woman of Condition riding astride wth her thick Legs uncovered except by her Stockings which attracted all Eyes to look on them.'[22]

Mrs Strickland had a wide circle of acquaintance in Paris: one of those to whom she introduced her English friends was the writer Marie-Anne du Boccage. Now in her sixties, Madame du Boccage presided over a celebrated salon. She had published French translations of *Paradise Lost* and of Johnson's *Rasselas*, and her writing had been praised by Fontenelle and Voltaire. A quarter of a century earlier she had boldly presumed to trespass on what was then widely regarded as a male preserve when her verse tragedy *The Amazons* received eleven performances at the Comédie-Française; in recent years the piece has attracted the interest of a number of feminist writers.

They were invited to dinner, and Hester was determined not to let the side down: 'The Morning was spent in adjusting our Ornaments in order to dine with Madame de Bocages at 2 o'Clock.' The house was a fine one, and first impressions were favourable: 'There was a showy Dinner with a Frame in the middle, & She gave us an English Pudding made after the Receipt of the Dutchess of Queensbury.' Some courses scored more highly than others, however: 'One Dish was a Hare not tainted but putrified, another was a leg of Mutton put on the Spit the moment the Sheep was killed & garnish's with old Beans, there was one Dish with three Sausages only & one with nothing but Sugar plumbs.'[23]

Such matters were clearly better ordered at Streatham. They passed into the drawing room, furnished with busts of Shakespeare, Milton, Pope and Dryden: 'The Lady sat on a Sopha with a fine Red Velvet Cushion fringed with Gold under her feet, & just over her Head a Cobweb of uncommon Size, & I am sure great Antiquity. A pot to spit in, either of Pewter, or Silver, quite as black & ill coloured, was on her Table; and when the Servant carried Coffee about he put in Sugar with his Fingers.'[24]

French morals were no more to Hester's liking than French manners: 'Panchaud, a Banker, invited us to his Country House where we found a Woman who went by his Name indeed but having all the Mien & Manner of a Harlot.' Hester made no attempt to conceal her indignation, and on the way home complained to both Baretti and Thrale at being introduced into such company.

She was obliged yet again to revise her league table of ecclesiastical architecture. 'We went to see St Roque's Church, which I like better than any I have seen upon the Continent, Amiens alone excepted.'[25]

Johnson, more prosaically, noted simply that the church was 'very large'.[26] There was also a visit to the Foundling Hospital in the Faubourg Saint-Antoine:

> The Place was wonderfully clean, cleaner than any I have seen in France, and the poor Infants at least die peaceably cleanly and in Bed – I saw whole Rows of swathed Babies pining away to perfect Skeletons, & expiring in very neat Cribs with each a Bottle hung to its Neck filled with some Milk Mess, which if they can suck they may live, & if they cannot they must die.[27]

The Thrales celebrated their twelfth wedding anniversary in Paris, and marked the occasion with a lavish dinner. 'Mr Thrale is very liberal,' Johnson wrote to Robert Levet, 'and keeps us two coaches and a very fine table.'[28] Hester's journal and the accounts kept by Baretti confirm that Thrale was extremely open-handed. 'I had the Pleasure to hear Mr Thrale offer me any Silk at any Price,' Hester wrote after a visit to a mercer's, 'and had the Pleasure to feel myself contented with his Kindness & unwilling to put him to any further Expence. Three Gowns is all I carry over, for it was all I wanted.'[29]

Baretti's accounts show that Hester's couturière's bill came to 679 livres; Thrale himself ran up a tailor's bill of 2,568 livres. Other expenditure included forty-eight livres for the physician who attended Thrale at St Germains, 144 livres for his surgeon in Paris and ninety livres for the dancing master hired to give lessons to Queeney. Twenty-four livres made up a louis d'or. The expedition lasted fifty-nine days, and the total cost to Thrale was 822 louis d'or; in today's money Thrale would have laid out close to £80,000.

The court was in residence at Fontainebleau. Hester thought the countryside lovely – 'like Tunbridge but more rocky'. They spent the next morning dressing to go to court, where they followed the curious tourist routine of observing the royal family at the dinner table: 'It is a mighty silent ceremonious Business – this dining in publick.' Hester felt sorry for the twelve-year-old sister of the king who was: 'not handsome but passable, if She was not so pinched in her Stays as makes her look pale & uneasy to herself. All Children through this Nation I perceive are thus squeezed and tortured during their early

Years, and the Deformity they exhibit at maturity repays the stupid Parents for their Pains.'[30]

In the next room they saw the King and Queen. Hester noted that the table was spread with a damask cloth, 'neither course nor fine', and that their dishes were silver – 'not clean and bright like Silver in England – but they were Silver'. Dinner consisted of five dishes at a course: 'The Queen eat heartily of a Pye which the King helped her to, they did not speak at all to each other.' Johnson, who saw a good deal more than his companions sometimes realized, noticed that the King fed himself with his left hand. Hester was confirmed in her view that Marie Antoinette was by far the prettiest woman at her own court. She was less impressed by Louis XVI. Shy, dull, corpulent, nearsighted, he had succeeded his grandfather only the year before at the age of twenty. 'The King is well enough,' Hester wrote '– like another Frenchman.'[31]

Then on to Versailles – 'a mean town' says a typically cryptic entry in Johnson's journal. His account of their journey, of which only a part survives, makes far less colourful reading than Hester's, consisting as it does mostly of brief descriptions of things seen, although he devotes the best part of a page to the menagerie at Versailles, which clearly intrigued him: 'Rhinoceros. The horn broken, and pared away which I suppose will grow. The basis I think, four inches across. The skin folds like loose cloath doubled, over his body, and cross his hips, vast animal though young, as big perhaps as four Oxen.'[32]

He was always curious to explore the contents of libraries, but his interest was mainly roused by anything that involved scientific or mechanical processes. One day he and Thrale left Hester to her interminable round of convent visits and went to inspect a mirror factory. They were also shown round the largest brewery in Paris.[33] Eighteen years later its proprietor, Antoine Joseph Santerre, would command the troops who surrounded the scaffold at Louis XVI's execution.

Hester did not share Johnson's enthusiasm for the Versailles menagerie, although she conceded that it was 'agreeable enough' to stroke a Siberian fox that was as tame as a lapdog. When they were taken to see the Versailles theatre, however, she was lost for superlatives. 'I had never known what Expence could do when pushed to the utmost had I not seen the King of France's Theatre,' she wrote. It had been built five years previously on the occasion of the future king's marriage to Marie-Antoinette – the palace had previously lacked a proper *salle de spectacle*. There were 712 seats, a perfect acoustic and a mechanical system that allowed the floor of the auditorium to be set at the level of the stage. Hester recalled their visit years later: 'As we stood on the stage looking at some machinery for playhouse purposes: Now we are here, what shall we act, Mr Johnson, – The Englishman at Paris? "No, no (replied he), we will try to act Harry the Fifth."'[34]

One last week of dining and shopping and theatre-going. The weather had grown cold, which had a bad effect on Johnson's breathing. It was time to turn for home. Hester had been much taken with the paintings she was able to see in Paris, particularly those in the Orléans Collection at the Palais Royale: 'I half cryed over some of them with mere delight,' she wrote: 'one View of one Room in this House is worth crossing the Seas for.' She spent a last morning there:

> I … staid among them three Hours & was treated with the Sight of many that are never shewn to common Observers – particularly those in the Bed-Chamber of the Duke of Chartres, who selected half a Dozen which he wish'd to open his Eyes on in a Morning; among these was a Landskip by Rubens over his Chimney which for a Moment effaced that of Carracci from my Memory: the Judgment of Paris only filled the Scenery, but the Paysage was the principal part of the Picture – & such a Paysage! I never saw anything to equal: Queeney made me observe a mighty pleasing Incident in it; Juno's Peacock pecking the leg of Paris for not bestowing the Apple on his Mistress.[35]

They left Paris on 1 November. 'Stricky' had gone back to Rouen two days previously:

> I have through her means made a more rational Figure where I have been, not staring about as I should have done a lone Woman with two or three Men about me … We have been long acquainted, but never lived much together till now, I think myself therefore particularly fortunate that She has proved as agreeable to all my Friends & to my Husband as to me – …[36]

Tiresome travelling companion as he was in some ways, Johnson's presence had also provided security and reassurance. Hester had caught a bad cold towards the end of their stay, and one evening did not feel well enough to accompany the men to the theatre: 'Mr Johnson sat at home by me, & we criticized & talked and were happy in one another – he in huffing me, & I in being huff'd.'[37]

They took a different route back to Calais – Chantilly, Cambrai, Douai, Lille, Dunkirk. Hester drank in fresh impressions as eagerly as she had done on the outward journey. At Chantilly they visited the magnificent castle which was the seat of the princes of Condé – 'which exceeds in Taste & Elegance all I have seen in France', she wrote.[38]

While they were visiting St Peter's Church in Douai the members of the Flemish Parliament arrived to hear high mass. This gave rise to a difference of opinion with Johnson as to whether they might have stayed through the whole service and witnessed the elevation of the Host:

> If you had staid, says Baretti, you must have kneel'd. I have no Scruples, said I, I was willing enough to kneel. Johnson said he would not have knelt on such an Occasion for the whole City of Douay. I was not in a humour to argue at that Moment, & besides I felt a Fear lest his force of reasoning might destroy my Quiet, for I have kneeled two or three Times or more at the Elevation since I have been upon the Continent & am firmly perswaded that in so doing I was not displeasing to God …[39]

They reached Calais on 10 November: 'Here I had the Mortification to find the things I sent by the Diligence cruelly mangled by injudicious Management & that fretted me.'[40] Hester also fretted about how they would be received at Dover: 'Custom House Officers indeed I have a dread of yet, though a three Livre piece has hitherto silenced the most sullen, but at Dover we are threatened with sad brutal Fellows – Nous verrons.'[41]

The weather was not good. Hester braved it out on deck throughout the crossing, but Queeney and Molly once again succumbed to seasickness. ('Sam,' Hester noted in the margin of her journal, 'was too ill to be Seasick.') The sad brutal fellows in the Custom House showed no interest in her three Paris gowns, the various pieces of Sèvres she had bought or the fine wig to which Johnson had been treated in Paris. 'My

Adventures are now at an End,' she wrote in her journal: 'I have at last brought my Niggey safe home again to England – which I shall now love on more rational Grounds than ever I did yet – I see now that it is better than France.'[42]

~ 11 ~

'An Unforeseen and Heavy Calamity'

THE HAPPINESS of the homecoming was short-lived: 'Here is little Fanny very ill & of her *head* too – it will turn my *Head* at last; Old Nurse is gone to Town to consult Dr Lawrence – Good News if it please God! Never happy long together!'[1]

Dr Lawrence had both good and bad news to impart. Hester's fear that the child's brain was affected was unfounded; the bad news was that the six-month-old was suffering from influenza. It was a disorder that the medical profession in the eighteenth century was ill-equipped to deal with; most doctors still believed it was spread by atmospheric factors. Fanny's condition steadily worsened; she died in early December, her death quickly followed by that of her wet-nurse. Hester, writing in the *Children's Book* on the day of the funeral, struck a note of anguished resignation: 'The other four are healthy active & vigorous as possible; I hope I may be permitted to keep them so – but be it as it may: I must endeavour not to provoke Gods Judgments on my Family ...'[2]

Harry, the only boy of the four children now left to her, was the apple of her eye. He was every bit as precocious as Queeney, although that precocity manifested itself somewhat differently. 'I have heard of my Son's naughtiness,' Hester wrote shortly after her return from France:

> It consisted in telling his Schoolfellows a staring Story about what was done at a Bawdy house, for w:ch Conversation Old Perny very wisely flogged him well ... The Truth is Harry is but *too* forward in some things; he told me yesterday he wondered Baretti was not ashamed of belonging to a Country where they cut the *Men*, as we cut the *Horses* – & all to make them *sing* forsooth. I bid him never talk to his Sisters on such Subjects ...[3]

'Old Perny' was Harry's master at the Loughborough House School;

the flogging clearly left no hard feelings, because he figured on the guest-list for the boy's ninth birthday party in February, along with Johnson, Murphy and Perkins, the brewery manager. Harry was much happier at Southwark than he was at school, and was a great favourite with the men at the brewhouse.

The Thrales had been so pleased with their French excursion that Baretti was set to work almost immediately arranging a more ambitious journey to Italy. 'A very rich gentleman has asked me to go with him on a long journey,' he wrote rather grandly to one of his brothers, and he gave thumbnail sketches of the Thrales: 'He only speaks a very little French, unlike his wife, who talks French and Italian fluently, without troubling about their quality, and likes to talk them, and is bright and lively.' He gave a warning, however, that Hester was 'shocked at the least offence against religion or morality'; she was, he said, *molto Bibbiaia*, a coinage of his own meaning 'devoted to her Bible'. He also asked his brothers to lay on a priest or monk 'who speaks Latin with some elegance' – this for Johnson's benefit; 'Then we will leave them to talk about literature together, and not trouble ourselves with his elephantine tricks.'[4]

By late March Baretti's plans were well advanced. He proposed conducting them as far as Sicily, and reckoned they must be away for the best part of a year. Johnson, greatly excited at the prospect of at last seeing Italy, set off on a round of farewell visits to friends in the Midlands, accompanied by Boswell. As they sat at breakfast in Lichfield one morning, Johnson received a letter that seemed to agitate him greatly. 'One of the most dreadful things that has happened in my time,' he exclaimed, 'Mr. Thrale has lost his only son!'[5]

Harry's death was a bolt from the blue. Several weeks passed before Hester could bring herself to record the sequence of events in the *Children's Book*. One moment he had been playing the fool in the nursery, the next he was writhing in pain – 'crying as if he had been whipt instead of ill', Hester wrote. Her first instinct was to scold him 'for making such a bustle ab:ᵗ nothing'. It seemed prudent nevertheless to summon a doctor. A message sent to her father's old friend, Herbert Lawrence, met with no response.[6] Meanwhile Harry started retching, and Hester made him drink a large glass of emetic wine. When this had no effect she began to be seriously concerned:

I sent out Sam: with orders not to come back without some Physician –
Jebb, Bromfield, Pinkstan … whichever he could find: in the mean time
I plunged Harry into Water as hot as could easily be borne, up to his
Middle, & had just taken him out of the Tub, & laid him in a warm bed,
when Jebb came …[7]

Richard Jebb, tall and thin, had a lucrative private practice and was
highly regarded in the profession. A Fellow of the Royal Society, he was
the friend of Wilkes and the poet Charles Churchill but also a favourite
of the King's. He had a reputation for blunt speaking and could be a
good deal less deferential to patients than some of his colleagues. He
began by giving Harry hot wine, and followed this with whisky and a
concoction known as Daffy's Elixir, a laxative made largely from alcohol
with senna as a chief ingredient:[8] Jebb then applied mustard poultices
to the boy's feet and administered a wine enema. 'But we could get no
Evacuation any way,' Hester wrote: '& the Inclination to vomit still
continuing Jebb gave him 5 Grains of Ipecacuanha & then drove away
to call Heberden's help.'[9]

Hester found there was little comfort to be had from either her husband or Baretti:

Mr Thrale bid me not cry so, for I should look like a Hag when I went
to Court next Day – he often saw Harry in the Course of the Morning:
and apprehended no danger at all – no more did Baretti, who said he
should be whipt for frighting his Mother for nothing … but soon a
universal Shriek called us all together to Harry's Bedside, where he
struggled a Moment – thrusting his Finger down his Throat to excite
Vomiting, & then – turning to Nurse said very distinctly – don't
Scream so – I *know* I must die.[10]

Years later, Baretti recalled the scene in the *European Magazine*:

Mr. Thrale, both his hands in his waistcoat pocket, sat on an arm-chair
in a corner of the room with his body so stiffly erect, and with such a
ghastly smile on his face, as was quite horrid to behold. Count Manucci
and a female servant, both as pale as ashes, and as if panting for breath,
were evidently spent with keeping Madam from going frantic (and well

she might) every time she recovered from her fainting-fits, that followed each other in a very quick succession.[11]

Queeney was so badly affected by the loss of her brother that Hester feared she too might die. When Jebb recommended a speedy change of scene, she decided to take her to Bath: 'Baretti kindly offered to go with me, so he conducted the Troop, & diverted Queeney's Melancholy with all the Tricks he could think on.'[12]

The letter conveying the news of Harry's death to Johnson had been from Perkins. Johnson wrote to Hester by return: 'This letter will not, I hope, reach you many days before me, in a distress which can be so little relieved, nothing remains for a friend but to come and partake it.'[13] He did not however, do so immediately; only after he and Boswell had paid a brief visit to Taylor at Ashbourne did he return, arriving at Southwark as the coach for Bath stood at the door. Baretti later expressed surprise that Johnson did not volunteer to accompany Hester in his place; 'therefore, after the sad exchange of a few mournful periods', he added, 'we got into the coach and were soon out of sight'.[14]

Johnson lingered at the house, but his attempts to comfort Thrale were rebuffed. Returning the next day, he was told that when he was wanted he would be sent for. He forwarded to Hester a letter of condolence from Boswell, and tried as best he could to comfort her with words of his own. 'Remember the great precept. *Be not solitary, be not idle,*' he urged her: 'I know that such a loss is a laceration of the mind. I know that a whole system of hopes, and designs, and expectations is swept away at once, and nothing left but bottomless vacuity. What you feel, I have felt, and hope that your disquiet will be shorter than mine.'[15]

Hester, slowly regaining a measure of tranquillity at Bath, was touched:

Shall I beg you to tell Mr Boswell that I feel myself but too much affected by his Friendship; Yours has long been the best Cordial to my heart, it is now almost the only one. I cold bathe here, & endeavour all I can to excite Appetite, & force Attention; I owe every Thing to Mr Thrale's indulgent Tenderness, and will bring him home the best Wife I can ...[16]

Boswell records an exchange with Johnson as they travelled back to London about the impact Harry's death would have on his parents: 'I said it would be very distressing to Thrale, but she would soon forget it, as she had so many things to think of. Johnson: "No, Sir, Thrale will forget it first. *She* has many things that she *may* think of. *He* has many things that he *must* think of."'[17]

Johnson for once was wrong. Thrale never forgot it and never got over it. He had borne the death of four other children with a degree of resignation. The loss of this lively, intelligent, knowing little boy was altogether more traumatic, as Johnson had been characteristically quick to perceive. 'This is a total extinction to their family,' he had declared to Boswell on first hearing the news, 'as much as if they were sold into captivity.' When Boswell observed that Thrale had daughters to whom he might leave his wealth, Johnson, impatient at such obtuseness, brusquely cut him off: 'Sir, (said he,) don't you know how you yourself think? Sir, he wishes to propagate his name.'[18]

From this time on, Thrale would become increasingly taciturn and his fits of depression more frequent. He had always been something of a trencher-man, but now his appetite became dangerously gross – but what could be done with a man, Hester once sadly asked, 'whose mouth cannot be sewed up?'

The cause of Harry's death remains obscure. Clifford wrote confidently in the 1940s of a ruptured appendix, but that seems improbable – the boy's illness lasted only a matter of hours. Bacterial meningitis seems a more likely diagnosis – it is possible that Queeney was suffering from a milder form of the infection that killed her brother.

Hester believed that she had had a premonition of Harry's death the previous autumn when she was going round a church in Lille with Thrale and Johnson, although more than two years would pass before she recorded the experience:

In one of the Chapels I observed myself to stumble in an odd manner, so as to give me uncommon Pain, & at the same time to excite strange Ideas of Terror, wholly unaccountable to me, who am neither timorous nor over delicate: I looked at the Altar-piece, & saw it was the figure of an Angel protecting a boy about twelve Years old as it should seem,

& somehow the Child struck me with a Resemblance to my own, and alarmed me in an unusual Manner.

She prayed for the safety of her children, and learning from an old man that the chapel was dedicated to the guardian angel of children determined to go into every other chapel to see whether she stumbled in them: 'I could not stumble, however, but when I returned with better Spirits to the Children's Chapel, I stumbled again and even hurt myself.' Later, when Thrale had taken Queeney to the theatre, she told Johnson what had happened: 'he bid me be careful not to encourage such Fancies, & talking the Thing through cleared my head of it for a Time'.

It was only for a time, however. Two days before the boy fell ill, she had another strangely disturbing experience. As she went down to receive the company at dinner she heard 'something like a preternatural Voice call me by my Name; but this I never mentioned to any one, lest I should be suspected of Madness'. Johnson's injunction had lodged securely in her mind: 'Mad notwithstanding all this Folly I am *not*; the Disorder never was in my Family, nor have I ever had any predominance in my Imagination which could cause me to suspect myself for an Hour ... My Mind is an active whirling Mind, which few Things can stop to disturb, & if disturbed, it soon recovers its Strength & its Activity.'

That defiant assertion was written more than two years after what she described elsewhere in *Thraliana* as the 'unforeseen and heavy Calamity' of Harry's death. Her mind had certainly by then recovered its accustomed vigour, but the heartache remained: 'I was too proud of him, and provoked God's Judgments by my Folly,' she wrote: 'Let this Sorrow expiate all my Offences Good Lord! ... Suffer me no more to follow my Offspring to the Grave.'

⁓⤳ ⤶⁓

The trip to Italy was put off, although Thrale spoke of postponement rather than abandonment. Baretti argued furiously against the decision – some of the baggage was already in Calais; his family and friends in Italy would be greatly disappointed; the loss the Thrales had suffered was an additional reason for going abroad. Johnson's reaction, generous and perceptive, could not have been more different: 'Mr. Thrale's alteration of purpose is not weakness of resolution; it is a wise man's compliance with the change of things,' he told Hester: 'Your business for the present is to seek for ease, and to go where you think it most likely to be found. There cannot yet be any place in your minds for mere curiosity. Whenever I can contribute to your tranquillity, I shall readily attend.'[19]

Hester, who had returned from Bath for Easter, was deeply touched: 'Every day every hour makes me more happy in your Friendship – it ought to take up a larger part of my Mind than I can just now afford it – nothing however out of my own Bosom is half so dear to my Heart as that is.' And she added a postscript: 'Mr. Thrale has seen your letter and shed Tears over the reading It – they are the first he has shed. – I can say no more.'[20]

Thrale now decided that Hester and Queeney would benefit from a further stay in Bath and by the middle of April they were installed, together with Johnson, in the Corner House on the North Parade: 'Mr Thrale slept on the 1:st Floor next the Dining room, Johnson slept on the 2:^{d} Floor, so did Queeney, so of course did I: and there were some dirty Irish people lodged in the Parlours. I think says Hetty our House is like the Tree in Sophy's Fable Book. The Eagles inhabit the top, the Fox possesses the Middle, & the *pigs* wallow at the bottom.'[21]

Boswell, who had never seen Bath, joined them for a few days and put up at the Pelican Inn nearby. He found Johnson in lively critical form. The historian Mrs Macaulay, whose republican principles Johnson so much detested, had moved to Bath two years previously for her health. It was rumoured, Boswell wrote, that she had recently taken to putting on rouge: 'Johnson. 'She is better employed at her toilet, than using her pen. It is better she should be reddening her own cheeks, than blackening other people's characters.'

At times even Hester did not escape 'his friendly animadversions', as Boswell called them: 'When she said, perhaps affectedly, "I don't like to fly." Johnson. 'With *your* wings, Madam, you *must* fly: but have a care, there are *clippers* abroad.'[22]

The bustle and chatter of Bath held no appeal for Johnson, however, and he was not unhappy to return to London to lend support to his friend John Taylor who was involved in a protracted legal dispute. Hester kept him supplied with the latest gossip from the balls and assemblies: 'The Politicians sigh here, & the Wits laugh at General Howe's walking out of Boston, & General Washington's walking in; but everybody agrees that Peace will soon be made, and an excellent Topick of Conversation taken from us all.'[23]

News still travelled slowly in 1776. Hester's letter is dated 8 May. General Howe had evacuated Boston on 17 March.

❧ ❧

The Thrales remained in Bath until the end of May, returning home by way of Stonehenge, Southampton and Portsmouth – 'seeing all we could find to amuse our Sorrows & heal our half broken hearts'.[24]

The return to Streatham was not going to be easy. With a long absence in Italy in prospect, most of the staff had been dismissed. 'What shall I do for Servants?' she wrote to Johnson: 'If you have any pity for me do not come home till I have got my house a little to rights, and if you can hear of a *Butler* or a *Footman* or a *Maid*, or almost anything do send them to me.'[25]

She was spared his company for a little, as he had been stricken by a severe attack of gout: 'I am a very poor creeper upon the earth,' he wrote.[26] Hester herself was laid low immediately on her return. The doctors spoke of Cholera Morbus, the name given to a dangerous form of gastro-enteritis. 'I mend gradually,' she wrote, 'but am as weak as a Cat now.' There was a further reason for her weakness: 'My three little Girls are all with me, the thin remains of my ruined Family; I find myself with Child again however, & perhaps if God Almighty spares me any very great Troubles during Gestation, I may see another Son to live …'[27]

Johnson expressed his satisfaction at her pregnancy: 'Compose your thoughts, diversify your attention, and attend to your health,' he urged her.[28] That was more easily said than done. Since Thrale's decision to call off the trip to Italy, Hester had found Baretti 'sullen and captious'. His devotion to Queeney – 'my Esteruccia', as he called her, with the Italian passion for diminutives, was not in question: 'I love her seven thousand times more than I ever loved any one else,' he wrote to his brother.[29] Since their return from Bath, however, Queeney kept telling her mother that he had become 'very odd and very Cross, would not look at her Exercises, but said he would leave this House soon, for it was no better than Pandæmonium'.

Hester and he had in truth never really liked each other. 'Baretti is for ever in the State of a Stream dam'd up – if he could once get loose – he would bear down all before him,' she wrote:

> Not a Servant, not a Child did he leave me any Authority over; if I would attempt to correct or dismiss them, there was ... instant Appeals to Mr Baretti, who was sure always to be against me in every Dispute. With Mr Thrale I was ever cautious of contending ... as I have no Friend or Relation in the World to protect me from the rough Treatment of a *Husband* shou'd he chuse to exert his *Prerogatives*, but when I saw Baretti openly urging Mr Thrale to despise my Requests, and to cut down some little Fruit trees my Mother had planted, and I had beg'd might stand: I confess I did take an Aversion to the Creature, & secretly resolved his Stay should not be prolonged by my Intreaties, whenever his Greatness chose to take huff and be gone.

That occasion now arose. Baretti's version appeared a dozen years later in the *European Magazine*. 'Madam took it into her head to give herself airs, and treat me with some coldness and superciliousness,' he wrote: 'I did not hesitate to set down at breakfast my dish of tea half drank, go for my hat and stick that lay in the corner of the room, turn my back to the house *insalutato hospite*, and walk away to London without uttering a syllable, fully resolved never to see her again ...'[30]

It was on 6 July that Baretti chose to 'take huff and be gone'. Two days earlier, far away in Philadelphia, the Continental Congress had formally adopted a rather more significant declaration of independence.

The Book with the Foolish Name

FOUR MONTHS into her pregnancy, Thrale told Hester something which caused her great anxiety: 'No peace saith my God for the wicked! No quiet Gestation for me! On Sunday Night the 3:ᵈ of Sept:ʳ Mʳ Thrale told me he had an Ailment, & shewed me a Testicle swelled to an immense Size …'

Thrale initially maintained that it had been caused when he leapt from the carriage in France the previous year, and Hester jumped to the conclusion that it must be cancerous. When Thrale talked of sending for a man called Osborne, however, her suspicions were aroused – she had read of him in the press – 'a sort of half Quack' who specialized in the treatment of venereal disease:

> I now began to understand where I was, and to perceive that my poor
> Father's Prophecy was verified who said If you marry that Scoundrel
> he will catch the Pox, /&/ for your Amusement set you to make his
> Pultices. This is now literally made out; & I am preparing Pultices as
> he said, and Fomenting the elegant Ailment every Night & Morning
> for an Hour together on my Knees, & receiving for my Reward such
> Impatient Expressions as disagreeable Confinement happens to dictate.[1]

It was not the first time Thrale had been obliged to seek such treatment, although Hester had made no previous mention of it. She now reflected with some bitterness in the *Children's Book* on an occasion in the late 1760s when he had paid out fifty guineas to be cured of an infection of the urethra: 'I thought I had so behaved on that last Occasion, setting him down myself at Daran's door, and keeping his Secret inviolable even from my Mother, as that he needed not have neglected any Ailment he might contract for fear of my Suspicion or Resentment …'[2]

Reassured that there was no cancer, Hester dismissed Thrale's

promiscuity with relaxed contempt: 'I do think it is only a Consequence
of Folly & Vice,' she wrote – 'as if I cared for any thing in Competi-
tion with a Life so precious to his whole Family.' She was realistic to a
degree – there were still debts to be paid from the crisis at the brewery
four years previously.

Thrale's 'elegant Ailment' put a question mark over their annual
autumn holiday in Brighton. In the middle of September, perhaps to
make amends for not being the easiest or most agreeable of patients, he
made Hester a handsome present:

> It is many years since Doctor Samuel Johnson advised me to get a little
> Book, and write in it all the little Anecdotes which might come to my
> Knowledge, all the Observations I might make or hear; all the Verses
> never likely to be published, and in fine ev'ry thing which struck me
> at the Time. Mʳ Thrale has now treated me with a Repository, – and
> provided it with the pompous Title of Thraliana; I must endeavour to
> fill it with Nonsense new and old.

This 'repository' consisted of six quarto volumes. Bound in undressed
calf, each cover bore a red label with the word 'Thraliana' stamped in
gold. Thrale's choice of title suggests that he was not such an ignoramus
in literary matters as has sometimes been supposed. The ana was a form
more familiar in France; Johnson, two decades earlier, had defined it in
his *Dictionary* as 'loose thoughts, or casual hints, dropped by eminent
men, and collected by their friends'. The only English examples Hester
could think of had both been published in the previous century – the
Table-Talk of the historian and antiquary John Selden and the *Remaines*
of William Camden, who had been Ben Jonson's headmaster at Westminster and modestly described the book as 'the rude rubble and out-cast
rubbish … of a greater and more serious worke'.

Not a commonplace book, then, and only intermittently a diary –
more a sort of literary ragbag: a voluminous receptacle for anecdotes,
literary trifles, gossip, reminiscences. It would take Hester until 1809
to fill her six volumes 'with Nonsense old and new'; Henry Thrale's
shamefaced gift made possible a vivid contribution to the understanding
of the life and culture of Georgian England.

On Queeney's twelfth birthday they went up to London to have her made heir to Hester's Welsh property in place of Harry – 'may she hold it as her Great Grandmother Lucy Salusbury did for 76 Years'.[3] And yet on almost every page of the *Children's Book* there is evidence of Hester's ambivalent feelings towards her eldest daughter. 'Have I not reason to rejoice in this dear Girl?' is followed a week later by 'There is something strangely perverse in Queeney's Temper, full of Bitterness and Aversion to all who instruct her.'[4]

This last observation was prompted by the recent appearance of a new instructor for Queeney. Hester had arranged for her to study music under Dr Charles Burney – 'who is justly supposed at present the first Man in Europe', she wrote, '& whose Instructions I have long been endeavouring to obtain for her'.[5] Burney had been apprenticed for a time as a young man to the composer Thomas Arne. Well known as a teacher of music to the upper classes, he also enjoyed something of a literary reputation – the first volume of his *General History of Music* had appeared earlier that year.

The arrangement was that Burney should come to Streatham once a week and that after Queeney's lesson, he should stay to dinner. Hester soon came to think very highly of him: 'Such was the fertility of his Mind, and the extent of his Knowledge; such the Goodness of his Heart and Suavity of his Manners that we began in good earnest to sollicit his Company, and gain his Friendship.'

Burney told Boswell of his many long conversations at Streatham with Johnson – 'often sitting up as long as the fire and candles lasted, and much longer than the patience of the servants subsisted'.[6] This willingness to relieve her of staying up half the night drinking tea with Johnson particularly endeared Burney to his hostess; many years later, in a letter to Queeney, Hester recalled sitting up so late with her insomniac house-guest that her legs 'began to swell as big as columns'.[7]

By September Thrale was well enough to travel and they spent several weeks in Brighton – sea-bathing in the morning, assemblies at night. Johnson, as usual, was bored: 'the place was very dull', he told Boswell, 'and I was not well'.[8] In another letter, shortly before Christmas, he reported on Hester's condition: 'Mrs. Thrale is big, and fancies that she carries a boy; if it were very reasonable to wish much about it, I should wish her not to be disappointed ... A son is almost necessary to the continuance of Thrale's fortune; for what can misses do with a brewhouse?'[9]

Hester's mood as she entered the New Year was sombre to the point of morbidity:

> The truth is I did pray earnestly for a son and I am strangely prepossessed with a Notion that God has heard my Prayers; but perhaps like poor Rachel I may pay my own Life for it – Well no matter! I shall leave a Son of my own to inherit my paternal Estate & for the rest M[r] Thrale may provide himself with Children & Chuse a Wife where he will: it is not his Principle to lament much for the Dead, so my Loss will not break his Heart ...[10]

The Thrales' eleventh child was born on 8 February: 'The Labour was rough & tight, but no Boy nor no Death ensued,' Hester recorded in the *Children's Book*; 'I was oddly prepossess'd that both was intended to happen.' Stricky, as a Roman Catholic, could not be a godmother, but the child was baptized Cecilia after her. 'It is a lovely Child sure enough,' Hester wrote, '– God grant it but Life & Grace.'[11]

She had had the company during the winter of a childhood friend called Margaret Owen, and in the middle of March, accompanied by Queeney, the two women spent a carefree fortnight in London. 'Did you stay all night at Sir Joshua's? and keep Miss up again?' Johnson enquired. 'You are all young and gay and easy. But I have miserable nights, and know not how to make them better.'[12] He joined them the following morning, however, when they called on the Burneys, who lived in Isaac Newton's old house in St Martin's Street. There is no mention in Hester's diary of her first encounter with Burney's shy, old-fashioned second daughter, then secretly completing the novel that would shortly make her famous, but she herself was closely observed by that young woman, shortsighted as she was: 'Mrs Thrale is a very pretty woman still,' Fanny Burney wrote to her elderly mentor 'Daddy' Crisp – 'she is extremely lively and chatty, – has no supercilious or pedantic airs, and is really gay and agreeable.'

It was also the first time she had seen Johnson, and her vivid portrait of him bears comparison with anything achieved by Boswell in the *Life*: 'He is, indeed, very ill favoured, – he is tall & stout, but stoops terribly,

— he is almost bent double. His mouth is in perpetual motion, as if he was
chewing; — he has a strange method of frequently twirling his Fingers,
& twisting his Hands; — his Body is in continual agitation, *see sawing*
up & down; his Feet are never a moment quiet ...'

He was, she noted, 'shockingly near-sighted, & did not, till she held
out her Hand to him, even know Mrs. Thrale'. And she recorded a
revealing passage of verbal jousting between the two:

> The whole party was engaged to Dine at Mrs. Montague's: Dr. Johnson
> said he had received the most flattering note he had ever read, or any
> body else had ever Read, by way of invitation. 'Well, so have I, too,'
> cried Mrs. Thrale, 'so if a note from Mrs. Montague is to be boasted of,
> I beg mine may not be forgot.'
>
> '*Your* note,' cried Dr. Johnson, 'can bear no comparison with *mine*; —
> I am *at the Head of Philosophers*; she says.'
>
> 'And I,' cried Mrs. Thrale, '*have all the muses in my Train*!'

At this point, clearly enjoying the contest, Burney intervened to egg
the protagonists on:

> 'A fair Battle,' said my Father; 'come, Compliment for Compliment, &
> see who will hold out longest.'
>
> 'O, I am afraid for Mrs Thrale!' cried Mr. Seward, 'for I know Mrs.
> Montague exerts all her forces when she attacks Dr. Johnson.'
>
> 'O yes,' said Mrs. Thrale, 'she has often, I know, flattered *him* till he
> has been ready to Faint.'
>
> 'Well, Ladies,' said my Father, 'You must get him between you to
> Day, & see which can lay on the paint thickest, Mrs. Thrale or Mrs.
> Montague.'[13]

Hester was also now belatedly presented at court. She was introduced
by Lady Gage, daughter of the wealthy Jewish financier Samson Gideon,
whose advice had been sought by both Walpole and Henry Pelham.[14]
'The ceremony was trifling,' Hester told Johnson, 'but I am glad it's over;
one is now upon the footing one wishes to be — and in a manner free of
the Drawing Room, I confess I am pleased at having been there.'[15]

Thrale meantime had been convalescing at Brighton, and Hester and
Queeney now joined him there — to 'take a Dip in the Sea by way of

refreshing ourselves & washing off London Smoak', as she wrote to
Johnson: '– but how was I astonished this Morning to see my Master's
Death in all the London Papers! The first Person I feared it might make
uneasy was you, I therefore make haste to write that you may be satisfied
he is alive & well, and just going out on horseback this Moment ...
Where can the Jest be of frighting a Man's Friends so foolishly?'[16]

Johnson sent Thrale a solemnly worded note:

> Dear Sir:
> This is a letter of pure congratulation. I congratulate you
> That you are alive.
> That you have got my Mistress fixed again after her excentricities ...[17]

He also had to reassure an anxious Boswell, who had clearly not yet
fathomed all aspects of the Sassenach sense of humour: 'It is supposed
to have been produced by the English custom of making April fools,'
Johnson told him, 'that is, of sending one another on some foolish errand
on the first of April.'[18]

Early in May, Queeney was confirmed. The service was conducted
at St Saviour's, Southwark, by Beilby Porteous, the recently appointed
Bishop of Chester: 'I had the Satisfaction,' Hester wrote in the *Children's
Book*, 'of being perfectly convinced that even his Lordship did not better understand the Nature End & Use of that Sacred Office than She
did.'[19] When Queeney celebrated her thirteenth birthday later in the year,
Thrale decided she should have an allowance of forty guineas a year: 'We
shall see how She manages it,' Hester wrote in the *Children's Book*.

A link with her young life was severed at the end of the month: 'The
Account of poor Doctor Collier's Death is this moment brought me; I
am sincerely concerned at it – the more as we did not part Friends, after
having been once so intimate; but he now knows that I could not do much
otherwise than I did, and that my Intentions at least were pure ...'

Hester now seemed resolved to spread her wings socially. She asked
Johnson whether the well-connected John Taylor, recently a guest at
Streatham, could procure tickets to a fête to be given by the Duke and
Duchess of Devonshire at their mansion in Piccadilly – Taylor had been
a friend of the Duke's father. 'Do write by the first Opportunity,' she
urged, 'as I really wish to see what Pleasure can do upon her Throne.'[20]

Johnson dutifully wrote to Taylor, although he warned Hester that 'the business is pretty much out of the Doctors way'. And, very gently, he teased her for what he clearly regarded as social pretention: 'You will become such a Gadder, that you will not care a peny for me. However, you are wise in wishing to know what life is made of: to try what are the pleasures, which are so eagerly sought, and so dearly purchased. We must know pleasure before we can rationally despise.'[21]

In the event the fête was postponed, but Hester did not lack for diversion: 'M^r & Mrs Garrick have been here,' she told Johnson in her next letter, 'so I have heard the Eagle & the Blackbird, & a very pretty Thing it is I think: he is to get us Places for Sherridan's new Play which is a *Thing* it seems.'[22]

Garrick had retired from the stage the previous summer at the age of fifty-nine. Summoned to perform before the Royal Family at Windsor, he had composed a somewhat embarrassing prologue in which he depicts himself as an ageing, greying blackbird called out of retirement by the royal Eagle:

> ... He never felt before such pride,
> Though crippled, old, and cracked his note,
> The royal smile each want supplied,
> Gave him a new melodious throat ...

Word had gone about that the royal smile had not been particularly broad and that Garrick, mortified by his reception, had vowed that he would read no more. But he had also written the prologue to *The School for Scandal*, and it was one of his best:

> A School for Scandal! Tell me, I beseech you,
> Needs there a School – this modish art to teach you?
> No need of lessons now, – the knowing think –
> We might as well be taught to eat and drink ...

Sheridan's new play had opened the previous month, and tickets for Drury Lane were like gold dust, in part because the piece was known to be a satire on the Devonshire House circle.

Later in the summer there was a visit to Thrale's friend John Cator, who lived in some style at Beckenham in Kent. The Thrales also dined at

Wick House, the villa Joshua Reynolds had built some years previously
on Richmond Hill. 'Some agreeable People were raked together, and we
intended to have a charming day of it,' Hester wrote in *Thraliana*:

> but Mr Garrick was sick, and Lady Rothes was troublesome; She
> brought two Babies with her both under six Years old, which though
> the prettiest Babies in the World were not wanted there at all, they
> played and prattled and suffer'd nobody to be heard but themselves –
> we ancient Maids, steril Wives or disappointed Parents were peevish
> to see others happier than ourselves in a little Boy who naughty as
> we called him – three People there would have been glad to purchase
> with ten thousand Pound – Garrick, Thrale, or old Deputy Peterson,
> who married a second Wife on purpose, but could not obtain his Wish
> ... I could hardly endure the day between peevishness Envy and the
> perpetual Regret to think that I once had a Son –

Within a matter of weeks she discovered that she was once again
pregnant. Thrale's reaction to the news came as an unpleasant surprise: 'I
am astonished ay & disgusted too to find Mr Thrale not at all rejoyced at
it: I confess I am as glad as possible, & I thought he would have wished
for a son but no, he seems rather offended than delighted, so indeed he
is commonly with all I do ...'

She was also becoming uneasy at what she saw as Thrale's extravagance; and dismayed at the eagerness with which he embraced the biblical
injunction to have no thought for the morrow:

> Mr Thrale's Affairs are now so very prosperous, that he thinks of
> nothing but to plan future Expences: and rejects Counsel as Insult, and
> Restraint as Injury – long may his Affairs be prosperous! though while
> they are so, he never plainly will lay up a Shilling, or admit the possibil-
> ity of a cloudy Day: – when his profusion has incur'd Distress – tis my
> Duty to assist, it is now my Duty to look on only, & throw in a gentle
> Warning when it will be accepted, and that is *seldom*.[23]

What Hester termed Thrale's 'profusion' found its principal expression in his passion for alteration and improvement. 'Dear Mr Thrale,'
she wrote after his death, 'had a Building Fever always lurking in his
Constitution.' The fever tended to flare whenever things were going

well at the brewery, and as profits for the previous year had amounted to £14,000, he had recently had a small lake with an island dredged out west of the house, and a two-mile gravel walk around the property rebuilt. 'Streatham is now I suppose the eighth wonder of the world,' Johnson wrote from Lichfield, 'I long to see it.'[24]

Thrale's reluctance 'to admit the possibility of a cloudy day' was also apparent in the running of his business. His desire to outbrew the Whitbreads and the Calverts verged on the obsessional, and he was constantly looking for ways of increasing the size and number of his vats. Johnson saw the danger as clearly as Hester: 'Next year will, I hope, complete Mr. Thrale's wish of an hundred thousand barrels,' he wrote to her from Ashbourne. 'When he has climbed so high, his care must be to keep himself from falling.'[25]

Johnson had been joined at Ashbourne by Boswell. 'I am glad M[r] Boswell is with you,' Hester told him, adding pertly, 'nothing that you say for this Week at least will be lost to Posterity.'[26] He had sent her a mock-serious rebuke for her failure to write often enough: 'Do you call this punctual correspondence? ... Instead of writing to me you are writing the Thraliana.'[27] Hester owned that it was so – 'If I do not write to you, and if I do work at the Book with the foolish name You are not the more out of my Head for *that*.'[28]

She had already filled the first volume: 'Writing as I do in a large loose hand, my Nonsense takes a prodigious deal of Room up.' Anecdotes of the living and the dead, translations of foreign verse, a sequence of 'Odd medical Stories' – much of that first volume makes tedious reading today. As she made a start on the second, she resolved that Johnson – 'his Life, his Character, and his Conversation' – would feature more prominently in it: 'All my Friends reproach me with neglecting to write down such Things as drop from him almost perpetually, and often say how much I shall some Time regret that I have not done't with diligence ever since the commencement of our Acquaintance ...'

Johnson was ready with advice: 'Do not remit the practice of writing down occurrences as they arise of whatever kind, and be very punctual in annexing the dates. Chronology you know is the eye of history.'[29]

The posts were unreliable, and now it was Hester's turn to complain of neglect:

I begin to be angry, uneasy at least in good earnest: you are used to be so punctual in writing even though there was nothing to be said: Sure it is Time to come home almost is it not? ... Sure you have not been taking Opium or Ipecacuanha or any dangerous Medecine again – sure you have not. Have patience with the bad Nights till you get them into Sussex, & try whether the Sea will wash them away.[30]

Thrale was impatient to get down to Brighton: 'If my Uncle was coming from the Grave – my Master says he would stick to his Word & go to Brighthelmstone on the 30th.' And so he did, although their own house was not ready for them and they had to go into lodgings for a week or so. 'Here we are, not very elegantly accommodated, but wishing sincerely for you to share either our pleasure or our distresses,' Hester wrote: ''Tis fine bathing, with rough breakers, and my Master longs to see you exhibit your strength to opposing them, and bids me press you to come, for he is tired of living so long without you.'[31]

They had brought Burney with them, and Thrale's sister and brother-in-law, the Nesbitts, were also in Brighton. Hester had no great opinion of her sister-in-law; 'Mrs Nesbitt was one of the *naïve* People,' she wrote in *Thraliana*: 'M' Thrale twitted her with bathing at that End of Bright-helmstone where the Gentlemen bathed: Lord Brother said She you think that I go there to see the naked men; God knows I would not give this now, – snapping her Fingers – to see all the Men of Brighthelmstone naked.'

Murphy appeared on the scene, and introduced the Thrales to John-son's rakish friend Topham Beauclerk. A great-grandson of Charles II and Nell Gwynn, Beauclerk was one of the original members of the Club. A noted bibliophile, with a collection of over 30,000 books, he had commissioned Robert Adam to design a library for his house in Great Russell Street – Horace Walpole said it reached 'halfway to Highgate'.[32]

Hester was less taken with another visitor: 'I have seen the famous J. Wilkes, he came hither to wait on Murphy; I like him not: he professed himself a Lyar and an Infidel.'[33] She was even less pleased when Wilkes invited Thrale to what she described as 'a Dinner of Rakes'. Beauclerk was to be there, and so was the Earl of Kellie, a dilettante Scottish

composer known for his coarse sense of humour and heavy drinking –
Samuel Foote said that the sight of his florid complexion would ripen
peaches.

Hester sometimes complained of Thrale's indifference, but he was
by no means indifferent to her appearance:

> Did I tell you that my Master grew ashamed of his Wife's Peruke since
> we came here & made me pull it off & dress my own hair, which looks
> so well now it is dressed that he begins innocently to wonder why
> he ever let me wear a Wig ... I did think to have burnt it for Joy of
> the great News from America but there comes no Confirmation of it
> they say.[34]

The 'great News from America' had been of early successes in General
John Burgoyne's plan to seize control of New York State and isolate New
England. He was to push south from Canada, while an army under Sir
William Howe marched north from New York City. News of Burgoyne's
capture of Fort Ticonderoga had reached London in late August. The
King had been so excited that he rushed unannounced into the apartments
of the Queen, finding her in her chemise. 'I have beat them!' he cried.
'I have beat all the Americans!' Not quite all of them. Howe, ignoring
his orders to move up the Hudson River, sailed south in the hope of
taking Philadelphia. Burgoyne, with a smaller force than he had been
promised, found himself outnumbered by four to one. The surrender of
his army at Saratoga marked a decisive turning point and led directly
to France's entry into the war.

By the time the humiliating news of Saratoga reached London, the
Thrales had returned to Streatham and Hester had entered the fourth
month of her pregnancy. 'Mrs. Thrale is in hopes of a young brewer,'
Johnson wrote to Boswell,[35] but an entry in the *Children's Book* shows
how deeply those hopes were tinged with anxiety: 'Just before I conceived I dream'd I was deliver'd of a Boy – all bathed in blood, and
last Night I dreamt there was a Mourning Coach at the Door to carry
my dead Son to the Grave. – I have nobody to tell my Uneasinesses to,
no Mother, no Female Friend – no nothing: so I must eat up my own
Heart & be quiet –!'[36]

It was not entirely the case that Hester lacked female friends. Shortly after the death of Dr Collier she had heard that he had been taken into the house of a rich widow in Tunbridge Wells and had been educating her children – 'and her eldest Daughter is just now coming out into the World with a great Character for Elegance & Literature'. She had been thrown together with this daughter in Brighton in the autumn: 'Her Face is eminently pretty, her Carriage elegant, her Heart affectionate, and her Mind cultivated. There is above all this an attractive Sweetness in her Manner, which claims & promises to repay one's Confidence, & which drew from me the Secret of my keeping a Thraliana to deposit all kinds of Nonsense in.'

At twenty-three, Sophia Streatfeild – 'S. S.' as she was known to her friends – was thirteen years younger than Hester. She would quickly become a member of the Streatham circle. And speedily make an effortless conquest of Henry Thrale.

~✺ 13 ✺~
Enter Little Burney

BY THE middle of January, Hester's spirits had risen dramatically: 'My Child within me is alive & the Pregnancy proceeds well,' she wrote in the *Children's Book*. 'My Master has given me a fine Gown too, & I am going to Court on Monday next with Mrs Montagu in little and great things now all goes well.'[1] The little matter of attending court certainly went most gratifyingly: the King spoke to her, she told Johnson – 'said I spent little Time in London because I lived so near it. Was not that fine too?'

What had been planned as a fortnight's stay in London with Queeney stretched out to seven weeks. She greatly enjoyed her 'Frolicks', as she called them, even if there was an occasional price to pay: 'I wish I had not caught this tingling Rash on his Majesty's cold Stair as I waited for my Chair,' she told Johnson. She dined at Mrs Montagu's, visited the studio of the sculptor Nollekens, was hugely flattered that the Duchess of Beaufort had requested leave to visit her.[2]

One *conversazione* that she attended, accompanied by Thrale and Queeney, was not the success her host had hoped to engineer. As a younger man, Burney had been the protégé of the diplomat and essayist Fulke Greville,[3] a man very conscious of his descent from that earlier Fulke Greville, Elizabethan courtier and friend of Sir Philip Sidney. Greville had expressed a wish to meet Johnson, and Burney had accordingly made arrangements for what he confidently expected would be 'a brilliant encounter of wits'.

He had invited an Italian musician called Gabriele Piozzi to play and sing to the company. Piozzi, who had come to London from Brescia two years previously, had a fine tenor voice, but his efforts went unappreciated; 'neither the Grevilles nor the Thrales', Fanny Burney wrote, 'heeded music beyond what belonged to it as fashion'. Piozzi's cantata did nothing to break the conversational ice. Greville, who would normally have thought it was for him to set the conversational ball rolling, was on his guard; he knew from Topham Beauclerk and others how easily one might be tossed and gored in exchanges with Johnson. 'Aloof, therefore, he kept from all,' wrote Fanny Burney; 'and, assuming his most supercilious air of distant superiority, planted himself, immovable as a noble statue, upon the hearth, as if a stranger to the whole set.'

Johnson, meanwhile, said not a word – Burney, clearly unaware that for some time now he had not been in the habit of initiating conversation, was greatly embarrassed, and asked Piozzi to sing again. At which point things began to get out of hand. The Italian had his back to the company and was accompanying himself on the pianoforte to what Fanny Burney described as 'an animated *arria parlante*'. Hester suddenly rose from her seat and tiptoed up behind him: 'She ludicrously began imitating him by squaring her elbows, elevating them with ecstatic shrugs of the shoulders, and casting up her eyes, while languishingly reclining her head.'

Burney, appalled at this display of bad manners, immediately remonstrated with her: 'Because, Madam, you have no ear yourself for music, will you destroy the attention of all who, in that one point, are otherwise gifted?' Hester, to her credit, nodded in acknowledgement of the rebuke and returned quietly to her place – where she sat, as she afterwards said, 'like a pretty little miss for the remainder of one of the most humdrum evenings that she had ever passed'.

She did not have to sit long. Johnson had observed nothing of her charade as he was sitting with his back to Piozzi, with a view only of Greville standing before the chimneypiece. Suddenly he broke his silence. 'If it were not for depriving the ladies of the fire,' he exclaimed, 'I should like to stand upon the hearth myself!' Greville managed the faintest of smiles, and seemed briefly minded to stay where he was, but the sight of everyone struggling not to laugh was too much for him. He moved back to his chair – ringing vigorously on the bell as he passed to order his carriage.[4] The party was over; but it was not Hester's last encounter with the man whose performance she had so crudely mimicked.

❧

Hester went on a spending spree while she was in London: 'Tis observable that I never bought any Baby things or Dresses for myself at Lying-In since the *first* Time till now; and this is the *twelfth*. I have now got myself a new Bed, new Sheets, new Bedgowns, Half Shifts &c besides Robes &c for the Kid —'[5]

She also splashed out on a harpsichord for Queeney's lessons with Burney — a purchase she soon regretted. 'Here is a new Agony,' she wrote in the *Children's Book* towards the end of April — 'My Master dispirited & almost in Despair about pecuniary Matters looks like death, & if any Disorder would seize/him/ is likely to dye himself instead of me.'[6] Thrale had seriously over-brewed during the winter. Credit was tight in the City, and he was having difficulty meeting his obligations. The situation was less serious than it had been in 1772, but just as she had done then, she immediately took matters in hand: 'I have been to Brighton for Counsel & Money of that Dear Creature Scrase whose Liberality of Sentiment & Behaviour charms and astonishes me. The Journey did me no harm I think, tho' in the 8:[th] Month of the 12:[th] Pregnancy and if Money or kindness could quiet the mind of M[r] Thrale I should still have a happy Lying In.'

Hester also suggested having some of the trees at Bach-y-Graig cut 'to pacify My Masters Uneasiness' — an offer which Thrale none too graciously refused: 'He or his Daughter,' she wrote bitterly, 'would at any Time rather suffer Misery in a slight degree than receive Consolation or Kindness from me.'[7] Thrale was possibly troubled by his conscience — unknown to Hester he had already raised £4,000 in this way some months previously.

Perkins came to dine at Streatham and was reassuring — 'says he pays every body with a high hand', Hester told Johnson, '& that the People all say there is no Money to be had at any house but ours, I mean Coopers & Ironmongers & common Tradesmen belonging to the Brewhouse'. It seemed, however, that nothing would lift Thrale's spirits. Hester appealed to Johnson for help:

On Wednesday you shall be fetched either by my Master's Coach or mine: he grudges every Candle's End just now in a manner that would be comical if one was at leisure to laugh ... If therefore you see my Master before I do — conjure him not to fret so, when he really has every Reason to be thankful. What shall I do tho' when Burney's fine

Harpsichord comes home? He grudges my new Bed so that it makes him half mad, & the other will be twice the Money of my poor Bed. – Oh Dear me! ... glad at heart shall I be to have you with us – for we grind sadly else.[8]

Sophia Streatfeild was frequently at Streatham during these last months of Hester's pregnancy. As one of the few people who knew of the existence of *Thraliana*, she was allowed to inscribe the title of the third volume at the top of the first page.

Thrale remained obstinately out of spirits: 'My Master is not much in a humour to be pleased, – he has not yet conquered his Panick: here is the 11:[th] of June however, & I still undelivered, much to my own astonishment; I expected this Baby the latter End of last Month ...'[9]

A week or so later she sent Johnson a letter, which in place of a date bore the words 'written during Labour':

Do huff my Master & comfort him by Turns according to your own Dear Discretion: he has consulted you now, & given you a Right to talk with Him about his ill Tim'd melancholy and do keep your Influence over him for all our Sakes. God be praised I have nothing to fear at present for my own Life or my Child's: all is regular & natural but very lingering and tedious –[10]

She gave birth the following day – 'My Baby is come at last – a Girl it is however,' she wrote.[11] Mrs Montagu and 'S. S.' were the godmothers, and the name chosen was Henrietta-Sophia: 'M[rs] Montagu offered herself as Godmother & said – to comfort us – that she would not have stood for a Boy; all our/other/Friends fret that it was not a Son – but my Master is in his *Aphelion* yet, and cares for nothing –'[12]

To Hester's alarm, Thrale now began to talk of sacking Perkins – 'who sets his faults before him some what too strongly indeed for policy, but not for Friendship'. If he was going to hate Perkins for telling him the truth, she reflected, 'he will of Consequence hate Johnson, & me most of all'.[13] But Johnson, never one to shrink from confrontation, came powerfully to her aid. Coming in from walking in the grounds one evening, she found him tackling Thrale head on:

M[r] Johnson observed that there was no need to be low spirited tho we had been Imprudent, that such was our Capital we might still be rich, might pay all our Debts, & lay up five Thousand a year, while we lived at the Rate of five Thousand more, if Mr Thrale would promise never to brew more than *fourscore Thousand Barrels of Beer* in a Winter ... says he I will allow you to spend three thousand rationally, & *two* Thousand foolishly – in building Digging Planting or what you will – only lay up the other five Thousand for your Children, who really have a Claim to it ...

Hester now weighed in equally forcefully, describing her husband's behaviour as 'mad Rapacity'. He was, she declared, 'the most unfit Man in the World to get into Dificulties':

He had so lost Flesh, Spirits & Appearance by this last Perplexity, that I thought few Things worth the Anxiety he had suffered since April; that it was very ridiculous to hazard his Health and Fortune nay his *Life* for the sake of a paltry Superiority to Whitbred & Calvert, Men whose Acquaintance he was ashamed of, & whose Persons he shrunk from if he met 'em in a Publick Place.[14]

It was a ferocious onslaught. Thrale held out stubbornly, and refused to give an undertaking never again to brew more than 80,000 barrels in one winter; he did, however, eventually promise that he would not do so for the next five years. 'And so the Wings of *Speculation* are clipped a little,' Hester wrote in *Thraliana*; 'very fain would I have pinioned her, but I had not Strength to perform the Operation.'

❧ ☙

Hester amused herself in this summer of 1778 by drawing up in *Thraliana* what a later age might call league tables:

Was I to make a scale of Novel Writers I should put Richardson first, then Rousseau; after them, but at an immeasurable Distance – Charlotte Lenox, Smollet & Fielding. The Female Quixote & Count Fathom I think far beyond Tom Jones or Joseph Andrews with regard to Body of Story, height of Colouring, or General Powers of Thinking. Fielding however knew the shell of Life – and the Kernel is but for a few.

She may well have been influenced in her view of the relative merits of Fielding and Richardson by Johnson. He also had a high regard for Charlotte Lennox, the daughter of a Scottish army captain, who had turned to writing after failing to establish herself as an actress. It was with *The Female Quixote* that she had made her name a quarter of a century earlier; Johnson, a friend as well as an admirer, cited her under 'Talent' in his *Dictionary*.

Hester also sat in judgement on friends and acquaintances, awarding them marks out of twenty under a range of headings. Nobody except Johnson scored full marks for 'Religion' and 'Morality', although he was given no marks at all for 'Good humor'; Garrick, with nineteen, led the field under both 'Wit' and 'Humor'. Thrale was awarded eighteen for 'Person & Voice' and seventeen for 'Manner'; rather more surprisingly, perhaps, he was given the same rating for both 'Religion' and 'Morality'.

Ladies were judged rather differently: 'As they must possess Virtue in the contracted Sense, or one w^d not keep em Company, so that is not thought about, & I would not be contracted about Beauty neither ...' Nobody scored higher than sixteen for 'Conversation Powers' and there were also quite a few zeros under 'Ornamental Knowledge'. 'S. S.' was one of only three who dropped no marks under 'Worth of Heart' (Queeney could manage only fourteen). 'I have run this foolish Amusement already out of Breath before half my Acquaintance are classed,' Hester wrote: 'if I was to endeavour to classing myself It should run thus' – and proceeded to rate herself more highly across the board than anyone except Mrs Montagu.[15]

A new novel called *Evelina* had been published anonymously at the beginning of 1778. It attracted favourable notices and the identity of the author was the subject of much speculation. Hester had had it read to her by Queeney during her confinement and liked it enormously. It was written, she enthused to Dr Burney, 'by somebody who knows the *Top & the Bottom, the highest & the lowest of* mankind' and she pressed her copy on him to take home.

Burney returned the three volumes on his next visit: 'Well,' cried she, & is it not a very *pretty* Book? & a very *clever* Book? & a very *comical* Book?' 'Why,' answered he, ''tis *well enough*; but I have something to tell you about it.' 'Well? What? –' cried she, 'has Mrs. Cholmley found out the author? –' 'No,' returned he; 'not that I know of; but I believe *I* have, – though but *very* lately.' 'Well, pray let's hear,' cried she eagerly, 'I want to know him of all things!'

At which point Burney undeceived her. Not him – her. *Evelina* was the work of his daughter Fanny.

It quickly went the rounds of the Streatham circle. Reynolds declared he would give £50 to know the author; Burke began it one morning at seven and sat up all night to finish it; Johnson pronounced that 'Harry Fielding never did any thing equal to the 2^d Volume'. Within a matter of weeks, Fanny found herself dining at Streatham – it was, she wrote in her journal, 'the most *Consequential* day I have spent since my Birth'.[16]

'Little Burney', as Johnson was soon calling her, was rapidly drawn into the Streatham circle: 'I know not how to express the *fullness of my contentment* at this sweet place,' she wrote to her sister Susanna:

> But I *fear* to say all I think at present of Mrs. Thrale, – lest some *flaws* should appear by & by, that may make me think differently: – & yet, why should I not indulge the *now*, as well as the *then*, since it will be with so *much* more pleasure? – In short, my dear Susy, I do think her *delightful*: she has *Talents* to create admiration, – *Good humour* to excite Love, *Understanding* to give Entertainment, – & a *Heart* which, like my dear Father's, seems already fitted for another World![17]

Hester came to regard her almost as a sister, and before long was referring to Streatham as Fanny's 'home'. And she and Thrale were soon busy matchmaking. 'Mr. Thrale says nothing would make him half so happy as giving Miss Burney to Sir John Lade,' Hester told Johnson one day in Fanny's presence. Lade, a dim and spendthrift youth of nineteen, was Thrale's nephew; Miss Burney was not amused.[18]

Hester was also quick to formulate literary plans for her new protégée, and thought she should collaborate with Johnson in writing for the stage: 'She stated the advantages attending Theatrical writing, and promised to *ensure* me success. "I have asked Mr *Johnson*," added she "if he *did* not think You could write a Comedy, – & *he* said *Yes*!"'[19]

Fanny received encouragement from both Murphy and Sheridan, and within a matter of months the writing was well advanced: 'Our Miss

Burney is big with a Comedy for next Season,' Hester wrote. It was called 'The Witlings', a lively satire on the female wits. A speech in the first scene by the hero, Beaufort, gives the flavour of the piece:

> My good aunt has established a kind of Club at her House, professedly for the discussion of literary subjects; and the Set who compose it are about as well qualified for the Purpose, as so many dirty Cabbin Boys would be to find out the Longitude. To a very little reading, they join less Understanding, and no Judgement, yet they decide upon Books and Authors with the most confirmed confidence in their abilities for the task.[20]

Initially, everybody who read it approved – Murphy liked it 'very well', Fanny's father liked it 'vastly'. 'I like it very well for my own part,' Hester wrote, 'though none of the scribbling Ladies have a Right to admire its general Tendency.' But Lady Smatter, Mrs Sapient and Mrs Voluble never got to strut their hour upon the stage. Nervous that Lady Smatter might be identified as Mrs Montagu and fearing the more general wrath of the 'scribbling Ladies' – the Blues – Burney lost his nerve. Together with 'Daddy' Crisp he wrote Fanny what she described as a 'Hissing, groaning, catcalling Epistle' urging her to abandon the project. Filial duty prevailed over literary ambition: 'I won't tell you I have been absolutely *ravi* with delight at the fall of the Curtain,' she wrote, 'but I intend to take the affair in the *tant mieux* manner.'[21]

Fanny Burney's journals and letters are a rich source for our knowledge of day-to-day life at Streatham in the late 1770s and early 1780s:

> Dr. Johnson came Home to Dinner.
>
> In the Evening, he was as lively & full of wit & sport as I have ever seen him, – & Mrs. Thrale & I had him quite to ourselves, for Mr. Thrale came in from giving an election Dinner to which he sent 2 Bucks & 6 pine apples so tired, that he niether opened his *Eyes* nor *mouth*, but fell fast asleep. Indeed, after Tea, he generally does.[22]

'Mrs. Thrale I like more and more,' she told Susanna:

> – for of all the people I have ever seen, since I came *into this gay & gaudy world*, I never before saw the person who so strongly resembles

our dear Father! … Since the first morning, she *seeks* me, – sits with me while I Dress, saunters with me in the park, or compares Notes over Books in the Library; there is an immediate communication from her Dressing Room to my Bedroom, & when she is up stairs, she flings open the Doors, & enters into Conversation. – And her Conversation is *delightful*; it is so entertaining, so gay, so enlivening, when she is in spirits; & so intelligent & instructive when she is otherwise, that I almost as much wish to record all *she* says, as all Dr. Johnson says.[23]

Which, happily for posterity, is precisely what she would do throughout the four years of her intimacy with the Thrales.

❧

Early in October, the Thrales took themselves off for two months to Brighton and Tunbridge Wells. Johnson, who was sitting again to Reynolds and preparing to make a start on his life of Milton, remained in London, but was eager to know whether Thrale's depression was lifting. Hester could offer only partial reassurance: 'My Master mends but it is gradually: he is not yet a good Tête a Tete but he behaves tolerably in Company – every body however says he is *strangely broke*.'[24]

The company was not very different from the company at Streatham or in London – Mrs Montagu was in residence, and so were Beauclerk and Sophy and Mrs Streatfeild. A new acquaintance, who would become a close friend, was Sophia Byron, the wife of Admiral John Byron – Foul Weather Jack as he was known, the grandfather of the poet. The Duchess of Devonshire was also in Brighton. Hester was flattered to discover that she had asked to be introduced to her: 'The Duchess of Devonshire, who has every thing that heaven can give except Health and a Son, will absolutely try for Celebrity among the Wits,' she told Johnson, '& to that Humour I am indebted for all her Civilities I suppose.'[25]

She might have been less flattered if she had known that the Duchess was the author of a novel called *The Sylph*, which was about to be published anonymously. Its depiction of sexual licence and violence won it some notoriety, and it quickly went through four editions. Hester found it obscene; the writing of it, she declared, required more knowledge of mankind 'than any *professed* Virgin should have'. There was outrage among the Streathamites when the publisher, T. Lowndes, who had also published *Evelina*, advertised the two books in such a way as to suggest they were by the same author. Charles Burney wrote to the publisher to remonstrate, and Lowndes promised to let him vet any future advertisement, but the damage was done.

There was better news from Southwark: 'All goes on well at the Brewhouse I hear,' Hester told Johnson: 'and the Money that was borrowed when the Leaves were coming out will be paid – or may be – before they are fallen.'[26] And better news about Thrale, who was following Sir John Shelley's pack of hounds over the Sussex Downs. Shelley had been Keeper of the Tower Records and Treasurer of the King's Household. Hester described him elsewhere as 'an absurd old Fellow, and much a Lyar', but that was all one to Johnson: 'Long live Sir John Shelly that lures my Master to hunt,' he wrote. 'I hope he will soon shake off the black dog, and come home as light as a feather.'[27]

By the end of November, he was becoming impatient for their return: 'You are by this time left alone to wander over the Steene, and listen to the waves. This is but a dull life, come away and be busy and count your poultry, and look into your dairy, and at leisure hours learn what revolutions have happened at Streatham.'[28]

They did so within a matter of days. Hester recorded in the *Children's Book* that Thrale had recovered from his anxiety and depression, 'and resolves to enjoy himself & his Friends as usual'. Her own anxieties were not entirely dispelled, however: 'Oh if we are to ruin a Fortune which might make me happy! Let my dear Hester get out of the house at least before it falls upon our heads.'[29]

She took time in the midst of her Christmas preparations to write a long letter to Fanny Burney, who had been reduced to a state of near hysteria by a pamphlet identifying her as the author of *Evelina*. 'Why will you, my lovely Friend, give Consequence to Trifles by thus putting your Peace in their Power?' she wrote:

> Your looking dismal can only advertise the paltry Pamphlet which I
> firmly believe no one out of your own Family has seen and which is
> now only lying like a dead Kitten on the surface of a dirty Horsepond
> – incapable of scratching anyone who does not take pains to dirty their
> Fingers for it ...[30]

Over Christmas and the New Year the house was filled with friends. 'We have had a charming Collection of Company,' Hester wrote, 'for Wit, Beauty, Literature, & the polite Arts I think few could match it.' Wit, literature and the polite arts were the province of Johnson and Murphy and Burney, who were all present; beauty was supplied by 'S. S.' and Thrale had eyes only for her: 'Mr Thrale is fallen in Love *really* & *seriously* with Sophy Streatfield,' Hester wrote:

> – but there is no wonder in that: She is very pretty, very gentle, soft & insinuating; hangs about him, dances round him, cries when She parts from him, squeezes his Hand slyly, & with her sweet Eyes full of Tears looks so fondly in his Face – & all for *Love of me* as she pretends; that I can hardly sometimes help laughing in her Face.
>
> A Man must not be a *Man* but an *It* to resist such Artillery –

The holidays drew to a close: 'Every body is gone now,' Hester wrote in *Thraliana*, 'and my poor Master is left to pine for his fair Sophia, till the meeting of Parliament calls him to London, and leaves him free to spend all his Evenings at her House.'

On the last day of 1778 she had reached the last page of the *Children's Book* and penned a final entry: 'I *think* I am again Pregnant, I *think* I am; then let us conclude the Old Year with humble Thanks to Almighty God for all his Mercies thro' Jesus Christ our Lord, & most of all for the Health of my dear Children, and for the Boon I hope I have obtained by my Prayers & Tears – That I shall never follow any more of my Offspring to the Grave. Amen Lord Jesus! Amen!'

The second Amen, big and bold, took her down to the very bottom of the page, but she managed to squeeze into what little space remained a pathetic rider to her petition: 'if so – I will not fret about this Rival this S. S. no I won't'.[31]

The Flight of Time

'MOST uncommon Weather,' Hester noted in *Thraliana* early in February:

> my Thorn as I call it which is always used to blossom on the 1ˢᵗ of April
> over against my Bed Chamber Window, is budded out now, and seems
> ready to burst into Flower – The Lilacs are coming out as fast as can
> be, & I see one Honeysuckle quite in Leaf … the Croakers expect a
> Comet or an Earthquake, but the rest of the World agrees that tis lovely
> Weather.

She needed all the solace she could draw from that lovely weather,
because those early months of 1779 were darkened by illness and death.
In January David Garrick died – a loss which 'has crushed the Spirits
of many People among whom I now live', she wrote: '*I* knew him only
just well enough to be proud of knowing him, not well enough to care
about his Death, except as at the stopping up a Source of Merriment in
the midst of a miserable World. But Johnson was his Friend, Murphy his
Enemy, & Burney his Obligée. Murphy felt it the deepest however …'

A week later, on her thirty-eighth birthday, she learned that her
childhood friend, Betsy Cumyns, mistress of the school in Kensington
attended by Susanna and Sophia, was suffering from breast cancer. The
news induced a mood of bleak despair: 'The Flight of Time is now so
shocking to me, I can hardly bear to see the *Winter* going – though
Spring is the nearer for it, & I live this Year wholly in the Country; yet
there are so *few* Winters *now* to be expected!'

The resolution not to fret over Sophy Streatfeild was fragile – and
Hester knew well enough that friends like Murphy were not blind: 'He
sees Thrale's Love of the fair SS. & I suppose approves my silent and
patient endurance of what I could not prevent by more rough & sincere
Behaviour. Men always admire a woman who tho' jealous does not rave

about it – & what sh^d one rave for!! would raving do anything but drive Mr Thrale *quite* away from me?'

When she recorded that Thrale was having a cold bath constructed for her at Streatham, she added a wistful footnote: 'Tho' he loves Sophy Streatfield, he has some Care for *my* Life I think; I *hope* so.' It was galling enough to know that when parliamentary business called him to London, Thrale should spend his evenings in Sophy's company; even more galling that it should be common knowledge among their friends and acquaintances. Years later, when she published her correspondence with Johnson, she made a marginal note of an unfeeling remark he made around this time: '"Why Mr Thrale is Peregrinus Domi," said Dr. Johnson; "he lives in Clifford Street, I hear, all winter;" and so he did, leaving his carriage at his sister's door in Hanover Square, that no inquirer might hurt his favourite's reputation …'[1]

Hester continued to take a keen interest in the proceedings of Parliament. The Lords had recently approved a bill barring those divorced for adultery from marrying those with whom the offence had been committed. Hester was contemptuous:

> The Bishop of Llandaff's Bill for the better preventing Adultery is a paltry Thing, they should inflict some real Punishment: was a Woman to have her Ring Finger cut off; her Lover would hesitate a little in marrying her I'll warrant him; & she well deserves a Punishment as severe as that at least, for thus madly transgressing – however provoked – the great laws of both God and Man.

If that makes her seem strait-laced by the standards of her class in the Age of Reason, the impression is modified by an anecdote she records in *Thraliana* shortly afterwards: 'Costollo an Irish Counsellor was retain'd in a Cause of Crim: Con: when a Footman was accused of Intimacy with his Lady. – why now Gentlemen of the jury says he let us not waste our Words – Here is a poor Footman d'ye see, indicted – & for what? Why for only doing his *Master's business*, & that by his *Mistress's Orders*.'

There were, however, limits to what she was prepared to commit to the pages of *Thraliana*:

> I have this Moment put into my Hand a Poem … so obscæne I will not

pollute my Book with it. Though nobody sees the Thraliana but my self, I can not bear that our Father who seeth in Secret & is of purer Eyes than to behold Uncleanness, should know my beastly privacies – though strongly tempted therefore to copy or get it by heart I have done neither, but returned it to Mrs Byron who lent it me – without any Comment.

At Whitsun the Thrales, together with their three eldest daughters and Fanny Burney, drove down to Brighton. 'It is barren enough of Conversation or Subjects of Amusement,' Hester told Johnson[2] (he had gone off on his annual jaunt to the Midlands), but Murphy was there to keep them amused, and they were flattered by the attentions of several well-heeled young officers of the militia. Hester was well pleased with their stay:

> I made a good fortnight's work enough of it, having added to my Friends & my Conquests – as I call 'em – the amiable Bishop of Peterborough. I have seldom on a short Acquaintance liked any Man so extremely, especially a Man of mean Birth and rough Temper; but really there is so much Dignity, so little *Pomposity*, so much Wit, so little Buffoonery, so much Christianity & so little Cant; that I have seldom seen a Character more truly to my Taste.

Back in London, there was family business requiring Thrale's attention. His sister Susanna's husband had recently died after several years of ill health, and Thrale was an executor. Arnold Nesbitt came from a prominent Irish banking family. Under his leadership the firm's interests had expanded to include the import of sugar and rum from the West Indies and the supply under government contract of money and provisions for troops in the American colonies. He and Thrale had done a good deal of business together over the years, much of it highly speculative.

On 8 June after going to his sister's house to hear the will read he stayed to dinner. Back at Streatham, Hester had dined with Fanny Burney and her father and Queeney. At about seven o'clock they were in the drawing room when Thrale's valet Sam Greaves appeared, in a state of agitation. 'My master is come home,' he announced, 'but there is something amiss.'[3]

Hester rushed into the library, where she found her sister-in-law holding the hand of the insensible Thrale. Burney was dispatched in a post-chaise to seek help. It was two hours before Dr Bromfield arrived, by which time Thrale had regained consciousness. Bromfield formed the view that he had suffered an apoplectic seizure and decided to call in Heberden and another well-known physician called Richard Huck, who had recently retired as physician to St Thomas's.

Fanny Burney described what had happened in a letter to her sister Susanna. During dinner Thrale's head had suddenly sunk on to the table, '&, as soon as he was able to raise it, they found that his reason had left him! He talked wildly, & seemed to know nobody.' He slowly improved, but for three days after he was brought home, his faculties were severely impaired.

Although she put a brave face on things to her guests – Thrale had insisted that the arrangements for a three-day house party should stand – it is plain from *Thraliana* that Hester was profoundly anxious:

> I'm confident he will recover, he has Youth and Strength, and general Health on his Side; but his Temper is strangely altered: *so* vigilant, *so* jealous, so careful lest one should watch him, & so unfit to be left unwatched. – Oh Lord have mercy on us! This is a horrible Business indeed. Five little Girls, too, & breeding again, & Fool enough to be proud of it! ah Ideot! What should I want more Children for? God knows only to please my Husband, who now perhaps may be much better without them.

Johnson, who liked to pontificate on medical matters, had originally made reassuring noises: 'The seizure was, I think, not apoplectical, but hysterical,' he wrote from Ashbourne,[4] 'and therefore not dangerous to life.'[5] Once he had a fuller account of what had happened, he was less dogmatic: 'I am the more alarmed by this violent seizure, as I can impute it to no wrong practices or intemperance of any kind,' he wrote. 'Mr Thrale has certainly less exercise than when he followed the foxes, but he is very far from unweildiness or inactivity, and further still from any vitious or dangerous excess.'[6]

But in speculating in purely physiological terms, Johnson was barking up the wrong tree. Thrale himself was in no doubt about what had brought on his attack; it was not something he ever brought himself to share with a living soul, although a curious conversation which Hester recorded in *Thraliana* only at a much later date indicates that he came close to doing so:

> One Evening at the Borough ... Mr Thrale said on a sudden: – when
> we see Heberden this Even^g – 'I'll tell him all the Truth.'
>   Do for Heav'n's sake replied I, and what *is* the Truth? 'Why that I
> am a ruined Man, and have undone my family.' – Which said I in return
> – the doctor will *know* to be a Dream, & set you down as one who has
> lost his Head – Ay Ay answer'd poor Mr Thrale, but *I know it for a*
> *Fact.* At these Words I ran to the Compting House, called Perkins to his
> Master, bid him bring the Ledger, Books &c. and *convince* him in good
> Time!! How well Things went ... So he looked grave & kept Silent, &
> saw Heberden & said *nothing* as usual; & I went to bed perswaded that
> he laboured under a Diseased Imagination only.

Several years would pass before she discovered the appalling truth of the matter.

⊸≺ ≻⊱

A number of entries in *Thraliana* in the summer of 1779 reflect Hester's increasing preoccupation with affairs in the wider world. It had become known in the middle of June that Spain had joined the Franco-American alliance:

> Even the Opposition People resolve no longer to impede, but chearfully
> assist the Government they so justly despise: 'tis indeed high Time
> to be in earnest; France & Spain are leagued against us, & add their
> Weight to the Miseries inflicted on the Mother Country by its revolted
> Colonies ...

Hester had also had to concern herself with the affairs of the brewery since Thrale's stroke. His passion for expansion was undimmed, and she now felt obliged to intervene decisively:

> Here is my mad Master going to build at the boro' House again: – new
> Store Cellars, Casks, & God knows what. I have however exerted

myself & driv'n off his workmen with a high Hand. – Is this a Time
as Elijah say'd, for oliveyards, & Vineyards? Men Servants & Maid
Servants? When our Trade & our profits are both decreasing daily? &
the Nation itself stagnating with Imbecility? I never saw anything so
absurd – surely his *head is still confused* …

And yet in spite of everything, she was very fond of him. Exasperation
at his recklessness went hand in hand with admiration for what she saw
as sterling personal qualities:

Few People live in such a State of Preparation for Eternity I think,
as my dear Master has done since I have been connected with him;
regular in his publick and private devotions, constant at the Sacrament,
Temperate in his Appetites, moderate in his Passions – he has less to
apprehend from a sudden Summons than any Man I have known, who
was young and gay, & high in health & Fortune like him.

She also entertained an extravagant opinion of him as a politician.
Contemplating the dangers to which the nation was exposed, her mind
turned, somewhat theatrically, to God's promise to Abraham that if ten
righteous men could be found there, Sodom and Gomorrah would not
be destroyed: 'If ten Men can be found in *either*, or indeed one may say
I believe in *both* Houses of Parl^t wholly clear from *Corruption* or *biass*
of any kind … ye whole may for ought I know be saved for the sake of
such *Ten* but I know only *one* myself, & that is Mr Thrale.'

He was still far from well, however; indeed Heberden told one of
their friends privately that he would never wholly recover. Hester, for
her part, had had a difficult pregnancy, and by the beginning of August,
with her confinement imminent, was concerned that she might miscarry.
'Abortions and Profluvia are not easily got through at my Age,' she
wrote grimly.

Thrale chose this moment to insist that she should accompany him to
Southwark to resolve a quarrel among the clerks at the brewhouse. The
matter was quickly settled, and Hester's only thought was to get back
to Streatham with the least delay. Thrale, however, stubbornly refused
to leave before the time originally set for their departure:

I beg'd him to make haste home, as I was apprehensive bad Consequences might very quickly arise from the Joulting &c. – he would not be hurried – the probable Consequences *did* begin to arise, I pressed him to order the Coach – he could not be hurried – I told his Valet my Danger, & begged him to hasten his Master; no Pain, no Entreaties of mine could make him set out one *Moment* before the appointed hour – so I lay along in the Coach all the way from London to Streatham in a State not to be described, nor endured; – *but by me*: – & being carried to my Chamber the Instant I got home, miscarried in the utmost Agony before they could get me into bed, after fainting five Times.

It was not a miscarriage but a stillbirth – 'a Boy quite formed & perfect', Hester wrote; 'once I wished for such a Blessing – now if my Life is left me no matter for the rest'. For several days she lay dangerously ill: 'this day Sunday 15: of August I go down Stairs like the Ghost of her who was carried up Stairs a Week ago'. She was full of bitterness towards her husband: 'Now tho' Mr Thrale's heart never much runs over with Tenderness towards me God knows, – yet common Humanity might have had a place here; no *Feelings* however, no *Shame* could induce him – to put himself in a hurry! –'

Those who saw him at the brewery ascribed Thrale's behaviour to his illness: 'Perkin's expression was that our master was *Planet-struck*,' Hester wrote. Whatever the reason, any hope of having a son for an heir was now blasted. 'Poor Mr Thrale looks like Death again,' Hester told Johnson, who was still in Lichfield: 'As soon as ever I can travel I must make him go some where, Change of Scene is actually necessary to his Recovery.'[7]

It is clear from *Thraliana* that Hester believed for some time that she might die – 'I thought about a fortnight ago that I was as likely to live two Centuries as two Days.' During her convalescence, she amused herself by composing three short 'Dialogues on the Death of Hester Lynch Thrale' modelled on Swift's *Verses on the Death of Dr Swift* which had appeared forty years earlier. The style and character of various friends and acquaintances are deftly and wittily caught – Burke is smooth and emollient, Johnson increasingly loud and truculent. One of the best lines is given to Mrs Montagu: 'Mrs Thrale, among her other Qualifications, had prodigious strong Nerves – and that's an admirable Quality for a Friend of Dr Johnson's.'[8]

The summer had continued exceptionally hot. 'It has been broad Summer this Year fairly from Aries to Libra,' Hester wrote in late September. But the fine weather did nothing to dispel the thoughts of death that still ran in her mind:

I have got a strange Fit of the horrors upon me to-day, something runs in my head that I shall die, or Mr Thrale die, & that we shall not – as we hoped – communicate together at God's Table next Sunday. – I will say nothing of it, for it may end in nothing, but I am not used to be low spirited, & tis very odd to be so now, for I ail nothing, tho' I tremble with Terror, just as I was the day before my Son died!

The mood passed, and in early October they set off for Tunbridge Wells and Brighton, accompanied by Queeney and Fanny Burney. They stopped on the way at Sevenoaks to show Fanny the beauties of Knole, at that time the seat of the Duke of Dorset. Fanny found the general air of the place 'monastic and gloomy'. She admired the pictures, but was disappointed not to see the library; the Duke, notorious for his womanizing, celebrated for his patronage of cricket, was not there, but his current mistress, the Venetian dancer Giovanna Baccelli, was in residence, 'and was not to be disturbed'. 'Mr Thrale longs to see his S: S: *that* makes us go to Tunbridge,' Hester wrote: 'I am glad he can think of anything external; & hope her Conversation will dissipate the Gloom which this paralytick Affection has cast over his Temper.' The two days spent in Miss Streatfeild's company were a disappointment, however: 'They met without Interest,' Hester recorded, '& parted without Pain.'

The sea air at Brighton seemed initially to do rather more for Thrale – 'he rode with Spirit, eat with Appetite, & his Friends observ'd a most agreeable Alteration in his Looks'. Johnson, who had stayed behind in London to write, plied Hester with advice: 'I do not see why you should trouble yourself with Physicians, while Mr. Thrale grows better. Company and bustle will I hope, compleat his cure. Let him gallop over the downs in the morning, call his friends about him to dinner, and frisk in the rooms at night ... Riding and cheerfulness will, I hope, do all the business.'[9]

Johnson also impressed on her the importance of Thrale's making a

will and urged her to enlist the help of Scrase: 'When he is gone our
barrier against calamity is weakened,' he wrote. 'Consult him, while his
advice is yet to be had.' A draft was drawn up, and Thrale invited Hester
to say who should serve with her as executors. Johnson was an obvious
choice; shrewdly, if more surprisingly, she also nominated Cator: 'Now
this was rather a Testimony of good Opinion too than of Fondness, for
who could be *fond* of Cator? & yet I really think him as fit a Man for
the purpose as either of the other two. Rough in his manners, acute in
his Judgement, skilful in Trade, and solid in Property is John Cator
Esqr of Wallingford ...'

None of Hester's letters to Johnson from this period survives, but his
replies show that she was plagued by toothache and found sea-bathing
less agreeable than before. 'What can be come to my Mistress,' he
wrote, 'when going into the sea disorders her. She was used to be quite
amphibious, and could hardly be kept out of any water she could get
at.'[10] He also entertained her with ironic bulletins concerning events in
the wider world: 'Of the capture of Jamaica nothing is known, nor do
I think it probable or possible. How the French should in a few days
take from us an Island, which We could not in almost a century take
from a few fugitive Negroes whom the Spaniards left behind them, is
not easily imagined.'[11]

By late November the weather had deteriorated and Thrale went
down with what Fanny Burney called a 'vile Influenza'. The journey
home was a nightmare. Thrale suffered dreadfully from the cold; servants were sent ahead to Reigate to order dinner; by the time they arrived
he had become inarticulate. 'I hoped it was accident,' Fanny told her
sister, '& Mrs. Thrale, by some strange infatuation, thought he was
joking.' Dinner was not ready; they were shown into a large unheated
room: 'Here the cold returned dreadfully, – & here, in short, it was
but too plain to *all* his Faculties were lost by it! – Poor Mrs. Thrale
worked like a *servant*, – she lighted the Fire with her own Hands, –
took the Bellows, & made such a one as might have roasted an ox in
10 minutes ...'[12]

It was late before they got him home. Hester debated with Fanny
whether to summon a doctor, but eventually ordered the butler to set
off at six the next morning to fetch Heberden. By the time he arrived,

Thrale had recovered sufficiently to be angry that anyone should think he required medical attention; Heberden settled for having him cupped – a procedure in which blood was drawn by scarifying the skin and applying suction with a cupping glass.

Hester recorded the detail of all this, but felt it was becoming tedious to do so: 'The Thraliana will be full of nothing but melancholy matters of Fact if we go on thus, I will write no more such things down if they do happen.' But even before going off to Brighton, she had been clear about the implications of Thrale's condition:

'Tis a dreadful Thing to think of a Man whose Brain has been injured having the Care & Management of such a Capital as ours – Perkins is of Opinion that he is not fit for his Business, so I see how it is all to end – I must go to the Boro' house this Winter, & hack at the Trade myself I hate it heartily, yes heartily! But if living in Newgate would be *right*, I hope I should be content to live in Newgate.

Johnson, still labouring to complete his *Lives of the Poets*, showed up at Streatham soon after the Thrales' return, and Hester had an early reminder of the proprietary interest he took in her appearance. The entry in *Thraliana* suggests she was flattered rather than offended: 'I had a Grave coloured Gown on today, & Johnson reproved me for calling old Age too soon; a gay Gown in a Morning said I is out of Rule – but thou art so little my Love he replied, that Rules may be superseded in Your Case –What! Have not *all Insects* gay Colours?'

The gay insect had begun to hanker after a house in a more fashionable part of town. She had mentioned this more than once to Johnson and been rebuked: 'I do not see with so much indignation Mr Thrale's desire of being the first Brewer, as your despicable dread of living in the borough,' he had told her: 'I am not vexed at you for not liking the Borough, but for not liking the Borough better than other evils of greater magnitude. You must take physick, or be sick; you must live in the Borough, or live still worse.'[13]

She knew well enough that he was right:

5: *January 1780*. Here is another New Year begun, but with no good Prospects: Mr Thrale's health declines apace, & the Palsy sometimes

seems to affect the Heart and Lungs. our Business too is in a cloudy
Condition, & every thing goes ill with us: we are settled once more in
Southwark the place I most abhor; but if residing there will contribute
to my Husbands's Ease or Entertainment – My Duty shall make it Pall
Mall to me.

~❧ 15 ❧~
'Like a Cock at Shrove Tide'

THERE WERE, unfortunately, only two things that contributed to Thrale's ease and contentment. One was gorging himself on rich food – he was now rapidly becoming a glutton. The other was the company of Sophia Streatfeild.

'Sophy Streatfeild is come to town,' Hester noted in *Thraliana* at the end of January:

> She is in the *Morning Post* too I see: she has won Wedderburn's heart from his wife I believe; & few married Women will bear *that* patiently if I do, they will some of them wound her Reputation so that I question whether it can recover.
>
> Lady Erskine made many odd Enquiries about her to me yesterday, & wink'd & looked wise at her sister. – The Dear S: S: must be a little upon her guard; nothing is so spiteful as a Woman robbed of a Heart She thinks She has a Claim upon …

Thrale and Alexander Wedderburn, the Scottish lawyer who was the Attorney-General of the day, were by no means Miss Streatfeild's only conquests – Beilby Porteous, the young Bishop of Chester, celebrated as a preacher and an abolitionist, was also for a time prepared to make a fool of himself: 'She shewed me a Letter from him,' Hester wrote, 'that was as tender, and had all the Tokens upon it as strong as ever I remember to have seen 'em.'

Everybody agreed that she was beautiful and that she had a remarkable knowledge of Greek, although Johnson once gave it as his view that 'taking away her *Greek*, she was *as ignorant as a Butterfly*'. She appealed mainly to older men, although as Hester's friend Mrs Byron shrewdly noted, she appeared to be 'Every body's Admiration and nobody's Choice'.

Sophy herself had for some years made no secret of her attachment to a parson called William Vyse, the Rector of St Mary, Lambeth. The son of a Lichfield contemporary of Johnson's, Vyse had made an imprudent marriage as a young man. He was separated from his wife, 'of whom' as Hayward puts it, 'he hoped to get rid either by divorce or by her death, as she was reported to be in bad health'.[1] Sophy appears to have regarded herself as engaged to him but the previous autumn, in Tunbridge Wells, she had confided in Fanny Burney that he had thrown her over. 'I am very sorry for her disappointment,' Fanny wrote primly to her sister, 'but *Ladies* chusing openly for themselves, never appeared to me a *right* thing, – nor does it prove *prosperous*.'[2]

In that age of sensibility, Miss Streatfeild possessed one devastating party trick – the ability to summon tears at will. It was an accomplishment variously deployed – to demonstrate sadness at parting or, more generally, to suggest the exquisite tenderness of her feelings. Hester, privately contemptuous of such coquetry, sometimes took malicious pleasure in inciting her to weep for the entertainment of the company. Fanny Burney describes one such occasion when she and Sophy and Hester were sitting at breakfast at Streatham with Sir Philip Jennings Clerke, the MP for Totnes and a great admirer of Hester's:

> *Sir Philip.* Well, I have heard so much of these Tears, that I would give the Universe to have a sight of them.
>   *Mrs. Thrale.* Lord, she shall Cry again if you like it.
>   *S.S.* No, – pray, Mrs. Thrale; –
>   *Sir Philip.* O pray do! – pray let *me* see a little of it! –
>   *Mrs. Thrale.* Yes, *do* cry, a little, Sophy; – (in a wheedling Voice) *pray* do! – consider now, you are going to Day, – & it's very hard if you won't *cry* a little; – indeed, S.S., you *ought* to cry –
>   Now for the wonder of wonders – when Mrs. Thrale, in a coaxing voice, suited to a Nurse soothing a Baby, had run on for some Time, – while all the rest of us, in Laughter, joined in the request, – two Crystal Tears came into the soft Eyes of the S.S., – & rolled gently down her Cheeks ...
>   'Look, look! Cried Mrs. Thrale, see if the Tears are not come already!'

Loud & rude bursts of Laughter broke from us all at once; – how indeed could they be restrained?[3]

Hurtful as Thrale's infatuation with Sophy was, Hester affected in public an air of ironic detachment, spelling out her true feelings only in *Thraliana*. But some things were too painful to record even there. Thirty years would pass before she could bring herself to describe to a friend a dinner party that had taken place shortly before her last confinement. She was in her place at the head of the table, flanked by Johnson and Burke. Thrale suddenly called out and unceremoniously asked her to change places with Sophy, 'who was threatened with a sore throat, and might be injured by sitting near the door':

I had scarcely swallowed a spoonful of soup when this occurred, and was so overset by the coarseness of the proposal, that I burst into tears, said something petulant – that perhaps ere long, the lady might be at the head of Mr. T's table, without displacing the mistress of the house, &c, and so left the apartment. I retired to the drawing-room, and for an hour or two contended with my vexation, as best I could.

When dinner was over Burke and Johnson sought her out:

On seeing them I resolved to give a *jobation* to both, but fixed on Johnson for my charge, and asked him if he had noticed what had passed, what I had suffered, and whether allowing for the state of my nerves, I was much to blame? He answered, 'Why, possibly not; your feelings were outraged.' I said, 'Yes, greatly so; and I cannot help remarking with what blandness and composure you witnessed the outrage. Had this transaction been told of others, your anger would have known no bounds; but towards a man who gives good dinners &c., you were meekness itself!' Johnson coloured, and Burke, I thought, looked foolish; but I had not a word of answer from either.[4]

Now, in the early weeks of 1780, Hester had further cause to be aggrieved:

M[r] Thrale is very unkind actually, sick or well: he has ordered some more of my Trees in Wales to be cut down, he knows I would lose both my Ears as willingly ...

So now because it was a bad Year forsooth – & all by his own Fault –
he goes and orders my Trees to be felled ... A Man has always his wits
well enough to cheat his Wife 'tis plain ...

Her bitterness was understandable, but the fault was not entirely
Thrale's: the war in America was inflicting severe damage on trade.
'We shall brew but sixty Thousand barrels of Beer this Year!' Hester
wrote in January: 'I wish the King would put an End to this destructive
War, I'm sure; the year before last we brew'd 96,000 Barrels – last Year
only 76,000 ... So horribly is the Consumption lessened by the War.'

One Saturday towards the end of February, the Thrales entertained
a large party to tea, cards and supper: 'Miss Streatfield was one, & as
Mr Thrale sate by her – he pressed her Hand to his Heart (as she told
me herself,) & said Sophy we shall not enjoy this long, & tonight I will
not be cheated of my Only Comfort.'

'Poor Soul!' Hester added sourly. 'How shockingly tender!'

Two days later Thrale suffered a second stroke. Hester was full of
praise for Sir Richard Jebb, whom she believed saved his life – 'Jebb is
the Man for Medical, as Lord Chatham for Political Courage'. Sophy
came and sat by his bedside, and Hester heard him say, 'Oh, who would
not suffer even all that I have endured, to be pitied by *you*!' This did not
go down particularly well with those family members who felt they had
made a more solid contribution: 'His Sisters who had alternately sate up
with him every Night & his Daughter, were offended; as they had never
been treated with a kind Word from him; but *I*, who expect none; thought
it rather good that he had *some* Sensibility for *some* human Being.'

By late March Thrale was well enough to travel and they set off in
leisurely fashion for Bath, accompanied by Queeney and Fanny Burney.
On the third night they put up at the well-known Black Bear coaching inn
at Devizes. They were greatly taken with their hostess, Mrs Lawrence,
who, as Fanny Burney put it, 'seemed something above her station in
her Inn'⁵ and by the good looks and skill in drawing of her ten-year-old
son. They were admiring the work of the future Sir Thomas Lawrence,
who in 1820 would succeed Benjamin West as President of the Royal
Academy.

In Bath they found lodgings on the South Parade in a house overlooking the Avon, and were quickly caught up in the familiar social round – concerts and card parties, visits to the Pump Room and the playhouse. One evening they saw Otway's *Venice Preserved*. The part of the heroine, Belvidera, was taken by the twenty-four-year-old Sarah Siddons, who after a disastrous London debut in Garrick's last year as manager had returned to the provinces; it was Hester's first sight of someone who would later become a close friend.

And of course endless calls made and received – what Fanny Burney described as 'our hurly-burly of visiting'. Her letters and journals give a colourful account of the events of the next few months – apart from a handful of letters to Johnson, still toiling away in London at his *Lives of the Poets*, Hester herself wrote little at this time. 'You are at all places of high resort, and bring home hearts by dozens,' he wrote plaintively to her; 'while I am seeking for something to say about men of whom I know nothing but their verses, and sometimes very little of them.'[6]

Thrale was now attended by Dr Abel Moysey, a fashionable Bath physician recommended by Mrs Montagu. 'He really seems as well as ever,' Fanny reported, 'except for violently swelled Legs & Feet, which keep him from *Beauism* in Dress.' Thrale's vanity imposed some constraint on their social life: 'We never go to the Rooms, as Mr Thrale will not exhibit his *Jambes* there, which are still much swelled, – & therefore we see nobody but by private chance.'[7]

Private chance served them generously, for all that, and they made a number of new friends. Thomas Sedgwick Whalley, a rich young clergyman, was the son of the Regius professor of divinity at Cambridge – Fanny Burney described him as 'immensely Tall, thin & handsome, but affected, delicate, & sentimentally pathetic'.[8] Marriage to a rich widow had brought him a large fortune. Some years previously he had bought the centre house in the Crescent at Bath, and there he wrote poetry and entertained lavishly.[9] The Thrales were also much in the company of a prominent Bath family called Bowdler, one of whose members, Thomas, would later add a word to the language with his expurgated *Family Shakespeare*.

Many of the Thrales' older friends and acquaintances were in town. They included Hester's Brighton conquest of the previous year, John Hinchcliffe, the Bishop of Peterborough. Hester thought him the most perfect reader of verse she had heard in her whole life: 'of all the Voices that I have ever heard, none are so round, so full, so sweet, so manly'. The Bishop, she wrote rather quaintly, treated her 'with a long Et Cætera of friendship & Flirtation'; she was especially flattered when he sent express to Cambridge to fetch a sermon he thought she would like – 'which he preached at the Abbey to please *me*', she told Johnson, 'for he had refused before'.[10]

She was also frequently together with Mrs Montagu:

> People think they must not ask one of us without the other, & there
> they sit gaping while we talk; I left it to her for the first fortnight, & She
> harangued the Circles herself; till I heard of private Discussions why
> Mrs Thrale who was so willing to talk at other Times, was so silent in
> Mrs Montagu's Company – then I began, and now we talk away regu-
> larly when there is no Musick, & the folks looks so stupid, except one or
> two who I have a Notion lie by to laugh, & write Letters to their Sisters
> &c. at home about us.[11]

Which was, of course, what Fanny Burney devoted a good deal of time to doing. 'We had a very entertaining Evening,' she told her sister, 'for Mrs. Montagu, Mrs. Thrale & Lord Mulgrave talked all the Talk, & talked it so well no one else had a wish beyond hearing them.'[12] Fond as she had become of Hester, however, and much as she admired her, she did not view her entirely uncritically. 'She is a most dear Creature, but never restrains her *Tongue* in any thing,' she wrote to Susanna: 'Nor, indeed, any of her feelings; – she Laughs, crys scolds, sports, reasons, makes fun – does every thing she has an inclination to do – without any study of prudence or thought of blame. And *pure* & artless as is this Character, it often draws both herself & others into scrapes which a little discretion w^d void.'[13]

Thrale's inability – or unwillingness – to control his appetite remained a matter of concern. Johnson offered what advice and encouragement he could from a distance: 'Mr. Thrale will never live abstinently, till he can persuade himself to abstain by rule. I lived on Potatoes on friday, and on spinach today ... When he comes home, we will shame him, and Jebb shall scold him into regularity.'[14]

Mrs Montagu also tried to help. When she saw him eat too much she sent Moysey to remonstrate, and Moysey was not one to mince his words: 'If says the Dr Mr Thrale will not mind the wisest Man & Woman in the World – let him listen to the foolishest; here's not an Apothecary's Prentice in this Town but what can see that he's *knockt down* like *a Cock at Shrove Tide*; & all by over feeding: For God's Sake dear Sir do not *stun* your Senses so ...'[15]

Now came unwelcome political news. Sir Richard Hotham, a wealthy and enterprising East India merchant who had started out as a hatter and hosier, announced that he intended to contest Southwark at the next election and began to spend liberally in the constituency. Hester told Johnson that one of Thrale's principal supporters had come posting down to Bath, partly to brief them, partly to form a view about Thrale's health: 'I asked the Man to dinner, & bid him observe (with an air) that my Master had not lost his Stomach – that is the Criterion of a good Constitution in Southwark I believe, so I did not fret at his eating that day.'

His supporters wanted Thrale to put in an appearance in the constituency, but Hester was clear that this would do him no good: 'Southwark is a Scene of Riot and Bustle and it would petrify him even to see & hear the Confusion,' she wrote to Johnson. 'He is not safe from another Apoplexy, he is not indeed, his Mind if it does not actually wander is enough disposed to do so ... There is a flutter & a Dejection at Times that will bear no Hurries.'[16]

Johnson urged her to come in Thrale's place. 'You should come for a week, and show yourself, and talk in high terms,' he wrote: 'A little bustle, and a little ostentation will put a stop to clamours, and whispers, and suspicions of your friends, and calumnies of your opponents. Be brisk, and be splendid, and be publick.'[17]

Which is what she did. 'I shall be fatigued and never thanked – no matter – it is fit he who is ill should rest & fit that I who am well should work,' she wrote in *Thraliana*. Leaving Queeney to look after Thrale, she posted up from Bath with Fanny Burney in fourteen hours and spent a week electioneering. 'Mrs. Thrale met with amazing success at the Borough,' Fanny wrote to her father, 'Every thing gave way to her, – her spirit, activity & dexterity made all difficulties sink before her, & the *Hothamites* will rue the day they ever projected supplanting Mr. Thrale.'[18]

Johnson, who had joined her at Southwark, was similarly impressed: She had 'run about the Borough like a Tigress', he told Queeney.[19]

After hurried visits to Streatham, where there were some alterations in progress, and to the Royal Academy Exhibition, held for the first time that year at Somerset House, Hester returned to Bath. She was not granted long, however, to enjoy the gossip and the bathing in Greenway's Grotto and the mellifluous cadences of Bishop Hinchcliffe. Early in June, reports began to reach Bath of serious rioting in London. The Roman Catholic Relief Bill had become law two years previously. It did away with the prohibitive oaths technically required of those who served in the armed forces; Catholics might henceforth be educated abroad without forfeiting their property, and Catholic priests would no longer be guilty of a felony.

The proposal to extend these measures of toleration to Scotland triggered anti-popish agitation. It was orchestrated by the president of the Protestant Association, an eccentric sprig of the Scottish aristocracy called Lord George Gordon. His hair was red and lank, and he wore it long; he occasionally sported bright tartan trousers. His contributions to debate in the Commons were infrequent and not always coherent, but in March he had informed the House that he had 160,000 Protestant men in Scotland at his command, and that if the King (who happened to be his godfather) did not honour his coronation oath, he would suffer as Charles I had done at the hands of Cromwell.

On 2 June a huge crowd had marched on Whitehall to present a petition. Some of them had been drinking. The approaches to Parliament were soon blocked; Lord Mansfield, the Lord Chief Justice, had the windows of his coach broken and his wig removed; later his house in Bloomsbury, with its celebrated library, was burned down. The chapel of the Sardinian ambassador in Lincoln's Inn Fields was destroyed; on 6 June the mob blew up distilleries in Holborn and swelled their numbers by bursting open Newgate prison. The initial response of the magistrates was feeble, and many property-owners fled the capital in panic. By Thursday, 8 June, more than 10,000 regular troops and militia had been assembled; by the weekend the cavalry pickets in the squares had become a tourist attraction for the returning quality and Gordon was safely tucked away in the Tower.

The violence now spread to several provincial towns, however, including Bath – described by one eighteenth-century priest as 'a veritable Mecca for Catholics'. Fanny Burney reported to her father that stage coaches arriving from London had *No Popery* chalked all over them.[20] Returning from drinking tea with the Bowdlers on 9 June, she and Hester were informed that a mob had surrounded a new Roman Catholic chapel that was due to be opened in two days' time. 'At first we disbelieved it,' Fanny wrote: '– but presently one of the servants came & told us they were knocking it to pieces, – &, in half an Hour, looking out of our Windows, we saw it in Flames! & listening, we heard loud & violent shouts!'[21]

In letters from Perkins and Sir Philip Jennings Clerke, Hester learned how close the brewery and the house in Southwark – where they had left Cecilia and Henrietta – had come to being destroyed. On 6 June the mob that had broken open Newgate moved on to the brewery, laden down with the prison chains they had seized as trophies. Perkins, with impressive presence of mind, told them 'it were a shame that *men* should be degraded by so heavy a load; and he would furnish them with a horse for that purpose'. He also shrewdly plied them with food and porter, and they left shouting 'loud Hourahs!'[22] Sir Philip later arrived with troops, carried the children to safety and gathered up plate and money and bills and bonds from the counting house, which he deposited at Chelsea College. Streatham also came under threat, and he had it stripped of furniture as a precaution.

There was worse to come. The same day a report in a Bath and Bristol paper asserted that Thrale was a papist – possibly because he had voted in favour of the pro-Catholic legislation two years previously. (But so had every other Member – the bill had passed without a dissenting vote.) 'This villainous falsehood terrified us even for his personal safety,' Fanny wrote to her father, '& Mrs. Thrale & I agreed it was best to leave Bath directly, & Travel about the Country.'[23]

They were on the road by eight o'clock that evening, heading for Brighton. They travelled by country roads, staying wherever possible in villages; this 'dawdling Journey cross the Country', as Hester called it, took eight days. They originally intended to remain in Sussex until the alterations at Streatham were complete, which might take two months or more, but Hester felt it imperative to see for herself how things stood at Southwark, and set off almost at once:

> We have now got Arms, & mean to defend ourselves by Force, if further Violence is intended. Whenever I come on these mad Errands, Dear Mr Johnson is sure always to live with me, & Sir Philip comes every day at some Hour or another ... I have presented Perkins by my Master's permission with two hundred Guineas, and a Silver urn for his *Lady* ...

She found time during the summer to return to a literary project begun three years earlier – character sketches in verse of those whose portraits by Reynolds hung in the library at Streatham. So far she had completed only those of Murphy, Baretti, Burke and Lord Westcote. Baretti and Burke both came in for fairly rough treatment, and Reynolds, when his turn came, fared little better:

> Of Reynolds what Good shall be said? – or what harm?
> His temper too frigid, his Pencil too warm;
> A Rage for Sublimity ill understood,
> To seek still for the Great, by forsaking the Good ...

She also had leisure to devote more time to *Thraliana*, and in one arresting and moving passage she lamented how little she had seen of Johnson in the course of the year:

> We never lived asunder so long since our first Connection I think, yet our mutual Regard does not decay that's certain – how should it? founded on the truest Principles Religion, Virtue, & Community of Ideas – saucy Soul! Community of ideas with Doctor Johnson: but why not? He has fastened many of his own Notions on my Mind before this Time, that I am not sure whether they grew there originally or no: of this I am sure, that they are the best & wisest Notions I possess; & that I love the Author of them with a firm Affection ...

Another visitor to Brighton that summer was Gabriele Piozzi. He had gone there in the hope that sea-bathing would be good for his vocal cords, which had become relaxed, but he had been persuaded to give fortepiano recitals each morning at a bookseller's in the town. One day in July, returning from an early dip in the sea with Queeney, Hester caught sight of him. With characteristic impetuosity she accosted him – in Italian – and asked whether he would give Queeney some lessons while they were in Brighton:

> He replied, coldly, that he was come thither himself merely to recover his voice, which he feared was wholly lost; that he was composing some music, and lived in great retirement; so I took my leave, and we continued our walk ... but on our returning home the same day, Mr. Piozzi started out of the shop, begged my pardon for not knowing me before, protested his readiness to do anything to oblige *me* ...[24]

The Thrales were soon seeing quite a lot of him: 'Piozzi is become a prodigious Favourite with me,' Hester wrote in *Thraliana*:

> He is so intelligent a creature, so discerning, one can't help wishing for his good Opinion: his singing surpasses every body's for Taste, Tenderness, and true Elegance; his Hand on the Forte Piano too is so soft, so sweet, so delicate, every Tone goes to one's heart I think; and fills the Mind with Emotions one would not be without, though inconvenient enough sometimes – I made him sing yesterday, & tho' he says his Voice is gone, I cannot somehow or other get it out of my Ears. – odd enough!

The plaintive lines that ran in her head spoke of love and betrayal and jealousy:

> Amor – non sò che sia,
> Ma sò che è un Traditor;
> Cosa è la Gelosia?
> Non l'hò provato ancor ...

'I instantly translated them for him,' she wrote, 'and made him sing them in English thus all'Improviso.'

And she noted in *Thraliana* one other thing about Piozzi which intrigued her greatly: 'He is amazingly like my Father.'

The apparent improvement in Thrale's condition naturally pleased Hester, but the likelihood of the dissolution of Parliament before the end of the year made her apprehensive: 'I dread the General Election more than ever; Mr Thrale is now well enough to canvass in Person, and 'twill kill him: had it happened when he *could not absolutely* have stirred – We would have done it for him, but now! Well! One should not however anticipate Misfortunes, they will come Time enough.'

They came early in September. There had been good news from America during the year as British troops advanced through the South and captured Charleston. At home the threat of invasion had receded. Soon after the Gordon Riots, North offered Rockingham a coalition, but the King baulked at the terms demanded by the Whigs. North called a snap election.

Thrale made such a feeble showing on his first day of canvassing that his supporters urged that Hester be by his side for the rest of the campaign. She complied, but paid an uncomfortable price: 'I worked at solicitation for ten Hours successively, without refreshment, or what I wished much more for – *a place of retirement*. This neglect, wch was unavoidable, surrounded as I was with *Men* all the Time, gave me an exquisite pain in my side – wch tho' relieved at my return home of Course, has never quite left me since –'

Johnson lent his support by drafting advertisements for the press and letters to electors. But by the end of the first week, Thrale was exhausted: 'On Sunday Morning he rose with a Diarrhea which fretted him the more, as he meant to appear at St George's Church that day, & face his Rival Candidates. Thither however I attended him, & had the Mortification to see him seized with such Illness as made him look a perfect Corpse in the full View of an immense Congregation ...'

He recovered sufficiently to make an appearance at the polling station two days later, but his support was ebbing fast: 'His friends now considered him as dying,' Hester told a friend, 'his Enemies as dead.'[25] The poll was not due to close until 17 September, but Thrale conceded the election on the thirteenth – '& we stole hither unobserved', Hester wrote, 'to refit our shattered Frames against the next great Storm'.

In spite of the parlous state of his health, Thrale was stubbornly determined to get back into Parliament. Johnson drafted a letter for him to send to the Prime Minister: 'Your Lordship knows my opinions and my practice, and therefore I hope I may without any impropriety desire a recommendation to some Borough where I may be chosen, through the influence of Government, at my own expence.'[26]

North was unable to oblige him. Henry Thrale's political career was at an end.

~ 16 ~

A Farewell to Trade

THE CAMPAIGN had taken a lot out of Hester:

> This last Election has hurt my Health radically and seriously: the great
> & long continued exertion of Voice for many days together deprived
> me for about 5 or 6 Days of all Power to speak at all ... I felt & still
> feel a pain across my Breast, & difficulty of Respiration which gives me
> reason to believe my Lungs are touched. I will however say nothing
> about it ... my Master will neither see the danger, nor care about it if he
> saw it –

Thrale's defeat had depressed him deeply. It also made him extremely
restless: 'He will go visiting everybody with whom he has any, or even
no Acquaintance,' Hester wrote to Mrs Lambart, the sister of Sir Philip
Jennings Clerke: 'We set out for Berks on Monday next, & have a thousand projects in View.'[1] She was too proud to admit it, but it is clear
that Sophy Streatfeild's hold on Thrale's affections continued to rankle:
'Here is Sophy Streatfield again; handsomer than ever, and flushed with
new Conquests ... Mr Thrale's preference of her to me never vexed me
so much as my Consciousness – or Fear at least – that he had Reason
for his Preference. She has ten Times my Beauty, and five Times my
Scholarship – Wit and Knowledge has She none.'

She was also incensed at this time by what she regarded as an imper-
tinent proposal from Perkins, the brewery manager:

> He wants to have a part in the Trade forsooth, & seems to think
> nothing will pay his Services but that. Mr Thrale's ill Health making
> His Death too probable, my Name may be joined with Perkins's com-
> modiously enough under an Alehouse Checquer. Good God! How such
> an idea shocks one! But ... who should expect a Clerk to behave like a
> Gentleman?

Thrale had suffered two attacks since the election, and early in December he suffered a third: 'Mr Thrale has been ill again,' Hester wrote; 'an Apoplexy succeeded by a Carbuncle; which however has made such a general Depuration, that we hope for a longer Reprieve than usual at least, if not a free Pardon.'

Christmas passed off surprisingly well. 'My Master keeps upon his Legs very prettily, and we have had a merry Xmas,' Hester wrote to her old aunt Cotton:

Two or three young Men & Maidens of an agreeable sort filled our Society – & that delightful Mortal Piozzi, the famous Italian singer spent a day or two in entertaining us with *his* astonishing Powers. What most amazed the people of the *Ton*, was *his* condescending to play Country Dances (for the 1:st Time of his Life) while we pretty Masters & Misses set to Dancing.[2]

But Hester's brave words to her aunt about Thrale's health masked a constant anxiety, as she confessed to Fanny Burney: 'I was terrified into Agonies by my dear Master's uncontrollable Spirit, made violent by Illness which kept me in such Terror.'[3] As 1781 dawned, her mood was one of despondency:

A Dutch War added to our Original enemies; a Hurricane which has almost depopulated Barbadoes, a Nobleman going to be hanged for promoting such a Spirit of Riot as half ruined the City of London itself[4] ... in our own Family, the death of its Principal hourly expected from a Repetition of dangerous Fits; the Trade going – as ev'ry Trade is – most rapidly to decay –

At the end of the month a ray of sunshine pierced the gloom and she was granted a long-held wish:

So now we are to spend *this* Winter in Grosvenor Square; my Master has taken a ready furnished Lodginghouse there, and we go in tomorrow: he frighted me cruelly a while ago, he would have Lady Shelburne's House – one of the finest in London: he would buy, he would build, he would give 20, 30, Guineas a Week for a House. Oh Lord thought I! the People will sure enough throw Stones at me *now*, when they see a dying Man go to such mad Expences, & all – as they will naturally think – to please a Wife wild with the Love of Expence.

The move to what Hester called 'the flashy end of the Town' was in fact dictated by Thrale's need to be closer to his doctors, but it chimed conveniently with Hester's social ambitions. Earlier in the month, on the Queen's birthday, she had gone to court, and her gown had been the talk of the town: 'The *toute ensemble* of the dress was magnificent as well as singular!' declared the *Morning Herald*.

Hester owed the inspiration for this remarkable confection to Fanny Burney's brother James, who had been with Captain Cook on his second and third voyages, and had presented her on his return with a scrap of cloth said to have been torn from the back of the native who had clubbed Cook to death: 'This Stuff I thought so pretty that I got Carr the Mercer to imitate it in Satten; & trimmed it with Feather'd ornaments to keep up the taste of the Character, still preserving in View the fashion of the Times.'

She was hugely pleased to have turned so many heads:

It was violently admired to be sure, and celebrated in all the Papers of the Day: – which I have a Notion was owing to my own willingness to be look'd at, by the people who sate in the Guard room, observing Dresses fashions &c.

My being us'd to Electioneering, prevents my Indignation from boyling at the sight of a few honest Fellows collected together, which The Ton-Folks call a *Mob*: so I turned to them & smiled, & I heard them say '*tis Mrs Thrale*, Oh She's a *good naturd Lady &c.* and so they put me in the News I guess.

In another age, like many another political wife, she would have been told that she was better candidate material than her husband.

❧ ❧

Installed in Grosvenor Square, Thrale advanced the hour of dinner from four o'clock to the more fashionable eight and Hester lost no time in mounting a strong challenge in the hostess stakes. 'Yesterday I made a *Conversazione* forsooth,' she wrote to Fanny Burney: 'Mrs Montagu was brilliant in Diamonds, solid in Judgment, critical in Talk. Sophy smil'd, Piozzi sung, Pepys panted with Admiration; Johnson was good humoured, Lord John Clinton attentive, Doctor Bowdler lame, & my Master not asleep.'[5]

'Old Master Pepys' as Fanny Burney called him, although he was no older than Hester, was panting after Sophy Streatfeild; Lord John Clinton, fourth son of the Duke of Newcastle, was being attentive to Queeney, although Hester did not rate his chances highly:

> Lord John is tame & gentle, & she doats on a *Flasher*; ill contrived
> that I must confess, for a sprightly fellow wou'd break her Heart in
> half a Year with Jealousy and Terror. Jack Fuller seems her Favorite:
> Jack Fuller of all People! Wild, gay, rich, loud, I wonder how a Girl of
> Delicacy can take a Fancy to Jack Fuller of Rose-hill?

But it was not all 'flashing about with my Quality Friends', as Hester put it. The brewery made increasing demands on her time. Soon after the move to Grosvenor Square, a clerk called Lancaster absconded with £2,000. Thrale was totally unconcerned, and it was left to Hester to pursue the matter. 'I have been running after him I think into all the hiding Places of this filthy Town,' she wrote: 'I am so afraid the Wretch will cut his own Throat, or do some desperate Act of Remorse – for he really *was* an honest Man *once*, & I feel Concern for *him* in the midst of the plagues he has been pleased to accumulate upon *me*.'

She was also increasingly exerting herself on Piozzi's behalf: 'I have set up Piozzi's Concert quite completely: we go every Fryday so prettily, & have such an elegant Room, & so select a Company, & he sings so divinely: all does well with this Project, & I got him 34 subscribers at 5 Guineas each by my own personal Interest.'

The attractions of a more fashionable address were proving illusory, however. 'Well!' reads an entry in *Thraliana*, 'now I have experienced the Delights of a London Winter spent in the Bosom of Flattery, Gayety, & Grosvenore Square: 'tis a poor Thing however, & leaves a void in the Mind.' Hester was also dismayed to discover that Thrale's enthusiasm for foreign travel had been rekindled – there was wild talk of visiting Spa and travelling on to Italy. The exasperation and bitterness that spilled out into her diary were not directed solely at her husband:

how shall we drag him thither? A man who cannot keep awake four
Hours at a Stroke, who can scarce retain the Fæces &c. Well! This will
indeed be a Tryal of one's Patience; & who must go with us on this
Expedition? Mr Johnson! He will indeed be the only happy Person of
the party: he values nothing under heaven but his own Mind, which is
a Spark *from* Heaven; & *that* will be invigorated by the addition of new
Ideas – if Mr Thrale dies on the Road, Johnson will console himself by
learning *how it is* to travel with a Corpse ...

Boswell was back in town, and was a frequent guest at Grosvenor
Square, sometimes without being specifically invited. ('I said I had a
silver ticket. "A gold ticket" said worthy Thrale.')[6] The next day he recorded disputing with Hester whether Shakespeare or Milton had drawn
the more admirable picture of a man. 'I was for Shakspeare; Mrs. Thrale
for Milton; and after a fair hearing, Johnson decided for my opinion.'[7]

Hester found him there again the following Sunday when she returned
from hearing the Bishop of Peterborough preach at the Mayfair Chapel.
The conversation ranged widely, but Thrale was listless and inattentive.
Hester ventured some words of praise for a kinsman of Lord North's
called Dudley Long, a shy man with a sharp wit and a bad stammer
who had entered the Commons the previous year. Johnson, who was at
his most combative, tore into her:

> Nay, my dear lady, don't talk so. Mr. Long's character is very *short* ...
> He is a man of genteel appearance, and that is all. I know nobody who
> blasts by praise as you do ... By the same principle, your malice defeats
> itself; for your censure is too violent. And yet (looking at her with a
> leering smile) she is the first woman in the world, could she but restrain
> that wicked tongue of hers; – she would be the only woman, could she
> but command that little whirligig.[8]

Johnson had recently started drinking wine again, and possibly it was
the wine that was speaking. Some days earlier at the Thrales', Boswell
had noticed him pour a quantity into a large glass and swallow it greedily.
'When he did eat,' he observed, 'it was voraciously; when he did drink
wine it was copiously.'[9]

But not as copiously or voraciously as his host. The very next day, observing how Thrale attacked his food, Hester decided to remonstrate, as she had been encouraged to do by his doctors: 'I checked him rather severely, & Mr Johnson added these remarkable Words. Sir – after the Denunciation of your Physicians this morning, such eating is little better than Suicide.' Thrale paid no attention.

An elaborate rout was planned for the middle of the week. Several Persian and Indian ambassadors who were in London to sign a treaty had been invited and Piozzi had engaged the celebrated Neapolitan singers Roncaglia and Sacchini on Hester's behalf. She was discussing these arrangements with him the day before the party when a letter was brought in from Dr Pepys. It contained nothing of particular significance, but in her overwrought state it triggered a flood of tears:

> I read the letter to Piozzi who could not understand it, & threw myself into an Agony, saying I was sure Mr Thrale would dye. The tender-hearted Italian was affected, bid me not despair so, but recollect some precepts he had heard Dr Johnson give me one day; & then turned to me with a good deal of Expression in his Manner, rather too much – it affected me – and sung Rasserena il tuo bel Ciglio &c &c.

'Rather too much expression.' Hester's worldly-wise friend Mrs Byron – the one who had once lent her an obscene poem – was present and watched Piozzi as he sang. 'I suppose that you *Know* that Man is in Love with You,' she said.

Thrale returned home shortly afterwards in high spirits. He had driven out in his carriage to deliver more invitations to what Hester called 'the morrow's Flash'. Once again, he gorged himself at dinner. The previous day he had eaten six courses, today he got through eight – 'with Strong Beer in such Quantities!' Hester wrote, 'the very Servants were frighted, & when Pepys came in the evening he said this could not last – either there must be legal Restraint or certain Death.'

Thrale retired to his room. When Hester looked in later, she found him sitting on his bed with his legs up. When she asked why, he replied, '*Because.*' 'I kiss'd him, & said how good he was to be so careful of himself.' Shortly afterwards Queeney found him lying on the floor. 'What's the meaning of this?' she cried. 'I chuse it, replies Mr Thrale firmly. I lie so o'purpose.'

Pepys had left word where he was to be found, but before he could return Thrale had suffered the first of a series of violent strokes. Jebb was also summoned, but 'seeing Death certain, quitted the House without even prescribing'. At eleven o'clock Johnson was sent for. Hester went into Thrale's room once, and saw them cutting off his clothes to bleed him; she ventured in no more.

Johnson recorded the events of the night in his *Prayers and Meditations*: 'I staid in the room, except that I visited Mrs. Thrale twice. About five (I think,) on Wednesday morning he expired; I felt almost the last flutter of his pulse, and looked for the last time upon the face that for fifteen years had never been turned upon me but with respect or benignity.'[10]

Hester, accompanied by Queeney, left immediately for Streatham – 'but finding myself pursued thither by officious Friendship, I ran forward to Brighthelmston where Mr Scrase, who like me had lost all he cared for *in earnest*; was a comfortable and useful Companion'. It was not then the custom for ladies to attend funerals, and she remained in Brighton for almost three weeks: 'There I had Time to collect my scattered Thoughts, to revise my past Life, & resolve upon a new one.'

Thrale was buried at St Leonard's in Streatham a week later. The elm coffin was placed in the family vault between those of his father and Hester's mother. 'With him,' Johnson wrote, 'were buried many of my hopes and pleasures.'[11] It was he who composed the Latin epitaph for the mourning tablet that was later placed on the south wall of the church. The stone was cut by the rising young sculptor John Flaxman.

Johnson wrote to Hester almost daily while she was in Brighton. 'Do not represent life as darker than it is,' he urged her: 'Your loss has been very great, but You retain more than almost any other can hope to possess ... Our sorrow has different effects, you are withdrawn into solitude, and I am driven into company. I am afraid of thinking what I have lost. I never had such a friend before.'[12]

He and his fellow-executors read Thrale's will on the day after his death. Hester had been generously provided for. Streatham was to be hers for life, and the contents there and at Southwark were left to her outright. So long as the brewery remained in operation she was to have £2,000 a year from the profits, together with a maintenance allowance for each daughter; if it were sold she was to receive £30,000, the remainder to be held in trust for her daughters.[13]

Hester, together with the other executors, was to be her daughters' guardian; the girls were also to be made wards of Chancery, which would give the courts wide jurisdiction over their welfare. The Crowmarsh property in Oxfordshire passed to Queeney; Hester's marriage settlement was not revoked, however, which meant that she would now receive £400 a year from the estate instead of £200 as formerly. Another provision of the marriage settlement – one that Hester had forgotten – was that she should receive a lump sum of £13,400 from her husband's estate if she survived him. This, for whatever reason, was not made over to her and became the cause of some recrimination when she realized her entitlement to it some years later.

She was in two minds about what to do about the brewery – 'my being entangled with the Trade perplexes me greatly', she wrote in *Thraliana*. Scrase argued that as she had only daughters it was madness to carry on – a view shared by Cator and Crutchley. Johnson, on the other hand, urged her to continue. He reminded her that a widow, unlike a married woman, was an independent legal agent: 'You are in your civil character a man. You may sue and be sued. If you apply to business perhaps half the mind which You have exercised upon knowledge and elegance, you will need little helps …'[14]

Knowing Perkins's eagerness to acquire a share in the business, Hester promised that if he found a purchaser, she would present his wife with the Southwark house and all its furniture.[15] In the meantime, she set aside three days a week to attend at the counting house:

> If an angel from heaven had told me 20 Years ago, that the Man I knew by the Name of *Dictionary Johnson* should one Day become partner with me in a great Trade, & that we should jointly or separately sign Notes Draughts &c. for 3 or 4 Thousand Pounds of a Morning, how unlikely it would have seemed ever to happen!

With the approach of summer some of her old sparkle and vivacity returned: 'Miss Owen & Miss Burney asked me if I had never been in Love; with myself said I, & most passionately. When any Man likes me I never am surprised, for I think how should he help it? When any

Man does *not* like me, I think him a Blockhead, & there's an End of
the matter.'

She was flattered when Mrs Montagu told her she ought to have a
statue erected to her for her diligence in attending to brewery business.
Then, in the middle of May, this excited entry in *Thraliana*: 'David
Barclay the rich Quaker will treat for our Brewhouse, & the Negotiation
is already begun. My heart palpitates with hope & fear, my Head is
bursting with Anxiety & Calculation ...'[16]

Two weeks later Hester went up early to town. 'This was the great &
most important Day to all this House,' Fanny Burney wrote to Susanna,
'upon which the sale of the Brewery was to be decided.' Hester was to
meet with Barclay and the executors. She was, Fanny wrote, 'in great
agitation of mind', and had promised that if all went well, she would wave
a pocket handkerchief from the coach window on her return: '4 o'Clock
came, & Dinner was ready, – & no Mrs. Thrale. 5 o'Clock followed, – &
no Mrs. Thrale. Queeny & I went out upon the lawn, where we sauntered,
in eager expectation, till near 6 – & then the Coach appeared in sight, – &
a white pocket Handkerchief was waved from it!'[17]

The documents completing the sale were signed on the last day of
May. Hester was ecstatic:

> Well! Here have I with the Grace of God, and the Assistance of good
> Friends, compleated – I really think very happily – the greatest Event
> of my Life: – I have sold my Brewhouse to Barclay the rich Quaker for
> 135,000^f to be in four years Time P^d I have by this Bargain purchased
> Peace & a stable Fortune; Restoration to my original Rank in Life, and
> a Situation undisturbed by Commercial Jargon, unpolluted by Com-
> mercial Frauds; undisgraced by Commercial Connections ... so Adieu
> to Brewhouse and Borough Wintering, adieu to Trade & Tradesmen's
> frigid Approbation.

She wrote in similar terms to Mrs Lambart: 'I have lost my Golden
Millstone from my neck, & float once more on the Current of Life like
my Neighbours – I long to salute You in my restored Character of a
Gentlewoman.'

Life in that restored character would be slow to become more
agreeable.

17

Hoarded Folly

THE DAY after Thrale was buried, Boswell dined together with Johnson and Reynolds at the Bishop of Chester's. At the end of the evening he returned alone with Reynolds to the painter's house in Leicester Fields. 'Let us diffuse,' he said to his host. Diffusion, possibly aided by a glass or two of wine, took the form of scrawling on two sheets of paper what he called 'I. Boswell's Epithalamium on Dr J. & Mrs T.' – fifty-six lines of verse in which he has Johnson addressing Hester on their supposed approaching marriage:

> While to felicity thus raised
> My bosom glows with amorous fire
> Porter no longer shall be praised
> Tis I myself am Thrale's entire …

Being Boswell, he was soon regaling the company on various social occasions with his 'Song'. His hearers would have required no explanation of the suggestive wordplay in that second stanza. Porter, as well as being a dark-brown ale, was the surname of Tetty, Johnson's late wife; they would also have known that 'entire' had two meanings – it was a kind of beer, but it was also short for 'entire horse' – a stallion. So it went on for fourteen sniggering stanzas:

> Charming Cognation! With delight
> In the keen aphrodisian spasm
> Shall we reciprocate all night
> While wit & learning leave no chasm.
> Nor only are our limbs entwind
> And lip in rapture glew'd to lip
> Lock'd in embraces of the Mind
> Fancy's enchanting sweets we sip …[1]

Boswell's latest biographer defends this exercise in prurience as not malicious: 'It has a kinship,' he writes, 'with folk verse in the native Scottish tradition.'[2] Some may prefer the pithier verdict of John Wain: 'Where ordinary bad taste leaves off, Boswell began.'[3]

That there was an erotic element in the complex knot of Johnson's feelings for Hester is plain; for the prurient modern mind to follow Boswell in his lubricious maunderings would be absurd. There is no evidence that Johnson ever made anything remotely resembling a sexual advance to his 'dear Mistress'; everything we know about Hester suggests that any such overture would have been briskly rebuffed.

Boswell was, of course, by no means alone in speculating about what the future held for Hester. Attractive, still only forty, celebrated for her wit, presumed to be in possession of a large fortune – plenty there for the wits and the bluestockings to gossip about and for the hacks to embroider.

The summer months following Thrale's death were spent quietly at Streatham. Fanny Burney, returning there in early June, found Hester far from well: 'Sweet Mrs. Thrale received me with her wonted warmth and affection,' she told her sisters, 'but shocked me by her own ill looks, & the encreasing alteration in her Person which anxiety & worry perpetual have made.'[4]

Johnson was once again in residence. He had at last finished his *Lives of the Poets* and devoted his time to instructing Queeney in Latin. Fanny Burney records that whenever she found herself alone with him, he talked incessantly of Thrale and of the sense of loss he felt. One day in June, as he so often did when he was anxious or troubled, he composed a prayer:

> Almighty God who art the Giver of all good enable me to remember
> with due thankfulness the comforts and advantages which I have en-
> joyed by the friendship of Henry Thrale ... O Lord since thou hast been
> pleased to call him from this world, look with mercy on those whom he
> has left, continue to succour me by such means as are best for me ...[5]

He clearly sensed that things must now be different and that those comforts and advantages were no longer as firmly assured as they had once been.

Queeney and Susan and Sophy were all having singing lessons from Piozzi, who had become almost as much a part of the household as Johnson, and was clearly assuming some importance in Hester's life. 'My Italian is going to his own country for a while,' she wrote in *Thraliana* in the early summer, 'to see his Friends, to fondle his Mother … He sung me a pretty Song t'other day – *a Venetian Partenza* I could not help translating it …

> The fatal Moment is arriv'd
> When of each tender hope depriv'd;
> I come to take my last Adieu,
> Of Love and Happiness and You …'

Piozzi's absence made her all the more reliant on the company of Fanny Burney. Always critical of the clannishness of the Burneys, she was furious when Fanny's father summoned her home to St Martin's Street: 'What a Blockhead Dr Burney is, to be always sending for his Daughter home so! What a Monkey! Is not she better and happier with me than she can be any where else? Johnson is enraged at the silliness of their Family Conduct …'

Hester went up to town to the Royal Academy Exhibition on 1 June, and a fortnight later made her first social call since Thrale's death. She paid several visits during the summer to the Albemarle Street studio of Robert Edge Pine,[6] who had been commissioned to paint her portrait. She is shown in widow's weeds, and wears a miniature of Thrale on a pendant. Pine painted her almost full face. Her hair is piled luxuriously high in the fashion of the day and crowned with a large black bow; there is a suggestion of a slightly sad smile. 'Not like, I think,' was Fanny Burney's verdict, 'but a mighty elegant Portrait.'[7]

In spite of an exceptionally long and fine summer, Hester was still far from well: 'I verily think that my Health which has stood so many Storms is now going to sink in the Harbour … now I am erisypelatous, & scorbutic, & I know not what: however I have had more than my Share …'

In the days before antibiotics a potentially severe streptococcal infection of the skin like erysipelas could be dangerous. The fact that she was also suffering from scurvy, which results from a deficiency of vitamin

C, suggests that she was not eating properly. Neither ailment is likely to have been helped by the discovery that she was considerably less well off than she had believed. 'My Coadjutors tell me I must have only 1200£ a Year instead of 1600£,' she wrote to Johnson: 'I find my possessions in Oxfordshire diminish upon close Inspection from 450£ to 300£ … in Consequence of all these Informations I have sent off a Pair of my Horses.'[8]

Two entries in *Thraliana* in October raise the possibility that Hester's continuing ill health was not due solely to physical causes or even to worry about her financial situation. 'I am growing excessively uneasy about Piozzi,' she wrote on the middle of the month, 'I have not heard from him so long.' Then, two weeks later, this remarkable passage:

> Concealed Fire burns very fatally … 'Tis this *Avarice* of mental
> Enjoyment, this *Hoarded* Folly; which now & then so blazes out of a
> sudden under the Name of Love; & I think the Reason of that Furor
> being more violent among the Female Sex is chiefly because being less
> tolerated to *declare* their Passion, it preys upon the Mind till it bursts all
> Reserve, & makes itself amends for the long Concealment.

Were her various maladies being aggravated by the repression of her feelings for Piozzi? She appears to have come close to confessing as much to Fanny Burney. The letter in which she did so is now missing, but Fanny's reply is revealing: 'What more bleeding! – more villainous Pill choaking! & Hemlock joined with *Mercury*! … Why a Feather, I should think, would make you stagger. Never Mind the foreign Letters, for depend upon it you will ere long have 2 or 3 at a Time; or else see the Abate suddenly at your feet when least expecting him …'[9]

Abate is the Italian for Abbot. Piozzi had originally been intended for the church. Hester and Fanny Burney had picked up the expression 'Signor Abate' from Pacchierotti, the Italian castrato, who habitually addressed Piozzi in this way – possibly ironically.

Several years later, when Hester published her correspondence with Johnson, she would be savagely attacked in a series of magazine articles by Baretti. One of his more sensational assertions was that Piozzi was the illegitimate son of John Salusbury and an Italian mother, and that he was therefore Hester's half-brother. The story was nonsense. Piozzi was born in 1740; Salusbury had returned from his Grand Tour several years before that and did not subsequently travel in Europe. What is intriguing, however, is that during Piozzi's absence in the summer months of 1781, and perhaps over a longer period, Hester appears at least to have played with the notion that she and Piozzi might be brother and sister and to have shared the idea with Fanny Burney. The evidence for this emerges from the letters that passed between them during November, when Fanny was visiting her 'Daddy' Crisp at Chessington.

Early in the month Hester received confirmation that Piozzi's return was imminent. 'Sweet Burney,' she wrote, 'Now that my stomach is lighten'd by Doses of Emetick Tartar, & my heart pacified by a Paris Letter, I can try for Flash again, at least rake up some old Embers.'[10] A week later, her spirits obviously greatly restored, she penned a much longer letter largely devoted to a version of a popular parlour game of the day, challenging Fanny to identify a number of their Streatham friends and acquaintances by quotations from Shakespeare.

She told Fanny that she was enclosing some 'treason', which she asks her to burn. Fanny dutifully (though not immediately) did so, but Hester retained a copy of most of it, and from that and from Fanny's reply, much of the exchange can be pieced together. One of Hester's conundrums concerned Piozzi. The wording is omitted from her copy, but Fanny's revealing response survives: 'Piozzi's *Father's Love* was, I think, not much, whatever his *Father's Daughter's* may be.' The exegesis offered by Fanny Burney's latest editor is convincing: 'Piozzi's *Father* here means HLT's father, an indication that FB and HLT still kept up the pretence that HLT's love was familial.'[11]

We cannot now know how this conceit came into her mind. Was she, perhaps unconsciously, using it as a device for denying or repressing her true feelings? Did she foresee the complications that would arise from an open declaration of attachment to Piozzi? She reverted more than once in *Thraliana* to the question of physical resemblance – "tis odd that none of my Children should resemble my Father – & that a Likeness of him – or I dream so – should in this Manner arrive from Italy'. Four years previously, she had recorded a conversation with Johnson about the nature of love. 'As My Peace has never been disturbed by the *soft*

Passion,' she wrote, 'so it seldom comes in my head to talk of it.' Now it seems her peace was being quite seriously disturbed.

❧

Johnson had stayed away for two months, although his thoughts turned frequently, sometimes anxiously, to Streatham. 'Piozzi, I find, is coming,' he wrote from Ashbourne towards the end of November: '... and when *he* comes and *I* come, you will have two about you that love you; and I question if either of us heartily care how few more you have. But how many soever they may be, I hope you keep your kindness for me ...'[12] Again, even more poignantly, from Birmingham: 'Do not neglect me, nor relinquish me. Nobody will ever love You better or honour You more ...'[13]

By the time Hester received this, Piozzi had already returned:

I have got my Piozzi home at last, he looks thin & battered, but always kindly upon me I think – he brought me an Italian Sonnet written in his praise by Marco Capello, which I instantly translated of course; but He prudent Creature, insisted on my burning it, as he said it w^d inevitably get about the Town how *he* was Praised, & how *M^s Thrale* translated & echoed his Praises, so that says he I shall be torn in Pieces, and you will have some *Infamità* said of you that will make you hate the Sight of me. He was so earnest with me that I could not resist, so burnt my Sonnet ...

He tells me ... if he does not fix himself for Life here, he will settle to lay his Bones at Milan: the Marquis d'Araciel his Friend & Patron who resides there; divides and disputes his Heart with me, I shall be loth to resign it.

Hester entered 1782 full of good resolutions: 'I am beginning a new Year in a new Character, may it be worne decently yet lightly! I wish not to be rigid & fright my Daughters by too much Severity: I will not be wild, & give them Reason to lament the Levity of my Life.'

Happily, she remained as avid a recorder of the gossip of the day in her new character as in her old: 'They say Pacchierotti the famous Soprano Singer is ill, & they say Lady Mary Duncan his frightful old Protectress has made him so by her *Caresses dénaturés* ...' And although she herself was no longer directly affected, Sophy Streatfeild clearly retained her ability to exasperate and discompose:

> She has begun the new Year nicely with a new Conquest – Poor dear Doctor Burney! He is *now* the reigning Favourite, and she spares neither Pains nor Caresses to turn that good man's head, much to the Vexation of his Family … How she contrives to keep Bishops, & Brewers, & Doctors, & Directors of the East India Company all in her Chains so – & almost all at a Time would amaze a wiser person than me …

Although her year of mourning was not yet over, Hester took a house in Harley Street for the first three months of the year; friends were reluctant to travel out to Streatham in the short dark days of winter, and she craved society:

> The World will watch me at first, & think I come o' husband hunting for myself or my fair Daughter: but when I have behaved prettily for a while, they will change their Mind … the first Seduction came from Pepys; I had a Letter today, desiring me to dine in Wimpole Street, & meet Mrs Montagu & a whole *Army of Blues*: to whom I trust my Refusal will afford very pretty speculation …

Her health continued both to preoccupy and irritate her – 'My face is all over Pimples like a drunkard, – twere better have a Hump-back.' But her mind turned increasingly to what shape her life should now take, even if her thinking was hedged about with an intricate sequence of provisos:

> …*if* neither I should marry, nor the Brewhouse People break; *if* the ruin of the Nation should not change the Situation of Affairs so that One could not receive regular Remittances from England: and *if* Piozzi should not pick him up a Wife, and fix his abode in this Country – If therefore & *If*, & *If* & *If* again – All should conspire to keep my present Resolution warm; I certainly would at the close of the four Years from the Sale of the Southwark Estate, set out for Italy with my two or three eldest Girls; and see what the World could shew me. I am now provided with an Italian Friend who would manage my Money Matters, facilitate my Continental amusements, & be faithful to my interest …

There was an even bigger if than all of these, however – 'my Monitor, my Friend, my Inmate, my Dear Mr Johnson'. He represented a formidable obstacle to these plans: 'Travelling with Mr Johnson *I* cannot bear, & leaving him behind *he* could not bear; so his Life or Death must determine the Execution or laying aside my Schemes: – I wish it were within Reason to *hope* he could live four Years.'

That seemed increasingly unlikely. 'Here is Mr Johnson very ill, ill indeed,' she noted in *Thraliana* on 1 February: 'If I lose him I am more than undone: Friend, Father, Guardian, Confident! God give me Health & Patience – what shall I do?' Holed up in his own house, depressed by the death of Levett, Johnson was in low spirits. To Hester, he sent this pathetic *cri de cœur*: 'I try to get well and wish to see You, but if I came, I should only cough and cough ... Do not add to my other distresses any diminution of kindness ...'[14]

By the middle of April Hester was preparing to return to Streatham:

> when I took off my Mourning the watchers watched me very exactly,
> but they whose Hands were mightiest have found nothing: so I shall
> leave the Town I hope in a good Disposition towards me tho' I am sullen enough with the Town, for fancying me such an amorous Ideot that
> I am dying to enjoy every filthy Fellow.

She elaborated in a footnote: 'Ld Loughborough' Sr Richd Jebb, Mr Piozzi Mr Selwin Dr Johnson every Man who comes to the House is put in the Papers for me to marry,' but she was in more buoyant spirits than for some time, and her mood was one almost of defiance:

> I am returned to Streatham, pretty well in Health, & *very* sound of
> Heart, notwithstanding the watchers & the Wagerlayers ... a Woman
> of passable Person, ancient Family, respectable Character, uncommon
> Talents, and three Thousand a Year: has a Right to think herself
> any Man's *equal*; & has nothing to seek but return of Affection from
> whatever Partner She pitches on. To marry for Love would therefore be
> rational in me, who want no Advancement of Birth or Fortune, and till I
> am in Love, I will not marry – *nor perhaps then.*

Unwanted admirers got brutally short shrift:

Here's a proposal of Marriage to me from a Man I scarcely know – I sent him an immediate & steady Refusal: 'My Acquaintance with you was always the slightest possible, & it is now two Years since I have seen your Face; yet in these two Years I have received two Letters from you, the first, a very strange one, the second stranger still; I beg I may never have a Third.'

But she also had to fend off would-be suitors from among the Streath-amites: 'Tis now Sir Philip Jennings Clerke's Turn to torment me; he makes Love to me now quite openly & seriously; says he shall marry me for that his Wife is Ill. Oh! What variety, what change of Torments from all but my Dear, my delicate, my disinterested *Piozzi*!'

Lady Salusbury, the widow of Hester's Uncle Thomas, had raised an action against Hester four years previously in the Court of Chancery to recover the money Sir Thomas had come up with many years before to pay off the mortgage on Bach-y-Graig. Hester had always believed that her uncle had never meant the debt to be repaid; her lawyers now found themselves unable to drag out the proceedings any further; the Court accepted that Lady Salusbury had documents to prove a legal obligation and found for her in the sum of £8,000 – about £750,000 today.

By the beginning of August Hester's mind was made up: 'The establishment of Expence here at Streatham is more than my Income will answer; my Lawsuit with Lady Salusbury turns out worse in the Event, & infinitely more costly than I could have dreamed on ... I must go abroad & save Money.'

She had already made arrangements to let Streatham for three years to the Prime Minister, Lord Shelburne[15] before she plucked up courage to tell Johnson and she was taken aback at the apparent equanimity with which he received the news – 'seemed even less concerned at parting with me than I wished him'. When she heard that he had told Queeney that he would not go with them even if asked, surprise turned to indignation: 'See the Importance of a Person to himself!' she wrote in *Thraliana*: 'I fancied Mr Johnson could not have existed without me forsooth, as we have now lived together above 18 Years, & I have so fondled and waited on him in Sickness & in Health – Not a bit on't! he feels nothing in parting with me, nothing in the least; but thinks it a prudent Scheme, & goes to his Book as usual.'

Only a few months previously he had been her 'Friend, Father, Guardian, Confidant'. Now, in a bitter footnote, she added what Walter Jackson Bate has justly called 'the ugliest and least honest remark' she was ever to make about Johnson:

> He *loved* Mr Thrale, I believe, but only wish'd to find in me a careful Nurse & humble Friend for his sick and his lounging hours: yet I really thought he could not have existed without *my Conversation* forsooth. He cares more for my roast Beef & plumb Pudden which he now devours too dirtily for endurance: and since he is glad to get rid of me, I'm sure I have good Cause to desire the getting Rid of *him*.

Hester had spoken to Johnson of 'the Necessity of changing a Way of Life I had long been displeased with' and in *Thraliana* she enlarged on her reasons:

> In Italy we shall live with twice the Respect, & at half the Expence we do here, the Language is familiar to me, & I love the Italians; I take with me all I love in the world except my two Baby daughters who will be left safe at School, & since Mr Johnson cares nothing for the Loss of my personal Friendship & Company, there is no Danger of any body else breaking their Hearts.

All of which would afford Boswell the opportunity for one of many feline thrusts at Hester when his *Life of Johnson* eventually saw the light of day:

> The death of Mr. Thrale had made a very material alteration with respect to Johnson's reception in that family. The manly authority of the husband no longer curbed the lively exuberance of the lady; and as her vanity had been fully gratified, by having the Colossus of Literature attached to her for many years, she gradually became less assiduous to please him. Whether her attachment to him was already divided by another object, I am unable to ascertain ...[16]

Hester was in truth manufacturing a grievance – forging a weapon to defend herself from the charge that she was treating her old friend ungenerously. She knew — everyone knew — how passionately he had longed to see Italy. But he was now old and infirm; it was by no means certain that he would survive the rigours of such a journey. Above all, Hester had decided that she now wanted to take control of her own life. By the time she came to compile her *Anecdotes* of Johnson some years later, she no longer felt the need to be defensive: 'Veneration for his virtue, reverence for his talents, delight in his conversation, and habitual endurance of a yoke my husband first put upon me ... made me go on so long with Mr. Johnson; but the perpetual confinement I will own to have been terrifying in the first years of our friendship, and irksome in the last ...'[17]

On Sunday 6 October Johnson attended the little church at Streatham for what he knew would be the last time. If Hester could have read his journal for that day, she might have felt a twinge of shame. He had composed a prayer for the occasion:

Almighty God, Father of all mercy, help me by thy Grace that I may with humble and sincere thankfulness remember the comforts and conveniences which I have enjoyed at this place, and that I may resign them with holy submission ... To thy fatherly protection, O Lord, I commend this family. Bless, guide, and defend them, that they may so pass through this world as finally to enjoy in thy presence everlasting happiness ...[18]

He was now very breathless, and had to rest several times on the short walk to the church. It seems likely that he was unaccompanied, but even so he chose to draw a partial veil over what he did as he left St Leonard's by lapsing in his journal into Latin: *Templo valedixi cum osculo* — 'I bade the church farewell with a kiss'.

Hester had plainly been deceived by his calm reaction to the news of her intentions. It had been achieved at colossal expense; Johnson had been obliged to call, in John Wain's phrase, 'on all his reserves of courage and generosity'. The next morning he was called early: 'I packed up my bundles, and used the foregoing prayer, with my morning devotions somewhat, I think, enlarged. Being earlier than the family, I read St Pauls farewel in the Acts, and then read fortuitously in the Gospels, which was my parting use of the library.'[19]

He would not see Streatham again.

18

No Mercy in This Island

FOR THE next two years, Hester's emotional life resembled a looping, roller-coaster ride of sickening twists and nightmarish descents. Shortly before leaving Streatham she had penned a lengthy entry in *Thraliana* agonizing over her feelings for Piozzi and the dilemmas they posed for her. It reads like an extended Shakespearian soliloquy:

> He is so amiable, so honourable, so much above his Situation by his Abilities ... but if he is ever so worthy, ever so lovely, he is *below me* forsooth: in what is he below me? In Virtue – I would I were above him; in Understanding – I would mine were from this Instant under the Guardianship of his: – in Birth – to be sure he is below me in birth, & so is almost every Man I know ...
>
> Here then I rest, & will torment my Mind no longer, but commit myself as he advises to the Hand of Providence, & all will end *all' ottima Perfezzione*, & if I *am* blest with obtaining the Man – the only Man I ever could have loved, I verily believe it will be only because the Almighty will not leave such Virtue as his – unrewarded.

Immediately on leaving Streatham she had gone down to Brighton with the girls. She invited Johnson to join them, and he did so, in spite of his dislike of such fashionable resorts. He received Fanny Burney 'with his usual goodness' when she joined the party, and one evening, to the general amazement, accompanied the ladies to a ball – 'it cannot', he declared, 'be worse than being alone'.[1] But he was far from being on his best behaviour. 'He has been in a terrible severe humour of late, and has really frightened all the people,' Fanny wrote in her journal: 'To me only I think he is now kind, for Mrs. Thrale fares worse than anybody.'[2]

The atmosphere in the house was not sweetened by continuing press interest in Hester's affairs. The *Morning Post* announced on 15 October that she and Johnson were to be married, and three days later embroidered the story considerably. Hester, they assured their readers, had stipulated that the Doctor should immediately discard his bush-wig, wear a clean shirt and shave every day, give up snuff, learn to eat vermicelli, and leave off red flannel night caps.

Hester was exasperated: 'There is no mercy for me in this Island,' she wrote: 'One day the paper rings wth my marriage to Johnson, one day to Crutchley; one day to Seward. I give no reason for such Impertinence, but cannot deliver myself from it. Whitbread the rich Brewer is in Love with me too; Oh I would rather as Anne Page says – be set breast deep in the Earth, & bowled to death with Turneps –'

There was even a proposal of marriage from a young member of the Irish parliament called Sir Richard Musgrave, whom Hester had met in Bath in 1776. 'A hot-headed Irishman' was how she had described him then to Johnson – 'rich, young, handsome & I fancy vicious enough'.[3] (She read him rather well; four years later, as High Sheriff of County Waterford, he would personally flog convicted rioters when nobody else could be found to do so.) 'He will get me to be sure!!' she wrote now in *Thraliana* – 'A likely matter! when My Head is full of nothing but my Children – my Heart of my beloved Piozzi!'

So full that it was making her fret and look ill, and Queeney – 'out of Tenderness perhaps' Hester surmised, somewhat improbably – pressed her for an explanation: 'I called her into my Room & fairly told her the Truth: told her the strength of my Passion for Piozzi, the Impracticability of my living without him; the Opinion I had of his Merit, & the Resolution I had taken to marry him.'

Queeney, now a highly intelligent, cold-hearted young woman of eighteen, plainly did not like what she heard:

To console her private Distress I called into the Room to her my own Bosom Friend, my beloved Fanny Burney; whose Interest as well as Judgment goes all against my Marriage ...

Such are the hands to which I have cruelly committed thy Cause – my honourable, ardent, artless Piozzi! ... the man I love, I love for his Honesty; for his Tenderness of Heart, his Dignity of Mind, his Piety to God, his Duty to his Mother, & his delicacy to me. In being united to this Man only can I be happy in this World; & short will be my Stay in it, if it is not passed with him.

Having poured out her heart in this way in *Thraliana*, she then showed what she had written to both her daughter and her friend:

Sweet Fanny Burney cried herself half blind over it: said there was no resisting such pathetic Eloquence, & that if She was the Daughter instead of the Friend, She should be even tempted to attend me to the Altar, but that while She possessed her Reason, nothing should seduce her to approve what Reason itself would condemn ... I will talk no more of it.

Back in London, Hester had to give her mind to how the money she must pay Lady Salusbury was to be raised. A compromise figure of £7,500 had been offered; she had Perkins's bond for £1,600, and thought that she might get £1,400 for her silver; Crutchley travelled to Wales on her behalf and established that the £4,000 she had hoped for from her trees would take too long to realize. Eventually, Cator found the interest and the security so attractive that he came up with the necessary sum from his own resources, although he did not think it necessary to inform Hester of this. 'Ah what a triumph will this wicked Woman have over me!' she wrote. 'God grant me but Charity enough to pray for & forgive her ...'

Hester had taken a house in Argyle Street for the winter, and her spirits lifted a little. 'I have given my Piozzi some hopes,' she wrote a week after her return from Brighton: ''Tis Time to be in earnest now, I have trifled too much with his Health & my own; I am ashamed of such poor Shifts & Tricks as I have used to ward off an honourable passion for a worthy Object; – yet how, how! shall I ever manage to obtain him? – Oh how indeed!'

She went out a good deal into society during the season: 'I am all the Mode this winter; no parties are thought highly of, except Mrs Thrale makes one of them: my Wit, & even my Beauty – God help me! is celebrated; and I have three or four Engagements of a Night among the very first Company this great Town can produce.'

Six years after her initial failure there, Sarah Siddons had made a triumphant return to Drury Lane that autumn, the intensity of her acting provoking scenes of near-hysteria. Hester and Fanny Burney encountered her at one of the *conversaziones* which the bluestocking Miss Monckton held at her mother's grand house in Charles Street. 'Why, this a leaden goddess we are all worshipping!' Hester declared, 'however, we shall soon gild it.'

Hester's popularity did not altogether please Piozzi: 'My Lover is jealous of me; how should he help it? He sees me surrounded with Fops & Fools, & Wits & Wise Folks; and I am angry because he is not pleas'd ... he fears my Faith my Honour may give way to the Seductions of Vanity, & Attachment to the gay World – Well let him!'

But then, as the conventions of romantic comedy require, the shoe was suddenly on the other foot: 'A fit of jealousy seized me the other Day; – some Viper had stung me up to a Notion that my Piozzi was fond of a Miss *Chanou*.' Hester, never happier than when playing with words, saw her presumed rival off with an atrocious pun: 'I called him gently to Account, & after contenting myself with slight Excuses, told him that whenever we married, I should however desire to see as little as possible of the Lady *chez nous*.'

She remained defiantly proud of her ability to hold her own, to keep her end up: 'While My Heart is penetrated by its Passion for Piozzi, my head confounded by various Schemes of future Life; my Purse pulled at on every side unmercifully, my Law Suit lost unjustly, my Friends treating me ungenerously, and every thing going most perversely: I have still Spirit to keep me from being frighted *out of my Wits* at least.'

The press still had Hester in their sights. Johnson remained their occasional butt, but they now increasingly homed in on Piozzi, as often as not dismissively referred to as a 'fiddler'. Matters were quickly approaching a point of crisis. It is impossible to chronicle the precise sequence of events, because several pages have been torn out of *Thraliana* at this point. On 26 January, a Sunday, Fanny Burney told Hester that she must either marry Piozzi immediately or give him up: otherwise she would lose her reputation: 'I actually groaned with Anguish, threw myself on the Bed in an Agony.'

Queeney is represented as looking on 'with frigid Indifference':

[She] said coldly that if I *would* abandon my Children, I *must*: that their Father had not deserved such Treatment from me; that I should be punished by Piozzi's neglect, for that she knew he hated me, & that I turned out my offspring to Chance for his Sake like Puppies in a Pond to swim or drown, according as Providence pleased: that for her part She must look herself out a Place like the other Servants, for my Face would She never see more –

Susan and Sophy said nothing – but with an unerring instinct for what would really hurt, they coached the two youngest children to cry 'Where are you going Mama? Will you leave us and die as our poor papa did?' At that point Hester's resolve snapped. She wrote asking Piozzi to come to her the next morning – her birthday, as it happened – took an emetic and passed the night 'in Torture not to be described'.

Informed of her decision, Piozzi asked to speak to Queeney: 'She had as I discovered afterwards, touch'd on the Magic String,' Hester wrote, 'by telling him *My Honour* was concerned in our immediate Separation.' To this, Piozzi could find no answer. He went off to his lodgings in Wigmore Street, returned with all Hester's letters, and handed them over to Queeney – who took them and turned her back on him. It had been an emotional morning, and his English buckled under the strain: 'Take your Mama,' he cried – 'and make it of her a Countess – it shall kill *me* never mind – but it shall *kill her too!*'

Hester, for her part, struck a distinctly theatrical note, lapsing for greater effect into the language of opera: 'Adieu to all that's dear, to all that's lovely. I am parted from my Life, my Soul! My Piozzi: Sposo promesso! amante adorato! Amico senza equale ...'

❧

As Piozzi prepared to return to Italy, Hester decided that she would go and live 'in a little way' at Bath:

I may in six or seven Years be freed from all Incumbrances; and carry a clear Income of 2500£ a Year, and an Estate of 500£ in Land to the Man of my Heart ... The Time indeed will be past in which I could have brought him Children – a Happiness I must now not hope for! – I may *yet* however bring him a useful and an entertaining Companion, and if

my Person is too much faded for his endurance, I will live at the next
Door to him as Brother, Friend, – or in *Honour* what he pleases ...

Her departure was delayed because Cecilia and Harriet became ill,
but by early April she judged it safe to leave. There is no mention in
Thraliana of her parting from Johnson, but he recorded the event in his
diary on 5 April: 'I took leave of Mrs Thrale. I was much moved. I had
some expostulations with her. She said that she was likewise affected. I
commended the Thrales with great good will to God ...'[4]

The next day Piozzi came to breakfast for the last time:

I perswaded him to bring his old Friend Mecci who goes abroad with
him & has been long his Confident, to keep the meeting from being
too tender, the Separation from being too poignant; – his Presence
was a Restraint on our Conduct, and a Witness of our Vows; which
we renewed with Fervour and will keep sacred in Absence, Adversity,
and Age.

When all was over I flew to my Dearest loveliest friend my Fanny
Burney, & poured all my sorrows into her tender Bosom.

'Bath 14: April 1783. Here I am settled in my Plan of Œconomy, with
three Daughters, three Maids and a Man.' But she had not been many
days in the house she had rented in Russell Street when a message came
from Cator to say that Harriet was dead and Cecilia dying. She dashed off
an agonized note to Johnson: 'My Children, my Income (of course) and
my health are coming to an end Dear Sir – not my Vexations ...'[5]

Breaking her journey only to lie down for two or three hours at
Reading she reached Streatham early on Easter Day. Cecilia was out of
danger; Harriet was laid to rest beside the others at St Leonard's. She
was received on her return to Bath with cold indifference: 'Mr Thrale
had not much heart, but his fair Daughters have none at all.'

She had heard from Dr Pepys that Piozzi had been ill – 'in Consequence of his Agitation I guess', she wrote: 'a sore Throat Pepys
said it was, with four Ulcers in it: the People about me said it had been
lanced'. She was unwise enough to mention this to the girls: 'Has he
cut his own Throat? says Miss Thrale in her quiet Manner.'

Small wonder that she longed for company: 'Not a person to speak to; not a soul. Dear Miss Burney at a Distance ...' A blustery day in Bath was enough to set her fretting about the weather in the Channel: 'Here blows a dreadful Wind, a Hurricane almost – God protect my best beloved, my Piozzi! he was to set out today, but *that* He will not; sure he will not. Oh but the Packet might set out last night & tempt him aboard –'

She had sent him some verses 'to divert him on his Passage'; distress and anxiety combined to produce the most atrocious doggerel she ever penned:

> Come friendly Muse! Some Rhimes discover
> With which to meet my Dear at Dover;
> Fondly to bless my wandring Lover,
> And make him dote on dirty Dover ...

She was determined that her daughters' education should not be neglected. The catalogue of what she drummed into them during their time in Bath makes remarkable reading – the Bible ('not Extracts, but the whole from End to End'), Milton, Shakespeare, Pope's translations of the *Iliad* and the *Odyssey*, *The Vicar of Wakefield*, the works of Young and Addison, Voltaire's *Zadig*, various travel books, not to mention 'Plays out of Number, Rollin's Belles Lettres – and hundreds of Things now forgot'. When she was not reading at home, she later wrote, she 'went wearying heav'n with Prayers to all the Churches & Chapels in town – watching the Post, too, & carrying my own long Letters to the Office'. In her distracted state she neglected on one occasion to pay any postage, an omission which brought her a delicately worded but hugely embarrassing letter from one Jackson, the Comptroller of the Foreign Post Office:

> Madam, – Let nothing add to your present pain, as no one surely
> deserves so much happiness. Your letter is gone safe; I transmitted the
> amiable contents to Mr. Piozzi, who will receive it in due time; but you
> should be careful not to send another packet unpaid for ... Your signing
> no name, and dating, forced me to peruse every word of a letter in three
> languages which no one could so have written but Mrs. Thrale ...[6]

In the middle of June came news that Johnson had suffered a stroke. 'I was alarmed and prayed God, that however he might afflict my body he would spare my understanding,' he wrote to Hester. 'This prayer, that I might try the integrity of my faculties I made in Latin verse.'[7] Hester has been criticized for not hastening to London to care for him – unjustly, however, as one of Johnson's many letters to her that summer makes clear: 'Your offer, dear Madam, of coming to me is charmingly kind, but I will lay [it] up for Future use.'[8]

'Dreadful Event! & I at a Distance – Poor Fellow!' Hester had written in *Thraliana*. 'I sincerely wish the Continuance of a Health so valuable; but have no Desire that he should come to Bath.' She described the letter in which he told her of his stroke as being written 'in his usual Style', which indeed it was, but it is plain from the sombre opening that he knew their relationship was no longer what it had been:

> I am sitting down in no chearful solitude to write a narrative which would once have affected you with tenderness and sorrow, but which you will perhaps pass over now with the careless glance of frigid indif-ference. For this diminution of regard, however, I know not whether I ought to blame You, who may have reasons which I cannot know ...'[9]

He was determined, for all that, to keep her fully informed about his health. 'I think to send you for some time a regular diary,' he announced three days later. 'You will forgive the gross images which disease must necessarily present.'[10] He was as good as his word, regaling her during the summer with accounts not only of the application of Spanish Fly to his head but of the hard fleshy enlargement of his left testicle: 'If excision should be delayed there is danger of a gangrene,' he informed her. 'You would not have me for fear of pain perish in putrescence.'[11]

Hester herself was still extremely unwell, and in August decided on a visit to Weymouth: 'I am come here chiefly on my own Account to repair my lost Health by Sea bathing: the past Agitations of my Mind have turned my Blood scorbutical: I will wash it well with Salt Water, & drink Dorchester Beer ...'

Salt water and beer proved equally ineffective:

> I am all burst out into an Erisypelas too frightful to look on without horror; it will ruin my Complexion for ever ... Oh me! What a World

this is! Yet I wish not to quit it till I have finally settled Matters with my Piozzi. I shall be grown too hideous for his Endurance by the Time I see him again perhaps – Oh God forbid!

The pages of *Thraliana* for the closing months of 1783 suggest that Hester was close to mental breakdown. She had hoped on her return to Bath to find a miniature which Piozzi had promised to send her from Paris – 'but no such Testimony of his Affection have I been blest with – surrounded by his Enemies, and my Tormentors, I live a Life of Vigilance & Constraint, ill suiting a liberal & expanded Mind'. The miniature eventually arrived – 'lively, lovely Resemblance of my adored Husband' – but then the flow of letters dried up: 'What is become of him for whom my Soul languishes? Dead! married! Lost for ever perhaps to his faithful Galesina who lives but in hopes to dye at last with him. Oh insupportable!'

Then she received a letter from her butler, Daniel, full of unwelcome tittle-tattle about the Miss Chanou who had caused a spasm of jealousy earlier in the year. Daniel had it from the girl's father that she had once been engaged to Piozzi, and was now preparing to go off and be married to him in Venice: 'Mr Chanou told Daniel that Piozzi used to carry my letters to his House, and laugh at them with his Daughter – a pretty Rival enough to be sure for a Descendant of the Duke of Bavaria but Love & Pride are incompatible, nor had I ever much of the latter –'

If the emotional turmoil of those months undermined Hester's physical and mental health, the generosity of spirit, which was one of her most marked characteristics, was unimpaired. There was further evidence of this some months later: 'My dearest Piozzi's Miss Chanou is in Distress – I will send her 10$^£$ perhaps he loved her, perhaps She loved him ... yet I have, and will have Confidence in his Honour, I will not suffer Love or Jealousy to narrow a heart devoted to him ...'

In the middle of November, Sophy fell dangerously ill, and Hester feared for her life:

I saved her in the first attack, by a Dram of fine old Usquebough given at the proper Moment ...

She lives, I have been permitted to save her again; I rubbed her while just expiring, so as to keep the Heart in Motion: she knew me instantly,

& said you warm *me*, but you are killing *yourself* – I actually was in a burning fever from exertion, & fainted soon as I had saved my Child.

Sophy's illness and Hester's subsequent collapse marked a turning point in her relations with her daughters:

all our Tenderness was called out on this Occasion: dear Creatures! They see I love them, that I would willingly *die* for them; that I am actually dying to gratifie their Humour at the Expence of my own Happiness ... they are weary of seeing me suffer so, and the eldest beg'd me Yesterday not to sacrifice my Life to her Convenience; She now saw my Love of Piozzi was incurable ...

Queeney's change of heart was undoubtedly prompted in part by the intervention of Matthew Dobson, one of the physicians attending her mother. He had not immediately appreciated the underlying cause of Hester's distress, but when it was explained to him he declared that there was no time to lose: 'Call the man home,' he told her daughters, 'or see your Mother die.'

Piozzi did not immediately heed the call. He was comfortably installed in the Palazzo Belgiojoso in Milan as the guest of Prince Alberico XII Barbiano di Belgiojoso – 'who loves him', Hester wrote, '& acknowledges his Merit'. It was only a matter of months since he had been sent packing; what if he was to encounter renewed hostility from Hester's family and friends and be subjected to a second humiliating rejection? Winter gave way to spring with no sign of Piozzi, and Hester became increasingly despondent.

For some time past she had harboured doubts about Fanny Burney: 'I am sometimes ready to think her treacherous,' she wrote, 'but tis a sinful Thought & must not be indulged.' She would have been much readier to indulge it if she had known of the correspondence Fanny had been carrying on in secret with Queeney since their arrival in Bath and of how divided that showed her loyalties to be. 'The excuse of Roads, &c, makes me sad,' Fanny wrote towards the end of February: '– little as is my haste for his arrival; yet it seems to me such *coolness*; – did not my Father travel home through Italy in December: – he could not, perhaps, have travelled fast, but *not at all* – O I much doubt the *ardour* of the desire! And to have Her throw away an affection that absorbs every faculty upon an *Ingrate*!'[12]

Slowly, Piozzi began to stir himself. At the end of March he travelled to Quinzano to obtain proof of his birth and christening; in late May or early June he set out for England.

Hester was gradually recovering her capacity for enjoyment. 'Here is the most sudden and beautiful Spring ever seen after a dismal Winter,' she wrote: 'so may God grant me a renovation of Comfort after my many and sharp Afflictions.' She went up to London for a week, saw a good deal of Fanny Burney, made enquiries about possible governesses for her daughters and spent some time discussing marriage arrangements with an Italian violinist called Aloisio Borghi – 'who *loves* my Piozzi, *likes* my Conversation, and wishes to serve us sincerely'.

A second visit to London was necessary to continue the search for a companion and chaperone for her daughters. 'Chance threw in my way a very *elegant Woman of Fashion*,' she told Fanny. Her name was Jane Nicolson, a tall, fair-haired young woman in her late twenties:

> what was my Amazement when on nearer Intimacy I discovered this charming Creature was a friend to Borghi, well known to Piozzi, & perfectly acquainted with our Story before I told it ... This sweet Miss Nicholson will make all still more smooth to me, She is a well-wisher to the Cause, and will when the Girls are parted from me keep them from hating or trampling on the Memory of a Mother who adores them ...[13]

It was arranged that Miss Nicolson and the girls should spend the rest of the summer at Brighton. Hester accompanied them part of the way: 'My Daughters parted with me at last prettily enough *considering* (as the Phrase is) We shall perhaps be still better Friends apart than together.' Then she returned to Bath, dashing off letters each day to Queeney as she awaited Piozzi's arrival – 'My poor heart is in a State wholly undescribable; *saltando, balzando*,' she wrote.[14] Then, the following day, '2: July 1784. The happiest Day of my whole Life I think – Yes, *quite* the happiest; my Piozzi came home Yesterday & dined with me: but my Spirits were too much agitated, my Heart too much dilated, I was too painfully happy *then*, my Sensations are more quiet to day, & my Felicity less tumultuous.'

The day before Piozzi's arrival, Hester had written to each of her fellow-executors, informing them that her daughters had gone to Brighton with Miss Nicolson:

> I waited on them myself as far as Salisbury, Wilton &c. and offered my Service to attend them to the Seaside myself; but they preferred this Lady's Company to mine, having heard that Mr. Piozzi was coming back from Italy, and judging perhaps from our past Friendship & continued Correspondence, that his return would be succeeded by our Marriage.[15]

With Johnson's copy of this not entirely straightforward communication she sent a covering letter. 'Our Friendship demands somewhat more,' she wrote:

> it requires that I sh[d] beg your pardon for concealing from you a Connection which you must have heard of by many People, but I suppose never believed. Indeed, my dear Sir, it was concealed only to spare us both needless pain: I could not have borne to reject that Counsel it would have killed me to take; and I only tell it you now, because all is *irrevocably settled*, & out of your power to prevent. Give me leave however to say that the dread of your disapprobation has given me many an anxious moment, & tho' perhaps the most independent Woman in the World – I feel as if I was acting without a parent's Consent – till you write kindly to your faithful Servt.[16]

She sent a copy to Queeney in Brighton: 'I want you to like my Letter to Dr Johnson,' she wrote, 'which is equally firm & tender, and will I hope defend me from his undesired Company.' She also sent it to Fanny Burney: 'Thinking the mere circular Letter too dry for dear Dr. Johnson, I sent it him inclosed in this for a Softener and Sedative.'[17]

Johnson was not to be so easily sedated. He responded with a great cry of anger and pain:

> Madam:
>
> If I interpret your letter right, You are ignominiously married, if it is yet undone, let us once talk together. If You have abandoned your children and your religion, God forgive your wickedness; if you have

forfeited your Fame, and your country, may your folly do no further mischief.

If the last act is yet to do, I, who have loved you, esteemed you, reverenced you, and served you, I who long thought you the first of humankind, entreat that before your fate is irrevocable, I may once more see You. I was, I once was, Madam, most truly yours,

Sam. Johnson

I will come down if you permit it.[18]

Hester met Johnson's rancorous ferocity with a dignified reproof: 'I have this Morning received from you so rough a Letter,' she wrote, 'that I am forced to desire the conclusion of a Correspondence which I can bear to continue no longer.' And she entered a sturdy defence both of Piozzi and of her own reputation:

The Birth of my second Husband is not meaner than that of my first, his sentiments are not meaner, his Profession is not meaner ... The Religion to which he has been always a zealous Adherent, will I hope teach him to forgive Insults he has not deserved ... to hear that I have forfeited my Fame is indeed the greatest Insult I ever yet received, my Fame is as unsullied as Snow, or I should think it unworthy of him who must henceforward protect it ...

You have always commanded my Esteem, and long enjoyed the Fruits of a Friendship never infringed by one harsh Expression on my Part ... but till you have changed your Opinion of Mr. Piozzi – let us converse no more. God bless you![19]

Johnson realized that he had overstepped the mark. The tone of the letter he now wrote was much more generous:

What You have done, however I may lament it, I have no pretence to resent, as it has not been injurious to me. I therefore breathe out one sigh more of tenderness perhaps useless, but at least sincere ... And whatever I can contribute to your happiness, I am very ready to repay for that kindness which soothed twenty years of a life radically wretched.[20]

She sent him a tender and conciliatory reply a week later,[21] but he wrote no more. Some months later Fanny Burney called on him at Bolt

Court. She asked whether he ever heard from Hester: 'No,' cried he, 'nor write to her. I drive her quite from my mind. If I meet with one of her letters, I burn it instantly. I have burnt all I can find. I never speak of her, and I desire never to hear of her more.'[22]

It had been discovered, belatedly, that residence of twenty-six days was necessary in the parish where a marriage ceremony was to take place, and the priest at Bell Tree House, the Roman Catholic chapel in Bath, made difficulties about officiating. Hester and Piozzi accordingly travelled up to London and were married on 23 July in the chapel of the French ambassador. 'My dear Piozzi trembled so violently during the Ceremony, that I was half sorry for him; when however we were pronounced *one* in the name of the Holy Trinity & declared *inseparable* by Mortal Man, he recovered *his* Spirits to a degree of Transport.'[23]

Immediately afterwards they drove back to Bath, where they repeated their vows in St James's Anglican Church. 'Wish me Joy then generously and like a Friend,' Hester wrote to Fanny Burney, 'and be not more severe than our gracious Sovereign himself.'[24] It is not clear how the views of the sovereign came to Hester's ears, but she retailed them with some satisfaction to Queeney: 'Oh but the King! King George the third told his Librarian that Mrs. Thrale had made an *odd* Choice, but he doubted not it was a *wise* one, as She was one of the *best* as well as one of the most accomplish'd Women in England ...'[25]

Not all the monarch's subjects agreed. The bluestockings were particularly exercised. 'I bring in my verdict lunacy in this affair,' Mrs Montagu wrote to Mrs Vesey. 'I am heartily grieved for Miss Burney and Doctor Johnson, female delicacy, and male wisdom, will be much shocked.'[26] She wrote on the same day to Mrs Carter, informing her that Piozzi had bought an estate in Italy with Hester's money: 'There she will probably weep out the rest of her days for bitter must be her reflections when her passions subside and give place to reason.'[27]

Another bluestocking, Sarah Scott, who was Mrs Montagu's younger sister, had also been keeping her ear close to the ground. 'I gave you an erroneous account of Mrs. Thrale,' she confessed to Mrs. Vesey. 'Piozzi it seems was in holy orders. She gave him 2,000*l.* a year ago with which he went abroad, it is supposed to purchase a Dispensation, and is but lately returned.'[28]

Grub Street naturally felt it would be falling down on the job if it allowed the Piozzi nuptials to pass without comment. Some of their efforts were more amusing than others. One of the less offensive appeared in the *Morning Herald* on 10 August:

'Lines on a Late Piozzified Marriage'

Most writers agree, and I know it a truth,
We all love a frolic in days of our youth,
But what shall we say, when such grave ones engage
And frolic in love, in the days of old age.

The newly-weds spent a little more than two weeks in Bath before returning to London to continue preparations for an extended honeymoon tour of Europe. Piozzi had ordered a coach from Hatchet, the Long Acre coachbuilder – 'a magnificent carriage capable of containing every possible accommodation', Hester wrote;[29] these 'accommodations' included a small portable harpsichord that could be placed under one of the seats.

Hester's friendship with Fanny Burney did not survive her remarriage. Fanny had not felt able to offer congratulations on a match which she had consistently opposed, and Hester took offence: 'I not only thought you unkind, but I think so still,' she wrote. 'True Tenderness does not express herself ambiguously.'[30] The rift was never healed, in spite of a number of overtures by Fanny and her family. Hester was always notably unsentimental in such matters. 'Life is not long enough for *Darning* torne *Friendships*,' she wrote many years later; 'and they are always a Proof however neatly done, that the Substance is *worne out*.'[31]

By early September they were ready to depart. The arrangement with Miss Nicolson had not lasted. Cator and Crutchley had taken against her, possibly because of her sympathetic attitude to the marriage, and she had been dismissed. Queeney eventually went to stay with the Cators, Susanna and Sophia were sent to school in Kensington and Cecilia was boarded in Streatham, but these arrangements were not in place until after the Piozzis' departure. Susan and Sophy visited them before they left – 'we part in Peace, and Love, and Harmony', Hester wrote. Queeney was less affectionate – 'we parted coldly, not unkindly: I hope we sometime or another shall meet again, still better Friends'.

An uncaring and neglectful mother? In a later age Hester might well have fallen foul of some of the more intrusive legislation that would find its way on to the statute book in such areas as child care and health and safety. But then is not now. No such charge was ever levelled by any of her contemporaries, even by those most scandalized by her remarriage. Traditional upbringing was stern; beatings were commonplace; sentimentality and worship of the child would get the wind in their sails only in the full flush of romanticism, and that time was not yet.

Queeney's coldness did nothing to cloud Hester's happiness. 'I have now been six Weeks married,' she wrote in *Thraliana*, 'and enjoyed greater and longer Felicity than I ever yet experienced.'

The next morning Mr and Mrs Piozzi set out for Dover in their custom-built coach. They had with them a small dog, which they took it in turn to have on their lap.

~❧ 1784–1821 ❧~
Hester Piozzi

~🙖 19 🙖~

Second Marriage, First Honeymoon

HESTER carried the volumes of *Thraliana* with her, but she also made a start on a new journal in a large leather-covered notebook which bore the title 'Italian Journey': 'I am setting out for the Country which has produced so many People & Things of Consequence from the foundation of Rome to the present Moment that my heart swells with the Idea, and I long to leap across intermediate France.'[1]

There was no wind, and they had to endure the tedium of a twenty-hour crossing. In the custom house at Calais – 'that foe to friendly Intercourse!' – Hester fell foul of French import restrictions and several flannel petticoats which she had brought for winter wear were seized.[2]

Their route took them by way of Boulogne to Amiens and Chantilly. Hester admired the grapes clustering on the tops of apple trees and noted that the rage for Lombardy poplars was as great in France as in England. It was immensely hot; she rose early and ran into the garden of the inn to sit by the waterfalls.

Soon they were installed in an elegant and comfortable lodging in the Quartier d'Angleterre, close to where she had stayed on her first visit to Paris. But travelling was proving a more strenuous business than she remembered – 'my Bones ache with jumbling on the stony Roads, and I am truly shaken to pieces'.[3]

She was eager to revisit the collection at the Palais Royal, which she had so greatly admired nine years previously: 'I shall let loose however in this Journey the Fondness for Painting which I was forced to suppress while Dr Johnson lived with me, & ridiculed my Taste of an Art his own Imperfect Sight hindered him from enjoying.'[4]

They did not go to the theatre during their stay in Paris – 'my Husband has no Taste for publick Shows I think' – but that did not inhibit Hester from having a view about a piece which had enjoyed a *succès de scandale* since its first public performance five months previously:

> They are all wild about a wretched comedy called *Figaro* full of such
> Wit as we were fond of in Charles the Second's reign; all Indecent
> Merriment, & gross Immorality mixed however with Satire as if Sir
> George Etherage & Johnny Gay had clubbed their Ingenuity to divert
> & corrupt their Auditors ... The Authour is Mr de Beaumarchais, &
> possesses so entirely the favour of the Public, that the Women weare
> Fans with Verses on 'em out of his Comedy as they did by the Beggars
> Opera in London 40 years ago.[5]

What escaped Hester was that the excited crowds that were flocking to
the Théatre de l'Odéon saw in Figaro the defender of liberty against
despotism and of equality against privilege – which was why the censors
had kept it off the boards for three years and why Louis XVI did not
wish Marie Antoinette to see it.

Hester owed her remarkably detailed knowledge of *The Marriage* to a
Count Turconi, whom she described in her brisk way as 'a hump-backed
Italian Nobleman'. Turconi had entertained them to dinner on Queeney's
birthday, made Hester 'a hundred Compliments' and generously offered
them the use of his country seat outside Milan. The Piozzis also met the
Italian dramatist Carlo Goldoni, now well into his eighties and at work
on his memoirs. 'We struck Fire vastly well,' Hester wrote, although
she found him extremely garrulous:

> The Italians talk a great deal, but he out talked 'em all: the Venetians are
> it seems eminent for their Eloquence even among their Countrymen,
> who seem to me all violent, all rapid, all fiery, to an Excess difficult for
> an English Mind to conceive, or an English Tongue to express – but one
> must see more before one pronounces on national Manners.

On to Lyons, where Hester had hoped there might be some mail
from home. 'No letters from Miss Thrale tho',' she complained, adding, in a tart non-sequitur, '– had she seen the Civilities paid us by the
Duke & Duchess of Cumberland, she would perhaps have thought some
Expressions of Tenderness from herself less disgraceful.' They met many
friends of Piozzi's there, and were lavishly entertained:

Such was the hospitality I have here been witness to, and such the luxuries of the Lyonnois at table, that I counted six and thirty dishes where we dined, and twenty-four where we supped. Every thing was served up in silver at both places, and all was uniformly magnificent, except the linen, which might have been finer ... I never received more kindness for my own part in any fortnight of my life ...[6]

'I should have liked to pass through Switzerland, the Derbyshire of Europe,' Hester wrote, 'but I am told the season is too far advanced.'[7] They passed instead through Savoy, where Hester experienced 'a sensation of fulness never experienced before, a satisfaction that there is something great to be seen on earth':

In these prospects, colouring is carried to its utmost point of perfection, particularly at the time I found it, variegated with golden touches of autumnal tints; immense cascades mean time bursting from naked mountains on the one side; cultivated fields, rich with vineyards, on the other ...

She caught a glimpse of a chamois, and spoke with a man who had just killed five bears that had been making depredations on his pastures: 'We looked on him with reverence, as a monster-tamer of antiquity, Hercules or Cadmus,' she wrote; 'we approached his cottage, and found the felons nailed against the wall, like foxes heads or spread kites in England.'[8]

By mid-October they were in Turin. 'My Health and Spirits mend every day thank God,' Hester wrote, 'and my husband's Kindness makes me amends for all I suffered to obtain him.'[9] She was writing to Samuel Lysons, a young man she had met in Bath earlier in the year. A talented artist and illustrator destined for the law, Lysons was one of the few people in England she corresponded with in the early years of her marriage to Piozzi.[10] She saw no reason to pretend that relations with her daughters were ideal: 'I correspond constantly and copiously with such of my Daughters as are willing to answer my Letters, and I have at last received one cold scrap from the eldest, which I instantly and tenderly replied to.'[11]

She was enchanted by all she saw in Turin. 'Model of Elegance, exact Turin! where Italian hospitality first consoled, and Italian arts repaid, the fatigues of my journey.'[12] The Prince della Cisterna called on them and handed her the key of his box at the Opera: 'Here's Honour and Glory for you!'[13]

At Genoa they stayed for a week at the country seat of the British consul. 'I fondled the Daughter of the house,' Hester wrote, '(because I had not my own Dears to fondle).' She also took a hand in the girl's moral education: 'I took Voltaire's Works out of her Closet, and charged her never more to look in such Books as She confessed had often poysoned her Peace, & put her on a Train of Thinking which as I told her could end only in Offence to God, and Sorrow to herself –'

Hester's own peace was also briefly poisoned at Genoa:

Yesterday I received a Letter from M[r] Baretti, full of the most flagrant and bitter Insults concerning my late Marriage with M[r] Piozzi ... he accuses *me* of Murder & Fornication in the grossest Terms ... he heard perhaps that Johnson had written me a *rough* Letter, and thought he would write me a *brutal* one ... Good Lord have mercy upon me! but I think the Man is fit for Bedlam.

In early November the Piozzis arrived in Milan. 'My heart is happy, & my Bones begin to get Flesh upon them,' Hester wrote in *Thraliana*, but her thoughts turned quite often to her life as it used to be: 'I have got D[r] Johnson's Picture here, & expect Miss Thrale's with Impatience. I do love them dearly still, as ill as they have used me, & always shall. Poor Johnson did not ever *mean* to use me ill, he only grew upon Indulgence, till Patience could endure no further.'

In a letter to Lysons in early December, she urged him not to neglect Johnson: 'You will never see any other Mortal either so wise or so good.'[14] Her injunction came too late. Even as she wrote, her old friend lay dying. His mind retained all its sharpness almost to the last – and his tongue its acerbity. He was very weak and helpless towards the end, and a man from the neighbourhood was paid half a crown a night to sit up with him. Johnson was asked the next morning how he liked his attendant. 'Not at all, Sir,' he replied, 'the fellow's an ideot; he is as aukward as a turn-spit when first put into the wheel, and as sleepy as a dormouse.'[15] He died quietly on 13 December, at about seven o'clock in the evening, and was buried in Westminster Abbey a week later.

1. Hester by Richard Cosway. A miniature painted when she was a young married woman.

2. Henry Thrale. A print by Edward Scriven of the portrait painted by Joshua Reynolds in 1777. Boswell described him as 'tall, well-proportioned, and stately'. The picture hung in the library at Streatham.

3. Hester and Queeney, painted by Reynolds in 1777–78. Hester was very proud of her eldest daughter. Queeney, she once wrote, 'looked so elegant among the Dowdies I have seen, that I restrain my Vanity with the utmost Difficulty'.

4. The house at Streatham, variously known as Streatham Place, Streatham Park and Thrale Place. An engraving by William Ellis published in 1792.

5. The Southwark Macaroni. A satirical print depicting Thrale published in 1772

6. Sophia Streatfeild. 'Take away her Greek,' Johnson said, 'and she is ignorant as a butterfly.'

7. The Brewery at Southwark. An engraving dating from 1829.

that Art — Hester is well & beautiful, Susan is a pretty Girl as need be; Cecilia is much liked, & Harriett quite a Cherubim. Sophy is much the plainest as to Countenance but her Form is most complete and her Temper enchanting. Hester & Susan are touchy, moody, & capricious.

Mr Thrale is once more happy in his Mind, & at leisure to be so in Love with S: S: that it is comical. She is a charming young Creature every body must love her. We have her, & F. Brown & Murphy, Seward & the D'Avenant & Johnson here, besides Tom Cotton & occasional Comers in. I think I am again Pregnant, I think I am; then let us conclude the Old Year with humble Thanks to Almighty God for all his Mercies thro' Jesus Christ our Lord, & most of all for the Health of my dear Children, & for the Boon I hope I have obtained by my Prayers & Tears —— That I shall never follow any more of my Offspring to the Grave — Amen Lord Jesus! Amen! if so — I will not fret about this Rival this S.S. no I won't

8. The last page of *The Family Book*. 'I will not fret about this Rival, his S.S. no I won't,' Hester wrote. But the evidence is that she fretted quite considerably.

9. Johnson as he entered his seventies. James Barry painted the picture between 1778–80 as a study for the Society of Arts mural, *The Distribution of Premiums*.

10. Dating from 1773, Reynolds's portrait of Giuseppe Baretti was one of the earlier pictures painted for the library at Streatham. 'Baretti,' Hester wrote, 'was the only Man I never could make attached to me by trying to do so.'

11. Fanny Burney. 'The most *Consequential* Day I have spent since my Birth,' she told her sister when she was invited to Streatham for the first time after the success of her novel *Evelina*. But Hester's marriage to Piozzi brought their friendship to an end.

12. Piozzi. A portrait painted during his extended honeymoon with Hester in Italy.

13. Hester was still in mourning for her first husband when she sat to Robert Edge Pine in the summer of 1781. He painted her in widow's weeds; she wears a miniature of Thrale on a pendant. 'Not like, I think,' wrote Fanny Burney, 'but a mighty elegant portrait.'

14. Mrs Montagu, 'Queen of the Blues'. 'Her form,' Hannah More wrote, '(for she has no body) delicate even to fragility; her countenance the most animated in the world; the sprightly vivacity of fifteen, with the judgement and experience of a Nestor.'

15. Sarah Siddons. Hester did not initially join in the general adulation when the greatest English actress of the eighteenth century first conquered the town in 1782 – 'Why,' she declared, 'this a leaden goddess we are all worshipping!' She was soon won over, however. A warm friendship developed between them, and 'Dear, lovely Siddons' could do no wrong.

16. James Boswell. His acquaintance with Hester could never ripen into friendship; what began as polite rivalry would eventually make them bitter enemies.

17. *Signor Piozzi ravishing Mrs Thrale* by Samuel Collings.
Johnson looks on disapprovingly; the menacing figure in the
doorway with a drayman's whip is presumably Thrale. 'Your
Music has ravished me, and your Instrument is large and
delightful,' Hester declares. 'And me like de Muzeek of your
Guineas,' he replies.

18. Rowlandson's *Bozzy and Piozzi: A Town Eclogue*, shows
Hester and Boswell trading insults. Sir John Hawkins,
Johnson's literary executor, makes a poor job of holding
the ring.

19. George Dance's pencil drawing of Hester dates from 1793. 'Mr.
Dance the Profilist is making a Collection of celebrated Heads,' she
wrote to her friend Mrs Pennington; 'I have sate, but nobody knows
me they say, so I am to sit again.'

20. 'Your precious Portrait is my only true & comfortable Companion at ev'ry Meal,' Hester wrote to Conway in 1821. A gift from the young actor, the picture was one of her most treasured possessions.

21. The only known portrait of Salusbury.

22. Salusbury's wife Harriet was an accomplished watercolourist. She presented Hester with this view of Brynbella shortly after her marriage in 1814.

23. Hester in old age. An engraving published in 1820 on the occasion of what she persisted in regarding as her eightieth birthday.

Hester figured prominently in much of the chatter engendered in London by Johnson's death. Foremost among the chatterers was Mrs Montagu: 'I am afraid Mrs Thrales imprudent marriage shortened his life,' she wrote.[16] She also gave currency to some of the more nonsensical gossip circulating in fashionable society about the Piozzis' new life in Italy: 'It is said accounts are now come in that she is confined in a convent in Milan. Her Husband says she is insane ...'[17] This particular *canard* did the rounds for some time and eventually, suitably embellished, found its way into the public prints. '*Signora Piozzi*, late Mrs Thrale,' the *Morning Post* told its readers, 'is at present immured in Italy by her husband, who having possessed himself of about 30,000£ of her cash, is striving, with use of it, to dissipate the remains of her affection.'[18]

Mail from London would normally take something like three weeks to reach Milan, and Hester cannot therefore have heard of Johnson's death until early in the New Year. She confined herself to a brief undated entry in *Thraliana* – 'Oh poor Dr Johnson!!!' – but his death gave her much to think about. By the end of January she knew from Lysons that the field of would-be biographers was already a crowded one. 'No less than Six persons have engaged to write his life,' he wrote – in addition to Boswell they included Sir John Hawkins, whom Johnson had appointed his literary executor, the bookseller Tom Davies and Dr Andrew Kippis, the minister of the Presbyterian congregation in Princes Street, Westminster, regarded by many as the leading biographer of the day.[19]

This placed Hester in a quandary. She recalled how she used to tell Johnson in jest that his biographers would be at a loss concerning some orange peel he used to keep in his pocket. 'Rescue me out of all their hands, My dear, & do it *yourself*,' came the reply. Piozzi now urged her to do just that, but eager as she was to do so, she hesitated: 'I think my Anecdotes too few, & am afraid of saucy Answers if I send to England for others – the saucy Answers *I* should disregard, but my heart is made vulnerable by my late Marriage, and I am certain that to spite me, they would insult my Husband.'

She decided to enlist the help of Lysons: 'I wish you would get *me* all the Anecdotes you can of the *early* and *late* Parts of a Life, the *middle* of which no one knows as well as myself ... Do not however proclaim either your Intentions or my own, which are scarcely settled yet ...'[20]

Meanwhile, life in Milan was proving very agreeable:

Here am I! With my Husband & his Friends passing my Birthday (after all past Anguish,) in the Bosom of Friendship, Love, & Good humour: with my health recover'd as far as it was recoverable; & even my Looks repaired by growing fat, so as to content my ever partial, my ever-kind Companion ... God has heard my Prayers, and enabled me to make happy the most amiable of his Sex. – Was I to wish for more, I might provoke Providence to lessen the Enjoyments I possess; let me suppress all inordinate Desire of a Child by the Man I so love – *that* only could add to my happiness.

The days that brought mail from home could still temporarily blight that happiness. 'I see the English Newspapers are full of gross Insolence to me,' she wrote at the end of January: 'Mr Boswell, (who I plainly see is the Authour) should let the Dead escape from his Malice at least. I feel more shocked at the Insults offered to Mr Thrale's Memory, that at those cast on Mr Piozzi's Person.'

The passage in question had appeared in a review of a *Biographical Sketch* of Johnson by Thomas Tyers: 'Poor Thrale studied an Art of which he loved the Produce, and to which he expired a Martyr ... Little did he think his Intemperance would have proved an Introduction to his Wife's Disgrace, by eventually raising an obscure and penniless Fiddler into sudden Wealth and awkward Notoriety.'[21]

This was certainly pretty poisonous stuff, but Hester was mistaken in ascribing it to Boswell – it was in fact the work of the literary editor and scholar George Steevens, a friend of Johnson's who made something of a profession of being obnoxious.

Lysons was not able to come up with very much, but Hester continued to badger him and others whose friendship she had retained: Sir Lucas Pepys – 'I keep no Corner of my heart from him,' she told Lysons – and the antiquary Michael Lort, who had been a notably idle incumbent of the Regius Chair of Greek at Cambridge – 'he is a Man whose esteem I am proud of'.[22]

Her letters from Johnson were in a bank vault in London; she was reluctant to allow anyone access to these, but equally hesitant about having them shipped to Italy. But she pressed on, even though she was not yet entirely clear about what precisely she was aiming to produce. 'My Book is getting forward,' she wrote to Lysons towards the end of March, 'and will run well enough among the rest; the letters I have of Dr. Johnson's are two hundred at least I dare say, and some of those from Skie are delightful: they will carry my little Volume upon their Back quite easily.' Pepys had advised her not simply to let friends know what she intended, but to let it be known more widely; 'You will therefore see it proclaimed in all the papers, I hope,' she told Lysons.[23]

~≈ ≈~

She was beginning to feel curiously at home in Milan. At a play performed by the monks of St Victor, she thought the friars resembled Welsh farmers – 'with straight Hair, grave Deportment, & Countenances full of intelligent Slyness & arch Penetration', she wrote: 'The Country People hereabouts all seem to have been transplanted from Merioneth, or Caernarvonshire; they like my Person, & fancy me something approaching to pretty – I dare say it is because I have the Welch Physiognomy so strongly marked in my Face & Features.'

The theatres remained dark during Lent – 'but every great house has a Weekly Concert, that we may not lose *all* Diversion', she told Queeney: 'that at Casa Piozzi is on a Monday'.[24] The unexpected entrance one Monday of Cardinal Angelo Durini, titular archbishop of Ancira, greatly impressed their guests – 'who all stood up astonished', she told Lysons, 'while he kissed Mr. Piozzi, and blessed him in a manner equally venerable and graceful'. The Cardinal, who wrote poetry and was a well-known patron of the arts, turned up again at breakfast time the next morning, invited them to spend a week at his palace and left Hester with his blessing – 'tho' my Faith was not totally the same as his own he said, but that I had given an Example at Milan of that Morality which it was the Business of all Religions to enforce'.[25]

It was not, by Hester's account, an example much followed by the local sisterhood: 'The grossness of the Women's Behaviour both high & low shocks my English Maid & myself excessively,' she wrote in *Thraliana*. She was also shocked, at a performance of Metastasio's *La Passione di Gesù Cristo*, to find the part of St Peter taken by a castrato, and she wrote at length in *Thraliana* about 'the depraved Morals & confined Ideas of

Religion reigning in this Country'. In a culture where marriage was widely regarded not as a sacrament but as a social convenience, she was particularly disturbed by the institution of the *cavaliere servente* – 'a settled Scheme of Vice, a System of Adultery', as she called it:

> I asked a very pretty Woman how *She* managed among them? ... 'What can I do replied She but follow the Crowd? My Husband will not go out into Company with me, nor sit an Hour Tête a Tête with his Wife – *lest People should laugh at him*: I would not else attach myself to other Men, none of which I ever should prefer to *him*; but what must I do? it is the Custom to have a Cavalier Servente, & when a Woman has no Money of her own, & dares not ask her Husband – why he lends me you see, & so the Connection draws closer ...

Hester was appalled: 'Good God interrupted I, what does the Confessor say to all this? is he contented too as well as the Husband? Not very *contented* replied the Lady, who spoke all the Time what they call *strett Milanes* – but he is already *assuefàà*.'

Having dealt with Milanese high life, she turned a disapproving eye on the lower orders. 'No Footman here is unmarried,' she continued, 'and no Footman's Wife other than a professed Harlot: which the Man recommends to his Master, & hopes for the Preference ... Well! These are the Vices of hot Countries – & as such let 'em pass ...'

Something which she found less easy to let pass was the flow of expletives with which the Milanese larded their speech – 'the Intercalations of these People are more horrible than Xian ears can endure with Patience: Blood of God! Body of the Lord Jesus! Father of Christ! Are the common Exclamations even of the Clergy.' She was also beginning to tire of the relentless efforts by many of the clergy to persuade her of the error of her Anglican ways:

> I have always been partial to *Peter* as elder Brother, tho' I acknowledge him neither for Padre nor Monsignore: but I shall now be a follower of dear *Martin* as much from preference as from being born and educated where his Heaven-dictated Reformation is the established Church. These People by treating my notions as Heretical, have made me a *Protestant* in despite of myself ... Could I but separate my Piozzi from these *Goats*!

Early in April they set out for Venice. 'Well! Now I *did* prepare to be happy,' Hester wrote; 'I had my husband to *myself* in the *Coach* which I began to consider as my favourite *home*; no Women to be jealous of, no Priests to be afraid of.'[26]

Leaving the coach at Padua, they completed their journey by barge down the Brenta – 'and Mr Piozzi's Forte piano never sounded so sweet I think as on that Water', she told Queeney.[27] Their lodgings were on the Grand Canal, and in the five weeks they spent in La Serenissima, Hester found more to write about than she had done in five months in Milan.

She enthused to Queeney about the castrato Luigi Marchesi – 'you may be sure that he will astonish England as he has done Italy, who crowd about him as if he was a Thing drop'd from the Moon'.[28] She told Lysons that she would not bore him with descriptions that he could find in any *Venezia illustrata*, but confessed that the general effect had about it something inexpressibly striking: 'From a Tower that I mounted yesterday the little Islands scattered about the Lagoon looked like Faery Cities formed in Water by the Touch of some Magical Wand.'[29]

Venice did not agree with her, for all that: 'I have never been the least indisposed since I left Dover till now.'[30] Perhaps it was all the coffee she drank: 'I have already had seven cups today, and feel frighted lest we should some of us be killed with so strange an abuse of it.'[31] They stayed to witness the Festa de la Sensa, the ancient festival held each Ascension Day to celebrate the republic's ancient dominion of the sea. Then they returned to Padua to retrieve their coach and cross the Apennines.

꙳ ꙳

She was not particularly taken with Bologna: 'This fat Bologna has a tristful look, from the numberless priests, friars, and women all dressed in black, who fill the streets, and stop on a sudden to pray, when I see nothing done to call forth immediate addresses to Heaven.'[32]

Some of the goods displayed for sale in the town were a stern test of character:

> I fear it requires much self-denial in an Englishwoman not to long at
> least for the fine crapes, tiffanies, &c. which might here be bought I
> know not how cheap, and would make one *so* happy in London or at

Bath. But these Customhouse officers! these *rats de cave*, as the French comically call them, will not let a ribbon pass.[33]

The university won her approval – it had, she discovered, 'been particularly civil to women; many very learned ladies of France and Germany have been and are still members of it'[34] – but she was not sorry when the time came to move on: 'I am glad, however, that we shall now be soon released from this upon the whole disagreeable town, where there is the best possible food for body and mind; but where the inhabitants seem to think only of the next world, and do little to amuse those who have not yet quite done with this.'[35]

They had arranged to stay in Florence at an inn kept by an English couple called Meghitt. Hester and her maid whiled away the long last miles in the coach in pleasurable anticipation of eating and sleeping once more 'all in the English way' as the maid put it.

Piozzi received an early visit from an old friend called Manucci – the same Count Manucci whom the Thrales had met in Paris ten years previously and who had later been their guest at Streatham. Hester described the occasion many years later for the benefit of Piozzi's nephew:

> The good natured Nobleman ... having been told that Piozzi was come
> to Florence with a rich Wife from England &c. made haste to wait on
> him – Wish him Joy &c. – They talked awhile in my Dressing Room
> whilst I was in an Inner Apartment. The Count asking particularly
> for *Mrs. Thrale* and whether She was married again or no, Your Uncle
> evading his Questions: till I rushed in: and Manucci exclaimed in French
> – Ah Madame! Quel coup de Theatre!![36]

Within days of arriving in Florence, Hester wrote to the bookseller and publisher Thomas Cadell: 'As you were at once the Bookseller and Friend of Doctor Johnson, who always spoke of your Character in the kindest Terms, I could wish you likewise to be the Publisher of some Anecdotes concerning the last twenty Years of his Life, collected by me during the many Days I had Opportunity to spend in his instructive Company ...'[37]

She explained that she would be abroad for at least another year, mentioned her collection of letters in England and expressed the wish to delay publication until she was able to assemble enough material to make two or three volumes; she nevertheless hoped that her intentions might be advertised immediately.

Cadell sent a prompt reply – 'I shall esteem it an honour to be engaged in any way most agreeable to you.' But he stressed the desirability of early publication, and suggested that the letters might be sent to her in Italy.[38] Hester was not prepared to agree to this, proposing instead that they should proceed initially with the Anecdotes as a separate exercise – 'if that should be the Case I am willing to double my diligence, and we may publish the two other Volumes when I get back'.[39] There for the moment the matter rested.

The summer heat was becoming troublesome: 'I drop one Petticoat after another like the Rope dancers,' Hester told Queeney.[40] Relations between them remained scratchy. A letter which she found waiting on her arrival in Florence she had thought delightful – had read it 'with infinite Pleasure'.[41] But Queeney's next letter prompted a totally different response:

> Surprise and Concern are my present Reasons for writing; what can be become of dear Susan & Sophy? Who never write themselves, & of whom you say not a Syllable ... why do you my sweetest Girl, write so coldly and so queerly? & why do you hinder your Sisters from writing at all? Is it because I am married to Mʳ Piozzi?[42]

She was writing the day after their first wedding anniversary, which they had celebrated with a dinner and concert; rather pathetically, she was at pains to impress on Queeney what a splendid and successful occasion it had been:

> The Prince Corsini, & his Brother the Cardinal honoured us with their Company, & paid Mr Piozzi every possible attention. Lord & Lady Cowper who are reckon'd difficult to many, are kind to us ... when every body expresses a just sense of Mr Piozzi's merit, and seeing his Value pays him a proper Respect – why should you be the only Person to stand out?[43]

Answer came there none. They both knew the question had been rhetorical. Queeney's infrequent letters remained as cold and formal and unforgiving as they had been before. It was two months before Hester wrote to her again.

~ ❧ ~

To her Johnson Anecdotes Hester now briefly added a new if rather less serious literary interest. 'I have been playing the Baby,' she told Lysons at the end of July: 'and writing Nonsense to divert our English friends here, who do the same thing themselves; and swear they will print the Collection ... Mr. Parsons, and Mr. Merry are exceeding clever, so is Mr. Greathead, and we have no Critics to maul us, so we laugh in Peace.'[44]

In their pleasant hotel overlooking the Arno the Piozzis had quickly found themselves drawn into a small, somewhat curious coterie. Bertie Greatheed, a wealthy young Warwickshire landowner, was a nephew of the Duke of Ancaster. He had been educated at the University of Göttingen, and for the last three years had been travelling in France, Switzerland and Italy with his wife Ann, with whom Hester rapidly struck up a warm friendship. Greatheed held radical views and wrote not very good poetry; the previous year he had become a member of a group calling themselves *gli Oʒiosi* – the Idlers – and some of his pieces had appeared in their privately printed collection called *The Arno Miscellany*.

Another contributor to this *Miscellany*, and a better poet than Greatheed, was Robert Merry, a grandson of the former Lord Chief Justice Sir John Willes. An Old Harrovian who had left Cambridge without a degree, he too had been travelling on the Continent for several years – a brief career in the Horse Guards had come to an end when his taste for high living and heavy gambling obliged him to sell out his commission. It was common knowledge among the English colony that he was carrying on an affair with Lady Cowper – who was also the mistress of the Grand Duke Leopold.

A third member of the group was already known to the Piozzis – they had encountered William Parsons – 'of the Sussex Militia' – both in Milan and Venice. Parsons would later define his ambition as 'merely to be classed among the mob of gentlemen who wrote with ease'. He certainly did that, although his facility was not matched by anything more substantial.

That could not be said of the Italian writers with whom they mixed. There was nothing of the dilettante about Lorenzo Pignotti, a physician as well as a man of letters, and well known as a fabulist; Ippolito Pindemonte's reputation as a poet was also well established. During that summer of 1785 Hester joined these new English and Italian friends in putting together what became known as *The Florence Miscellany*, which was printed privately later in the year. Hester was not a major contributor – of the seventy-nine poems in the collection only nine are hers, and in the introduction, which her friends persuaded her to write, she made no great claims for them: 'We wrote them to divert ourselves, and to say kind things of each other; we collected them that our reciprocal expressions of kindness might not be lost, and we printed them because we had no reason to be ashamed of our mutual partiality.'[45]

Her fellow-contributors, English and Italian, had more serious intentions, not all of them literary, and it is difficult to believe that someone whose antennae were as sharply attuned as Hester's could be unaware of this. Two years previously the Habsburg Grand Duke Leopold had decreed that the Accademia della Crusca, an important repository of national culture which had been founded in 1582 to maintain the purity of the language, should be merged with two other Florentine institutions. This had been widely resented as a manifestation of Austrian despotic rule, and much of what the patriotically minded Italian poets who contributed to the *Miscellany* wrote there – poems in Italian and French, translations from Petrarch and Dante, imitations of classical Italian forms such as the elegy and the sonnet – can be seen as a defiant assertion of Italian identity. Even though the book was printed privately, blanks were left on some pages. The full sense of the verses could only be read by the insertion of a number of slips, which were printed even more privately and allowed only a limited circulation. Hester cannot have been unaware that this was a device to avoid the unwelcome attentions of Austrian censorship.

During her stay in Florence she met the celebrated Maria Maddalena Morelli. Courtesan, salonnière, *poetessa improvvisatrice*, this daughter of a violinist from Pistoia, briefly married to a Spanish officer, had been controversially crowned as poet laureate on the Capitoline Hill in 1776 and taken the name of Corilla Olimpica. She had entertained the youthful Mozart, enchanted Casanova (although he thought she had a squint), served as official poet to the grand duchy of Tuscany and the imperial court at Vienna. Hester approved of what she saw and heard of her: 'Corilla, without pretensions either to immaculate character (in the English sense), deep erudition, or high birth, which an Italian esteems above all earthly things, has so made her way in the world, that all the nobility of both sexes crowd to her house; that no Prince passes through Florence without waiting on Corilla ...'[46]

In recent years Hester has attracted the attention of a number of feminist writers. One of them takes the above passage to mean that she identified with the famous *improuvisatrice* because she saw striking similarities between Corilla's situation and her own:

> What impressed Piozzi the most about Corilla was how her genius and enthusiasm seemed to triumph over social prejudice ... In addition to her ambiguous social status, Corilla ... was also rumored to have abandoned her husband and children for her career ... Witnessing Corilla's tremendous success in the public sphere – overcoming many of the kinds of obstacles that Piozzi herself faced – was an incentive for Piozzi to begin writing professionally.[47]

Whether Hester's words can bear that weight of speculative scrutiny is doubtful, although her renewed enthusiasm for writing is obvious enough from her work on the Anecdotes and her travel journal and what she referred to dismissively as the 'nonsense' written to divert her new English friends. Her own most interesting contribution to *The Florence Miscellany* was the one entitled 'To Wm Parsons Esqr' – not because it is a particularly good poem, but because of what it reveals about her state of mind and how she now saw herself:

> Thus Fancy was stagnant I honestly own,
>> But I call'd that stagnation repose.
> Now wak'd by my Country-men's voice once again
>> To enjoyment of pleasures long past,
> Her powers elastick the soul shall regain,
>> And recalls her original taste.

What these rather prosaic lines suggest is that in the free space afforded by her marriage to Piozzi Hester was beginning to rediscover not just her voice but also herself. She was coming alive again, beginning to feel for the first time since her youth that she was an autonomous person – not an experience that all that many eighteenth-century women were able to enjoy.

❧ 20 ❧
The Day War Broke Out

PIOZZI found the company of their English friends at Florence so congenial that he would have stayed longer, but early in September Hester went down with a fever, and it was decided to seek a change of air.[1] They went first to 'the sweet Republick of Lucca', as she called it. 'It lies in the middle of Tuscany, like a Parenthesis in a Sentence,' she told Queeney, 'but I sh^d be sorry if it were *left out*.'[2]

There had been a slight thaw in relations with 'the Misses': 'I received your letter at Florence, & one from each of your Sisters, in Consequence of my Lamentations − they protest it was nobody's fault but their own that I remained 12 Weeks without hearing of 'em, and when you say it was not yours, I hold myself bound to believe it.'[3]

She was writing on Queeney's twenty-first birthday: 'It is now more than time to wish you Joy, which I do from the bottom of my heart,' she wrote, although by the time she had filled her paper, a slightly acerbic note of defiance crept in: 'I have scarcely left Room I see for the Initials of a Name which you profess so much to *abhor*, but of which the Possession is regarded as an honour by/Your H: L: P.'[4]

She was enchanted by everything they saw during their brief stay in Lucca. Much of the charm lay in the Lilliputian scale of the place:

> Their armoury is the prettiest plaything I ever yet saw, neatly kept, and capable of furnishing twenty-five thousand men with arms. Their revenues are about equal to the Duke of Bedford's, I believe, eighty or eighty-five thousand pounds sterling a year; every spot of ground belonging to these people being cultivated to the highest pitch of perfection that agriculture, or rather gardening (for one cannot call these enclosures fields), will admit …[5]

Later in her travels, her enthusiasm for Lucca and the Lucchesi would earn her a memorable snub:

I once mentioned this place with warm expectations of delight, to a Milanese lady of extensive knowledge, and every elegant accomplishment worthy of her high birth ... 'Why yes,' said she, 'if you would find out the place where common sense stagnates, and every topic of conversation dwindles and perishes away by too frequent or too unskilful touching and handling, you must go to Lucca.'[6]

Hester, the veteran of many bruising verbal encounters at Streatham, was not to be easily put down: 'Had she been battered through the various societies of London and Paris for eighteen or twenty years together, she would have loved Lucca better, and despised it less.'[7]

Pisa was memorable, less for its conventional tourist attractions than for the 'Gnats, Bugs, Spiders, Scorpions, & Serpents which keep one in perpetual Terror'[8] although she thought the 116 camels kept by the Grand Duke in his park 'pretty creatures' and the marbles in the baptistery superior to those of Florence.

On to Leghorn – 'a Place of no small entertainment in its way', she wrote to Lysons:

Like Noah's Ark, it contains all manner of Creatures, but *un*like that here are all Religions, Dresses, Customs and Languages. Armenian Christians, Greek Church, Turks, Jews, – and even the poor *Church of England* are all established at Leghorn; shame to our Ministers that keep no Chapel in any other Town of Italy, while the Merchants and Captains of Ships who report hither, have provided decent Conveniences at their own Expense for serving God in their own way.[9]

Here Hester finished work on the Anecdotes. A copyist was found to produce a clean manuscript and Piozzi busied himself looking for a trustworthy sea captain to carry it to England. 'Cadell will have his little book to print in Spring, or even earlier if he chuses,' Hester told Lysons, and she allowed herself a thrust at the London gossips – 'People will see by this, that I am *alive and at Liberty*.'[10]

She was still not wholly restored, and as there were no facilities for bathing at Leghorn, Piozzi now took a small house at Bagni di Pisa, known to the Romans and the Etruscans before them for its waters. 'I enjoyed the finest Cold Bath in all Europe,' Hester told Queeney, '& try'd to swim every Day, but never could attain to the power.'[11]

It was very delightful to me to have a Cottage in the Country after running from one great Town to another for so many long Months ... I therefore call'd the Chickens under my Window, tasted the new Wine in the Barrel, caress'd the meek Oxen wch do all the Work in these Countries, and felt a Sensation of Pleasure so unaffected, that I soon began to teize Mr Piozzi to stay here till quite dead Winter at least ...

The idyll was short-lived. Piozzi developed a putrid throat infection; Arcadia, as Hester quickly discovered, is ill-equipped to deal with sickness: 'Here was no help to be got ... except the useless conversation of a medical gentleman whose accent and language might have pleased a disengaged mind, but had little chance to tranquillize an affrighted one.'[12]

To make matters worse, the house was full of vermin. Hester remembered when they had first taken the house her maid jumping on to a kitchen chair while a local lad disposed of seventeen scorpions; now suspicion centred on Piozzi's mattress, and she and the maid ripped it open: 'Nondescripts in nastiness I believe they are, like maggots with horns and tails; such a race as I never saw or heard of, and as would have disgusted Mr. Leeuenhoeck himself.'[13] A terrifying thunderstorm three nights later, accompanied by earth tremors, settled the matter. Hester packed up the coach and they set off for Siena.

❧ ☙

The town was clean and airy. On a nearby hillside stood a suppressed convent, where the land was being sold off for a song. Briefly, Hester began to dream: — 'With half a word's persuasion I should fix for life here. The air is so pure, the language so pleasing, the place so inviting; — *but we drive on.*'[14]

To Rome — and to a measure of disappointment: 'You ask me if Rome answers my Expectations,' she wrote to Samuel Lysons:

I answer *No* as far as relates to the external Appearance of ancient Buildings which Piranesi gives one so pompous an Idea of ... you know the Art and the *Artifices* of Drawing well enough to be sensible that keeping down mean Objects is tantamount to exalting great ones — and he judiciously leads one's Attention away from the disgusting Sight of that Wretchedness and dirt, which is here every where mingled with the Monuments of ancient Magnificence ... they are all like Rembrant's Pictures composed of the strongest Lights and darkest Shadows possible ...[15]

The surrounding countryside also failed to impress: 'We found it arid, desolate, harsh, and so full of noxious Vapour, (tho' they told us the Malaria was at an End;) that I saw a Flame look nearly globular in the Night; and smelt a Stink which as Trunculo says, *much offended my kingly Nostrils* —'[16]

Early in December they moved on to Naples. They had seen Vesuvius thirty miles off; now, from her bedroom window Hester had a grandstand view of the mountain — 'which called me the first night twenty times away from sleep and supper'.[17] Naples quickly came to rival Venice in her affections, and they spent a happy three months there.

Christmas came and went with no confirmation of the safe arrival of the manuscript of the Anecdotes, and Hester became anxious. The *Piedmont*, the ship to which it had been consigned, had reached Dover at the end of November, but Cadell did not receive it until two months later. 'I began to fear it would never arrive,' Lysons told Hester, 'and the Papers began to be witty about it.'[18] The *Morning Herald*'s idea of wit was, as always, rather special: 'Report frequently whispered that a connubial knot would be tied between Mrs. Thrale and Dr. Johnson: — that event never took place, and yet Mrs. Piozzi and the Doctor, it seems, are shortly to be *pressed* in the same *sheets*.'[19]

Hester finally heard from Cadell in the middle of February. He offered either to buy the property outright, or to divide the profits: 'The latter mode I have followed with Mr. Gibbon, Bishop Lowth, Adam Smith ... and many other of my capital Authors.' Hester opted for a division of profits, and enclosed a list of those who were to have complimentary copies; the twenty names included those of Mrs Montagu — and of Charles Jackson, the Post Office official who had come to her aid three years previously when she had forgotten to pre-pay one of her letters to Piozzi.[20]

Meanwhile, Boswell's *Journal of a Tour to the Hebrides with Samuel Johnson, LL.D.* had been published. Reynolds was lavish in his praise;

Wilkes told the author he thought much of the detail 'a horrid deal of trash'; Burke did not take kindly to learning that Johnson thought little of his sense of humour. Horace Walpole pronounced the book 'the story of a mountebank and his zany'; [21]Sir Alexander Macdonald of Skye was so incensed that he threatened violence: 'Damn me if with a heavier weapon I do not tickle your ass's head, till the blood flows down and the bare skull reeks horridly where I have ripped off the hide.'[22] Boswell, highly alarmed, consulted a friend about how to handle duelling pistols.

The verbatim recording of actual conversations was novel and controversial – some thought scandalous. The book sold well; a first impression of a thousand was exhausted in less than three weeks. Hester soon heard from several correspondents that one short passage in it had given grave offence to Mrs Montagu. It related to her *Essay on Shakespeare*, and Boswell recorded Johnson as saying, 'Reynolds is fond of her book, and I wonder at it; for neither I, nor Beauclerk, nor Mrs. Thrale, could get through it.'

We now know from Boswell's correspondence that he had dithered over whether to include Hester's name, striking it out in the manuscript, reinstating it in proof and then removing it a second time. Eventually he was swayed by the opinion of his friend John Courtenay, a witty Irishman who was the MP for Tamworth. Courtenay argued, possibly maliciously, that Boswell had no right to deprive Hester of the honour of having been quoted as an authority on taste by Johnson. The passage was restored.

A misunderstanding with the Queen of the Blues was the last thing Hester needed, but she found herself in a cleft stick. Friends in England urged her to make an immediate denial, but that was something she could not in conscience do – she had, after all, read Boswell's Journal in manuscript ten years previously and raised no concerns.[23] She decided that her best tactic was to huff and to puff; the letters she fired off to Sir Lucas Pepys, Michael Lort and Lysons were an object lesson in obfuscation:

> Mr Boswell did me very great Injustice in saying I could not get
> through Mrs Montagu's performance, for the Elegance and Erudition
> of which I hope I am not wholly without Taste or Cognizance; and as
> for Dr Johnson, he had to my certain Knowledge a true Respect for her

abilities, and a very great regard & Esteem for her general Character. It is hard upon me that I am not at home to defend myself, but Mr Boswell is well qualified to be witty on the *Dead* and the *Distant*.[24]

She also wrote to Mrs Montagu herself, and succeeded, rather against the odds, in mollifying her. It was a lucky escape – which she owed in part to Boswell's fondness for the bottle. Mrs Montagu told her in reply that she would have been mortified if Hester had found her essay dull, but that her mortification was mitigated by the 'very moderate degree of credit' she gave to everything Boswell had attributed to Johnson: 'Poor man! he is so often in that condition in which men are said to see double, the hearing in the same circumstances may probably be no less disorder'd.'[25]

Malone appears to have had a sight of what Hester had written; it was, he told Boswell 'a most flaming letter of panegyrick', and Mrs Montagu considered it the greatest honour ever done to her: 'So the ladies, you see, will be bien d'accord when Mrs P. arrives ...'[26]

Which is more than Boswell himself and Hester would be. Glancing through the proof pages of *Anecdotes*, young Samuel Lyson's eye was caught by a passage that set alarm bells ringing. Hester had not forgotten the offensive letter about herself and Thrale which had appeared the previous year in the *St James's Chronicle*. She remained convinced it had been written by Boswell, and had decided to retaliate. She inserted in the manuscript of *Anecdotes* the Latin epitaph which Johnson had composed for his dead friend. 'Such was the Character of Henry Thrale, when given by Samuel Johnson,' she wrote: 'but what must be the Character of him, who ... dares even to deride the sacred Dead, and represent the greatest writer of our Age and Nation, as a wretched Retailer of Latin Scraps, gather'd up to ridicule an Infirmity caused by his best Friend's Illness and ending in his Death!'

It is a measure of her fury that she reaches, in conclusion, for words from *Titus Andronicus*, Shakespeare's sensational and blood-soaked drama of double revenge:

Oft have I digg'd up dead Men from their Graves,
And set them upright at their dear Friends' Doors,
Even when their sorrow almost was forgot;

And on their Skins as on the Bark of Trees,
Have with my Knife carved in Roman Letters,
Let not your Sorrows die tho' I be dead.[27]

Lysons was appalled. Not without difficulty, he managed to dig out
back copies of the newspaper and satisfy himself that in this matter at
least, Boswell was as innocent as a lamb. There was no time to refer to
Hester. He consulted Pepys, Lort and the Bishop of Peterborough, all
of whom agreed that the passage should be removed. The gap left on
the page was filled by a translation of the epitaph hastily undertaken by
Lort. This meant the cancellation of an entire sheet, and publication was
delayed by several weeks.

Hester saw at once that she had been saved from huge embarrassment
and was suitably grateful. 'Oh pray thank them all, and say how much
I love them, how much I feel obliged to them,' she wrote to Lysons.
'Why my Shoulders would have ached for a Year with the Blows I
should have received!'[28]

Having saved her bacon by a judicious deletion, Hester's friends then
did her an injury by an officious insertion. Instead of leaving well alone
on the Mrs Montagu front, they decided on Pepys's initiative to paint the
lily, and cobbled together from her various letters to them a postscript to
the *Anecdotes* purporting to have been written by Hester in Naples at the
beginning of February: 'Since the foregoing went to the press, having
seen a passage from Mr. Boswell's Tour to the Hebrides, in which it is
said, that *I could not get through Mrs. Montague's Essay on Shakespeare*, I
do not delay a moment to declare, that, on the contrary, I have always
commended it myself, and heard it commended by every one else ...'[29]

Boswell was out of London when the *Anecdotes* appeared. He had recently, in spite of an almost total ignorance of English law, been admitted
to the Bar and joined the Northern Circuit; the book was dispatched to
him in Lancaster, where he was attending the Lent Assizes, dancing with
the ladies and taking medicine for his seventeenth bout of gonorrhoea.
'She is a little artful impudent malignant Devil,' he wrote to Malone the
next day. 'It is *clear* that she *means* to bite me as much as she can ...
I must have the patience of *Job* to bear the Book of *Esther*. But I shall
trim her *recitativo* and all her *airs*.'[30]

The ill-judged postscript impugned Boswell's veracity. Rivalry now gave way to enmity. The opening shots had been fired in a famous literary war. It would be protracted and bitter. And it would add greatly to the gaiety of the nation.

21

'Our Magic Lanthorn of Perpetual Motion'

THE BOOK sold like hot cakes. The first edition was exhausted in a matter of hours. When the King sent out for it at ten o'clock that night Cadell was obliged to beg one from a friend: the sovereign sat up all night reading it.

A second edition was announced on 5 April, a third the following week and a fourth early in May. Several newspapers printed extensive extracts, and there was much critical attention in the magazines. The *English Review* was complimentary: 'Of the *nine lives* of this giant in learning, as he is called, which have been promised to the public, Mrs. Piozzi's is the fifth that has been published, and in our judgment the best.'[1] The *Gentleman's Magazine* thought the writing showed some signs of haste, but conceded that the book was 'evidently the production of a vigorous and cultivated understanding'.[2]

The small worlds of fashionable and literary London were more hostile. Dr Burney, writing anonymously in the *Monthly Review*, criticized Hester for exposing Johnson's failings 'to the curious, yet fastidious eye of the Public'.[3] The *Anecdotes* were not well received in bluestocking circles. Hannah More, in a letter to her sister, deplored 'this new-fashioned biography'; it seemed, she declared, 'to value itself upon perpetuating every thing that is injurious and detracting'.[4] Horace Walpole, writing to Mann in Florence, was savage: 'I am lamentably disappointed ... I had conceived a favourable opinion of her capacity – but this new book is wretched – a high-varnished preface to a heap of rubbish in a very vulgar style, and too void of method even for such a farrago.'[5]

The print shops, he wrote, were full of satiric prints of both Hester and Boswell: 'A Dr Woolcot ... has published a burlesque eclogue, in which Boswell and the Signora are the interlocutors, and all the absurdest passages in the works of both are ridiculed.'[6]

Wolcot, who wrote under the name of Peter Pindar, was a quarrelsome Devon man who had qualified in medicine at Aberdeen and had later, for purely mercenary reasons, taken holy orders. He had already fingered Boswell in February with *A Poetical and Congratulatory Epistle to James Boswell Esq. On his Journal of a Tour to the Hebrides with the Celebrated Doctor Johnson*:

> O Boswell, Bozzy, Bruce, whate'er thy name,
> Thou mighty shark for anecdote and fame;
> Thou jackall, leading lion Johnson forth
> To eat M'Pherson midst his native North ...[7]

Pindar now followed this with *Bozzy and Piozzi: or The British Biographers. A Town Eclogue*, in which Sir John Hawkins, Johnson's official biographer, is cast as umpire in a mock contest between the two rivals:

> A Scotchman one, and one a London dame;
> *That*, by th'emphatic JOHNSON, christen'd BOZZY;
> *This*, by the Bishop's license, DAME PIOZZI;
> Whose widow'd name, by topers lov'd, was THRALE,
> Bright in the annals of election ale ...

They briskly trade anecdotes for several pages like a pair of modern base-line tennis players, but then tempers begin to fray and they become abusive:

> MADAM PIOZZI
> *Who* told of Mistress Montagu the lie –
> So palpable a falsehood? – Bozzy fie!
> BOZZY
> *Who*, madd'ning with an anecdotic itch,
> Declar'd that JOHNSON called his mother *b-tch*!

It is, of course, this 'anecdotic itch', deplored by so many of their contemporaries, which commends both Hester and Boswell to a modern readership. Credit for devising the technique is normally accorded to Boswell, but here is Hester employing it in 1786, independently of Boswell's recently published *Tour* and a good five years before the appearance of his *Life*. When she referred to her book, no doubt defensively, as 'a piece of motley Mosaic' and 'an ill-strung selection' she was being unnecessarily modest.

Much of the criticism – and abuse – she encountered came from former friends and acquaintances who saw her as betraying Johnson. 'It was not handsome,' declared the bluestocking Hester Chapone (whom Johnson had much admired), 'to repeat things of him which she must know would mightily detract from the hyperbolical praise she affects to give him. I do not love such inconsistencies.'

The inconsistencies, however, the contradictions, were Johnson's, not Hester's. For all its shortcomings, *Anecdotes* is a very honest book. It paints a darker picture of Johnson, certainly, than Boswell would do, but in many ways a more perceptive and less sentimental one. 'Mine is a mere candle-light picture of his latter days,' she writes self-deprecatingly, 'where every thing falls in dark shadow except the face, the index of the mind.' But it is because, unlike Boswell, she shared something of Johnson's toughness of mind that her portrait of him tells us more of the man that the innocently admiring Boswell was able to. The American scholar William McCarthy, in his illuminating study of Hester as a writer, concedes Boswell's superior literary skill, but regards *Anecdotes* as psychologically more penetrating: 'As interpretation of Johnson it is pretty clearly superior to Boswell, largely because it mounts resistance to him at points where Boswell cheerfully embraces or blandly steps aside.'[8]

It is many years now since Katharine Balderston pointed out how radically, in the *Anecdotes*, Hester departed from the text of *Thraliana*, the raw material on which it was principally based: 'She expanded, contracted, telescoped, confused the time sequence, changed general statements into specific ones and specific into general, invented occasions for conversations floating in a vacuum, transferred speeches from one person to another, and repeatedly gave in the form of direct quotation from Johnson statements for which there is no hint at all in her diary.'[9]

In some cases this was due to carelessness, in others to the conditions in which she wrote. For the most part, however, it is clear she was deliberately shaping her material for artistic effect – very much as Boswell would do in the *Life*.

In the spring of 1786, however, Boswell's immediate concern was to strike back at Hester. He was not only indignant about her postscript – he was also offended at how little he himself featured in *Anecdotes*. There was, for instance, no mention of him in her account of a discussion with Johnson about who his future biographer might be, and he did not figure in the list of friends – Reynolds, Burke, Murphy – for whom Hester said he had the greatest affection.

From Lancaster he sent Malone a draft of a statement to be sent to the newspapers. Malone and Courtenay persuaded him to tone it down – to refer to Hester as 'Mrs' rather than 'Signora' and to remove phrases like 'the oblique stiletto' and 'the great Brewer's Wife in all the pomp of Wealth'. It appeared in a number of papers, and also in the third edition of the *Tour* later in the year. Boswell, reluctant to see some of his best thrusts disallowed, characteristically incorporated them in a sequence of doggerel, which he called *Piozzian Rhimes*. He submitted it, without telling his friends, to *The London Chronicle* – where it appeared in the same issue as his signed statement.[10]

The Piozzis, meanwhile, had returned to Rome and Hester resumed what she called 'my old Employment of seeing Palaces & Churches; examining Statues, Pictures &c'. She marvelled at the scale of St Peter's – 'Warwick castle would be contained in its middle *aisle*' – and admired its freedom from decoration. She could not, however, prevail on the Vatican librarian to show her any books or manuscripts except some love-letters from Henry VIII to Anne Boleyn: 'which he said were the most likely to interest *me*: they were very gross and indecent ones to be sure; so I felt offended, and went away, in a very ill humour, to see Castle St. Angelo ...'[11]

Hester did not, she announced in *Thraliana*, find quite as much 'rank Idolatry' in Italy as she had expected: '– the worst Shock was given to my Blood by seeing the Pope kiss St Peter's Statue on the Foot with fervent Devotion; and that not quite for Ceremony's Sake I think, but *tout de bon* as the French say – what could the Man think he was doing?'

She formed a favourable impression of Pius VI, for all that:

No prince can less affect state, nor no clergyman can less adopt hypocritical behaviour. The Pope powders his hair like any other of the Cardinals, and is, it seems, the first who has ever done so. When he takes the air it is in a fashionable carriage, with a few, a very few guards on horseback, and is by no means desirous of making himself a shew ... The money he has laid out on the conveniences of the Vatican, the desire he feels of reforming a police much in want of reformation, joined to an immaculate character for private virtue and an elegant taste for the fine arts, must make every one wish for a long continuance of his health and dignity ...[12]

In the middle of April the Piozzis headed once more for Venice. Their splendid coach had taken a lot of punishment since leaving London, and finally, high in the Umbrian Apennines, it came to grief. By great good fortune two English travellers appeared on the scene, and with their help it was possible to continue. Their rescuers were a young Berkshire landowner called Charles Shard and a clergyman called Leonard Chappelow, a keen naturalist and amateur poet who would become a lifelong friend.

When it turned out that the coach could not be properly repaired at Bologna, Shard and Chappelow gallantly insisted on giving up their post-chaise to Hester and her maid while they followed behind in the damaged coach with Piozzi. They had barely made a start, however, when the post-chaise lost a rear wheel and the women had to rejoin the men in the coach as it crept towards Ferrara.

It was only when they reached Venice that Hester got news of how *Anecdotes* had been received, and it would be July, when they had moved on to the Italian lakes, before she received a copy. The book's commercial success was confirmed in a letter from Cadell – the sale, he wrote, had been 'more rapid than any Book I ever published'.[13] Hester was jubilant: 'Nothing can exceed my Sense of the Public's generous Approbation,' she told Lysons, 'for Curiosity might easily have sold the first Edition of any Book about Dr. Johnson, but the other Copies must have owed their reception to kinder Motives.'[14]

Mrs Montagu's verdict was particularly gratifying: 'Your Anecdotes of Dr. Johnson my dear Madam are very different from Mr. Boswell's. Yours do honour to the subject, the Writer, and harm to no one; He indeed tells the World that *Mr. Boswell* thought highly of Dr. Johnson, but all he relates of him tends to diminish the Worlds esteem of his friend ...'[15]

George James, an eccentric and uneven portrait painter to whom Hester had sat in Bath, expressed himself rather more racily. 'Every body goes on admiring you and your pretty book,' he told her: '– and says how nicely You have cooked your Ragout of Elephant – that you have given all the Flavor of the Substance – without the Rankness and Heaviness of the Beast – and done with such pure clean Hands too – whereas Boswell has *pawed* his Scotch Collops about so – that they stink of himself to such a degree that they turn every body's stomach.'[16]

The Piozzis had bought a Canaletto in Rome – a view of St Mark's Square – and now in Venice they acquired several more. They also found an original sketch of Guido Reni's *Aurora*, and bought paintings by Domenichino, Bassano, Amigoni and Salviati. 'Living at Venice is like a Journey to the Moon somehow,' Hester wrote to Queeney, 'and a sweet Planet it is!'[17] but her thoughts were plainly turning more insistently towards England: 'These amiable Venetians seek to detain me among *them* by paying Mr. Piozzi every possible, every respectful Attention; it is certainly the *only* way for *any* Set of People to detain me; but my Desire of seeing him caressed by my own Country will draw me away from this in a short Time now.'[18]

By early June the heat was intolerable. Hester became unwell. She was uncertain whether to blame the stench from the canals or an over-indulgence in anchovies; she was terrified of going down with a putrid fever. They moved on to Padua, where their coach, now fully road-worthy, was returned to them: 'the man says it will now carry us safely round the world if we please'. They contented themselves with moving in easy stages to Milan – 'dear Milan, where we have cool apartments and warm friends'.

Since leaving there the previous year she had recorded her impressions only in her travel journal. She now once more began to make entries in *Thraliana*, reflecting on her experiences of the past fifteen months. When she left London she had been confident she was setting off for 'the finest Country in the World'. Her view was now more nuanced: 'Oh if one could live alone in Italy – who w^d ever leave it? Not H: L: P. God knows. But these Priests do so buz about my Husband, and so try to make him hate me for a Heretic – it is very dangerous to stay.'

The extent to which she was preoccupied by what she had under-

taken to write next emerges from a letter to Lysons: 'If I really had the
Assurance to fancy that I or my Book were seriously *wanted* and *called
for*, either by Country, or Countrymen; Mr. Piozzi would willingly go
home with me this Autumn, and it might yet be published (I mean the
letters from Johnson) before the World was quite wearied from variety
of Publications ...'[19]

To escape the worst of the summer heat they took a villa near Varese
– 'with a full Table of Friends never fewer than 15 at a Time to dinner'
she told Queeney; 'who laughed, and made Rhymes to every Toast,
with a degree of Humour and *Good* Humour, wholly uncompatible with
the more reserved Manners of English Society'.[20] They also spent some
days in the Italian lakes, where Count Borromeo put his vast palazzo on
l'Isola Bella at their disposal:

> Guess you if we made Lago Maggiore resound? having one Bargefull
> of Friends, another with a band of nine performers the best in Italy,
> to divert us and them upon the Water. And of an Evening when by
> Moonlight we returned home to our Calypso-like Dominion, & the
> Fragrance of the Orange Grove met us by the Time we were half way
> thither, I really fancied myself in a sort of Mahomet's Paradise ...[21]

Hester learned while she was in Milan of Fanny Burney's appointment as second Keeper of the Robes to the Queen. This prompted an
intriguing entry in *Thraliana*, which demonstrated the ambivalence of
Hester's feelings towards both Italy and England:

> What a glorious Country is ours! where Talents & Conduct are suf-
> ficient to draw mean Birth & original Poverty out of the Shades of Life,
> & set their Merit to ripen in the sun. No such Hopes, no such Pos-
> sibilities in these wretched nations; where pride & prejudice, Pedigree
> & Pomp chain up every liberal Idea, and keep the Mind enslaved ...
> Yet I do not now as formerly, feel a fondness for England: Esteem and
> Preference over evry other Place is all that's left. I shall be half sorry in
> earnest to leave these rascally Italians – prying, pilfering, and paltry as
> they are ...

Her reluctance to return home is partly explained by the unwelcome
tittle-tattle that continued to appear in the press. 'We hear that Madam

Piozzi, with her *cara sposa*, will soon return to England,' the *General Evening Post* had informed its readers on 4 May: '– when she intends to have him naturalized, and take the name of her ancestors; how far the name and family of Salusbury may be enriched or ennobled by such an alliance and union, she certainly can best explain to the public'.

For his part, her *caro sposo* could apparently not get back to England soon enough, as she made plain in a gossipy letter to Chappelow: 'Mr. Piozzi in the midst of Luxuries cheaply purchased, and Prospects of Health and Abundance; sighs for a clean Floor, a neat Breakfast, Tables that will stand fast, and Windows that will open and shut ... and to find himself in the neighbourhood of Cavendish Square where he used to visit a certain Lady who is now his Affectionate Wife ...'[22]

Hester's daughters continued to be indifferent correspondents, and whenever friends were returning to England she begged them to visit the girls. Chappelow and Shard obligingly called at Mrs Murray's school in Kensington to do so: 'The Eyes of the Youngest sparkled with joy when we mentioned you,' Chappelow reported. 'They are 2 very different characters, different are their features, but both I am sure Good Girls, with good hearts.'[23]

It was for Susanna's benefit, while she was in Milan, that Hester wrote a short treatise expounding Anglican doctrine – although it may also in part have been a reaction to what she saw as the importunate attempts by various Italian clerics to convert her. She described it as being 'somewhat upon the Plan of Abbé Fleury's historical Cathechism'.[24] It was intended, she wrote, 'to shew the Necessity of that Union between Religion & Morality, which Bigots & Scepticks are alike diligent to destroy'.

By September Hester and Piozzi were ready to turn for home:

Well! I am now about to close my Residence in Italy, at the same Moment as I close my 4th Vol: of *Thraliana*. and must confess that no Days since I began it, have been so happily spent by me as those I have past in this beautiful Country ... Five Years have elapsed since this last Vol: was begun; the next if I live to open & begin it at all, will be opened & begun in old England – I wish Mr Piozzi may like that Country to fix in, because it is *my* Country: & the Religion & Government is such as I approve ...

> Farewell fair Italy say I,
> Whilst other Modes & other Climes we try.

~❧ ❧~

Those other climes further to the north proved less congenial. The Tyrolean Alps failed to impress – 'you find Italian Sublimity sinking off into German Minuteness', she informed Queeney; 'no Cascades or Mountains like those of Savoy'.[25] She had a good word for Innsbruck, however – 'it is no small comfort to find one's self once more waited on by clean looking females'.[26]

In Munich the Piozzis discovered they were staying in the same inn as the marchese Trotti, a young Italian nobleman they had met in Paris two years previously, and he and Hester immediately rushed out to look at pictures: 'Brughel,' she wrote, 'seems to pique himself on putting on a 15 Inch Board more than Claude or Poussin would have found sufficient for six large Pictures of four Feet each.'[27]

A detour allowed her to conduct some gratifying genealogical research:

> Saltsburg was pleasant to me from the Ideas it excited: myself the last Heir of its old Princes! ... the Benedictine Convent on the Hill contains the Sepulchre of my Ancestor, & the Records of the Town prove the migration of his youngest Son Adam to Great Britain with William the Norman who conquer'd it, and gave him Lands to settle on – in the year 1070.

By late October they were in Vienna. Passing her travels in review after her return to England, Hester wrote that she had disliked both the town and the people, but that is not altogether the impression given by her letters, or by the account of the imperial capital she subsequently published in *Observations*. 'I have an agreable Intimacy here with two ladies in whose House the famous Metastasio lived and died,' she told Chappelow, 'and they tell me pretty Anecdotes about him.'[28]

The two ladies were Marianna von Martines and her sister Antonia, the daughters of a papal official. Marianna was highly regarded both as a composer and a performer. She had been taught as a child by Haydn and often played pianoforte duets with Mozart, who was a frequent guest at her parties. The young Irish singer Michael Kelly was also in Vienna at this time – six months previously he had taken the roles of Don Curzio and Don Basilio when *The Marriage of Figaro* had its première at the Burgtheater. Kelly was often at Marianna's house, and there is a passage in his *Reminiscences*, which makes tantalizing – and exasperating – reading:

> At one of her parties I had the pleasure to be introduced to Mrs. Piozzi ... there appeared to me a great similarity in the manners of these two gifted women, who conversed with all around them without pedantry or affectation. It was certainly an epoch, not to be forgotten, to have had the good fortune, on the same evening, to be in the company with the favourites of Metastasio and Dr. Johnson; and last, not least, with Mozart himself. [29]

It was not, unfortunately, an evening which made any impression on Hester. Her marriage to Piozzi had not sparked any real interest in serious music; there is, alas, no mention of Mozart in either her travel journal or her correspondence.

She was impressed by how well acquainted 'these dear Germans' were with English literature – they were already familiar with the work of William Cowper, whose long poem *The Task* had achieved critical and popular success in England the previous year. And she was gratified to discover that her reputation as an author had gone before her: 'my Book about Dr. Johnson is in ev'ry Body's hands at Munich & Vienna', she reported proudly, '& they are translating it away – as if it was the finest Thing in the World'.[30]

The Piozzis had once more fallen foul of import restrictions. 'The Custom House Officers are a terrible Scourge to us,' Hester complained to Queeney: 'We have been completely stript here not only *to* the Skin, but *of* the Skin; for they have seized all my Furs ... If I were to buy good Sables they would perhaps tear 'em off my back, & burn 'em at Dover; you can't conceive what a perpetual Worry those vexatious Animals are to People that travel –'[31]

They had been on the road long enough. 'It would be a comfortable Thing to sit quiet and stir the Fire,' she wrote to Lysons, 'a Pleasure we never enjoy for the Stoves here warm, but do not divert one ...'[32]

Dresden, however, diverted her very considerably – once they got there. 'The road from Prague hither is too bad to think on,' she wrote, 'while nothing literally impels one forward except the impossibility of going back.'[33] Near Lobositz, the site of Frederick the Great's first victory over the Austrians in the Seven Years' War, they were obliged to go forward on foot:

> Our coach was held up every step of the journey by men's hands, while we walked at the bottom about seven miles by the river's side ... As soon as we arrived, tired and hungry, at Aussig, we put our shattered coach on board a bark, and floated her down to Dresden; whither we drove forward in the little carts of the country, called chaises, but very rough and with no springs, as our very old-fashioned curricles were about the year 1750.[34]

The coach was in such a state that they had to stay a month in Dresden 'to careen & refit' as Hester put it. She spent three hours each day at the celebrated Old Masters Picture Gallery, its collection spectacularly enriched by the purchase in 1746 of a hundred masterpieces from the Duke of Modena: 'I have now seen all the Correggios the World has to shew,' she told Queeney, 'and am never weary of admiring such proofs of human Genius.'[35]

It was the one German city that completely won her heart. 'Was I sixty Years old I should like to settle at Dresden,' she later wrote in *Thraliana*. Although she was dismissive of much of what she had seen since leaving Italy, she was deeply impressed by the accomplishments of her own sex in the German-speaking countries through which they passed: 'The Ladies all speak many Languages, and value themselves on literary Accomplishments which they display in a Manner that our English Gentlemen would hardly suffer from their Wives and Daughters lest Pedantry should be the Cry ... but here the Musick is learned, the Painting deeply studied, the Workmanship finished to the utmost nicety, and the Conversation correct to minuteness.'[36]

She did not take kindly to an officious letter she received about this time from Sir Lucas Pepys, warning her that not everyone was likely to welcome her home with open arms. She would be well advised, he suggested, to take her younger daughters to live with her in a house in

London – or 'perhaps you will find it much more Comfortable to go First to Bath, & not settle in London for the first 6 Weeks or Two Months'. A further suggestion was received even more frostily:

It has been said that an Italian Name makes an awkward Jumble with the Smiths, Thomsons, Jacksons & all the Usual Names of John Bull's Children, & that You being aware of this have Thought of getting your Name changed to your Mothers Name of Salisbury; an Excellent Idea & Mr. Cater could get it done for you before you arrive.[37]

Hester's reply, if she returned one, has not survived, and there was a coolness between them for some months after the Piozzis' return to England: 'Sir Lucas Pepys has been but a half-faced Friend at last,' she noted in *Thraliana*.

The Prussian capital held little appeal. 'Berlin is a dismal Place,' Hester wrote to Queeney, 'the Coaches and even the Churches are all in Mourning for the late King.'[38] Frederick the Great had died in August, and in the garrison church at Potsdam Hester placed a hand on the unadorned silver coffin in which his body lay. 'A Propos to Heroes, I have seen Sans Soucy,' she wrote to Queeney: '– have heard his Memory curs'd by the Saxons, sung by the Italians, and adored by his own Servants & Subjects. I have stood on the Fields which he drench'd with the Blood of Enemies that applauded his Courage, & of Friends that willingly spilt it in his Company.'[39]

They hurried on now through north Germany – 'Brunswick, Hanover, & Osnaburgh, form a Climax of Misery; God keep one from ever seeing those Places again.' By early February they were in Brussels, and here they found a batch of letters from England and numbers of familiar friendly faces – Robert Merry, whom they had last seen in Florence and the Whalleys among them:

Ay Brussells was something like indeed … The Duke & Dutchess of Arenberg quite adore us, Lord & Lady Torington professed themselves jealous of our fondness for *them*: the *Princesse Gouvernante* invited our further residence in her City, & asked me if *nothing* she could do, would induce us to stay? – the Archdutchesses learned English out of my Book (Johnson's Anecdotes) – and Prince Albert would not have Mr Piozzi out of his Sight.

Brussels was one of the last scenes exhibited by what Hester described in a letter to Chappelow as 'our magic Lanthorn of perpetual Motion'.[40] The travellers arrived back in London on 10 March, and put up at the Hotel Royal in Pall Mall. Hester dashed off a note to Queeney, who had engaged a lady companion and was now living in Lower Grosvenor Street:

> My dear Hester will see by the Date of this that we are arrived, but upon my Honour to the very worst Hotel I have been at in any Capital City of Europe; and we have seen above a dozen: I told one of the Women so two Minutes ago, & She replied *Indeed my Lady and everybody that comes to the House says the same Thing.*[41]

Streatham was still let. The next morning – it was a Sunday – the search began for a furnished house in town.

22

Pen and Ink Conversation

ONE OF Hester's first visitors at the Royal Hotel was Cadell, who came with an offer of £500 for the completed copy of her *Johnson Letters*. She accepted his terms, speedily retrieved Johnson's correspondence from the bank and enlisted the help of Lysons to push the work of editing forward as quickly as possible.

Her return had not gone unremarked. 'The lady's visit is highly seasonable at this time,' declared the *Morning Herald*, 'as she may survey her learned friend *Dr Johnson laid in state* by that grave undertaker Sir John Hawkins.'[1] Hawkins's recently published *Life* was generally thought to make turgid reading and was much pilloried in the press, but Boswell regarded it as a threat. (He was also furious at being mentioned only once, and then as 'Mr. Boswell, a native of Scotland'.) He hastened to assure the public that his own work was 'in great Forwardness', which was a considerable exaggeration.

Hester's bargain with Cadell was quickly public knowledge. One paper, noting that Hawkins's 600 pages were to be followed by Boswell's 'gleanings' and Hester's 'gatherings', suggested that the Johnson industry must be running short of its essential raw material: 'The Doctor's bones must be acknowledged to be the bones of a giant, or there would be poor picking, after their having furnished *Caledonian Haggis*, and a dish of *Italian Macaroni*, besides slices innumerable cut off from the body [by] Magazine mongers, anecdote merchants and rhyme stringers.'[2]

Hester was undeterred, and from the end of the month was able to work in more comfortable surroundings. 'Mrs *Piozzi* has taken a house in Hanover-square,' the *World* reported on 27 March. 'Mrs *Piozzi*, if not again admitted to the *Blue-Stockings*, will probably establish a similar meeting of her own. The intervals of Conversation to be relieved by Music.'[3] Towards the end of the season, Hester was ready to make just such a test of her social acceptability. 'Mrs. Piozzi and her *caro sposo*

seem very happy here at a good house in Hanover Square,' her friend
Michael Lort wrote to Bishop Percy; 'I am invited to a rout next week,
the first I believe she has attempted, and then will be seen who of her
old acquaintance continue such.'⁴

The evening was a success. 'We had a very fine Assembly,' Hester
wrote in *Thraliana*, 'in my best Days I never had finer; there were near a
Hundred people in the Rooms which were besides much admired.' There
was one notable absentee: 'Miss Thrale & her Companion were asked
& refused: – pass'd my Door, & looked insultingly up at the Window,
as they went to Mortellari's Benefit. Was that worth the while?'⁵

Relations with the 'Miss Thrales' – Queeney, Susan and Sophy were
now twenty-two, sixteen and fifteen respectively – had been cool since
Hester's return: 'As for seeing our Daughters why we never do see them
here, any more than when the Sea parted us – or hardly,' she wrote in
Thraliana. 'The eldest has called twice, and we have called twice on Susan
and Sophy, who refused dining here at our Invitation' – 'perhaps,' she
added sourly, 'from an idea that *they* are superior to the petty Sovereigns
of Germany.'

Little Cecilia, who was now ten, was at a fashionable boarding school
kept by the Misses Stevenson in Queen Square, Bloomsbury⁶ – Queeney
had taken it upon herself in their mother's absence to move her there
from Streatham on the ground that she was not making sufficient progress. Hester now heard something concerning Thrale's cousin, Henry
Smith, which understandably enraged her: 'I find Mʳ Smith one of our
Daughters's Guardians told that poor Baby Cecilia a fine staring Tale,
how my Husband locked me up at Milan & fed me on Bread & Water, to
make the Child hate Mr Piozzi: Good God! What infamous Proceeding
was this?'

Piozzi was captivated by Cecilia, but Hester was not entirely convinced
by her show of affection: 'while she is at School [she] will honour us with
her Visits no doubt, but her Tenderness will end there ... her Spirit is
the same to that of her Sisters', she wrote: 'Well! never mind, my heart
is vastly more impenetrable to their unmerited Cruelty than it was when
last in England. Let them look to their Affairs, & I shall look to mine.'

Hester's heart was more penetrable than she knew, however. Before
the summer was out Cecilia would become the unwitting cause of a

bitter confrontation with Queeney, which would blight relations between mother and daughter for several years.

❧

With the honourable exception of Murphy, most of the old Streatham set – the Burkes, the Burneys, Reynolds and his sister – had remained coldly aloof since the Piozzis' return. Hester was unperturbed: 'This is a pretty House here in Hanover Square, and we live very comfortably ... Dr. Lort is attentive and kind, so is Mr Selwin ... Mrs Byron seems glad of my Return, but hates my Husband cordially, Perkins's respectful Behaviour surprizes & pleases me much ...'

Cadell had emphasized the importance of surfing the continuing wave of interest in Johnson and argued strongly for publication of the *Letters* before the summer holidays. This seems a tight deadline even by eighteenth-century standards, but Hester and Lysons had made a determined attack on the material even before she had moved in to Hanover Square. There was an early setback when Queeney showed herself hostile to the whole enterprise and refused to agree to the inclusion of the letters Johnson had written to her, of which there were more than thirty. Hester harboured dark suspicions: 'perhaps she keeps them for some professed enemy of mine: it would be droll enough if after refusing then to her Mother She should give them to Sir John Hawkins as a Reward for having insulted me with every unprovoked, & undeserved Abuse ...'

Outwardly she was philosophical: 'We will do without, and very well too,' she told Lysons.[7] Within a matter of weeks they had accumulated some 400 of Johnson's letters. Some were too short, or dealt in too great detail with business matters. Others Hester decided to suppress for different reasons – the strange letter Johnson wrote to her in French in 1773, for instance, and his first intemperate response to the news of her remarriage. She would claim in her preface that Johnson's letters remained 'just as he wrote them' but that is not strictly the case. Some fifty of the letters she printed were abridged, and in a dozen or so she made verbal changes.

None of this represents a major departure from general eighteenth-century practice.[8] One particular piece of doctoring stands out from the rest, however. 'Do you read Boswel's Journals?' Johnson had enquired in a letter from Lichfield in the summer of 1775. 'Boswel's narrative is very natural, and therefore very entertaining,' he continued. 'He is a very fine fellow.'[9] Here was conclusive proof that in the controversy about Mrs Montagu's *Essay on Shakespeare* the previous year, Hester's rival had been in the right. Not only was the incriminating paragraph erased in the original letter before it was sent to the printer, but a quotation was cut from another letter and pasted over the top – an elaborate deception uncovered only in the 1950s when R. W. Chapman published his edition of Johnson's letters.

Johnson had burned many of Hester's letters after she married Piozzi, but his executors discovered a hundred or so which had escaped his rage, and Joshua Reynolds had handed these over to Cator two years previously. Cadell thought that some of them would add spice to the collection. Hester was initially in two minds, but after a week's hesitation told Lysons that she was 'now resolved to be patiently tyed to the Stake' and that a handful might be included. Her guidance to him on how he should proceed would make a modern editor want to lie down in a darkened room: 'No need to *expunge* with Salt of Lemons all the Names I have crossed – let the Initials stand: 'tis enough that I do not name them out; Civility is all I owe them, and my Attention not to offend is shewn by the Dash.'[10]

Twelve letters were eventually selected for the first volume and fifteen for the second; and once she had looked them over it occurred to Hester that they might be improved. In some instances she did little more than tidy up the grammar or reword the occasional sentence, but others were almost entirely rewritten, often in a more literary style that robbed them of their spontaneity. Some of her shorter notes were run together; several letters had material from *Thraliana* spatchcocked into them.

It soon became apparent that the extra work involved made the original deadline unrealistic. It was also plain that still more material would have to be found to fill the projected two octavo volumes; Cadell was persuaded to delay publication until the following year.

With the pressure off, Hester was able to lay aside work on the letters for a time, and she and Piozzi set off for Bath, accompanied by a Count Martinéngo, a friend of Piozzi's from Brescia, whom, as Hester put it, 'we carried about to see Sights'. They showed him Salisbury and Southampton, and Hester was particularly keen that he should see the fleet at Portsmouth – 'which we English are justly proud of ', she wrote: 'Foreigners have a much stronger Manner of setting their Possessions off than the natives of Great Britain, whose cold Way of mentioning all that does not relate to War or Politics, makes People think they care less about 'em than they really do ... We cannot puff – We are above it.'

While they were in Bath, she received an extraordinary letter from Queeney – 'thanking me for my *polite Attentions* to Cæcilia, but observing that they were superfluous, for that *She* intended removing her from the School She is in, to another *further from me*; and that She should take her immediately away to the Isle of Wight'.

Hester was enraged – and would have been even more so if she had known that in correspondence with Fanny Burney Queeney had written of her as a corrupting influence on Cecilia. 'Dear Miss Thrale,' she wrote coldly in reply:

> I have very few Letters from you, and this last is an odd one. I had no Notion till I read it, that Cecilia was either generally unhealthy, or at this Time particularly ill: when we parted She made no Complaints: and Mrs. Stevenson – under whose Care I am told You placed her, said She was perfectly well. If London however disagrees with her – why is She there? I left her in the Country at Mrs Ray and Fry's School Streatham, where She enjoyed the Air of her native Place and if you removed her thence, on pretence of Improvements which you now say are Trifling Matters at so early an Age – it will be found necessary perhaps some day for you to produce your Authority for so doing.

She reminded Queeney that under the terms of Thrale's will it was she who was Cecilia's guardian: '... and I must add, that to bathe a lean growing Girl of large Expectations, whom *you* say is unhealthy – in the Sea, without more and nearer Medical Advice than the Isle of Wight would afford – seems somewhat a rash Step when taken by a young and single Lady who cannot pretend to the smallest Degree of Legal Power over the Child's Person'.[11]

The tone of Queeney's reply made Hester suspect it had been dictated by Baretti: 'I have got the Child home to us however, & Piozzi doats on her. — I hold her to my heart all Day long, as Niobe did little Chloris; if they steal her away from me now, I shall lose my life: 'tis so very comfortable to have *one* at least saved out of *twelve*.'

The price she paid was a total severance of relations with Queeney. The estrangement between them would last for six years.

✧ ✧ ✧

Hester's greatest desire was to have a child by Piozzi, and she had been overjoyed to think at the age of forty-seven that she was once again pregnant. A short, bleak entry in *Thraliana* appeared to record the death of her hopes: 'The Harrass of these Letters made me miscarry tho'; and that was a bad Thing; we laid the Blame on a fall, but external Causes affect my health but little; if I *did* miscarry, (and all the doctors say I did,) the Letters caused the Misfortune.'

As soon as she was well, they set off on their travels once more, partly to let Piozzi see something of the English and Welsh countryside, but mainly with a view to acquiring more material for the second volume of *Letters*; mistrustful of Queeney, they took Cecilia with them. They spent several agreeable weeks with the Greatheeds in Warwickshire: 'Mr Greatheed is very clever & is now employed in writing a Tragedy,' Hester noted; she advised him to take it to London and show it to the managers and agreed to write an epilogue.

They followed much the same route as she had taken with Thrale and Johnson thirteen years previously: 'Mr Piozzi likes England vastly,' she wrote to Mrs Byron, 'and Cecilia seems a very dapper Traveller.'[12] Hester had hopes of garnering more letters and anecdotes in Lichfield, but discovered that Boswell had been there before her. She was cordially received, however, by Anna Seward, the witty, sharp-tongued daughter of a canon of the cathedral whose poetry had increasingly won acclaim during the 1780s, and who was very much the queen bee of social and intellectual life in the town.[13] Hester had heard a great deal from Johnson of 'the Swan of Lichfield'; both women were eager to size the other up.

'Dr Johnson told me truth when he said she had more colloquial wit than most of our literary women,' Seward wrote to the poet William Hayley: '... but he did not tell me truth when he asserted that Piozzi was an ugly dog, without particular skill in his profession. Mr Piozzi is a handsome man, in middle life, with gentle, pleasing, and unaffected manners, and with very eminent skill in his profession.'[14]

Seward had already supplied Boswell with what she could in the way of anecdote, but now offered to help Hester secure letters written by Johnson thirty years previously to Hill Boothby, a cultured and pious young woman to whom he seems to have considered proposing marriage.[15] These letters – they were for some reason in the keeping of Johnson's friend John Taylor at Ashbourne – had already been promised to Boswell, but Seward worked hard on the Boothby family, whose property they were. Taylor proved hostile. He declined to hand over any of his own letters from Johnson, and when Sir Brooke Boothby eventually asked him to let Hester have those addressed to his sister, he forwarded them with a distinctly crotchety covering note:

> Dr. Johnson's Mental Powers and extreme good Heart, all Men very well know, and his Enemies acknowledge; but I shall be greatly grieved to see the ridiculous Vanities and fulsome Weakness's which he always betrayed in his Conversation and Address with his amiable female friends exposed; I cannot forbear to entreat you to change your Resolution about printing these Letters.[16]

The Piozzis pressed on northwards. At Liverpool Hester encountered her old butler Daniel, now a waiter at an inn. 'He was a cheating fellow I believe,' she wrote, 'but not as bad as he was painted by the old Nurse and her Associates ... Besides he used to bring my Piozzi's Love Letters to me of a Morning in Argyll Street, that dreadful Winter which I spent there.' They moved on to Chester, and an older memory stirred that was bitter-sweet: 'Chester Wall put me in mind of poor dear D^r. Johnson who said one day very drolly; *now have I known my Mistress sixteen Years*, & never saw her out of *Humour yet – except once upon Chester Wall.*'

When she had travelled this way with Thrale and Johnson, Hester had been deeply disappointed at their indifference to the beauties of her native land. Piozzi did not disappoint her. 'Our Tour was a delightful one,' she told Mrs Byron: '... you can scarce think how happy it made me to see dear Wales again; and to find my Husband so caressed by my

oldest Friends – he is satisfied with My Country, and in Love with its
Mountains and Castles; more resembling Lombardy to be sure than any
part of England does –'[17]

They had travelled in greater comfort than on that earlier journey,
but there was a canker in the bud:

> The Inns are now as much above mere comfortable Inns, as they were
> below that State 13 years ago, when dear, cruel, unkind Queeney was
> my sweet Companion. Will Ciceley ever treat me as She does now?
> Hope & Fondness answer no sure; but reason, Experience, & Knowl-
> edge of the World all agree to say 'expect no better Behaviour from any
> of the Breed – they are all true Sisters'.

At Shrewsbury on the way home Piozzi fell ill. The horses were
whipped up and they drove on in a day to Warwickshire. The Greatheeds
were away, but they stayed at their house until Piozzi's fever subsided.
By early October they were back in Hanover Square, and Hester sent
off what little she had acquired to Lysons. She was still very much in
two minds about the worth of her own contribution: 'Write me word
what you do with *my* Stuff, and pray take care to scratch Names out.
Yours is a very serious Trust, & tho' you live to be Lord Tetbury, you
will never again have the heart of any one so completely in your hand
to rummage every Sorrow out as you now have …'[18]

They had returned to London a matter of days before the anniversary
of her marriage to Thrale. 'Why do the People say I never loved my
first Husband? 'tis a very unjust Conjecture,' Hester wrote:

> Ours was a Match of mere Prudence; and common good Liking,
> without the smallest Pretensions to Passion on either Side: I knew no
> more of him than of any other Gentleman who came to the House …
> yet God who gave us to each other, knows I did love him dearly; &
> what honour I can ever do to his Memory shall be done, for he was very
> generous to me.

For all her extraordinary toughness and resilience, she was by her
own admission something of a 'croaker', and these reflections about her
first marriage led on to one of her occasional bouts of hypochondria:
'My Health is going very fast. It has lasted surprisingly, & has held out

against many storms: perhaps the Jury Masts may just serve to carry me into harbour, (as they *have* done,) and then the ship is to sink ...'

She had sought Murphy's advice about Greatheed's play. 'If there be a Leading female Character,' he told her, 'you know that nobody can do it justice but Mrs. Siddons. With her my acquaintance is very slender. You know her I believe ...'[19] Hester accordingly arranged a dinner party – the Greatheeds, Mrs Siddons, Murphy and William Parsons – 'who is likewise a Conspirator in forming this new Play'.

No great conspiracy was required. When she was in her teens, Sarah Kemble as she then was had fallen in love with an actor called William Siddons, a member of her parents' touring company. Sarah was fifteen, Siddons twenty-six; her parents disapproved, not least because they had been encouraging the advances of a local Brecon squire. An angry confrontation with Sarah's father resulted in Siddons's dismissal from the company; when Sarah refused to marry the squire, she was sent into service, first as a maid, later as a companion to the lady of the house – who was Greatheed's mother.[20] Now, seventeen years later, the first lady of the English stage graciously agreed to do as she was asked (although Hester suspected that she did not much like her epilogue); she also undertook to persuade her brother, John Philip Kemble, that he too should take a major role.

At the end of October work on the *Letters* was complete. Hester awaited publication with some apprehension: 'I *know* of only six professed Enemies who are determined to write against the Book, but there are doubtless six and twenty of whom I know nothing. Well! Johnson always said that nothing could sink a Book except its own dullness ...'

The Piozzis now drove down to Bath and Hester tried to put her own literary affairs out of her head for a time. There were old friendships to be renewed, notably with Mrs Byron and Mrs Lambart – 'Mrs Byron is converted by Piozzi's Assiduity, She really likes him now,' she wrote, 'and sweet Mrs Lambart told every body at Bath She was in Love with him.'

And there were new friendships to be made. Harriet Lee was one of four sisters who kept a boarding school for girls. The previous year she had brought out a five-volume novel called *The Errors of Innocence*, and her comedy, *The New Peerage, or, Our Eyes may Deceive Us*, had just had a successful run of nine nights at Drury Lane. Her elder sister, Sophia, was also a writer of note: 'Miss Lees are charming Women, and appear to deserve their very uncommon Success,' Hester wrote to Lysons.[21] She made a perceptive – and barbed – comparison between Harriet's work and that of Fanny Burney:

> The Books written by that Lady are valuable only as they are an exact and perfect Copy of those Manners which at this Moment prevail in this Nation; – every body may see their own picture, & read their own Character in her Novels, which are the truest representation of the very commonest Life: while the Author's Conversation & Behaviour is all unnatural, all stilted, all Affectation ...

At Christmas she amused herself by composing for the small daughter of George James, the painter, 'The Book of Genesis put in easy Verse for Babies':

> The first Man was Adam, the first Woman Eve,
> God made them, & plac'd in fair Eden to live,
> But early transgressing his single Command,
> They were turned from the Garden to till the rough Land.
> Then Cain kill'd his Brother for Malice & Spite,
> And looked like a Murderer black as the Night.
> The World was so wicked and Noah so good,
> He was sav'd in the Ark, and they drown'd in the Flood ...

She began the New Year in good spirits:

> How little I thought this Day four Years that I sh^d celebrate the 1st of Jan: 1788 here at Bath surrounded with Friends and Admirers? The Public partial to *me*, and almost every Individual whose kindness is worth wishing for, sincerely attached to my Husband ... These Waters have done my Health good too, and I shall begin the Winter quite pert again, if it please God. –

She spoke too soon. By the time they reached Hanover Square, there was yet another entry to be made in the melancholy catalogue of her blighted hopes. They had broken their journey to visit her friend Charlotte Lewis, and there Hester suffered a miscarriage. The doctors had been mistaken in August:

I did *not* miscarry *then*, only was very ill; but the Bath Waters gave me Strength, and *now* I *have* miscarried of a Daughter at Mrs Lewis's House at Reading in my Road hither — *She is Witness*, but not thinking even that sufficient, would have every possible examination made in order to satisfy me that bringing Children is still *possible*.

She held stubbornly to that belief: that although she was now approaching her late forties, she might still bear Piozzi a child — a child who could inherit her Welsh estates. Years later, she remembered how differently they had reacted to their loss: 'Oh how that Event did vex me! — Ten times more than it vexed my Husband, to whom it certainly was More Important — but he seemed never to regret his Loss ... It was a mortifying Circumstance.'[22]

Miscarriage or no, Hester had, in the few days they had spent with Mrs Lewis, entertained her friend by composing an amusing mock review of the *Letters* — 'imitating the Style of those I expect to abuse it':

The Care and Attention with which we have review'd this Work,
was rather excited by our long Expectation of it, than repaid by the
Instruction or Amusement it affords; let it not however be consign'd to
Oblivion without a few Remarks on its Excellencies & Defects, which
to say Truth are neither of them numerous, & we should do the Publick
double Injury in covering much paper with Criticisme upon what the
Rambler himself would call *Pages of Inanity* ... If our fair Editress
publish'd this Correspondence to shew with how much Insipidity people
famed for their Wit & their Learning might maintain a twenty years
Intercourse by Letter and Conversation; She has succeeded admirably —

Back in London, there were proofs to be read and an old friend and admirer to be mourned — Sir Philip Jennings Clerke had died. '*There* was a Man who would have gone through Fire, nay he *did* go thro' Fire to serve me,' she wrote. 'If I had not loved him I had been a Monster, if I were not sorry for him I were a Jew! ...'

Relations with her daughters continued to plague her:

Here comes Mr Cator to ask me what School Cecilia is to go to — I tell him *Mrs Piozzi's*, and that the World considers it as *the first in England*. He replies that the three eldest Miss Thrales having often complain'd to him that I neglected *their* Education, was the chief Reason of his Fears that Cecilia should *lose her Time* in my Company. What a strange Combination of Malice, Envy, Avarice & Ingratitude is here! ... I think I shall never see my Girls again; what I mean is, we shall never more embrace like Parent & Child – I fear not! & Oh good God! How dreadful is that idea!

On 13 February London was lit up by a blaze of pageantry unequalled since the Coronation as Warren Hastings went on trial for his alleged misdeeds in India. 'Hastings's Tryal takes up all the Conversation,' Hester wrote, 'the eloquence of Burke, Fox &c are much talked on.' Cadell sensibly decided not to compete for attention with the sensational proceedings in Westminster Hall, and publication was deferred.

The book finally appeared on 8 March. 'The Letters are out,' Hester wrote in *Thraliana*. 'Cadell printed 2000 Copies, & says 1100 are already sold ... the Book is well spoken of upon the whole – yet Cadell murmurs – I cannot make out why.'

IT IS not clear what Cadell had to murmur about – the edition sold out within days. He may have got wind of the pirated edition that would appear almost immediately in Dublin, infringing his copyright. Possibly he didn't like the tone of some of the reviews: 'MRS PIOZZI, after the pleasure of publishing her own unrivalled excellence in her letters, and enjoying the more substantial happiness of 500£ in hard cash, is determined to spread her peacock tail, and on adulation "sup most royally". At her Concerto to-night this lady expects to be installed a tenth Muse.'[1]

The *Morning Post* condemned the Letters as a breach of trust, and was predictably abusive: 'Poor DR. JOHNSON has been served up to us in every shape – we have had him boiled to a rag, roasted, fricasseed ... The letters of DR. JOHNSON, for the most part, form a salmagundi, composed of *bulls, cows, calves, cats, and Mr. Piozzi*.'[2]

The *World*, on the other hand, was distinctly friendly – unsurprisingly, as its editor was the Reverend Charles Este, chaplain of the Chapel Royal, Whitehall, whom Hester knew socially. The paper had been puffing the book since shortly after it went to press; Este was full of praise for Hester's preface, and advanced the doubtful proposition that her letters compared favourably with those of Johnson.[3]

The monthlies were divided. One of the most considered notices appeared in the *Monthly Review*. The writer maintained that the picture painted of Johnson in no way detracted from his greatness – 'We see him in his undress, that is the undress of his mind, which, unlike that of the body, was never slovenly.' Hester's letters were praised for their elegance and vivacity – 'they exhibit a mind enriched with literature, and provided with a plentiful store of images'.[4] She was not to know it, but the writer was Murphy.

Bluestocking opinion of Hester's own contribution was generally favourable. 'Good sprightly letters', was Hannah More's verdict[5] while Mrs Montagu, although wrinkling her nose at what she considered a number of stylistic vulgarities, confessed that she had found the letters amusing: 'She writes like a Woman of parts; her accounts of things are lively and clever, and her observations often very ingenious and sensible.'[6]

The most virulent attack on the *Letters* by a member of Hester's own sex would come only four years later with the publication of Mary Wollstonecraft's *A Vindication of the Rights of Woman*. Hester had chosen to include a letter of advice addressed in 1773 not to Johnson but to a young man who had eloped with a fifteen-year-old niece of Thrale's. 'My letter to Jack Rice on his Marriage seems the universal Favourite,' she wrote in *Thraliana* shortly after publication, and it was frequently reprinted over the next few years both in England and America.

In it she offers the bridegroom her 'rules for felicity' in marriage. William McCarthy describes it as 'a prescription for companionate marriage on the Bluestocking model'[7] and even detects in it a mildly feminist tinge — 'let your wife never be kept ignorant of your income, your expences, your friendships, or aversions ... consider all concealment as a breach of fidelity'. Wollstonecraft, squinting through the distorting prism of her own more radical feminism, might have been reading a totally different letter: 'Indignantly have I heard women argue in the same track as men, and adopt the sentiments that brutalize them with all the pertinacity of ignorance ... Mrs. Piozzi, who often repeated by rote, what she did not understand, comes forward with Johnsonian periods.'

She is particularly incensed by a passage warning that women do not like to feel neglected by their husbands: 'There is no reproof however pointed, no punishment however severe,' Hester had written, 'that a woman of spirit will not prefer to neglect; and if she can endure it without complaint, it only proves that she means to make herself amends by the attention of others for the slights of her husband.' Wollstonecraft was contemptuous: 'Noble morality! ... A woman must know, that her person cannot be as pleasing to her husband as it was to her lover, and if she be offended with him for being a human creature, she may as well whine about the loss of his heart as about any other foolish thing.'[8]

William McCarthy, by way of comment, quotes the poet and essayist

Anna Letitia Barbauld, a near contemporary of Hester's. She had been invited to associate herself with a literary journal to be managed by women, but declined: there was, she wrote, 'no bond of union among literary women, any more than among literary men' – a proposition that would have found a ready seconder in Hester.[9]

Boswell's publisher, Charles Dilly, had managed to get him a copy of the *Letters* the day before publication. His first reaction was one of disappointment at what he felt was the triviality of much of the correspondence. But what hurt most was the clear evidence of Johnson's deep affection for Hester – and his own near-invisibility. 'This publication cooled my warmth of enthusiasm for "my illustrious friend" a good deal,' he wrote in his journal. 'I felt myself degraded from the consequence of an ancient Baron to the state of an humble attendant on an Authour.'[10] To make matters worse, Malone thought much better of it than he did: 'The letters are, I think, in general very pleasing and exactly what I expected. I think you rate them too low.'[11]

Boswell's *magnum opus* was still nowhere near completion. Depressed and angry at the apparent ease with which Johnson's 'dearest dear Lady' could capture the attention of the reading public, he resolved to do her an injury – he would publish 'Johnson's supposed Nuptial Ode' which he had composed at Reynolds's house just after Thrale's death. He embellished it with a 'Preface by the Editor' and an 'Argument', two coarse passages of prose in which Hester is described as this little woman 'of pregnant parts'. To Boswell's chagrin, it was largely ignored. He also composed 'A Thralian Epigram', which appeared in the *Public Advertiser*:

> If *Hesther* had chosen to wed mighty SAM
> Who it seem, drove full at her his BATTERING RAM
> A wonder indeed, then, the world would have found
> A woman who truly prefer'd SENSE to *sound*.

Nobody read the *Letters* with closer attention than Baretti. He filled the margins with savage annotations – 'You lie, you Bich, and Johnson never wrote this damn'd paragraph,' he wrote beside one letter. As he worked his way through the two volumes, his long-standing dislike and resentment of Hester turned into blind hatred. Two letters particularly enraged him. In one Hester had asserted that after Harry's death, he alone had been unsympathetic; in the other, Johnson had expressed the hope that Thrale would soon rescue her daughters – 'the fair captives' – from Baretti's tyranny. He lashed out in three so-called 'Strictures', which appeared in the *European Magazine* during the spring and summer. They are full of coarse abuse of 'La Piozzi' – 'the frontless female who ... in the great wisdom of her concupiscence ... has degraded herself into the wife of an Italian singing-master'.[12]

The onslaught was so intemperate that it backfired. Anna Seward wrote of 'the base, ungentlemanlike, unmanly abuse of Mrs Piozzi by that Italian assassin Baretti';[13] even Boswell thought he had 'clipped rather *rudely*, and gone a great deal *closer* than was necessary'. Hester herself took it all rather calmly. 'It was the heat of the Summer exalted Baretti's Venom so,' she wrote to Lysons '– I am told *all* the Vipers sting terribly this Year.'[14]

The vipers were also to be found in the print shops. The caricaturist James Sayers, better known for his influential political prints,[15] entered the fray with his *Frontispiece for the 2ᵈ Edition of Dʳ. J...n's Letters.* Hester, seated at her writing desk, is visited by the shade of Johnson, who upbraids her with disturbing the repose he sought in the grave:

> When Streatham spread its plenteous Board
> I opened Learning's valued hoard
>   And as I feasted, prosed.
> Good things I said, good things I eat,
> I gave you knowledge for your Meat
>   And thought th'Account was closed.
> If Obligations still I owed
> You sold each Item to the Crowd,
>   I suffer'd by the Tale;
> For God's sake, Madam, let me rest,
> Nor longer vex your quondam Guest.
>   I'll pay you for your Ale.

Hester could see no good reason why this sort of traffic should be all one-way. Anticipating a new salvo from 'Peter Pindar', she decided to get her retaliation in first:

Now Peter Popgun, Pill-Box Pindar! Hail!
Feast for one Week on Johnson and on Thrale;
Or to that Rhyme if Readers should grow dozy,
Change it at once to Johnson and Piozzi.
With hungry haste dispense your dirty Drug
And clasp these Letters with a Cornish Hug ...[16]

A Cornish Hug was a lock used in wrestling, but for the moment Wolcot chose not to enter the ring, and Hester's verses were not published.

In England, as in the rest of eighteenth-century Europe, the aristocracy had a passion for amateur theatricals. None more so than Charles Lennox, third Duke of Richmond, a member of Pitt's cabinet as master-general of the Ordnance. In the spring of 1788, Nathaniel Lee's tragedy *Theodosius, or the Force of Love*, was in rehearsal at the private theatre in the Duke's house in Whitehall. The cast included a young woman called Jane Hamilton, a talented amateur singer related to the Dukes of Hamilton. Hester described her in *Thraliana* as 'now upon the first Rank in the World as a Woman of high Fashion', and she was not a little flattered when Miss Hamilton applied to her for help in finding an appropriate song for the moment in the play when the heroine has resolved to die rather than receive the addresses of the emperor. 'The Lord & Lady Performers would not suffer an Italian Song to mingle with the Distresses of Athenais,' Hester wrote; she therefore took an air of Sacchini's, and with Piozzi's help, devised some English verses to meet the situation:

Vain's the Breath of Adulation,
Vain the Tears of tend'rest Passion,
While a strong Imagination
　　Hold the wandring Mind away:
Art in vain attempts to borrow
Notes to soothe a rooted Sorrow
Fix'd to dye – and die tomorrow
　　What can touch her Soul today?

They were pronounced a success, and Hester was jubilant: 'Miss Hamilton who is *Italian Mad*, says they are better than the Words of the Original Language, I mean better for *Musick*.' Her engagement book for 1788 shows a number of invitations to Richmond House, giving her the entrée to a social circle somewhat grander than those she had previously moved in. What was especially gratifying was that Piozzi was included – something which the more rigid conventions on such matters in Italy had frequently prevented.

Hester was also much taken up with Greatheed's tragedy *The Regent*, which had its first performance at Drury Lane at the end of March – '& with prodigious Eclat', she recorded excitedly. 'Everybody agreed that such a first Tragedy had never been presented to an English Audience since Shakespear's Romeo & Juliet,' she declared, although she conceded that there had been more than one view about the denouement: 'There was some hesitation in the Public about the 5th Act, whether the last Scene of it might not be deem'd too horrible for Endurance, when the Tyrant is preparing to cut off the Boy's head in his Mother's presence ...'

But then the play ran into difficulties. After two performances Mrs Siddons suffered a miscarriage and was obliged to withdraw; two weeks later her youngest child died. Hester wrote a prologue for the play's return, but noted sadly in *Thraliana* 'They have shelfed it.' There were six further performances later in the season, however, and a few stagings in Dublin during the summer.

There was no improvement in Hester's relations with her daughters – Bertie Greatheed had dubbed them Goneril and Regan: 'The inflexible Sisters continue their Behaviour, which the youngest appears not to condemn, but seeks perpetual Connection with them: they have made some fruitless Attempts to get her from me, but we are setting out together now for a very distant Province, so that they can scarce hear or see anything of each other for Six months ...'

The 'very distant Province' was Devon. They had found a pretty house for the summer on the Strand at Exmouth – 'with the Water quite washing yᵉ Wall on one side, & a smart little Garden on t'other, I shall sit down to work with much Chearfulness & Comfort'. Hester had already decided what her next literary venture would be – 'I will write my Travels & publish them – why not? 'twill be difficult to content the Italians & the English but I'll try – & tis something to do.'

'Here is very little Society,' she noted in *Thraliana*, although she added, 'What there is to be *had* – we *have* it.' Their best country neighbours, she told Lysons, were Sir John Duntze and his family – 'but 12 miles is a long way to drive'.[17] She was rather taken with Lord Huntingdon – 'When I fall in love next,' she wrote, 'it shall be with Lord Huntingdon, who is a most agreeable Man indeed.'[18] Dinner parties – evenings of shilling whist – an Assize ball at Exeter – the Piozzis quickly settled into an agreeable routine, which provided material for a steady stream of letters, mainly to Hester's friend Sophia Byron. 'Mr Piozzi laughs at my facility of accommodating myself to every Place,' she told her: '... here I bathe and write (by the by the 1st Volume is done) and go to bed at 10 o'Clock, and comb my Hair clean out of the Powder, washing it every Morning in the Sea and on Sundays tell my friends at a Distance how I love them.'[19]

At the end of July, they celebrated their wedding anniversary – 'it is the 5th we have passed together, & I trust the happiest, and that we love one another as well, if not better than ever'. Piozzi rode and walked and relished the peace of the Devon countryside: 'Mr. Piozzi is very nervous,' Hester told Mrs Byron, 'but the air agrees with his Voice so, that the increase in its Compass is to me almost miraculous.'[20] Early in August he went off up to London 'for a Week's Business & Pleasure' and Hester resolved to be '*double diligent*'.[21] She was a good as her word: 'The Book I have really not read yet, only written, which sounds odd, but *so it is*,' she wrote:

> I shall now read, correct and copy it over – beginning next Thursday at soonest, for just now I hate the sight of it.
>
> *You* will like the description of Naples best: but there will be great Censure upon the whole, *that* I expect and shall willingly compound for. The first thing for a Book is to be *read*, the second to be *praised*, the third to be criticized – but the irremediable Misfortune is – *to be forgotten*.[22]

When she was not transcribing her manuscript or washing her hair in the sea, Hester devoted herself to Cecilia's education, but with scant success: 'I cannot make a Scholar of Cecilia, I never shall; tis impossible, but there are Scholars enough in the World without her: she has many good Qualities – among her bad ones a Spirit of total Idleness is the worst.'[23]

The weather continued fine and hot into September, but as autumn drew on, Hester succumbed to a bout of depression:

> I am strangely lowspirited somehow – a Horror over my heart that I cannot express: Something is going to happen I am sure – something that will separate me from my Husband – I *feel* some unaccountable Terror every Time I look at him, & every Time I do *not* look at him: What in the World can be coming? We have had so many Storms before we met – Are they not over now?

Her forebodings proved groundless, but she did shortly afterwards become quite seriously unwell – 'a cold, a fever – a deal of Plague', she wrote to Lysons; 'I began to think you would have had a stroke at the Thraliana soon' – she had had it in mind to make him her literary executor. Piozzi, she told him, had been 'worse frighted' than she herself had been. She intended to recover 'by dint of Bath Water if possible, and get hardened there for the Winter'.[24]

Although she had no contact with them, the three elder girls were often in her thoughts. 'My fair Daughters have been seen at Bath I hear,' she wrote to Mrs Byron: 'Is it not silly to feel that they are well and happy? Who wish me no good I am sure either of Health or any other Enjoyment ... Yet glad I am at my Heart – for after every thing is said they *are* my Children – at least *Mr. Thrale's* to whom I owe many Obligations.'[25]

A few weeks later she had a further sighting of them to report: 'Well! I hear my young ladies are gone into Wales, what can that Frisk be for? was it because we were coming within ten Miles of them?'[26]

The Piozzis reached Bath early in October – 'I do love the Place passionately and the Waters gratefully,' Hester wrote. They had been having problems with the valet who travelled with them:

> Flood is never sober for a Day together, and his Hand shakes, and he cannot dress one after drinking so, and we are at our Wits End with him – and yet he is very *agreeable* somehow, and we are as sorry for his

Ruin, as for our own Inconvenience. The Maid is sober, and decent, and does no harm, and one *hates her*. She is so *dis*agreeable: don't you know how all that feels exactly?[27]

Piozzi had gout in his toes and found Bath a shade tedious. 'He is an ungrateful Creature,' Hester wrote: 'There is no Place where one lives so *well* for so little Money, no Place where so many Beauties meet, no Place where there are such Combinations of Gayety and such Opportunities of Snugness.'[28]

Here she managed at last to finish making a fair copy of her manuscript, and in the middle of November she wrote to Cadell:

I have finished the book of observations and reflections made in the course of my journey thro' France, Italy, and Germany, and if you have a mind to purchase the MS I make you the first offer of it ... The price at a word (as the advertisers say of their horse) is 500 guineas, and 12 copies to give away ... No creature has looked over the papers but Lord Huntingdon, and he likes them exceedingly ...[29]

~✹✹~

By the autumn of 1788 it was widely known that George III was seriously ill. 'Nothing is so much talked of here, you may suppose as the King,' Lysons wrote to Hester in the middle of November. 'There is now certainly no danger of Death but what is much worse I think, a confirmed madness.'[30] He talked unceasingly and sometimes indecently, was mentally confused and occasionally became violent – when the Prince of Wales was summoned, his father seized him by the collar and flung him against the wall. In December Francis Willis, the celebrated mad-doctor was called in, bringing with him a straitjacket and a restraining chair. 'The King's Illness is a very dreadful Event,' Hester wrote in *Thraliana*. She was greatly exercised by the political implications of the sovereign's illness: 'Fox, Burke, Sheridan, all the Opposition People want an unlimited Regent: – how unconstitutional! how dreadful! Pitt I think wants a settled Republick; how unconstitutional is that too, but far less dangerous – anything but Despotism for God's sake ... The Prince's Character makes his Elevation to power extremely perilous to the State; his Connection with a Catholic Lady increases our Peril ...'

Hester had delivered her manuscript a week before Christmas, but Cadell's commercial sense told him that the moment was not propitious. The talk of a regency was also bad news for Bertie Greatheed:

Among ten Thousand *private* & petty Mortifications produced by the present State of Affairs, I am sorriest for the Effect it has had on poor Greatheed's Play: the *Name* of which is so *odious*, that the Managers are forced to lay it by, lest the People should pull their House down.

So he loses his ninth Night, and all his Fame poor Fellow; it is exceedingly provoking to be sure ...

The proceeds from the second and ninth nights of a run went to the author, although as things turned out Greatheed was not denied his second benefit performance. The King's health began to improve; the Lord Chamberlain gave permission for the play to be revived. Greatheed's temperament, however, was ill-suited to the uncertain world of the theatre. He had become ill the previous year when the play had first been withdrawn; his piece would enjoy two brief subsequent revivals, but he never wrote for the stage again.

The official bulletin on the King's health for 26 February spoke of 'an entire cessation of illness'. Hester was ecstatic:

Our King, our dear & invaluable Sovereign recovers; recovers is not enough, he is convalescent, convalescent is not enough – he is *well*, he is returned to the enjoyment of his Senses, his Friends, his People: no – not his People, they love him *too much*, their Joy would be too clamorous, his new-strung Nerves could not support *our* Exclamations of tender, but Violent Transport.

The Piozzis joined enthusiastically in the official celebrations marking the King's recovery. The *World*, which obligingly acted as the eighteenth-century equivalent of a fan magazine for Hester, told its readers that Mrs Piozzi's house in Hanover Square was 'alight – from the roof to the area, With a Transparency in the Heart of the building – God Save the King ...'[31]

Hester speculated darkly on what might have befallen the country if the King had not recovered: 'Had the Regent been made wth out Limitation, and his Brother been appointed Generalissimo of the Army, we had never seen our King again ...' It occurred to her that there were similarities between the King's position and her own, and she offered up a somewhat melodramatic prayer: 'So may God of his mercy ever preserve all virtuous parents from the Hands of *Their own Children*!'

She also leapt into print. A number of newspapers accepted from her an 'Ode on the Rejoicings for the King's Providential Recovery', although Hester grumbled that it had been 'mangled and falsely printed in twenty Places'. Some of the eight stanzas read better than others:

> Mark! How th'unwilling gates of Death
> Close heavy on their Caves beneath,
>   Defrauded of their Prey;
> While Britain's Guardian Angel bears,
> His sacred Charge to purer Spheres,
>   Restor'd to Life and Day.

Some of the most revealing – and entertaining – passages in *Thraliana* are those where Hester records how she sees herself and how she believes she is regarded by the outside world:

> I have a great deal more Prudence than People suspect me for; they think I act by Chance, while I am doing nothing in the World unintentionally ... Often I have spoken what I have repented after, but that was want of *Judgment* – not of *Meaning*; what I said, I meant to say at the Time ... when I err, tis because I make a false conclusion, not because I make no Conclusion at all. When I rattle, I rattle *on purpose*.

She had rattled to good effect since returning from Italy. Regular Monday concerts at Hanover Square had also played their part in her efforts to remake a place for herself in London society. One evening the guests included Miss Nicolson, who had briefly been Queeney's companion: 'She says Piozzi and I are grown each ten years Younger since we parted from her in Welbeck Street; and She thinks My Misses now live in the house we had *then*. How astonishing as She says that they are able to resist the Vortex which brings every one beside them to our Feet!'

Not *quite* everyone: 'Mrs Siddons dined in a Coterie of my unprovoked Enemies yesterday at Porteus's – She mentioned our Concerts and the Erskines lamented their Absence from One we gave two days ago, at which Mrs Garrick was present, and gave a good Report to the *Blues*. Charming Blues! Blue with Venom I think; I suppose they begin to be ashamed of their paltry behaviour ...'

Another evening, across a crowded room, she caught sight of Reynolds:

> We hardly looked at each other – yet I see he grows old, & is under the Domination of a *Niece*: Oh! That is poor Work indeed for Sir Joshua Reynolds. I always told Johnson they overrated that Man's mental Qualities; he replied Everybody loves Reynolds except *you*. The Truth is I felt that he hated *me*; and suspected that he encouraged Mr Thrale's attachment to Sophia Streatfield ...

Inevitably, it was not long before she encountered her old rival: 'I met Sophy Streatfield at an Assembly the other night, and was thrust by the Crowd quite close to her: nothing could exceed her Confusion, & Distress; when I said coldly *How do you do Miss Streatfield? I hope you have been well since we last met &c.*'

Murphy was not the only member of the old Streatham circle who remained loyal: 'Mrs Garrick more prudent than any of them, left a Loop-hole for returning Friendship to fasten through, and it *shall* fasten. That Woman has lived a *very wise Life*; regular and steady in her Conduct, attentive to every Word she speaks, & every step She treads – decorous in her Manners, & graceful in her Person.'

One of the most interesting of the new circle of friends which Hester gathered round her in Hanover Square was the Scottish physician John Moore. A distant cousin of Tobias Smollett's, Moore had retired from medical practice some years before and had earned a considerable reputa-tion for his travel writings, which included accounts of visits to Voltaire at Ferney and conversations at Potsdam with Frederick the Great.

It was to Moore that a fellow-Scot who had recently had a slim volume of poetry published wrote a lengthy and revealing account of his early life and education. Moore lavished advice on his young compatriot, urg-ing him to abandon Scots and write in standard English – a misguided suggestion which, happily, Robert Burns largely ignored.

Moore's first novel, *Zeluco*, had just appeared, and Hester found it

'charming'. 'I love Dr More,' she wrote, '& it is such an entertaining
& such a well-intention'd Work, one dotes on it: *but it won't be liked.*'
She was mistaken. It went through thirteen editions in his lifetime. The
death of Moore's eldest son at Corunna during the Peninsular War would
inspire one of the most celebrated elegies in the English language.

Another new acquaintance was Lord Fife, a landowner with large
estates in the north-east of Scotland.[32] In a fragment of autobiography
written many years later, Hester recounted how Fife had retailed some
gossip calculated to stoke her suspicions of the Burneys:

> One day ... when I was airing my lap-dogs in a retired part of Hyde
> Park, Lord Fife came up to me, and after a moment's chat, said, 'Would
> you like to know your friends from your enemies?' in a Scotch accent.
> 'Yes, very much, my lord' was the reply. 'Ay, but have you strength of
> mind enough to beat my intelligence?'[33]

He then told her that when Baretti had been hawking round his
'Strictures', the only magazine that would touch them was that edited
by 'the female Burney'. It wasn't true, of course – Fanny never edited a
magazine in her life, and Hester seems to have brushed the story aside.
What was true, however, is that until her dying day she *did* believe that
it was Fanny's brother Charles who was the villain of the piece. She
was misinformed. He was for a time the editor of the *London Magazine*,
but never of the *European*.

Early in May of that year Baretti died. 'Poor Baretti! I am sincerely
sorry for him,' Hester wrote in *Thraliana*, and quoted a line from Edward
Young's *The Revenge*:

> And art thou dead? So is my Enmity;
> I war not with the Dust.

She did, however, compose what she termed a character sketch of him,
which was published in the *World*:

> ... Long supported by the private bounty of friends, he rather delighted
> to insult than flatter; he at length obtained competence from a public
> he esteemed not; and died, refusing that assistance he considered as
> useless – leaving no debts (but those of gratitude) undischarged ... the

description of Menelaus in Homer's 'Iliad' as rendered by Pope exactly
suits the character of Baretti:

So burns the vengeful Hornet, soul all o'er,
Repuls'd in vain, and thirsty still for gore;
Bold son of air and heat, on angry wings,
Untamed, untired, he turns, attacks, and stings.

Baretti was buried in Marylebone on 9 May. He had instructed his
executors to destroy all his papers and manuscripts. On the day of his
funeral, a curious paragraph appeared in the *Morning Post*: 'If Bar-
retti had not unfortunately *slipped his wind*, the world would soon have
been favoured with some anecdotes respecting the musical *Signora* of
Hanover-Square and her *pseudo-brother*, of a very interesting kind.'

Hester would shortly discover that the vengeful Hornet possessed a
vicious posthumous sting.

～ 24 ～
Land of the Mountain and the Flood

PIOZZI had talked of going to Italy in the spring, but Hester was apprehensive: '– if I go with him I lose Cecilia, & for every Reason am *sure* to lose her: the moment we are off, Cator sends for her, which as he is her Guardian, I have no right to hinder; the Sisters seize her *Person*, & her *Mind*, & by the Time we return back, *both* will be alienated, & *She* will treat us as *they* do ...'

They decided instead on a journey to Scotland. Hester was far from being tired of life, but she was tired of London: 'I long to see Green Fields, & get out of hearing of these naughty Boy Princes; who do nothing but spite their Royal Parents, and make Talk for all the Fools in Town – one's Ears are fatigued with Stories of their various Pranks; now a Drunken Fit, and now a Duel: I am so sick of them and the Conversation they cause.'

By early July they were installed at Walker's Hotel in Edinburgh. As before, she kept a journal, and maintained a generous stream of letters to friends. 'We shall not present our Recommendations till Tomorrow, for I am as tired as a *Dog*,' she told Lysons. 'Cecilia bears her Journey like a Stout Girl,' she added, 'but her Heart sighs after Phillis.' Phillis was the family's red and white spaniel, which was pregnant and had been left behind in London. 'Do ask at Hanover Square if the poor little Creature is alive and well, and her Puppies safe in the Straw.'[1]

Hester's expectation of what she would find in Edinburgh – 'a second hand London set in a second hand England' – was confounded. Forty years earlier it had been little more than a small, crowded market town; now it had expanded dramatically. Hester, standing on Calton Hill, liked what she saw: 'The new City all Symmetry and exactness, every Street crossing the other at right Angles – and looking like a Cork Model when one views it from the Hill ...'[2]

If the sight of the New Town was pleasing, the smell of the Old, running from the Castle down to Holyrood, was not: 'The Scots have never turned their Thoughts towards making a Common Sewer, nor ever considered Cleanliness an Ornament, much less a *necessary* of Life. Every thing most odious is brought and thrown out before the owners door at 10 o'Clock of an Evening without Shame or Sorrow ...'[3]

A fellow-guest at Walker's Hotel was a wealthy young Englishman called Samuel Rogers, later a successful poet and well known as an art collector. He thought Piozzi played the piano most beautifully, and became a close friend.[4] The Piozzis had been furnished with letters of recommendation from both Dr Moore and Lord Fife, and these opened many doors, including those of Robert Dundas of Arniston, who had just, at the age of thirty-one, been appointed Lord Advocate, and Thomas Erskine, the future Lord Chancellor, whose rhetorical brilliance had secured the acquittal of Lord George Gordon eight years previously. They also met the Reverend Hugh Blair, celebrated both as a preacher and a man of letters; it would have delighted Hester to know that early in the American War of Independence he had preached a fast-day sermon against the colonists, which caused such offence to James Boswell that he stopped attending Blair's church for a time.

It would have delighted her even more to know in what glowing terms Blair wrote about both Piozzi and herself to the young George Husband Baird, then the minister of Dunkeld, later professor of Hebrew at Edinburgh and principal of the university:

> Mr. Piozzi (who understands and speaks English very imperfectly) is an obliging and amiable man, and I am informed of very respectable character. Mrs. Piozzi (late Mrs. Thrale) is exceedingly accomplished and agreable. She is not only mistress of all the modern Languages, but understands Latin perfectly, and is much conversant in all the parts of classical Literature. Her Conversation is lively and instructive; her information extensive; and her taste Excellent. I have seldom known any of the Learned Ladies with whom I have been so much pleased as with her.[5]

^{~→ →~}

'My Book is budding,' Hester had written just before leaving London, 'it will be in Blossom when I am gone.' It had in fact been published the day after their departure, and now, in Edinburgh, she had from Lysons the first news of its reception: 'I am glad the Book swims poor Thing,' she wrote.[6] The 'poor Thing' consisted of two octavo volumes each of some 400 pages. Short titles were not in vogue for travel books, and Hester's was called *Observations and Reflections made in the Course of a Journey through France, Italy, and Germany*. The *World*, as might be expected, had nothing but praise; the *Morning Post*, equally unsurprisingly, was hostile: 'the literary crudities of this lady afford a lamentable proof of what *vanity* will do when it is associated with wealth'.[7]

The *European Magazine* was ponderously unflattering:

Beauties and defects are so closely intermingled in almost every page of this desultory and heterogeneous performance, that the acutest powers of criticism might find it an arduous and perhaps impractical task entirely to decompose them. Sentences, the harmonious and accurate structure of which would certainly not discredit the pen of a Johnson or a Gibbon, are frequently surrounded by a context crowded with familiar phrases and vulgar idioms ...[8]

Horace Walpole, in his waspish way, made much the same point rather more pithily in a letter to Mrs Carter. He reminded her that someone had said of Addison's *Travels* that he might have written them without going out of England: 'By the excessive vulgarisms so plentiful in these volumes, one might suppose the writer had never stirred out of the parish of St Giles. Her Latin, French, and Italian too, are so miserably spelt, that she had better have studied her own language before she floundered into other tongues.'[9]

For vulgar, read colloquial. And it is, of course, precisely because Hester does not deal in the florid periods of so many of her contemporaries that *Observations* still appeals to modern readers. Her friend Leonard Chappelow wrote her a reassuring and perceptive letter two weeks after publication: 'One Observation I can most conscientiously make, which is this – should anyone say to me, that 'twas a desultory Publication, I shall immediately reply – Twas intended to be so – for to read 20 pages and hear Mrs. P. talk for 20 minutes is the same thing.'[10]

Until the middle of the eighteenth century, travel writing in English had been an almost exclusively male preserve. Lady Mary Wortley Montagu's *Letters Written during her Travels* had appeared in 1763 and the letters Lady Miller had sent to a friend during a tour of Italy had been published in 1776. Hester makes belligerently plain in her Preface why she has not adopted that formula: 'A work of which truth is the best recommendation, should not above all others begin with a lie. My old acquaintance rather chose to amuse themselves with conjectures, than to flatter me with tender enquiries during my absence; our correspondence then would not have been any amusement to the Public.'[11]

Which, being translated, means that she had not forgotten – or forgiven – the absurd rumours that had circulated about her being confined in a convent. *Observations*, as the record of a happy and fulfilling honeymoon journey, hammers that message home, and defiantly asserts the rightness of her decision to marry Piozzi. Her aim, she declares, has been 'to obtain from a humane and generous Public that shelter their protection best affords from the poisoned arrows of private malignity'[12] – the book, in other words, is a form of retaliation against the likes of her daughters and such faithless former friends as the Burneys.

William McCarthy suggests that in *Observations* Hester had a score to settle not just with family and erstwhile friends but with English society more generally, and highlights a number of passages where she draws an unfavourable comparison between what she knows of England and what she finds in Italy. Conceding, for instance, that Italians do not enjoy the political liberty of which the English so frequently boast, she points out that the English enjoy very little *social* liberty – 'It is a choice delight to live where the everlasting scourge held over London and Bath, of *what will they think?* And *what will they say?* has no existence.'

Another example is drawn from Hester's reflections on what she observed of the role of women in Venetian society: 'At first the passage seems antifeminist,' McCarthy says, 'but it is more properly anti-English':

Here is no struggle for female education as with us, no resources in study, no duties of family-management; no bill of fare to be looked over in the morning, no account-book to be settled at noon; no necessity of reading, to supply without disgrace the evening's chat; no laughing at the card-table, or tittering in the corner if a *lapsus linguae* has produced a mistake, which malice never fails to record. A lady in Italy is *sure* of applause, so she takes little pains to obtain it.[13]

McCarthy is on less solid ground when he instances Hester's strictures on the unrelenting attempts at conversational one-upmanship with which she was so familiar in England: '*Here* no man lies awake in the night for vexation that he missed recollecting the last line of a Latin epigram till the moment of application was lost.'[14] There was quite a lot of that at Streatham in the old days, after all; and Hester did not have Johnson under her roof for all those years without learning a good deal about the gentle art of verbal pugilism.

However people chose to read it, *Observations* was a success. An edition quickly appeared in Dublin, and the following year it was also translated into German, where it boasted an even longer title than in the original and carried a foreword by Georg Forster, the well-known traveller and naturalist who had accompanied Cook on his second voyage. A new edition was published as recently as 1967 by the University of Michigan Press.

꙳ ꙳

The Piozzis had reached Glasgow on 25 July. The plan was to leave their coach there and, as Hester put it, 'scramble about in the Carriages of the Country to see Sights'. But there was a limit to how far they were prepared to scramble: 'Lord Fife has sent his Nephew *Macduff*'s Representative to court us Northward,' she told Lysons (Fife's estates were mainly in Aberdeenshire and Morayshire), 'but 170 Miles rough road is no Joke ... besides I long to be in Wales ...'[15]

Glasgow she damned with faint praise – first, perhaps, 'among the second Rate Cities of Europe'. She conceded that the university was handsome – 'and that the Cathedral would have been so too, but for the violating hand of hasty and rapacious Reform'.[16]

News of attempts at hasty and rapacious reform elsewhere had begun to appear in the papers while they were in Edinburgh – the Bastille had fallen on 14 July and the head of its governor, the marquis de Launay, had been paraded through the streets on a pike to the Palais Royal. Hester did not at first view the turmoil in France too seriously. 'My Notion is *strictly* this,' she wrote to Lysons:

> the present Sovereign will have much to suffer, but that if the little Dauphin turns out a Youth of good Parts, and personal Accomplishments, the French will have fatigued themselves with their own violent Exertions just by the Time that his Merit or Figure will strike them ... How do you like my Prophecy? Mrs. Siddons always says what a good *Hoper* I am.[17]

From Glasgow they drove south, admiring the English Lakes, visiting Mrs Strickland, spending time at Liverpool with John Philip Kemble and his wife Priscilla.[18] 'I think Mr. Piozzi must write the Account of *this* Town,' Hester wrote to Miss Weston; 'he is all Day upon the Docks, and all night at the Theatre.' But she too was impressed by Liverpool, particularly by how clean it was – 'the Streets embellished with showy Shops all Day, and lighted up like Oxford Road all Night. A Harbour full of ships: a chearful, opulent, commodious City.'[19]

In Wales there was business to attend to. 'Mr. Piozzi will tell you how severely our Affairs have suffered by Neglect,' she told Mrs Byron. 'He is excessively active and diligent to mend Matters however; is adored by the Tenants, and delighted in by the Neighbouring Gentlemen.' The estate consisted of some 600 acres, but was made up of a dozen or so so-called 'tenements', the largest of 273 acres, the smallest no more than three: 'These nasty Steward's Accounts crack my Brains, I know no more of Business now than Cæcilia does: and have at best just Sense enough to see that I am cheated, without knowing how to extricate myself. Had not God given me always a large Fortune, I must have been in Prison Years ago.'[20]

It became plain that Hester's steward, Edward Edwards, had been embezzling rents from the tenants. He was dismissed and replaced by a mercer in Denbigh called Thomas Lloyd. The Piozzis now began to buy up parcels of meadow and woodland in Tremeirchion parish; by the following year the estate had grown to more than 800 acres, with an annual value of £502. Thoughts of returning to her roots were forming in Hester's mind: 'My best Amusement here was planning a House with Windows every way,' she wrote in her 'Journey Book' and she told Miss Weston, 'In a few days I intend to go to see our Little estate, and choose the place for building a Little Cottage.'[21]

Word reached her from time to time that Queeney, now twenty-five, had become engaged. She received the latest rumour with some detachment: 'Well! I have heard *some* body say *some*thing of Colonel Balfour *some* time or other,' she wrote to Mrs Byron: 'but it was good, by what I can remember: an Irishman is often honest, and almost always brave, whatever Defects he may have.'[22] Nisbet Balfour was in fact the son of a Scottish laird and at forty-six, much closer in age to Hester herself than to Queeney. He had distinguished himself in the American War of Independence and on his return was made aide-de-camp to the King. The rumour of an engagement was unfounded. The following year Balfour entered Parliament, where he gave his loyal support to Pitt. He was promoted to general during the Napoleonic Wars and would die, unmarried, in 1823.

Having brought some order into their affairs in Wales, the Piozzis moved on to Bath. Although she felt that 'Bath Chat' would benefit from an injection of 'solid London Talk', Hester liked the company well enough to stay for six weeks. 'Do not speak ill of Bath,' she adjured Chappelow: 'it is a lovely Place, and our Master's Lungs were never in better Order; everybody said last Night that he sung beyond himself: and Mrs. Siddons has felt the Benefit of Bathing here, and how can one hate a Town that does such People good!'

She was, she told him, 'impatient to write upon a Subject which engrosses the Attention of everybody here'. This was the appearance of a child prodigy called Bridgetower, who had made his début in Paris earlier in the year at the age of nine. 'This wonderful Child is a Mulattoe,' Hester wrote, 'offspring of an African Negro by a Polish Dutchess ... such are his Powers upon the Violin as to have extorted Money and Applause from the professors themselves.'[23] If she was excited by the boy's playing, she was swept off her feet by his father, who had been a page to Prince Esterhàzy and was referred to as 'the Abyssinian Prince':

Languages, Address and Elegance of Person he possesses to a Wonder:

Was he less eager to display his Talents it were better, but he is a fine
Fellow with all his Faults ... Was he sent hither by Providence to prove
the Equality of Blacks and Whites I wonder, he would make a beautiful
Figure at the Bar of the House of Commons ... he is so very flashy a
Talker, and has a Manner so distinguished for lofty Gayety, and univer-
sality of Conversation, I can but think all Day how Dr. Johnson would
have adored that Man![24]

The Piozzis returned to Hanover Square at the end of December,
and before many weeks had passed Hester began to have doubts about
her newfound paragon. 'In return for the best News here – that of our
charming Siddons' gradual Recovery; let me beg some Truths from
Bath,' she wrote to Thomas Whalley:

> Is Bridgetower in prison for having had to do with Sharpers? He was
> here last Week, – and calling on us asked Mr. Piozzi to lend him 30£
> which was no Proof of his *Sharpness* I think, to suppose one should
> throw such Sums into the Lap of a Man one had not seen Six Times,
> and whose Son never played at our house ...[25]

Soon she was describing him in *Thraliana* as 'this Negro Mountebank':
'Poor Bridgetower! That thou art a fine Fellow I can see, that thou art
a Scoundrel I can only believe – but how in Nature thou shouldst be
an honest Man, I certainly cannot imagine.'

❧ ☙

There was fresh unpleasantness with Queeney and her sisters in the
early months of 1790; Hester let off steam in *Thraliana* with near-Gothic
intensity: ''Tis now productive of Sensations exceeding disagreeable to
hear the Names of my Daughters, or meet the Countenances of their
Guardians: At Sight of a Murderer the wound even of a dead man whom
he has killed unclose & bleed afresh – *so do mine*, when chance has
thrown those Ladies, or their Adherents in my Way.'

She recorded what she described as 'a nasty Transaction with Miss
Thrale'. It appeared that Tibson, the old family nurse, who had stayed
with Queeney since Hester's remarriage, had made several visits to
Streatham in their absence, 'and seldom left it without carrying somewhat

away'. On one occasion she had taken a locksmith with her and broken open John Salusbury's old sea chest, in which Hester had left a number of things she did not care to leave with tenants:

> ... Mr Piozzi talked *half an hour* of seizing & imprisoning the old Woman, sending her a Letter to give her some hint of his Intentions – but Miss Thrale, instead of concealing or softening the Story setting steadily to protect the Thief – We let the Business drop, lest old Nurse should swing on a Gallows – or take a Trip on a new Discovery to Botany Bay.

Hester also recorded about this time a chance encounter with Fanny Burney:

> I met Miss Burney at an Assembly last night, 'tis Six years since I had seen her: She appear'd most *fondly* rejoiced – in good Time! And Mrs Locke, at whose house we stumbled on each other, pretended that She had *such* a Regard for me &c. I answered with Ease & Coldness, but in exceeding Good humour; and we talked about the King & Queen, his Majesty's Illness & Recovery – and all ended as it should do with perfect Indifference.

Several friends had suggested that Hester should publish an account of her recent travels. The idea did not appeal, but the manner in which she dismissed it is extraordinary:

> They say it to ensnare me: was I to act according to such Advice I should deservedly lose the little Fame I have already acquired. How false the Creatures all are!!! But I *know* them ... They have always played the same Game with me whatever my Name or Place was, and how has it answer'd? – why always the same way I think. Those who have aimed at shortening my Life, lowering my Reputation or emptying my Purse, have had the constant Torment of seeing my Health stronger, my Fame fairer, and my Pockets fuller than almost anybody else's.

This is either silly or paranoid. Johnson's *Journey* was one of the books she had carried with her to reread in Scotland: 'I look it over now every day with double Delight,' she had written to Mrs Byron from Edinburgh,[26] and she was certainly wise not to contemplate publishing anything that might be compared unfavourably with it. But who are these nameless 'false Creatures' lying in wait to ensnare her? And if, as she boasts, she has consistently outsmarted them in the past, what has she to fear from them now? We are not told. Perhaps they are creatures of her imagination, pressed into service to mask an underlying fear that she might not be able to equal the success of *Observations*.

She had in any event for some time past had it in mind to attempt something different. 'If all goes well this Time,' she had written when *Observations* was still with the printer, 'I'll have a Stroke at the Stage another Year.' Now she had made a start: 'I am writing for the Stage a Dramatic Trifle from poor Dr. Johnson's Floretta: will it be liked I wonder?' Floretta was the heroine in a piece called 'The Fountains: a Fairy Tale' which Johnson had contributed to Anna Williams's *Miscellanies*, not long after the beginning of his friendship with the Thrales. 'Come Mistress,' he had said to Hester, 'now *I'll* write a Tale and your Character shall be in it.'

By a strange irony, Hester now heard that her character was to figure in a rather different tale: 'I hear Baretti's Enmity towards me outlived his Powers of exerting it; and that he left a Libel behind him desiring it might be printed to vex me. – Can such Malignity inhabit the heart of any thing but Dæmons? ... Mr James of Bath said he saw it, but I scarce believed him –'

What Mr James of Bath had seen was the text of a play called *The Sentimental Mother, a Comedy in Five Acts*, published anonymously the previous June. The subtitle announced it as *The Legacy of an Old Friend, and His Last Moral Lesson to Mrs. Hester Lynch Thrale, Now Mrs. Hester Lynch Piozzi*.

It was pretty poisonous stuff. The main character is Lady Fantasma Tunskull – vain, affected, parsimonious, nymphomaniac. Her husband, Sir Timothy, is an amiable nonentity who thinks of nothing but eating and sleeping (was Baretti ignorant of Thrale's philandering?). Their daughter Caroline, on the other hand – as Queeney was in Baretti's eyes – is a paragon of all the virtues. Lady Fantasma, when not lusting after their suitors, intrigues to cheat her daughters of their dowries, an enterprise in which she is aided by their singing-master, the odious Signor Squalici.[27]

It was an elaborate revenge; whether Hester ever saw the full text of the play is unknown. She had in any case more important things to occupy her mind in the spring of 1790:

> We are going to Streatham on Saturday next – for *Good* as the Phrase is, – yet I am in no high Spirits about it. Mr Piozzi had a slight Spitting of Blood a Week ago, & it alarmed me, & my Nerves now will bear no more Shocks ... My charming Husband has changed the furniture of every Room that convey'd black Ideas, & perpetuates the remembrance of every Circumstance likely to please me with extreme Tenderness and kind Solicitude: he spends Treasures of Money upon the Place, tho' it belongs to his & my most inveterate Enemies ...[28]
>
> I *ought* to be happy & thankful, & go to Streatham in the best Humour possible – & *so I will too*.
>
> Addio Londra!

STREATHAM had been knocked about a bit in the eight years since it had been let to Lord Shelburne. The lease had been taken over in 1786 by General Dalrymple, a brother of the Earl of Stair, who had bred pigs; the latest tenant, Thomas Steele of the Treasury, had kept a goat.

The Piozzis spent freely to renovate and refurbish the property. 'Well! We have lived more merrily than wisely, to be sure,' Hester wrote; 'the Expences fright me: *such* Improvements! & a Chimney Piece that costs 100 Guineas for a House not our own.' Adorned with the numerous art objects they had acquired in Italy – the paintings by Ruysdael and Cipriani and Canaletto, the Etruscan vases from Cicero's villa in Tusculum – Streatham was now much more opulently furnished than it had been in Thrale's day. 'The Misses will be told how fine Piozzi has made their House – & will wish him & his Wife dead the more I suppose,' Hester wrote in *Thraliana*: 'If I go first, he w^d be turned out in a Day I trust, and might take my dead Body with him, for from their Toleration nothing could be hoped – I never knew so rancorous a Hatred ...'

They celebrated their sixth wedding anniversary in style. 'Seventy People eat at our Expence,' Hester recorded proudly:

> – the Plate so fine too, the China so showy, all so magnificent, and at the Time of Dinner Horns Clarinets &c wch afterwards performed upon the Water in our new Boat that makes such a beautiful, such an elegant Figure ... at Night the Trees & Front of the House were illuminated with Colour'd Lamps, that called forth our Neighbours from all the adjacent Villages to admire & enjoy such Diversion. Many Friends swear that not less than a Thousand Men women & Children might have been counted in the House & Grounds ...

Her mind ran insistently through the summer months on religious matters. Her beliefs were what a later age would describe as fundamentalist. Chappelow said in her hearing one day that the story of Adam and Eve was an old wives' tale — 'that he believed the World was five Hundred thousand years old at least, with many other equally *impious* Positions'. Hester was profoundly shocked. 'Surely to doubt *one Word* of the Sacred Scriptures, is no other than a direct *Sin against the Holy Ghost.*'

Her musings occasionally took an apocalyptic turn: 'I do myself verily think that the World is drawing on to a Conclusion which is scarcely further off now than 210 Years — & the ten odd ones are probably swallow'd up by the Days lost in our Calculations since Cæsar's Divison of the Months &c.' She speculated on the nature of the happiness enjoyed by the saints in heaven, and concluded that it was progressive; she also disposed briskly of a matter of doctrine that over the centuries had furrowed the brow of countless theologians: 'With Regard to Identity of Body at the Resurrection, I see little more Difficulty than in many a Proposition less cavilled at ... My Grandmothers were old Women when I knew them, to me therefore they must at the Day of Judgement appear Old; how else shall I know em? ... To their Parents & Nurses however they must appear Babies ...'

She would have loved Stanley Spencer.

Sarah Siddons, still struggling with ill health, was a guest at Streatham for several weeks in the spring and early summer. 'I think mighty well of her Virtue, & am amazed at the Cultivated State in which I have found her Mind,' Hester wrote: 'that She loves *me* I am not so sure, but I love her exceedingly.' She became convinced that her condition had been hopelessly misdiagnosed, and persuaded her to turn to Sir Lucas Pepys. 'Poor pretty Siddons! A warm Heart, & a cold Husband are sad things to contend with, but she'll get thro.'

As indeed she did. Pepys quickly recognized that he was dealing with a case of recurrent depression. In a letter to a friend, William, her 'cold Husband' — his infidelities were common knowledge — reported a remarkable improvement:

> To be as brief as possible, either from Sir Lucas, the air, or Mrs. Piozzi's attention and witty concorse, she is amazingly better, and sleeps the whole night without waking — what she has not known for a year and a

half past. She has got her flesh again, and I think looks as well as ever she did in her life.[1]

By early summer, Hester had completed the first two acts of her 'Stroke at the Theatre'. In Johnson's cautionary fable – essentially a version for children of *The Vanity of Human Wishes* – the heroine, Floretta, is granted fairy powers. By drinking from an alabaster fountain fed by the Spring of Joy, her every wish will be granted; a wish can only be retracted by drinking from a fountain of dark flint fed by the Spring of Sorrow. As she takes the golden cup for the first time, she is given a warning – water from the spring of sorrow will be as bitter as the water of joy was sweet. She wishes for beauty, for a faithful lover, for a great fortune – but returns each time, disillusioned, to the fountain of flint. Finally she conceives the desire to be endowed with something traditionally associated with men – wit. The results are predictably painful. There is no happy ending to Johnson's bleak tale. Floretta drinks one last draught from the flint fountain and resigns herself 'to the course of nature'.

Hester fashioned from this a masque set in thirteenth-century Derbyshire, complete with knights and their ladies. She wrote a part for Oberon, 'Tyrant of Faery Land', who decrees that Floretta's fairy powers must come to an end; it was at once more elaborate and more romantic than Johnson's unadorned tale, and written in verse, not prose. 'Kemble and his sister both pretend to like my little Drama,' she wrote in *Thraliana*, 'but I dare say would see me hanged, rather than bring out at the very slightest personal Hazard of ten pence Loss, as well as they pretend to love me –' Like Floretta, with whom she so clearly identified, she has drunk more than once from the bitter waters of the dark fountain: 'My last Set of Friends have however done me *one* Favour; they have cured me of suspecting Kindness from any one. I am not cured of loving *others*, but shall never more believe that any one loves *me*.'

※ ☙

It was a warm summer. 'The thermometer stood this day at 87 1/2 placed in the Shade at South Lambeth,' Hester noted in late June. She also recorded that the hay harvest had been 'eminently prosperous – in many Places two Load to an Acre, a Proportion scarce ever known before'. And it pleased her that her husband was settling contentedly into his new role as an English country gentleman: 'Mr Piozzi gave his Haymakers and servants a *Festa di Ballo* with Roast Beef and Rum Punch for sixty Persons – so we had a gallant Harvest home –'

Hester had qualms about the cost of the recent improvements: 'Poor Piozzi has sure enough, a little *over*-done the Business; & put us into a little Distress for Money, to pay these last Bills: which amount to no less than two Thousand Pounds Sterling, a Sum perhaps imprudently laid out on a Seat whence if I dye tomorrow, he must instantly be gone.'

It was perhaps these concerns which prompted Piozzi to suggest they should make enquiries about several tracts of land granted to Hester's father in Nova Scotia forty years previously. Thrale had at one time made an abortive attempt to regain possession of them; Hester now wrote to a lawyer called Sterns in Halifax asking whether he could ascertain the present value of the properties and granting him power of attorney.[2]

It turned out that there had been four such tracts, covering between 200 and 300 acres, but that they had all been forfeited after twenty or thirty years for want of any kind of improvement. It seemed for a time there might be some prospect of repossessing them. It would be necessary to provide Stern with the original patents, and to furnish proof that Hester was indeed her father's daughter and 'only legitimate issue'.[3] This sent her on a journey into her past: 'Dr Parker, Mr Hale of Kings Walden, & poor Mr Lawrence all named in the very early Vol^s of Thraliana as my very earliest Friends, Admirers & Sweethearts, were hasty to come forward & give what help they could. I shed Tears of Tenderness over dear Lawrence's Letter; –We had once half loved – and once half quarrel'd – but never met for many, many Years ...'

The matter dragged on for eighteen months. Initially, Hester's hopes ran high. 'My Property in America is likely to turn out of more Value than I thought it,' she wrote; an acquaintance newly arrived from Nova Scotia had told her it was 'well worth looking after'. But eventually it became clear that an appeal to the Court of Chancery would be necessary. The Piozzis quailed at the prospect of wading into a costly legal quagmire; the attempt was abandoned.

It seemed possible in the autumn of 1790 that there would be war with Spain. Two years previously the English explorer John Meares

had established a trading post at Nootka Sound on what is now Vancouver Island; the Spanish, laying claim to the whole Pacific coast of the
Americas, had seized the post and a number of ships. Parliament voted a
military credit of £1 million and at the beginning of October Pitt issued
an ultimatum. 'War is now once more hourly expected,' Hester wrote:
'I am not sorry, tho' the Stocks *do* fall ... A War will open the Eyes of
our silly pretended Patriots; and shew them that France still preserves
its original Aversion to us, & preference of Spanish Connections, tho'
here there has been such a Talk about their Tenderness tow'rds England,
and desire of imitating its Constitution ...'

She viewed the Spanish ambassador with a particularly baleful eye:

> The Marquis de Campo is a *Traitor sure*; I marked him one Night, he
> knew me not, it was in a mixed Company with ten Card-Tables ... he
> spoke Spanish with a Friend ... and little imagined there stood near him
> one who understood a Tongue so little studied.
>
> His Discourse was very contemptuous, very cruel I may say, towards
> the Person of our unfortunate Sovereign; whose utter extinction he
> seemed as eager for – as if his King were to have been immediate Heir ...

French support was not forthcoming, and Spain backed off. The first
Nootka Convention, negotiated by Captain George Vancouver[4] and his
Spanish counterpart, was signed at the end of October; the war clouds
lifted.

Piozzi was considering visiting Italy by himself the following year
'to take a farewel Leave of Father Bro[rs] Family & old Friends'. Hester
fretted a good deal at the thought – 'they will try to keep him from
ever returning; or if he does return, will send him home perhaps with a
Heart alienated from England & from me'. She regarded the Romanists,
as she called them, as an unscrupulous lot: '... the most pious among
them would think himself not only justified but meritorious in the Sight
of God & his Confessor to throw a Woman of his own Language &
Perswasion in his Way, to make what they would hope an irreparable
Breach between us'.

She did not really know her man. Piozzi could think of nothing more
agreeable than the life of an English – or Welsh – squire. After Christmas they went down to Bath; while they were there, he delighted her

by sketching plans for a cottage on Tremeirchion Hill in her beloved Clwyd.

❦

Hester was now close to fifty, and the ranks of her older friends were beginning to thin: 'Poor dear dead Mrs. Byron! Nobleness, Elegance, Animated Beauty – Promptitude of Wit, Capacity for Thought – could no longer avail her it seems ... Sweet Soul! In her Way she loved *me* dearly ...'

Michael Lort died on the same day: 'I loved Dr Lort; he was a Man one could tell one's whole heart to – I have now no Creature that I really confide in – all Acquaintances & no Friends ... Delap would be my next Choice for true Worthiness of Heart, & Cultivation of Mind; but one never sees him, & he knows beside no more of the World than a Baby ...'

Bath had its usual tonic effect, and she quickly regained her customary resilience. 'Here I have good air and good Water and good Company – and at last – *good Nights*,' she told Miss Weston, 'so that I mean to be among the merriest immediately.'[5] She was in equally good spirits when she wrote to Chappelow a fortnight later: 'Bath is a mighty pretty Translation of London, and I like it better than the original – for the same Reason as I do Pope's Homer – because I *understand* It better and because 'tis *easier*.'[6]

The 'perpetual Nothingnesses' in which she told Chappelow she was engaged eventually palled, and by early April they had returned to Streatham, 'not sorry to come home'. She noted that fifteen years had elapsed since she had first, as she put it, 'made the *Thraliana* my Confident, my solitary Comfort, and Depositary of every Thought as it arose'. Now she recorded in it the start of the menopause:

> I believe my *oldest Friend* is at last going to leave me, and that will probably make a Change in my Health ...
>
> When I was a Girl of ten Years old perhaps, the Measles attacked & put me in some Danger[7] – leaving at their Departure a small red swelling on my Cheek ... & it remained there till the *Change of Life* took it quite away. That very mark is now upon this second *critical Change* returned ...

I am now exactly 50 Years old I think, & am possessed of great
Corporal Strength blessed be God, with ability to endure Fatigue if
necessary. The Nerves however so shaken between the years 1779 and
1784 cannot be expected to recover their Tone ...

Within days of writing this, Hester's nerves were once more to be
severely shaken. The year 1779 was the year in which Thrale had died,
but only now did she learn from Cator and Perkins the true cause of
the seizure he had suffered at his sister's dinner table, and which marked
the beginning of his decline. He had been stunned to discover that Nesbitt had died insolvent and that he himself could in consequence face
bankruptcy.

Possibly he had forgotten that nineteen years previously, three years
before his marriage to Hester, he had entered into a joint venture with his
brother-in-law involving a liability of £220,000.[8] Nesbitt had purchased
some French annuities; discovering shortly afterwards that he was in
need of ready money, he sought Government permission to offload them
to English investors. This was granted on condition that he offered
suitable security; Thrale agreed to join him as co-signatory to a bond
guaranteeing this, and the annuities were sold at public auction.

Nesbitt's insolvency, however, made Thrale and his heirs solely liable;
hence his anguished outburst – 'I am a ruined Man, and have undone
my family' – which Hester had brutally dismissed at the time as the
talk of a man who had 'lost his Head'. It now dawned on her that for
all those years she and her daughters had been perched on the rim of
a volcano. With the onset of revolutionary turmoil in France, payment
of the annuities had ceased; if therefore the Pitt administration were to
demand payment on behalf of the English investors – something which
both Perkins and Cator thought likely – the volcano would erupt:

Thus have his poor Girls been living as Women of Fortune when all
they have on Earth will not suffice to answer the Claims of Government, should the Talons of it be laid on their Possessions after ten Years
Enjoyment. Cruel Supposition! Dreadful Misfortune! curst imprudence!
But Friendships formed in Debauchery and Profaneness – how should
they end? That Nesbitt was a shockingly wicked Fellow always – how
could Mr Thrale adore him so! ...

She recalled her father's angry reaction all those years ago when her uncle had been pressing Thrale's suit: '*if the* Child does marry that Puppy, I know he'll be a Bankrupt'. She did her best to look on 'the *hoping* Side' as she called it: 'Our fears of a War with Russia are all over, the Stocks rise, and our gallant Minister will not 'tis to be hoped, want Money ... We tell Cæcilia nothing, because the less is said about such Matters – the less will be done: Government may *forget*, if our Clamours do not *remind*; & prompt sleeping Justice to Arm his red right Hand to plague us. Milton.'

Her main concern was for Queeney, and 'that hereditary Disposition She has from her poor Papa of sinking down, even from Apprehension of a Change in Fortune'. The barrier built up by years of mistrust and misunderstanding was temporarily breached by a flood of maternal feeling: '... may she dear Soul! Never increase her own Vexations by a thought of *me*! Unless it should dispose her to fly into my Arms, and in the Warmth of the Embrace receive full Conviction of my pure, my fond forgiveness ...'

She and Piozzi had felt for some time that they were over-extended financially, and an arrangement had been made to let the Hanover Square house to the Earl of Dumfries: '...our Establishment here is too magnificent for the admission of other Expences, and if we are prudent even Bath must be given up for this Season, for one cannot do every thing; tho' by Dint of Management I see that a great deal may be done with *3000*£ o'Year. Mr Piozzi is a capital Manager.'

Although she was deeply attached to Piozzi, she did not romanticize their relationship; she read his character every bit as clearly as she had read Thrale's. She records in *Thraliana* a conversation with a Mrs Jackson of Jamaica who had been with her husband and children on a ship that caught fire; the husband could have escaped, but refused to abandon her:

Now I have had two Husbands; and as good ones as can be hoped
... yet neither of them I am confident would have paid me any such
Compliment: Piozzi would have hasten'd to save himself, & have said
Bisogna pensar all'individuo, che così Dio vuole. Thrale would have
been so tardy in escaping, that he would only have reflected on his own

good Luck; & laughed heartily at any one supposing he could at such a moment be thinking *on a Wife* ...

Although this throws revealing – and entertaining – light on both husbands, it casts even more on Hester herself. The entry in *Thraliana* was made on the very day she heard the appalling tale of Thrale's financial recklessness.

᷍ ᷍

She continued to read widely, and not only in English: 'I have been reading Gasparo Gozzi; 'tis inconceivable how Baretti imitated that authour in all his lighter Pieces.'[9] *Reflections on the Revolution in France* had recently appeared and she was full of admiration: 'How finely does Burke beat them down under his feet!'

She also read William Beckford's *Vathek*, although she disapproved of what today would be described as the author's sexual orientation: '... 'tis a mad Book to be sure, and written by a mad Author, yet there is a Sublimity about it – particularly towards the Conclusion. Mr Beckford's *favourite Propensity* is all along visible I think ...'[10]

Hester awaited the publication of one particular book with a mixture of eagerness and apprehension. It had been long in the making. Boswell himself had kept the pot boiling by planting the occasional puff in the papers, some of them crude thrusts at Hester, as often as not loaded with crude sexual innuendo. 'The Wits expect me to tremble,' Hester wrote: 'what will the Fellow say? – that has not been said already.' The *Morning Post* had reassuring news for its readers. Mr Boswell, it declared, was 'honest and benevolent' – he was 'pursuing an Eagle', not 'plucking a feather from a *tom tit*'.[11]

The two volumes appeared on 16 May. 'I have been now laughing & crying by turns for two Days over Boswell's Book,' Hester wrote: 'That poor Man should have a *Bon Bouillon* and be put to bed, – he is quite light-headed. Yet Madmen, Drunkards, & Fools tell Truth they say: and if Johnson was to me the back Friend he has represented – let it cure me of ever making *Friendship* more with any human Being – let it cure me!'

⁓❧ 26 ❧⁓
Bozzy's Revenge

WHAT HURT most was the way it made her relive the day that Harry died:

> The Death of my Son ... so shockingly brought forward in Boswell's two Guinea Book, made me very ill this Week, very ill indeed; it would make the *modern* Friends all buy the Work I fancy, did they but know how sick the *ancient* Friends, had it in their Power to make me: but I had more Wit than tell any of 'em.

Susanna had just come of age. 'We drank her Health & sincerely do I wish it her,' Hester wrote, but she added bitterly, 'I wonder whether those Girls read Boswell's Book? & whether they enjoy the Insults offered to their Mother ...' Boswell had, in fact, taken Courtenay's advice, and toned down some of the more intemperate things he had written about Hester and her *Anecdotes*, but enough remained that was deeply wounding. James Clifford puts the matter succinctly: 'As an artistic achievement in depreciation it remains a masterpiece.'[1]

To the end of her days, Hester would continue to reread the *Life*, annotating both a fifth edition which appeared in 1807 and an eighth edition published nine years later. She never knew that the *Ode* on her approaching nuptials with Johnson was Boswell's – 'Whose silly Fun was this?' she wrote mildly in the margin. Accusations of inaccuracy or carelessness she countered by pointing to infelicities of style or bad taste on Boswell's part, or simply dismissed with a shrug.

She launches an occasional barb at Johnson. In 1774, when they were touring Wales, he had described it in a letter to Boswell as 'a very beautiful and rich country, all enclosed and planted'. Hester was indignant. 'Yet to please Mr. Thrale,' says her marginal note, 'he feign'd Abhorrence of it.' In another letter, Johnson had written, 'She has a great regard for you.' The record is briskly corrected: 'Not I – never had: I thought him a clever and a comical fellow.' Wearily, she offers what might just be mistaken for a small compliment: 'Curiosity carried Boswell further than it ever carried any Mortal breathing.'

Hester had herself started work on a new project. 'I have written a pamphlet or thin flat octavo Book on popular Subjects – the Title Una and Duessa,' she wrote '– but Mr Piozzi won't let me print it, for fear of making Enemies, & such Stuff.' She took her title from Spenser's *Faerie Queen*, an allegory in praise of Elizabeth I where Una represents the True Church, and Duessa the 'false religion' of Catholicism – and Mary Queen of Scots. They engage in six dialogues on a range of subjects – liberty of the press, the relative merits of painting and poetry, Negro emancipation.

In one of them Una attacks the French *philosophes* – 'See you not that they are seeking to infect England with their Folly?' Elsewhere she refutes the arguments in Paine's *Rights of Man*, which had recently appeared, and advances a no-nonsense Tory defence of property and social mobility. The Dialogues have none of the liveliness that characterizes the best of Hester's letters or travel writing. Whether Piozzi was equipped to make a judgement about their potential for making enemies is doubtful. In a footnote to *Thraliana* Hester sets out a more likely reason for his lack of enthusiasm: 'Piozzi likes the Money I get well enough, but dislikes ye Manner of getting it; he married a Donna not a *Virtuosa* he says.'

In the late summer Hester accepted an invitation to spend some time with Mrs Siddons, who was staying on the estate of Lord and Lady Harcourt at Nuneham Courtenay near Oxford. It was not the most successful of visits. Siddons suffered another miscarriage, there was a violent storm in which they saw a woman killed by lightning, the food was 'insupportably ill dress'd, dirty & scanty' and Hester's spaniel Phillis went on heat.

It had all begun so idyllically:

The View from our Cottage window was enchanting, Mrs Siddons sate spinning under a great Tree at the Door, reminding one of Circe as Homer describes ... but her Illness laid an Extinguisher on every Comfort, & that settled Despair of Recovery with which nervous

Patients are particularly afflicted, preying on *her* Spirits, stole mine too imperceptibly away –

By early September she was back at Streatham, where the temperature stood at ninety-six in the shade. 'Very astonishing at close of the year so,' Hester wrote, '& I fear bodes no Good, – *nous verrons*.' The phrase global warming had not yet entered the language.

Piozzi kept a close eye on Hester's financial affairs, and had become increasingly suspicious of Cator. The immediate matter at issue was a sum of £186.0.6d – rent due from Thomas Lovegrove at Crowmarsh – which had not been paid. Hester drafted a letter for Piozzi to sign: 'I am very earnest to have done trifling and very weary of our way of going on,' she wrote, and having reiterated their grievance, ended with a threat of legal action: 'Then good Sir let me this last Time be seriously listened to; nor force upon me a suit so scandalous to yourself – for if there is Justice in England, it will not be refused by the Courts thereof to your humble Servant/Gabriel Piozzi.'[2]

That did the trick; Cator paid up at once. He wrote ten days later defending his management of Hester's affairs, adding lamely, 'But in order to have no more trouble Mr C. will give Mr. Piozzi all the Information in his power, which is only from Memory.'[3] Hester was unimpressed. 'This Man is a Hero of Rascality,' she wrote, '– when Hanging Time comes, he should have the right Hand of all the Thieves in the Cart I think.'

She had not given up hope of having her play produced. Some of her friends, after all, had seen good things in it: 'You have catered here for my Tooth exactly,' Bishop Percy had told her. The fairies, he declared, were 'the best since Shakespeare's'. Now, just before the start of the new season, there was encouraging news: 'Mr Kemble has sent for my little Drama ... My Fairies would cut a nice Figure! I wish he may want them: – & if poor Siddons is sick, & Miss Farren – *called to the Upper House* there will be neither Tragedy nor Comedy, & so *my* Stuff may come in Play.'

In September Hester noted that it was twenty-seven years since she had given birth to Queeney: '...who is God be praised – (at least as I hear) – still alive, and my *beautiful Daughter* yet: but never married: a thing apparently strange enough, as her Person is agreeable, her

Knowledge extensive, and her Fortune high, (if the Government lets her enjoy it in Peace.)'

Cecilia, meanwhile, not yet fifteen, had an admirer called James Drummond, a member – or so he gave Hester to understand – of the banking family. 'Well! There's no great harm in that to be sure; he expects to rise & be one of the Partners: a proper Ambition for a young Clerk,' she wrote: 'Yet my Duty teaches to give no Encouragement where a large sum of Money must be sunk I suppose to purchase a perhaps imaginary Joynture: Cecilia w^d take to the house we'll say 40 or 50,000^£ and what *Certainty* can they give her of a competent – I mean adequate Annuity after his Death should She survive him.'

Of greater immediate concern was her husband's health. Piozzi was afflicted by that ubiquitous Georgian disorder, gout, and as winter came on he suffered a severe attack: 'Mr Piozzi has had Gout upon his Throat, his Voice – all that could agitate and terrifie me: but now *Safe's* the Word, and I care little for his *Pain* poor Soul if we can but keep away Danger.'[4]

She was briefly cast down in December when she heard that Kemble had decided against *The Fountains*: 'Mr Piozzi is angry & I am sorry – but what cares Kemble for either!' Her spirits revived over Christmas – 'Here is fine frosty seasonable Weather, & all goes well' – only to plunge again before the New Year was more than a week old: 'Here is a dreadful event! A dreadful Discovery rather!' The Piozzis had a neighbour at Streatham called Daniel MacNamara, a well-known Irish lawyer who acted as the London agent for several public men, including the Irish chief justice and the Duke of Bedford. MacNamara had discovered that their marriage settlement, by which her Welsh estate would pass to Piozzi, had not been properly drawn up and was invalid:

Pretty News! and if I dye tonight it seems poor old Bachygraig &c. falls to the King. Strange I should not have a power of leaving to whom I please what was transmitted to me from so many Ancestors! Horrible that my poor Husband should have nothing to live on after my Death; when he has been spending so liberally on me & mine during our Joynt Lives! ... Mr Piozzi bears it a great deal better than I do – but I have had so many Mortifications! will this be the last I wonder –

It was not. Worry over MacNamara's discovery had laid Piozzi low again with gouty spasms in his stomach, and they decided to go to Bath to take the waters. They were pursued there by young James Drummond, who made such a nuisance of himself that Hester felt obliged to write to Henry Drummond,[5] a senior partner at the bank:

> Mr James Drummond has visited at our House since last September and thought fit to make open Declaration of Love, and formal proposals of Marriage to my Daughter Cæcilia Thrale when only 14 Years and 8 Months old. A strange Impropriety sure! ...
>
> We all know the Dangers and Disadvantages of Engagements begun in Babyhood, a Folly which would lead to Circumstances peculiarly vexatious in Cecilia's case who being a Ward in Chancery cannot command her own Fortune for six Years to come.[6]

Drummond sent a courteous reply. There was, he wrote, no family connection, but 'if my advice can influence his future conduct, I hope you will have no further reason for complaint'.[7] Hester returned to Streatham mollified, if not entirely reassured: 'The sight of our Family settled so near London frights me tho' – for he certainly *may* bribe himself into the Girl's Bedchamber, if he'll pay handsomely – at least I should fear so: and then *we are all at his Feet*.'

Young Drummond did not give up easily. He wrote to Cecilia in April urging her to convince her mother that 'the happiness of children ought not to be sported with'. Cecilia dutifully showed the letter to Hester and asked her to draft a reply, although she made it plain that her surrender was not unconditional:

> My darling Mother you will not be a little surprised to find by this that *for the present* I give up James Drummond. At a *future time* however, if I find I *really* love him why as we shall neither of us be superannuated I hope all will go on well but *now* I will neither *see*, *hear*, or *think*, of him ...

Hester's suspicions – and fears – were not so easily dispelled, particularly after she discovered not only that Drummond had bribed a servant to carry his picture to Cecilia but had had the effrontery to have the banns read at Christchurch, Southwark.[8] The problems arising from her marriage settlement proved less intractable. She wrote a new will, and Piozzi embarked on the lengthy process of becoming naturalized. By August of the following year he was a British subject – 'he is now empowered to take whatever I am willing to leave', Hester wrote, '& my Children lose nothing'.

Joshua Reynolds died in February of that year. 'Poor Sir Joshua! Another of our Library Portraits gone,' Hester wrote: '... dismal enough – this Man was never much of a personal Favourite with me however; so I only feel that kind of general Sullenness rather than Sorrow, which Death & Defalcation naturally produce'.

It was rumoured – Hester heard it from the Bishop of Dromore – that Reynolds's Life was to be written by Boswell. 'Let us be careful of our health my Lord said I – or he will write our Lives too.'

She was turning over in her mind a new literary project:

a two Volume Book of *Synonymes* in English, like what the Abbé Girard has done in French, for the use of Foreigners, and other Children of six feet high ... I have not depth of Literature to do it as one ought. – a good parlour-Window Book is however quite within my Compass, and such a one would bring me Fame for ought I know, & a hundred Pounds which I want more; for this last Bath Journey has been marvel- lously expensive – between giving Balls & Suppers, & Stuff to divert Cecilia Thrale's empty head from this paltry Fellow ...

For a time, however, synonyms had to compete for attention with more material matters: 'We are going to Wales, where Piozzi thinks of building a Cottage ...' By mid-September they were installed in the Crown Inn at Denbigh. Work had already begun on the new house. It stood on higher ground than Bach-y-Graig and they originally thought of calling it *Belvedere* but eventually settled on a curious Welsh/Italian coinage meaning 'beautiful hill' – *Brynbella*. Returning from an expedi- tion there one day they were caught in the rain, and their stay turned into something of a nightmare. They had taken with them as company for Cecilia Sarah Siddons's daughter Sally, a good-looking girl of seventeen. Both girls became ill, Cecilia quite seriously so, with difficulty in breath- ing and spitting of blood. 'We sent for Haygarth from Chester,' Hester wrote, '& he bled her copiously, so *She* recovered poor Soul, but *I* was nearly finished up with such dismal Suffering.'

Not long after their return Hester was distressed – and indignant – to discover that the true cause of the ill-health which had dogged Mrs Siddons for so long was a venereal infection from her husband. 'Poor Siddons pities my very Soul to see her,' she wrote:

> … as indignant Melancholy sits on her fine Face, and Care corrodes her very Vitals I do think. God only can comfort her, and his Grace alone support her – for She is all *Resentment*; and that Beauty, Fame, and Fortune She has now so long possessed, add to her Misery – not take from it.
>
> … How Shall I do to endure the Sight of her odious Husband?[9]

She was writing to Penelope Weston, who at the age of forty, and after much hesitation, had just married William Pennington, an American Loyalist ruined by the War of Independence who for some years past had been master of ceremonies at Bristol Hot Wells. Hester, a compulsive matchmaker, had been urging her for months past to take the plunge. 'Have him, Have him,' she had written, '– and try not to disappoint his Romantic Expectations of Felicity never to be found.'[10]

She had few secrets from Mrs Pennington. 'We have no Money for Bath this year, Brinbella drains all away,' she told her early in January: 'and Cecy prefers a Week's flash in London to a Month at Bath She says –'[11] Cecilia's flightiness remained a worry, and her mother was by no means confident that young Drummond had been seen off for good: 'I'm told London has a violent Influenza in it, and will keep my Miss out while I can; but one's arms do so ache with pulling at an unbroken Filly, that longs to hurt herself by skipping into some Mischief or other …'[12]

Hester's letters and the pages of *Thraliana* at this time reflect deep foreboding at the train of events in Europe:

> 'Tis now expected that the French go to Rome; and if they do destroy the great City that in St John's Time did most certainly reign over all the Kings of the Earth; why we know what is coming. Mean time the all-conquering Canaille carry every Thing before them, and plant their Tree of Liberty in Holland, threaten Spain, ruin Austria, destroy Brabant, & declare their Intention of coming to plunder Great Britain. We have at this Moment doubled the Guards at the Tower and the Bank for fear of Accidents …

Louis XVI went to the scaffold on the morning of 16 January 1793 in the Place de la Révolution – the present-day Place de la Concorde. Two weeks later France declared war on Britain and Holland. 'I suppose we shall send a Fleet into the Mediterranean for Protection of Italy,' Hester wrote to Mrs Pennington; 'they will all be contented to see us pay the Expence of a War they have not Spirit to fight for themselves. Fye on 'em all!'[13] She was still greatly exercised by the French King's execution two weeks later: 'Why does not that hapless Queen of France dye of Grief at once, and spare Frenchmen the crime of murdering an Emperor of Austria's Daughter whom they have already reduced to the Disgrace of begging a Black Gown of his Murderers to wear for her Consort's Death.'[14]

The hapless Queen – 'Prisoner No. 280' as she had by then become – was guillotined the following October.

⊸≫ ≪⊱

'A new & strange Event for *Thraliana* – The Miss *Thrales* have been to visit Mrs *Piozzi*. What an Honour! What a Favour! What a Wonder! Tis impossible to guess the motive of their coming, any more than of their staying away ...'

Hester was hugely excited. She had been staying at the house of a cousin in Cavendish Square while Cecilia enjoyed her London 'flash'. 'I have covered Cecy with finery,' she told Mrs Pennington, 'and sate up till Morning at every Place without repining while She was diverted I hope.'[15] The 'Miss Thrales' who descended on them out of the blue: '... spoke of no Business, but conversed about the French and the Fashions, as if we had been separated a Month only ... This Morng I returned the Visit, & then came home after inviting them to Dinner on Easter Monday next; and to My Astonishment the Eldest rather eagerly catched at the Invitation.'

The occasion passed off marvellously well – Hester and Piozzi had pulled out all the stops. 'The Flash is over, my charming Master made his new found Friends a flaming Entertainment,' Hester wrote:

Dinner Concert Supper and *Ball*. Miss Hamilton sung her best, so did Piozzi ... I danced a Pas de deux with Pisani – a first Rate Nobleman

of Venice ... *Our* Performance was much applauded – What a Mercy
'tis that I could so perform, after having been a married Woman just 30
years! ...

Well I do think that all is completely healed up between *my* Daughters & myself – on my Side it certainly is ...

On her side perhaps, but it was not long before she realized that her
daughters were not moved principally by a reawakened sense of filial
duty. Hester and Piozzi remained convinced that Cator had been sys-
tematically defrauding them of substantial sums of money. The previous
autumn she had drawn up a lengthy paper entitled 'Memorial of H: L:
Piozzi against John Cator Esq.'[16] The charges related not only to the
administration of Thrale's estate will but also to the collection of rents
in Oxfordshire and Caernarvonshire and to the cutting of timber on her
estates in Flint and Denbighshire. Her arithmetic is not impeccable, but
Piozzi had decided to pursue Cator in the Court of Chancery.

Two months after the reconciliation which had so surprised and
delighted her, Hester realized what was actually going on: 'Miss Thrale
has been here to solicit our Mercy for Cator; She has heard that Piozzi
drives him by these Bills in Chancery, and he had frighted her wth the
Notion that Gov^t is coming to fall upon us. – perhaps he himself has
informed the Gov^t ...'

Hester's immediate response was both philosophical and generous:
'In the Ladies's Return to my House & Friendship then, – was Interest
more than Affection or Duty, 'tis plain, – but no Matter; they are come
again, & I am happy to see them: and if we wait till some Action is
discovered of which the Motive itself & every separate part was pure – I
suppose we may wait till the Millenium.'

That generosity, as she made plain in *Thraliana*, did not extend to
Cator, although in speculating about how matters would end, she displays
a remarkable degree of detachment.

Remarkable, however, only until one recalls that although she was
living in the Age of Enlightenment, Hester was also living in a world
ordered for the convenience of men. Blackstone, in his *Commentaries
on the Laws of England*, had pronounced that 'the very being or legal
existence of the woman is suspended during the marriage, or at least

is incorporated and consolidated into that of her husband'. Unless she
happened to be a queen regnant, a wife was under the authority of her
husband – together with her moveable property:

> I wonder whether God Almighty will suffer Cator to escape thro' this
> Stratagem of frighting Miss Thrale so as to make her stop Piozzi's
> Enquiries into his Peculation. *I* will stand Neuter – the Rascal shall have
> all the Advantage he can make of them, for *me*: but all our Lawyers,
> some from Desire of Gain, some from Desire of seeing Cator's head
> (which has so often been too hard for *them*) in the Pillory; – excite my
> Innocent & unmeaning Master to drive forward – *Nous verrons*; I have
> long remained a mere Spectator – no Actor in this human Life; & shall
> yet perhaps Live – tho' ill enough too – to see this farce out, & possibly
> speak the Epilogue.'

~ 27 ~

Land of Her Fathers

WITH THE approach of autumn Hester buckled down to her book of synonyms. Unusually, she made no entries in *Thraliana* between the middle of September and the end of the year, although she kept up her correspondence. Thanking Chappelow for a present of game, she told him that it came most opportunely: 'I make a little Dinner for an old Acquaintance Mr. Murphy, and a new Acquaintance Robinson the Bookseller, who is to buy my Synonymes; – and your good game, with my Master's good wine, will I hope procure me an excellent Bargain –'[1]

It did. George Robinson – a six-bottle man it was said – was renowned for his *bons mots* and his generosity to authors. The family firm was at the time the greatest trading bookseller and publisher in England. Murphy happened to be acting for them in a literary property case, and Robinson had asked him for an opinion on what Hester's manuscript was worth; recognizing the handwriting, Murphy had offered to act for her, and negotiated a sum of £300 for the copyright.

Soon after his return from Brynbella, Piozzi became ill again. Hester seldom spared her friends the details. 'It certainly was Gout in the Collar bone,' she told Chappelow: '... he really suffered sad anguish for a whole Week: unable to be touched, yet wanting Assistance every Moment, and screaming while the Paroxysms were upon him like a Woman in Labour. Light-headed besides and raving of the French Poissardes with their Bonnet rouge &c.'[2]

Piozzi suffered three successive attacks in the course of December and January. Once he was strong enough they went up to London, partly to keep Cecilia amused, partly, now that the book was in the press, to make it easier for Hester to correct proofs. She was anxious about Piozzi. 'I hope this Frisk to London will not hurt him,' she wrote to Queeney: 'We shall go home every Saturday to Dinner, and come up every Tuesday to *fraternize* our Friends till the Lease is over, but without

Thought of moving our Family, this nasty Place could not be endured but as a sleeping Hole ...'

She was writing from their old house in Hanover Square – now 'the dirtiest Lodging in London'. Lord Dumfries had clearly not been an ideal tenant; in a later age he would have done well as a squatter:

> How People should delight so to live in a Dust-Basket I cannot guess, but they have made such Beasts of the furniture you would not believe. Well, never mind, they can't eat the Pictures ... I never saw such Tricks played, but then our Tenants were *Democrates*. They have torne Mr. Pitt's Print out of the frame and burned it.[3]

Cecilia was clearly enjoying herself. Hester had noted in *Thraliana* some months previously that she was being 'courted underhand' by Sammy Lysons; the London season now afforded her a steady stream of conquests. 'She does lead a Life much like that of *sweet Anne Page* in the Merry Wives of Windsor,' Hester told Mrs Pennington: 'Did I tell you Mr Rogers had made formal Proposals, or that Count Zenobio offered himself to her, before he was seized by Bailiffs, or dismissed by Ministry.'[4]

British Synonymy, or an Attempt to Regulate the Choice of Words in Familiar Conversation was published in April. Horace Walpole thought there were good things in it, but not for the first time wrinkled his nose at Hester's style: 'Here and there she does not want parts, has some good translations and stories that are new, particularly an admirable *bon mot* of Lord Chesterfield, which I never heard before, but dashed with her cruel vulgarisms.'[5]

Walpole does not seem to have read Hester's Preface. 'While men teach to write with propriety,' she asserts, 'a woman may at worst be qualified – through long practice – to direct the choice of phrases in familiar talk.' She was concerned, that is, not with the measured periods of the written page, but with the way people actually speak: 'I profess to teach *talk* only, not *language*,' she writes elsewhere 'and to teach that only to foreigners.'

The *Monthly Review*, describing the author as 'this lively female Philologist', was roguishly patronizing:

We were glad to see that so useful and desirable a work was undertaken in our own country by a lady of a classical education, who had spent the chief part of her life in the study of literature and in conversation with the learned. We could not help being a little envious and ashamed that the honour of this enterprise should have been usurped ... by a female ... and who shall say that this envy may not vent itself in a little severity, in our remarks on a work which has defrauded our sex of that superiority to which it has long laid claim?

In other words, 'How did this bloody woman get into the club?'

The *Bath Chronicle* was complimentary: 'As Lord Peter's brown loaf contained every thing that was eatable,[6] so Mrs. Piozzi's ingenious book on the British Synonimies, contains every thing cognoscible; a taste, at least, of law, physick and divinity, chymistry, natural history, logick, rhetorick, and what not.'

As indeed it did. The book is by no means simply an early forerunner of Fowler's *Modern English Usage*. Many of the entries are less about particular words than about what lies behind them. From the cluster of words she assembles around Bravery, for example – Valour, Fearlessness, Fortitude, Intrepidity, Courage – she fashions a seven-page essay illustrated with references to Julius Caesar, Marshal Turenne, Mary Queen of Scots, and Gideon in the Book of Judges. The book also tells us a great deal about Hester's religious and political views, a good many of the entries expressing her revulsion at the French Revolution: 'FRIGHT-FUL and HIDEOUS may well be appropriated to delirious dreams; to the sight of mangled bodies, or human heads streaming with blood, such as France has lately exhibited for the savage amusement of a worse than brutal populace.'

'I have not depth of Literature to do it as one ought,' Hester had written when she was first mulling over the idea of *British Synonymy*. False modesty. Its range of reference demonstrates the remarkable breadth of her reading, not only in English but also in classical and European literature. A second edition appeared in Dublin later in the year, and in 1804 substantial sections of it were reprinted in Paris as part of Parsons & Galignani's *British Library*.[7] Hester described it to a friend many years later as 'the best thing I ever wrote'.[8] It would have gratified her to know that the first edition of her entertaining bran-tub of a book was reprinted in facsimile as late as 1968.⁹

Hester registered in *Thraliana* her contempt for a growing fashionable trend. 'I see my Neighbours at Putney or Fulham or Croydon all migrating for *finer air* towards July: how ridiculous!' Ridiculous or no, by the end of July the Piozzis had themselves migrated to the finer air of Denbighshire. The change did not immediately agree with Hester: 'I have not had one day's health here at Denbigh, yet know not why,' she wrote in *Thraliana*.

Teenagers had not, of course, been invented in 1794, but Cecilia, bereft – briefly – of beaux, contrived an uncanny prefiguration:

> When Mr Piozzi rides to Brynbella, She goes the other Way; professing with more Sincerity than Politeness her Hatred of Wales, and of our House in particular … She has, and She shews She has, an ineffable Contempt for us both; but why do I say of *us*? She despises every body, I know, except her own Sisters & her Father's Family.

Brynbella was still far from finished, and visits to the site could be hazardous. 'The Drawing Room had only Planks and Joysts laid,' Hester told Queeney, 'and down thro' a large Space left uncovered, *fell four Yards perpendicular* this Morning, my poor dear Darling foolish Phillis.'¹⁰ The poor dear foolish darling survived: 'Immortal Phyllis,' Hester reported to Mrs Pennington, 'to the Astonishment of Physicians, Friends and Nurses, now promises to be once more – her own Dog again.'¹¹

It was all very different from Streatham and Hanover Square. 'After half a Century Spent in this empty yet bustling World,' she wrote to Queeney, 'here am I like a Hare ending at the Place I set out from.'¹² She was well aware that they would have to make their own amusements. 'Mr. Piozzi's Forte piano is now as near us as Chester, I think we shall all be out of our Wits for Joy when it arrives,' she wrote: 'Here is very little Society indeed, half a Dozen people I believe that like reading – not more, and they suffer sad intellectual Famine: I reproach myself daily that I forgot to bring them down the Mysteries of Udolpho – it would have had such an Effect read by Owl-light among the Old Arcades of our ruined Castle here —'[13]

If there was intellectual famine, there was also natural plenty. 'Here are fine Rides, and fine Prospects, and a glorious Harvest, and Heavenly Weather,' she wrote to Chappelow. 'I hope our Master will sell his Hay at a fine Price. He was right enough to build in this Country, for never did any Country so agree with him.'[14]

Eager as she was to expand their social circle, Hester was not prepared to lower her standards: 'Mr. Yorke of D'Affrenalli has been introduced to me as a Wit & a Flasher: it was supposed that we were to admire one another's Abilities, – but I fancy the project failed on both Sides; – I *dis*liked him, and Dislike is commonly reciprocal: he is clever though, but rough & coarse, and has too little polish ...'

She did however encounter one kindred spirit – 'our Philosopher Mr Lloyd of Wygfawr'. It turned out that their grandmothers had been close friends:

> Yet tho' I have had my Share of driving about the World as well
> as he; tho' I have shone among the Shiners, & plodded among the
> Traders, tho' the Roar of a Fox Chase has roused my Spirits to even
> a Wildness of Delight; and the Music of an Opera has melted me into
> Tears of Rapture – never did I hear of this Gentleman, at any Place,
> much less see him, till in our own Country we meet it seems, I the *Wit*
> forsooth, and he the *Philosopher* of our little Circle ... I consider his
> acquaintance as a Treasure.

Physical remoteness did nothing to blunt Hester's compulsive interest in France, where under the Thermidorian Republic the revolution was now devouring its own children. That summer Robespierre, a slight figure in a sky-blue coat, mounted the scaffold in the Place de la Révolution just as Louis XVI and Danton had done before him. '153 Persons guillotined the very day after him show plainly that his Successors love the Sport as well as he did,' Hester wrote in *Thraliana*. 'Is Tom Paine among the Number I wonder.'

Cecilia's manners did not improve:

> Cecy vexes me by her unprovoked Insolence to the few People round

us, & her apparent Study to disoblige Mr Piozzi, till She makes me *so* nervous, & my Head *so* dizzy, I can not sit down to Study any more than *She* can ... Well! The other three are *busy Misses*; dancing & frolicking with the Princes at Weymouth & Brighthelmstone: I like that no better; & tis so tedious to like nothing –

They were still in Denbigh on Hester's birthday in January. She had not celebrated it in Wales since 1748. 'A good Dinner and a harp was all the festivity we could have *in Doors*, but the merry Maids & Men had a Ball at the Crown Inn.' One of the men was a local doctor: 'Doctor Thackeray is a pretty young Man of elegant Manners and an excellent Heart; he loves my Cecy – poor fellow! ... What chance has mere Merit with our Cecy I wonder! ... Settlements, Settlements, Equipage, Equipage, Pin money &c. are the Things we must look for in a Lover of hers ... Poor dear Doctor!'[15]

Cecy's eyes were fixed elsewhere:

Well! Cecilia Thrale has given her Word to the Family of Llewessog that she will marry Young Mostyn, and no one else; and we are going to London – to Streatham Park at least, in order to ask the Chancellor's consent – will he give it? Or shall we want it? Does Cecilia *mean* what She says? ... Mr Mostyn is a very honourable & a very handsome Youth: his Fortune not high, but his Character excellent – I only wish him older, & with a more authoritative Manner: he is too much under Cecilias Feet, & She has too much Disposition to keep him there –

Days before they set out to travel south, Denbigh was the scene of a riot provoked by the price of corn. A mob of three hundred armed with bludgeons surrounded Hester's new friend John Lloyd and two other magistrates. A woman wielding a long knife attacked the tail of Lloyd's horse; the ringleader 'talked the true Language of Democracy' Hester wrote to Queeney: 'You have worne Boots and we have worne wooden Shoes long enough now,' he told Lloyd; 'try how you like the Exchange.' Thanks to Lloyd's coolness, there was no violence.[16]

The Piozzis arrived in London a matter of days after the marriage of the Prince of Wales. Hester was inclined to think well of Caroline of Brunswick: 'if *any* thing will do, *She* will do: 'twas a good measure to bring her over'. Confusingly, however, she then went on to express strong disapproval of the marriage:

> One is not oneself quite Young enough to think well of any Woman's
> Principles who could solemnly accept our Heir Apparent's Hand at
> the Altar if he ever did – as is still asserted – marry Mrs Fitzherbert
> according to the Rites of the Romish Church ... had I been Archbishop
> I would not have joined their Hands for all this World could give. Will
> the Almighty bless such polluted Nuptials with Children? And will he
> bless those Children? I *think not.*

She had more pressing matrimonial concerns nearer home. Cecy's beau had followed them to Streatham: 'Mostyn has been introduced to all our Intimates, and all seem to like him excessively.' So did she – he was handsome, he was Welsh, he was the grandson of an old friend of her father's. But Thrale's will had stipulated that so long as Cecilia was a minor, she might not marry without Hester's consent; and until she came of age her legal heirs were her sisters. Mostyn was also under age – he would not reach his majority until August of the following year. Until then, whatever assurances he might offer, he was unable to make a binding settlement in return for Cecilia's dowry; without such a settlement, Cecilia's estate, if she were to die before coming of age, would be lost to her sisters.

Hester, naturally reluctant to do anything that might damage her fragile relations with the elder girls, was nevertheless in an agony of indecision:

> if they wait till he is of Age, 'tis a mighty silly Life, Courting &
> Cornering for fourteen Months together so ... If I give my Consent
> wch freely would I do – her Fortune w^{d} be instantly thrown into the
> husband's Power, & Mr Thrale's Intent of its reverting to his other
> Daughters w^{d} be defeated by my Partiality for a Countryman – This,
> tho' I am certainly very partial to him, – *shall never be* ...

She also still felt threatened by Drummond, who was apparently in the habit of waylaying the Streatham servants – and 'throws out threatenings that *He will* have Cæcilia, Spite of my Arts & Efforts as he calls them'.

My Heart half wishes they would run away –' Which, three days later, was precisely what they obligingly did:

> Oh Lord! Oh Lord! Mostyn and Cecilia are run away to Scotland sure enough, and here is Mr Piozzi in an Agony about *his Honour* wch he fancies injured by the Step ... Oh my poor Cecy! – for the 1st five Minutes I knew not but Drummond might have tricked her off with *him* pretending to be the other: but No, She is in safe & honourable hands, and happy with her dear Mostyn at Llewessof Lodge ...

Cecilia wrote from Gretna Green the day after they were married. She was eager to know how her sisters had taken the news and enquired teasingly about Piozzi, whom she called Papa: 'What does he say to the Affair? *May godda bless, never I see such a people* ... How will he be able to live without *Miss Cecil* to scold and row I wonder.' She urged them to come and stay until Brynbella was ready. 'Don't be ill or fidgetty now any more,' she told Hester, 'for all will go on well.'[17]

The marriage attracted a certain amount of sly attention in the press. 'Mr. Mostyn received from the sooty hands of the *Gretna Green Black-smith*, Miss Cecilia Thrale, the daughter of Mrs. Piozzi, and 55,000£ sterling!' the *Oracle and Public Advertiser* informed its readers.[18] The *True Briton*, describing Mostyn as 'an accomplished and amiable young man' – and noting that Cecilia was a ward of Chancery – expressed the sanctimonious hope that the Court would not, as it put it, 'call the gentleman to a severe audit, because he did not wait for the awful sanctions of her legal guardians'.[19]

Hester soon found something else to fidget about:

> This House is too expensive – I must give it up. Here have we dined 30, 40 People every Day for three Weeks together, tis a *Ruin*! and Brinbella going on all the while – Impossible, Impracticable! We must dye in a Prison at last if we live thus; & Streatham Park will not do with a small Family & little Money spent – We must let it – & live in Wales ...

Piozzi looked into the matter, but having established that there was interest only in an indefinitely long let, decided not to proceed. Hester was greatly relieved: 'I have been happier since Mr Piozzi gave up the Idea, & since I feel myself writing this Nonsense at poor Dr Johnson's dear old Inky Slab; with my Mother's trees in Sight, planted by *her* Hand; & not to be *given out* of *mine. I am happier!*'

It was not the only reason she had to feel happier: 'Drummond is Married I hear; to Miss Castell. Well! God bless them – now my Fear of him is over, my Hatred sh^d be over too.'

⁓∾ ∿⁓

Something which she heard from Murphy that summer both intrigued and disturbed her. He was amazed, he said, that Thrale had left so little money in the bank. For three years before his death, he had, to his certain knowledge, held a lucrative government contract – 'by Virtue of wch Whitbread & he divided 23000£ a year A'piece'. Hester could only share Murphy's amazement: 'What *could* become of that Money? What *could* become of it?' She had been closely involved in Thrale's electioneering. Did she remember a passage from one of his last appeals to the voters before losing his seat in 1780? He had, he declared, 'Not only scorned to receive either Pension or Contract, (the frequent Reward and Encouragement of venal Representatives) but pledged himself to the Public, by being one of those who voted against the Possibility of a Contractor's ever sitting in Parliament, never to accept any.'

How certain was Murphy's 'certain knowledge'? Was his old friend a liar and a hypocrite? 'What on Earth did he do wth the Money?' The questions hang unanswered in the air.

Preparations for the move to Wales were now well advanced. Boxes of books and linen were dispatched by sea. Some furniture from the house in Hanover Square had already been sent, but £2,000 was laid out on new furniture, much of it from Gillow of Lancaster, one of the leading cabinet-makers of the day. Hester and Piozzi set out from Streatham early in September. Brynbella was still full of workmen, but habitable: 'On this happy Morn^g the Birthday of my eldest Daughter, do I open my eyes – and My Thraliana, at *My own house*; my new beautiful Residence built for me in *my own* lovely Country, by the Husband of my Hearts Choice. Never was so Charming a Spot, never ought there to be so grateful a Creature as I.'

Hester Lynch Piozzi had come home.

'Justice! The Law! My Ducats, and My Daughter!'

BRYNBELLA was hardly the 'little cottage' Hester had originally envisaged. The architect was Clement Mead, whom the Piozzis had employed to renovate and refurbish Streatham; he had now, at a cost of £20,000, presented them with a substantial Italianate villa.[1] Hester was eager for 'the Misses' to come and admire it: 'Mrs. Mostyn will entertain you much in the same manner at Segroid, & you will see how we live in Wales.[2]

Hester took them about the Vale of Clwyd, and Piozzi, quickly recovered from an attack of gout, exerted himself to entertain them: 'Mr. Piozzi gallants his Wife's four daughters to Holywell Assembly tomorrow.' When they left at the end of November, she cast up a sober account of the visit:

> They have behaved very well; not loving Piozzi, not liking Mostyn, nor approving the Connexion Cæcilia has made with one – and I with the other, it was no easy task to behave very well, yet all went as it should do without fawning & without Rudeness – with no assumed Transports of Delight, and no expressions or even Appearance of Disgust: of so much Use is Good Breeding.

She later had cause to revise that charitable judgement when she heard from her maid, Allen – 'who knows ten Gossiping Tales for my one' – that her daughters had been heard to speak disrespectfully of Piozzi. Hester asked the butler, Sam Hodgkins, whether it was true – 'or whether he thought my Maid romanced a little'. 'Lord Madam! said he Twas I who called Allen to witness their Dialogue, Twas I who heard 'em 1st.'

She had got on well with Queeney – 'She is a person greatly to my Taste, independent of relationship or Vanity.' There was one nagging question she had been sorely tempted to broach: 'It was often at my

Tongue's end to talk to Miss Thrale concerning her Father's Contract with Government, & concerning his being bound for Mr Nesbitt &c. but I always checked myself wth the Certainty that She has no Confidence in *me* ...'

＊＊＊

The times continued troubled. In London, the mob, enraged by the tax burden of the war and the cost of living, stoned the state coach as the King drove to open parliament. 'Good God!' Hester wrote in *Thraliana*, 'here is the King insulted in his own Park – & in danger of being torne to Pieces.' She noted that there remained 'strong Dispositions towards Rioting' even in the Vale of Clwyd: '... they have threatened to stick poor Pennant's head upon a Pike – What Rascals! His Literature, his Virtue, his Piety, – his Charity & perpetual Almsgiving will not perhaps secure his Safety and his Peace ...'

Thomas Pennant's Chairmanship of the Flintshire Loyalist Association made him an obvious target. Celebrated for his writings on travel and natural history, he was a distant cousin of Hester's and now a near neighbour. They quickly struck up a warm friendship. 'All his Letters are signed Your Affectionate Kinsman,' she told Chappelow; she was, she said, 'not a little proud of his Connection'.[3]

The views from Brynbella were incomparable, but the Piozzis decided they might be enhanced. 'We set up our new Telescope and saw a large Fleet of forty one Sail pass by,' Hester wrote to Queeney.[4] Occasionally her enthusiasm for their new toy got the better of her. They had made the acquaintance of a family called Williams, who lived five miles away at Bodylwyddan. One day John Williams lost his watch, and spent the best part of an hour looking for it in the grounds. Just as he was about to abandon the search, a servant arrived with a message from Mrs. Piozzi: 'Had he found what he was looking for?'[5]

Her new circle of friends could not satisfy her hunger for gossip of the world she had left behind. 'You can scarcely imagine how much a Cargo of London Chat enlivens our Conversation here in the Country,' she wrote to one acquaintance,[6] and she was even more delighted whenever friends came to visit. 'We have got Mr. Chappelow with us, and are showing him about just as we showed you about,' she told Queeney:

He is prodigiously admired, just as you were prodigiously admired; and we are very proud of him: and he can tell us of Lords and Ladies, and Wits and Beauties, and Duels and Gaming Debts, and all *desirable* Topicks ... But I don't tell him about my Book, I tell nobody that but You, and I am dying to see whether you will like it.[7]

She had mentioned this new literary venture more than once to Queeney; now, early in 1796 she announced she had made a start: 'Well! 'tis a Sign my Spirits are not low, for last Monday I begun upon a Literary work of no inconsiderable Magnitude. Its Title would be anticipated if I let any body know it, but when we meet I shall tell it *you* under promise of Secrecy ...'[8]

No promise of secrecy was required from *Thraliana*:

This Day I determined on a Project my Brain has long been hatching – that of getting a Book ready for Publication this time five Years if possible to come out early in *1801*: – containing a summary of Events, & general Ideas of what has happened in the World during those Centuries ... I must make the Title of it

RETROSPECTION

... if by Gods Mercy the Volumes should be completed – they may be really useful to some, & entertaining to others, and may bring me in a thousand Pounds first & last.

A regretful footnote indicates that even this represented a scaling down of her original ambitions: 'I should like to begin with the very beginning, but Life is not long enough,' she wrote. 'We must commence yᵉ Work at ye Xtian Æra.' It would occupy her for four and a half years.

~⤞ ⤝~

Before long the Mostyn marriage became the subject of gossip in the neighbourhood. Cecilia had told her mother that she had been 'frightened into fits' on her wedding night. Hester found it all very puzzling: 'Mostyn's Grandfather was a famous Fellow among the Women – & this Boy is near six Feet high, & particularly well looking.' In her direct way, she asked Mostyn's mother whether the marriage had been consummated. She was told it had — but discovered that was not the view in the servants' hall: 'Cecilia's Maid says her Mistress is a *Maid now* after being married *a Year*. She tells my Servants so, but says 'tis Mrs Mostyn's Fault. — She will not let her Husband touch her ... This all seems to me stark Nonsense; no Man that *is a Man* will be so kept at a Distance.'

It was also believed below stairs — and, apparently, by Piozzi — that there was a subplot involving Dr Thackeray: 'The Maids think there is something between him & Cecy, but I can scarce believe it; if She had liked him She would have married him: Who hindered her?'

Of rather greater concern than Cecilia's presumed frigidity was her husband's reluctance to address the question of a marriage settlement. Although Cecilia was a ward in chancery, her income was still essentially controlled by Cator; Murphy, to whom the Piozzis increasingly turned for advice, urged them to apply for a transfer of this control to the Accountant-General, an officer of the Court of Chancery charged with receiving all monies lodged in court and disbursing them.

In April, in spite of their obviously scratchy relations, the Mostyns took themselves off to London. 'I am sorry for it,' Hester wrote to Mrs Pennington, 'but she felt very tired of Wales, and he felt disposed — not to *indulge* but to *obey* her: I am sorry for *that too*, a little Bridle is not amiss to a Young Filly Foal like her ...'⁹

The Piozzis, meanwhile, decided on an excursion to Anglesey: 'We are going to take a little Sea Dip at Beaumaris,' Hester wrote in *Thraliana* — 'no Money for Streatham Park or Bath yet.' She retained throughout her life a capacity to wring enjoyment from the most unpromising situations. 'So here are We in a little dirty Fishing Town,' she wrote to Chappelow, 'living on Grey Mullet cheaper than Mutton and nice boyled Whiting and Flounders.'¹⁰ And in a long, chatty letter to Queeney she boasted that she had 'obtained the Reputation of a capital Whist-player and a Complete Fashionist': 'Tying my Waist round with a Cord instead of a Ribbon procured me the last advantage, and I think leading from the Head of a Suit — Knave for example when followed by ten, nine &c. gained me Triumph the first.'¹¹

She still kept a close eye on what went on at Westminster. She disapproved of the legislation sponsored by Sir John Sinclair, the President of the Board of Agriculture, for the enclosure of waste land. 'It will,' she wrote, 'be a ruin to one Staple Commodity, our Wool Trade.' She was even more exercised by the repeal of the Game Laws. It would 'bring on a Democracy quicker than any Step could be taken', she wrote:

> Such Proceedings will drive Country Gentlemen to London in Shoals, for Cheapness – education of Children &c. those will be the Pretences I mean: but the tru reason – hurt Pride. A Man will easier bear to be jostled by his Taylor at Ranelagh or Vauxhall, than to see a Tenant's Son cock his Hat and his gun in his Landlord's Face ...

By late July they were back at Brynbella. 'My Master mends very slowly,' Hester told Chappelow, ' and likes a Fit of Gout in Anglesea so little he resolves to have the next at Bath.'[12] Cecilia continued to accumulate entries in her mother's black books. She had gone off to London without calling to say goodbye; she had written only once while they were away; they had spent several weeks at Streatham without so much as a by your leave; a wine bill for £16.15s which Mostyn had run up there remained unsettled a year later.

No Welsh valley is without its rumour-mill, and in the Vale of Clwyd that October the water in the mill-race flowed even faster than usual. Cecilia had a maid called Mason, a local farmer's daughter. She was observed to be pregnant, and the whisper was that it was John Mostyn who had made her so. 'The Boy has proved his Manhood quite *Classically*,' Hester observed acidly in *Thraliana*, and found an apposite quotation from Martial's *Epigrams*; but to her various correspondents – to Chappelow, to Mrs Pennington, to her other daughters – a pose of ironic detachment was less easy to maintain. 'Our unfashionable Neighbours cry Shame,' she wrote to Queeney:

> and Cecy laughs and says – *it is the Way*, and what signifies making a Bustle about nothing? ... After hearing these *Infamità* repeated in my Ears by every Creature round me for a whole fortnight ... I watched my Opportunity ... She heard me negligently – expressed her Weariness of the Tale – looked into an old Annual Register as we talked, or rather as I talked, for She said little, till I observed that Mr. Mostyn never called here, and I suppose says I he stays away for Shame. She then looked off the Book, and at me, with much Amazement. For Shame! said She – why

what is there to be ashamed of? I suppose he is not the first Man who has got a Pretty Girl with Child ... what a blessing her Fortune has not been paid into the hands of such a Man!!! The little Power *I* have shall be exerted he may assure himself, to keep it long out of his Reach.[13]

'Dear Murphy behaves like an Angel in the Business,' Hester wrote. Her head told her how much she stood in need of disinterested professional advice, although her heart was not always disposed to accept it. Murphy wrote in late November urging her to go to London; he stressed the importance of forcing a settlement before Cecilia came of age in February 1798 – at that point the Lord Chancellor would lose all power over her fortune. They set out shortly after Christmas: 'We are going to Streatham Park I think I will *take*; no, I think I will *not* take Thraliana: but leave it locked in our new Iron Chest here ... My heart is sorry to leave this Majestic View of Nature ... Adieu! ever charming Valley! lovely in the gay Season, sublime in the severe one – Adieu dearest Brinbella – Adieu!'

It was late summer before they returned, and it would have been better if they had stayed put in the 'ever charming valley' and left the lawyers to get on with it. Relations with Cator were already bad enough. 'Permit me to ask,' he had written to Hester in November, 'if your Experience in the World has not yet convinced you that acting under the Motives of Violence, Passion, and Revenge, seldom prove Salutary.'[14]

Hester's reply had been shrill and uncompromising, but now Piozzi, casting about for some way of bringing further pressure to bear on Mostyn, came up with the extraordinarily foolish idea of trying to recover all the expenses incurred on Cecilia's account in the years preceding her marriage. 'The Sisters consider our Claim of 1400£ for eight Years & a half as Enormous,' Hester noted in *Thraliana*. So did John Eardley Wilmot, master in chancery, who initially disallowed it altogether, although he ultimately made a compromise award of £500. The lawsuit disposed of what remained of the friendship with Cator.[15]

Relations with Murphy also came under strain. Hester had been bombarding him almost daily with her views on how to proceed, and his patience was wearing thin: 'I have had nothing to disconcert me,' he told her, 'Except your Letters veering and shifting from one point to another, Capricious, *flickering*, Inconsistent, and Contradictory.'[16]

Exasperation on Murphy's part was succeeded by indignation on Hester's:

> Mr Murphy plagued me wth calling ye Prince of Wales and actually *inviting* him what Madness! to Streatham park ... The Prince wanted an Opportunity wth ye young Thrales no doubt, but Murphy should have known better. I kept the Prince away however, no Prince shall court my Daughters in my House certainly: but I was forced to be quite rude to our fine Heir Apparent ... Murphy has hated Me ever since, & I have loved him less; What an old Goose he must be – or an old – something worse than Goose. Did he mean to sell the Girls? What *did* he mean? I am afraid to think.

The news that Cecilia was pregnant took the Piozzis back to Wales and Hester dug *Thraliana* out of the iron chest: 'Cecy who always said She hated Wales would come hither to Lye In – very contradictory & very absurd; – 'Tis just the *only* Thing I would have had her do at London.' Cecilia went into labour in late August; Queeney had ridden up from Sussex to be with her. 'They never sent to *me*,' Hester wrote bitterly, 'They will not let me go to *Her*: her Husband keeps me off perhaps – perhaps her Sister – She cross'd the Country hither to attend Cecilia, 285 Miles from the Coast of Sussex, with no Companion, no female Servt – nothing but a Groom & Saddle Bags: all the way on one Horse, as People travelled in Days of Yore. They are astonishing Girls.'

Cecilia was in labour for three days and three nights. Mostyn called in help from Chester, but the child – a boy – was stillborn. Hester, who knew all too much about such matters, vented her anger and frustration in the pages of *Thraliana*:

> I hate these Country Accoucheurs – these *Demi Savans*: they are so forward to produce their *Instruments* ... With Opium & Encouragement, & not putting her too soon upon Labour, I verily do think that a skilful Practitioner might have brought the Baby forward with the *Forceps* at worst ... but since the horrid death-doing Crotchet has been found out,

& its use permitted – oh! many & many a Life has been flung away. M^r
Mostyn however, Enemy as he is to me, *must* on this Occasion be pitied.
he spared no Expense, no trouble: he called in help 30 Miles round the
Country.

Mrs Strickland, now confined to a wheelchair, came to visit from
Westmoreland, but even the company of her oldest friend could not
lift Hester's spirits and a kindly suggestion from Piozzi provoked an
uncharacteristic outburst:

> Mr Piozzi asked me Yesterday if I did not want Company to divert me,
> now Mrs Strickland is gone ... the Company replied I, never divert
> me at all, – 'tis I divert the Company ... All I can do to entertain
> them is seldom sufficient either: I must call in Company, or take them
> abroad – show them the Places about – at hazard of my Neck, or fetch
> in *Society* for them, as they Phrase it – at certain loss of my own Time,
> & hindrance of my own Comforts ... Life has been to me nothing but
> a perpetual *Canvass* carried on in all parts of the World – not to make
> *Friends* neither – for I have certainly found very few – but to keep off
> *Enemies*.

They had planned to travel south in October, but Piozzi fell ill again
and was still unwell as the year drew to a close. He came down to dinner
on Christmas Day for the first time for more than two months, but found
it impossible to get back upstairs again. His condition was not improved
by the news of events at home. He had originally been convinced that
Napoleon's Italian campaign would end in failure – Italy, he maintained,
had always been 'Il Sepolchro de Francesi'. Now, Hester told Mrs Pennington, the letters he received told a very different story: 'Narrations
of what Brothers, Sisters, Friends &c. endure from the Rapacity of these
vile French, false as they are cruel, and insolent as they are Successful:
His own particular Town has been the Immediate Seat of Distress –'[17]

Brescia, Piozzi's native town, was then part of the territory belonging
to Venice. Having conquered the Most Serene Republic, Napoleon, by
the Treaty of Campo Formio, ceded it to the Habsburgs in return for
the Ionian Islands – but not before subjecting it to wholesale plunder.
The 'exploits' of the French, Hester wrote, 'have frighted Mr. Piozzi's

good old Father out of what *remained* of Life at fourscore Years of Age'.[18] Much of the family property was destroyed, and Piozzi's favourite brother, Giovanni Batiste – Giambattista – had been driven from his home.

Hester had met Giambattista twice during their travels in Italy: 'I liked M[r] Piozzi's Brother whom I saw at Venice excessively: he is the very Image of my Husband,' she wrote. The regard was mutual; some years later Giambattista had named one of his sons John Salusbury in honour of his wealthy English sister-in-law. When the boy was a year old, Giambattista had asked whether the Piozzis would like to adopt him; Hester replied that she was not able to send for him then, but would do so in a few years' time.

On the first day of 1798, she passed in bleak review the state of her relations with her daughters and her son-in-law:

> Oh what a Melancholy New year. My poor Husband confined to his Bed since y[e] 20: Oct[r] & myself *ill now*.[19] And Bills pouring in for Goods taken up by M[rs] Mostyn during the Time 8 years y[t] she lived with us a Minor – from Houses & Shops I *never heard of* ...
>
> Now M[r] Mostyn has written me an insulting Letter saying where's my *fine Breeding &c* & accusing me of interfering in his *private Affairs* – because I censured his keeping his Wifes Maid for a Mistress I suppose. He knows Piozzi & I are both ill, & Cecy sets him on to pinch us to Madness. A pretty Nest of Wasps they are to be sure. *I will get out on't tho'* before 'tis long.

One strand of her strategy for doing so had already been determined: 'Italy is *ruined*, & England *threatened*: I have sent for one little Boy from among my husband's Nephews, he was christened *John Salusbury*: he shall be Naturalized, & we will see if He will be more grateful, & rational, & comfortable than Miss Thrales have been to the Mother they have at length *driven to Desperation*.'

～ 29 ～

Piccolino

BY THE middle of February Piozzi was well enough to travel. 'I am ill myself but desirous to go because I want to get rid of Streatham Park,' Hester wrote, '– & come home here to lay my Bones with my old ancestors at Dymerchion. We cannot now afford to keep two Houses, nor expect to live long in any.'

Two days of their journey, she told Mrs Pennington, 'were delightfully disposed of with the Recluses at Llangollen Cottage'.[1] 'The Ladies' as they were known locally had long been urging the Piozzis to visit them: 'Lady Eleanor Butler and Miss Ponsonby present their best Compliments to Mr. and Mrs. Piozzi, and at any time will be extremely happy to see them at Llangollen Vale. – Mr. P. must bring his Forte Piano.'[2]

Eleanor Butler, the elder of the two Ladies of Llangollen, was the daughter of impoverished upper-class Irish parents. When she was almost thirty, this difficult, convent-educated bluestocking had formed an intense friendship with Sarah Ponsonby, a thirteen-year-old orphan related to the Earl of Bessborough. A decade later, a first attempt to run away together, disguised as men and armed with pistols, was thwarted, but in 1780 they set up house in a rented cottage on the outskirts of Llangollen and settled down to a carefully planned life of Rousseauesque retirement.

They dressed in the riding habit and beaver hat commonly worn by Welsh countrywomen; they read, they gardened, they studied foreign languages; they furnished their cottage with Gothic extravagance and conducted an extensive correspondence; they disapproved of the French Revolution and called one of their dogs Sappho.

Their reclusiveness was relative. They received a stream of visitors – Josiah Wedgwood, Erasmus Darwin, William Wordsworth and Walter Scott were all drawn to call on the two dumpy women whom the Prussian travel writer Prince Pückler-Muskau gallantly described as 'certainly the most celebrated virgins in Europe'. Curiosity about the nature of their 'romantic friendship' made them the subject of endless gossip; in 1790, when a newspaper suggested they were lesbians, they asked their friend Edmund Burke whether they should sue – and accepted his advice not to.

For Hester, it was the beginning of an enduring friendship. The 'famous Hermitesses' as she called them were added to her list of correspondents: 'They conquer and keep in their Enchanted Castle all Travellers passing that particular Road,' she told Mrs Pennington.[3] Over the years the Piozzis would quite often stop at Llangollen on their way to Bath, and the 'Ladies', who seldom ventured away from home, also visited Brynbella. The record of one visit notes that the date was carefully chosen because there was a full moon to light them safely back over the mountains.[4]

By the end of the month the Piozzis were in Streatham, and before taking any action on the house they decided to offer it to the 'Miss Thrales' rent-free. 'I thought Mr. Piozzi most paternally kind in his offer,' Hester wrote to Mrs Pennington, '– but they refuse with Disdain.'[5] The offer was not perhaps quite as irresistible as Hester thought. Queeney, Susan and Sophy would still have been responsible for taxes and for the upkeep of the property, and considered that for their mother's lifetime these remained her responsibility. The property was accordingly advertised to be let, with entry offered at Midsummer-day: 'The house makes twelve beds, and has every conveniency of good offices, stables, dairy, etc. The library and the pictures are well known; the whole suitable to a great family, desirous to be near London. The family is in the house, and will shew it to any Nobleman or Gentleman who previously sends his name ...'[6]

A tenant was quickly found – not, as it happened, a nobleman desirous to be near London, but a corn factor called Giles who already lived there: 'He pays 550£ pr ann, & we stand to the Taxes, but the getting quit of all Establishment there, is the great Advantage; – we were ruined by keeping Servants & Dogs & Horses &c. and one could not shut the *House up*: This dear Mr Giles will keep it aired & repaired, & insured from Fire – '

Quarrels with her daughters – Piozzi's frequent bouts of illness – overnight visits to the houses of friends and neighbours – endless legal wrangling – none of these appeared to affect Hester's extraordinary ability to retreat into herself and give her mind to whatever literary project was currently on the stocks. She had now been plugging away at *Retrospection* for the best part of two years, and she quite often appealed to Queeney for help: 'Oh! Do look over some Bookseller's Catalogues for Knollys's History of the Turks: Second hand *Runs* of that Sort are very cheap.'[7] Many of her own reference books were still at Streatham. She was reluctant for some reason to have them shipped to Wales, but when she resorted to borrowing from neighbours she was terrified of spoiling them: 'You would laugh to see my Anguish about Mrs. Heaton's *beautiful Infidel Gibbon* – lest a Spot of Ink should penetrate the Papers I have wrapped him in, and make him black on the *Outside*.'[8]

Now, in the spring of 1798, she felt confident enough to show what she had written to Robinson, and to ask £1,000 for it. Robinson, shrewd businessman that he was, was affable but stopped short of committing himself: 'he said we would not *Quarrel* about the Price of *such* a Perform-ance: In good Time! so I believe in him like as Sir Francis Wronghead did in the prime minister's Smiles I suppose. I shall go on with the Stuff however ...'

They went up to London for a time, staying at Warrens Hotel in St James's Square. Hester found the town much changed. 'There is a visible stagnation upon business and upon Pleasure too,' she wrote to a friend in Wales, 'even Public Places are coldly attended unless the Royal Family animates them with their Presence or the singing of some popular Air calls the People's attention.'[9] But they dined with Sarah Siddons, and saw her create the part of the adulterous Mrs Haller in *The Stranger*, a translation from the popular German dramatist Kotzebue.

Hester was also able to indulge her passion for pictures at an auction held at Christie's – 'the Spoil of Italy and Flanders – which the French sell to those who bid highest', as she wrote to Mrs Pennington.[10] The French government, eager to raise money in any way it could, was ingeniously exploiting the permeability of eighteenth-century frontiers and selling off many of the art treasures looted from conquered ter-ritories. Without, understandably, revealing their provenance – Christie's advertised the sale simply as 'A Valuable and Capital Collection of Italian, French, Flemish, and Dutch Pictures, a few Bronzes ... the property of a Gentleman, deceased'.[11]

In the charged atmosphere created by the continuing threat of a French invasion, Hester laid *Retrospection* aside for a time to enter the crowded field of political pamphleteering. While she was at Warrens she dashed off *Three Warnings to John Bull before He Dies*, a brisk appeal for loyalty to the government, regard for the established church and 'an immediate Amendment in our Manners'. It was published anonymously – Hester signed herself only 'an Old Acquaintance of the Public'; it did not make a great stir, and did not run to a second edition.

Early June saw the Piozzis back in Wales. The summer was hot and dry – not good for the Piozzis' young tree plantations, but excellent for the wheat harvest. Hester continued to delight in the beauties of the Welsh countryside: 'I have seen this Year in N. Wales what England – no nor Italy ever shewed me,' she wrote to Chappelow '– Yellow Roses! large, double cabbaged Roses, the Colour of a Jonquil.'[12]

She buckled down at once to *Retrospection*. It was lonely work, and much as she relished the company of new friends like the Ladies of Llangollen and her kinsman Pennant, her craving for news of events in the wider world was undiminished. 'This is a letter of mere request,' she wrote to Daniel Lysons: 'Do pray write now and then, and make me up a good long letter of *small London chat*: you can scarcely think how welcome *living* intelligence is to those who have chiefly the *dead* to converse with, and I work hard at *old* stuff all morning, and sigh for some *evening* conversation about literature and politics …'[13]

An unlikely visitor to Brynbella during August was Philip Francis, the presumed author of the *Letters of Junius* – unlikely because it is difficult to conceive of any political question on which he and Hester might remotely agree. Three years previously he had been one of the shrinking band of Fox's supporters who had divided the House against the Seditious Meetings Bill; in 1793 he had been a founding member of the Society of the Friends of the People. They might have little in common, but even conversation with a staunch Whig was better than no political conversation at all. And she would reward him with a walking-on part in *Retrospection*: 'Junius, clad in complete darkness, darted malignant, and yet undetected flashes of wit and anger through the gloom …'[14]

Hester had heard next to nothing from her daughters since her return from Streatham, but now, in September, a letter from Queeney brought news that Cecilia had been safely delivered of a son. If she expected an early invitation to inspect her first grandchild, she was disappointed: 'Strange Conduct. I *hear* that Cecilia Mostyn has a Son, & yᵗ his Name is *John Salusbury*. I never have *seen* the Child at all; – The Mother I met one Night by Chance at Denbigh Assembly.'

Drawn to society like a moth to the candle, Hester had been appointed Queen of the County Assembly, with their neighbour Lord Kirkwall as her King Consort. 'We take it by *Quarters* here, and *our* Quarter expires next Thursday sennight – the full Moon,' she explained to Mrs Pennington: 'Tis our third and last Night, and I shall come home at five in the Morning – change my Dress and drink my Coffee, and set out for the famous Cottage of Llangollen Vale, where dwell the fair and noble Recluses of whom you have heard so much …'[15]

They were on their way to Bath – 'chiefly for my Health – it certainly is going, but it has lasted surprisingly', Hester noted in *Thraliana*, although Piozzi too had been laid up for a fortnight in the early autumn and succumbed again within days of their arrival. One heel was particularly badly affected; when Alexander Hay, the local apothecary and surgeon, called on the morning of Boxing Day, Hester speculated that he would find there 'a terrible Chalk Stone': '– a *Stone* of Chalk madam – replies the Man – a *Quarry* I believe you must mean – So I expect seven or eight Weeks Confinement to his bed at the very lowest Computation'.[16]

Piozzi's nephew had at last arrived in England. He was taken to Streatham and put in the care of Reynold Davies, the curate at St Leonard's, who had leased ground from Streatham Park and built a preparatory school for boys – 'Streatham University', as he jocularly described it. 'I am glad you like our dear little Boy – we are very impatient to see him,' Hester wrote to Jacob, her Streatham coachman:

He is in the right to say that his Name is John Salusbury, for so he was Christened just five years ago, and he is my Child now. It is a Blessing that he has had the Smallpox and I am glad he has a good Spirit to get through this Stormy Life – Poor fellow he has begun trouble very early to take such a long Journey at his Age.[17]

Her first impressions of the little boy were favourable – 'active and well proportioned, intelligent and merry-hearted', she wrote to Chappelow: 'You never saw a little Creature sharp and busy and tidy and helpful so at 5 years old. He can put on and off his own clothes, tye them all up in his little Bag, and see that nothing is lost ...'[18]

The child walked one day through the Bath flesh market with Hester. '*These are* Sheep's Heads are they not Aunt?' he asked. 'I saw a Basket of *Men's heads* at Brescia.'[19] He seemed curiously untouched by the horrors he had witnessed:

> Poor Rogue! he has seen early Service; and gave me yesterday a very clear account of the battle he saw somewhere – in the Square he says – between French and Germans; how their Legs were broken – and the Surgeons tyed them up with Bandages &c. I asked him if they loved the French at Brescia – my Mama hates them says he because they dirtied Count Fenarolis fine House – (*Citizen* Fenaroli I mean –) – and threw his best Pictures out at Window.[20]

Tongues were already wagging however. 'Mr. Ray says he has heard heavy Censures on me for saving this poor innocent Baby Nephew of Mr. Piozzi's from Destruction,' Hester told Chappelow:

> Comments as if I meant to disinherit my own beautiful and deserving Daughters, and give *all to him*. People are exceedingly premature in their Comments, and very unkindly ready with their Censures (quoth I). Little is the *all I have to bestow* compared to theirs and their Father's noble Fortunes ... To no Mortal did I ever say that I would *give him all*: He comes here for Refuge, for Instruction, for Education – I will give him the best of each which my Country affords –[21]

The winter passed very pleasantly at Bath, in spite of Piozzi's 'quarry of chalk' and one minor social unpleasantness – 'Mrs Wynne & Miss Mostyn – mother & Sister to Cecy's Husband, turned their backs upon me at Bath. What car'd I?' 'This Place is more beautiful than ever,' Hester wrote to her cousin Margaret Owen, '– finer Streets, Newer Squares, London looks dirty and *Commercial* to it. Bath is the head Quarters of Pleasure and Gayety.'[22]

She was a frequently in the shop of John Bull, a bookseller who had a circulating library at 6 Lower Walks:

> Bull hates the very Sight of me the while, because I come to his Shop at
> 8 or 9 o'Clock in the Morning always – the only Leisure hour the man
> has from Readers who sit round his Table all Noon, and Footmen who
> ferret after him for Novels all Night –: and I make him clamber for me
> and reach Books which do not answer, and then he has to mount the
> Steps again …[23]

The Theatre Royal was enjoying a season of exceptional brilliance. Sarah Siddons had returned to the scene of her earlier triumphs, and for several weeks the town flocked to see her in some of her best-known roles. Her last appearance was as Millwood in Lillo's *George Barnwell*. The theatre historian John Genest, who lived in Bath, records that the noise was so great that the opening scenes could not be heard: '– it was expected that when Mrs. Siddons made her app. the noise would cease, but it did not, and she was obliged to retire – when the tumult subsided, the play was begun again from the 1st speech'.[24]

Thraliana was almost entirely neglected during the winter, but Hester's letters continued to reflect her consuming interest in public matters. She had shared the general joy at Nelson's victory over the French fleet in the Battle of the Nile the previous August (Lord Spencer, the First Lord of the Admiralty, had fainted on hearing the news) and subsequent events in Egypt had commanded her close attention. 'The odious Ægyptians, after worshipping crocodiles so long, will perhaps worship Buonaparte,' she wrote to her friend Robert Gray, the vicar of Faringdon in Berkshire. 'Surely those are the basest of nations who accept the yoke of French democracy.'[25] She had greatly admired the pious tone of the letter in which Nelson had announced his victory to the secretary of the admiralty: 'I hear our warrior's father is a clergyman – how must his and Lady Nelson's hearts leap for joy!'

Lady Nelson and her father-in-law were in Bath at the time, as it happened, and Hester had a choice piece of gossip to retail:

> Have you dear Madam heard another Story? How Nelson's brave
> Defence of Italy is not – tho' warm and tender – quite disinterested.

'Tis said a Neapolitan lady holds *him* Captive, and very sorry am I for his Wife, who looks so pretty and seems so happy with her husband's Father here; the People quite delight to look on them, and clapped one Night when they came into the Playhouse.[26]

The hero of the nation had already been drawn into that bizarre relationship with her husband and herself which Emma Hamilton quaintly referred to as *tria juncta in uno*. Nelson, as his most recent biographer unimprovably puts it, 'had, like many naval officers entering the Mediterranean, left his marriage vows at Gibraltar'.[27]

※ ✄

By early February Piozzi was well enough to return his nephew to the care of Mr Davies, and before long one of the Misses went riding down to inspect this new and unwelcome member of the family – 'The Pretence a Visit to Mr. Macnamara's Niece now she is Ill,' Hester told Chappelow: '– but the true Reason I conceive merely *to see that Child* – and so the Curiosity was gratified; and our Piccolino was produced, with *My Name* and my *Husband's Face* – I wonder which would be the greatest *Recommendation*!'[28]

She returned to Brynbella to the sombre realization that the ranks of her friends were thinning fast: 'Since I left Wales – what a Diminution, what Deaths among my Old & among my new Acquaintance.' Thomas Pennant had died during her absence in Bath, and this affected her particularly – she had intended to dedicate *Retrospection* to him.

They received a warm reception: 'Lady Orkney, Lady Williams, Lady Blaquiere – *all* the Neighbours, even from Plâsnewydd have either come, or sent, or both – to welcome us home.'[29] There was no welcome from Cecilia. 'We hear in the Country that Mrs. Mostyn and her Son prosper exceedingly,' she wrote drily to Chappelow:

She sent the old Nurse who has lived with Miss Thrale these 15 Years and is now at Llewessog on a Visit – to see *this Place* while we were at Bath. The Gardiner and his Wife walked over it with her of Course – and Lord Bless me! says the Woman – 'what Fools must the Owners be to build such a Seat which they *never can live to enjoy*!!! but they have sent for an heir from Italy it seems; so *no matter*'.[30]

'I shall not begin Work till after Easter,' she told Mrs Pennington, 'we have enough to employ us now in surveying our sweet Place.'[31] Matters below stairs also required some attention. 'I seldom talk in my Letters of Domestic Arrangements – *Kitchen Griefs* as I call them,' she wrote to Queeney:

> Mrs. Beckwith's Conduct however amazed even *me* who am not easily astonished at proofs of human Depravity. She married the Gardiner but just in Time it seems, and is ready to lye In at 3 Months End. A poor, meek, mortified, unhealthy, unhappy, but completely *Ladylike* Person as She appeared to me; and as She really *was* in Birth and Manners: but too much Opium, and too many Modern Novels were certainly the Cause.[32]

She worked hard at *Retrospection* through the year, but there was time to visit Llewenney Hall, the old Cotton family home, to celebrate young Lord Kirkwall's coming of age – '& I *danced* in the *old Hall* with the *young Heir* 50 Years since I last remember to have seen it lighted up in hon^r of my own Uncle's Birthday'. And she still made time to read, and did so as voraciously as ever. Hannah More's *Strictures on the Modern System of Female Education* appeared during the year, critical both of Rousseau's doctrine of sensibility and of the strident feminism of Mary Wollstonecraft. 'Glorious Creature!' Hester wrote, 'how She writes! finding new Reasons to enforce old Virtues.'[33] She was less taken with Mungo Park's *Travels in the Interior Districts of Africa*. The young Scottish explorer, she felt, told her little she did not know already: 'I thought to gain a Thousand new Ideas from such *new Ground*: he has given me but one; he has cured me of my Uneasiness for those African Slaves that arrive *safe* at our Sugar Islands. They are really in a State of Preferment to the Situation awaiting them at home ...'[34]

Cecilia was pregnant again – 'and grown fat besides', Hester told Chappelow, 'and looks exceedingly well, and is packing up for *Town*, and for *Ton* and for all fine Things of Course'.[35] She was learning to keep her distance. 'I hope She will get happily thro' her lying in,' she wrote, 'but will not subject myself as last year to be driven almost from her door.'[36] The question did not arise; the child was born in London in the late autumn, and christened Henry Meredith. Hester was outraged to hear that Cecilia had gone out to dine with the MacNamaras at Streatham when the boy was two weeks old: 'Can such Things *be*? She returned to London at 11 o'clock at Night!!!! Shame!'

Hester had formed the view that John Salusbury – 'our Titmouse' as she called him – was not making as much progress as she had hoped and wrote critically to Reynold Davies; she also believed that the fees charged for his tuition were excessive. Davies entered a spirited defence. 'What an admonition!' he wrote:

> At a very serious expence I have taken into the house a preceptress whose labour was for a long while confined to him alone. He is hard at his books for above eight hours every day with one of us teachers at his elbow ... Labour is the characteristic of the university at the expence of one hundred pounds per annum. Idleness and extravagance are the characteristics of Eton at the expence of three hundred pounds per annum ...[37]

Hester was disarmed and accepted his blunt advice that to spend a month with them in Bath over Christmas would retard the boy's progress in English. Their departure was delayed when Piozzi suffered an attack of gout, but by the middle of December they were installed in a small house in Laura Place. As winter closed in, Hester's mood had been distinctly apocalyptic: 'The Plague is come from Barbary to Lisbon. Oh dreadful! America is desolated by the yellow Fever, Fine Times! ... If we do not feel Pestilence War and Famine before the Century ends, I think 'tis nothing but miraculous Interposition of Providence yᵗ protects us ...'

In France, the coup d'état of 18–19 Brumaire had brought Napoleon to power as First Consul. On Christmas Day, he wrote directly to George III offering to open peace negotiations. 'All things are odd now, and contradictory,' Hester wrote to Chappelow: 'We are looking for Peace to the very Man whose Genius and element is War – and who – had not the World been in a State of Contest and Distraction never would have acted any Part upon it at all.'[38]

There was more than one view, both in the administration and among the public, about how to respond to Bonaparte's initiative. And there was also, as the old year gave way to the new, more than one view about a quite different matter – was 1800 the end of the old century or the beginning of a new? Hester was in no doubt: 'I will not let this month Slip away without sending the Dear ladies at Bodylwyddan a letter with a *new Date*, which confounds many People so that they fancy a *new Century* begun, forgetting that Number *one* is the first of all numbers.'[39]

Hester Lynch Piozzi had every intention of living one more year in the century in which she was born.

30

Buzzers and Stingers

'TELL ME some London Chat of Literature or Scandal, or any Thing to keep Law Suits and Lawyers out of my Head.'

Hester's *cri de cœur* was addressed to Chappelow:

> Scarce were we returned from Bath … before a Bunch of Letters surprized and terrified me into a new Agony; when I was made to comprehend that Miss Thrale – the eldest – had written to our Oxfordshire Tenant Mr. Newton charging him not to pay any more Rent to *us* – but to *her*; who had at length examined her Father's Will, and found it would bear her out in the Demand.[1]

The estate had indeed been left to Queeney. But it was also the case that in Hester's 1763 marriage settlement, she had been granted £200 a year from Crowmarsh during her husband's lifetime and £400 after his death – provisions which had never subsequently been revoked. She was in despair: 'And I was so well after the Bath Waters!' she told Mrs Pennington, '– and now nothing but Law and Letters, and Chancery Suits, and false Accusations and every Evil Plague.'[2]

Both sides took the advice of counsel; by early summer, after protracted exchanges, Hester was able to report that the matter had been settled without further litigation: 'Miss Thrale *withdraws* (somewhat disgracefully) the Claim She could not *substantiate*: A tedious Suit against this never-dying Mother would have eaten up all the Profits of her hoped-for-Estate; and nobody would have benefited *but* the Lawyers …'[3]

A chance visitor to Brynbella that summer was the young Lord Henry Petty, son of the Earl of Shelburne who had taken Streatham when the Piozzis went off to Italy. Petty was still a Cambridge undergraduate at the time – six years later, at the age of twenty-six, he would become Chancellor of the Exchequer in Grenville's 'Ministry of all the Talents'.

Towards the end of his long life, the Whig elder statesman – Lord Lansdowne as he had by then become – recalled the visit:

> I remember her taking me into her bed-room to show me the floor covered with folios, quartos, and octavos, for consultation, and indicating the labour she had gone through in compiling an immense volume she was then publishing, called 'Retrospection.' She was certainly what was called, and is still called, blue, and that of a deep tint, but good humoured and lively, though affected; her husband, a quiet civil man, with his head full of nothing but music.[4]

If Lord Henry had done more than stay to dinner he might have formed a rather different impression of Piozzi. The Italian music master had slipped easily into the role of country gentleman. When he was not prostrate with gout, he took a keen interest in the estate, planting trees, deciding what crops should be planted, visiting the tenantry. In April that year he was appointed Overseer of the Poor for the parish; in July, he decided they would celebrate their wedding anniversary – it was the sixteenth – rather differently. 'Instead of feeding the Rich, We fed the poor,' Hester told Mrs Pennington: '... and every one of our 35 Haymakers had a good Noggin of Soup and a Lump of Beef in it and a Suet Dumpling and they were like the People in the Deserter who Sing – Joy Joy to the Duchess wherever She goes.'[5]

Careful with the pennies, Piozzi was an excellent steward of Hester's affairs. He was also generous. He made constant improvements at Brynbella and also turned his attention to Bach-y-Graig, which had been in a ruinous state when Hester visited it with Thrale and Johnson in 1774:

> Our neighbours advised him to tumble the venerable Ruin quite down, and build a snug Farmhouse with the Materials – but he would not – and so poking about we found some very curious Bricks with Stories on them composed in 1500, and one large one with Catherine de Berayne's Arms derived from Charlemagne ... I have set her Atchievement in Front – and a Stone to say the Mansion was repaired and beautified by Gabriel Piozzi Esq. in the year 1800.[6]

Some years later Hester described to Queeney the extensive restoration work they had set in hand at the local church:

We are now putting little Dymerchion Church in order; paving, glaz-
ing, slating, painting it &c. and we give them a new Pulpit, Desk, and
Cloths besides – with a brass Chandelier.

It *was* a Place like a Stable you know; and we have made a Vault for
ourselves and my poor Ancestors, whose Bones were found by digging
under the Altar; Dear Grandmamma's Skull had a black Ribband
pinned tight round it with Two Brass Pins ...[7]

Although Hester had written *British Synonymy* partly for his benefit,
Piozzi never really mastered the finer points of the English language.
When they were first married, Hester had told Queeney that her maid,
Johnson, 'laughs herself blind at Piozzi's English'. Not a great deal had
changed – when Hester was ill one year at Bath he wrote in his diary,
'Mrs. Piozzi she got the influenza, and find herself very ill with fever.'
The poet Thomas Moore, in his *Memoirs*, has a story about his calling
on an old lady of quality and being told by the servant that 'she was
indifferent': 'Is she indeed?' answered Piozzi huffishly, 'then pray tell
her I can be as indifferent as she,' and walked away.[8]

By mid-August *Retrospection* was almost complete. 'The Difficulty
will be to sell it,' Hester wrote in *Thraliana*, and so it proved: 'Here is
a letter from Robinson to say he is grown sick, and old, and going to
leave off, and will take no new Engagements: but wishes me success,
and doubts not but many in the Trade, – (those are his Words) – will
give the Money I have asked from him.'[9]

Hester had pinned her hopes on having the book appear by the first
day of 1801, which she regarded as the beginning of the new century,
and decided that her best hope was to take the manuscript to London
and hawk it round herself. Before their departure, she made an alarming
discovery:

– an Indurated Gland in the *Mammelle droite*; a Sentence of Death I
take it: – I shall then follow my poor Mother Step by Step: may I but
arrive where She is in Bliss eternal! ... At my Age, cutting is nonsense;
the Complaint's Hereditary. If 'tis *not* true, as I am not yet *quite sure*;
The People would say that I had lost my Senses.

At all Events Silence is the best & wisest Measure ...

It was a false alarm. The lump presumably disappeared; it was at any rate mentioned no more.

They stopped at Oxford on the way south, and Hester was shown over the Bodleian Library. This prompted Piozzi, possibly tired of stumbling over books and papers at home, to offer a dry suggestion: 'Mr Piozzi says if I was to undertake any thing ever again (which I shall not) the best way would be to take a house at Oxford and study in some College Library.'[10]

She was agreeably surprised by what they found at Streatham. The library seemed cluttered, because it now accommodated a billiard table, but Giles had laid out a thousands pounds on rare prints and books in fine bindings – 'I felt as if transported by Magic into Edwards's Shop Pall Mall,' she told Chappelow. Improvements were not confined to the house: 'The Garden gains surprisingly by our Tenants heavy Purse and liberal Hand; He has new planted the Espaliers – new clothed the Wall & even brought Earth at an immense Expence to promote the growth of Trees he takes no visible Delight in ...'

She was intrigued by her tenant's unorthodox domestic arrangements:

> He sleeps wth a fat Housekeeper at home ... lives in London getting Money all Morn^g and comes home on a Saturday to drink hard and play Billiards till 5 or 6 o'Clock o' Monday – leaving old Streatham Park a *Brothel* for his Servants: each of whom is a Relation: Brother, Sister, Niece or Nephew to the fat bedfellow who stays behind ...
>   So live the Rich Men of England!

She eventually found a publisher in John Stockdale, a native of Cumberland noted for his eccentric behaviour and coarse manners who had been a blacksmith and a valet before drifting into the book trade. He had published Johnson's works in 1787 and his bookshop was a fashionable lounging place favoured by supporters of Pitt (Whigs preferred the rival establishment of John Debrett).[11] Hester did not get the £1,000 she had asked for. Stockdale would agree only that the book should be published at his expense and that any profits should be shared equally between author and publisher, who would also jointly own the copyright.

The contract was signed on 3 November, and the Piozzis moved shortly afterwards to Brunet's hotel in Leicester Fields so as to be near the printer's – 'Stockdale plies me pretty hard with Proofs, and promises to present *Retrospection* as a New Year's Gift to the Town,' she told Chappelow: 'Mean while my *best Friends* must make Enquiries about the Work, and desire to be put down for some of the *first Copies* &c. because that will heighten his hopes, and possibly induce him to give me my 1000£ and let me go.'[12]

Retrospection: or a Review of the Most Striking and Important Events, Characters, Situations, and Their Consequences, which the Last Eighteen Hundred Years Have Presented to the View of Mankind was indeed in circulation early in the New Year. The two quarto volumes sold for two guineas. To serve as a frontispiece, a portrait of Hester was commissioned from two émigré artists living in London; it was painted by Pierre-Noël Violet, a native of Flanders who had been miniature painter to Louis XVI and engraved by the Neapolitan Marino Bovi. Some of her friends thought the likeness unflattering – Murphy said it made her look like the Witch of Endor.

It was a pretty ragged piece of publishing. The printer was Thomas Gillet, who had a shop just off Fleet Street; during December some of his compositors withdrew their labour in pursuit of higher wages, and there were a great many typographical errors – Hester was particularly irritated by those that had crept into her Latin and French quotations.

She was persuaded by Piozzi and Lady Eleanor Butler and others that it would be a good idea to send a copy to her uncle Thomas's widow – who would then, they argued, 'remit all past Malice, & embrace the Author'. They were mistaken. The eighty-year-old Lady Salusbury was as unforgiving as ever – 'She returned it back by the Servant,' Hester told the Ladies of Llangollen, 'and gave the Man a verbal Message that She had left off reading now on Account of bad Eyes.'[13]

The Piozzis returned briefly to Streatham, and from there travelled down to Bath. Sales of the book were slow. It had not yet brought her a shilling, she told Mrs Pennington – 'and it was upon that I fully depended for our Reimbursement of these few Weeks charges here in Bath'.[14]

Retrospection was roughly handled by the reviewers – Buzzers and Stingers, as Hester called them. Some were merely patronizing – 'a pretty piece of female patch-work'.[15] The *Anti-Jacobin Review* was withering –

'History cooked up in a novel form reduced to light reading for boarding school misses, and loungers at a watering place during the Dog-Days'.[16] The *Critical Review* was equally severe – 'To the learned, it must appear a series of dreams by an old lady.' Its conclusion was particularly offensive: 'In regards to her sex we are anxious to treat her with all possible lenity; but we should totally fail in our duty if we suffered the minds of youth, or of female readers, to be contaminated by such a flood of idle tattle and innumerable blunders.'[17]

Hester put a brave face on it. 'I am still alive,' she wrote to the Ladies of Llangollen, 'notwithstanding the feeble attacks of our Critical Reviewers, meant no doubt to break my Peace and ruin my Reputation for the Learning which I never boasted.'[18] Kind words from friends buoyed her up from time to time but she wasted a good deal of the summer dashing off spirited rebuttals of the reviewers' criticisms. In the end it was the gentle Piozzi who persuaded her that they were not worth her powder and shot.

One of the few favourable reviews appeared in the *British Critic*. 'How shall we characterize a work so perfectly singular?' the writer asked: 'An universal history from the Christian æra, translated into chit-chat language; the result of much, very much reading, containing facts and characters put together certainly as they were never put before; a string of reflections chronologically arranged, full of good sentiments …'[19]

Unfortunately, this did not appear until more than a year after publication – too late to persuade Stockdale to bring out a second corrected edition. By the end of 1801, only 516 sets of the original edition of 750 had been sold. Hester's share of the profits amounted to £124. 3s. 9d, and once she had paid for the complimentary copies she had sent to friends this was reduced to £99. 3s. 5d – something over £5,000 at today's prices.

She knew well enough what she could expect as a female writer – indeed she produced her own witty parody of how the reviewers would treat *Retrospection*:

Tho' we have been lately accustomed to the Style of *Female* Dramatists, *Female* Wits, Female Politicians, & Female Astronomers – It has not been quite in our Practice to travel wth y^e *fair* Creatures thro' the *Dark* Ages … Mrs Piozzi upon the Strength of a Three Years Tour thro' Italy,

& Three more pass'd in Meditation upon its distant Beauties, strongly contrasted by her present Prospects in the County of Flint, North Wales – bursts on us in the Character of *Serene Instructress* w[th.] regard to Religion & Politics ...[20]

She undoubtedly offered a broad mark to the reviewers. Some disapproved of anecdotal history; there were those who thought it inappropriate to include jokes; others deprecated her religious fundamentalism, and in particular her belief that the events of recent years in France validated the biblical prophecy of the approach of the last days. (She also believed, a shade prematurely, that the Jews were shortly to be recalled to the Holy Land.) And there were undoubtedly some who disliked, and were perhaps unsettled by, the prominence given to the achievements of women. '*Retrospection*,' Margaret Anne Doody declares roundly, 'is really a feminist history. The whole is not only a retrospection but a retaliation.'[21]

What Hester could most reasonably hold against her critics was that they had not measured performance against declared intention. She had not set out to write a work of scholarship like Hume's *History* or Gibbon's *Decline and Fall* – was not, indeed, equipped to do so. But she had declared her aim clearly, if orotundly, in her Preface: 'Whilst the deep current of grave history rolls her full tide majestick, to that Ocean where Time and all its wrecks at length are lost: our flashy *Retrospect*, a mere *jet d'eau*, may serve to soothe the heats of an autumnal day with its light-dripping fall, and form a rainbow round ...'[22]

Well before *Retrospection* appeared, the *Oracle* had carried a friendly puff – it reads suspiciously as if Hester had written it herself: 'Mrs. Piozzi, almost forgotten in the Metropolis, besides building a fine house in *Wales*, is busily engaged in adding another *tier* to the Temple of her *Literary Reputation*.'[23] The best laid schemes ... The years she had devoted to the book – the first attempt by an Englishwoman at a history of the world – brought her scant financial reward and dented her literary reputation; the crowning tier of the temple remained unbuilt. *Retrospection* was certainly Hester's most ambitious and original book, and she continued to believe it was her best. But in the twenty years of life that remained to her, she would make only one more at attempt to have anything published.

31

'Cruel Death'

'YOUR LIVELY friend Mrs. Piozzi, is our next neighbour, and the expense of strength and spirits which two such quartos would suppose, have not one whit diminished her gaiety, animation, and cheerfulness.'[1]

Thus Hannah More to their mutual friend Thomas Whalley. If Hester was cast down by the disappointing impact of *Retrospection*, she was not going to show it to those she encountered in the Pump Room or John Bull's circulating library. She returned to Brynbella well satisfied with their stay: 'I had more Pleasure from the Bath Society this Spring than ever ... all seemed proud to love and court the Authour of Retrospection. Mr. Piozzi was in high Looks & Voice, and charmed all Ears & never was ill an hour ...'

Thraliana now once again begins to read like a running commentary on current events – the health of the King ('They will soon break that dear Creature's heart – & then – all's over'); Nelson's victory over the Danes at Copenhagen ('I suppose he will add the Order of the Elephant to his other Plumes, now Prince Alexis or Alexander reigns in Russia'); advances in medicine ('Well! the Smallpox will soon be a Thing only to talk of, & on wch to make Conjectures; – Jenner extirpates it I see, for ever.')[2]

Freed from the tyranny of required reading, she could now explore whatever took her fancy: 'Here is a pretty Book concerning the Prolongation of Life come out from the German of Huffland – not Atheistical or wicked as I see – & that's a Wonder – in these Days.' She also devoured a book by a member of the Irish Parliament called *A Concise View ... of the Great Predictions in the Sacred Writings*: 'Mr Dobbs of Ireland must be quite a Lunatic surely; he says Jesus Christ is coming to *Armagh* to judge the World in the Valley of *Armagheddon*.'

There was now time to give more attention to Piozzi's nephew. The boy had been brought to the house each day during their brief stay at

Streatham. 'No child of his own age is before him *now*,' Hester had written proudly to Lady Williams, 'which says very well considering he could not speak or understand a word of English 20 Months ago.'³ Now, in the late summer of 1801, John Salusbury, accompanied by 'Professor' Wood, spent several weeks at Brynbella. 'I have every possible Reason to be pleased with Mr Wood, and flatter myself that between him and you and I; our little Black Eyed Salusbury will be a fine fellow,' she wrote to Davies:

> Reading English is what he does worst: I have begged of Mr. Wood with your leave to buy that oldfashioned but very valuable and too much neglected Book, Watt's Art of Reading for his Use ... these empty Tales of Titty Mouse and Tatty Mouse, and Miss Polly and Master Tommy, are but thin Food if the Children *did* remember and digest them; – which I think they never do.⁴

She was not happy about the boy's teeth, however, and urged Davies to take him to the local surgeon-dentist in Streatham:

> Let Parkinson look to his Mouth directly, for it is so constructed he shews his Teeth every Time he speaks – and there *are those* who regard *them* more than the *Words* you know, which will *at any Rate*, come with a better Grace from between Two Clean Rows of Fencibles in fair Uniform, than from an illformed and masked battery of black Fascines.⁵

Pitt, unable to persuade the King that Irish Roman Catholics should be admitted to the Westminster Parliament, had fallen from power at the beginning of the year. He was succeeded by Addington and on 1 October, after almost a decade of hostilities, Britain and France signed 'Preliminaries of Peace'. Hester was in two minds about the merits of the settlement. 'The terms are certainly in no sense disgraceful,' she wrote to Mrs Pennington; 'the Gold and Silver and Rubies and Rice from Ceylon, sweetened by sugar from Trinidad will keep Great Britain in perfect Good Humour.' But she also struck a more sombre note: 'Little did I dream seven Years ago of seeing Peace proclaimed between Great Britain and the *Consular State* of France – Little could I *ever* have dreamed that I should see Venice annihilated, Genoa forgotten: Piedmont's Alpine Barrier insufficient to keep out Invasion even in the

Depth of Winter – and old Rome divided against herself – dropping into her Enemies' Mouth almost without Invitation.'[6]

The Piozzis had been planning extensive improvements at Brynbella and decided to absent themselves while work was in progress. They went to Bath for four months and then moved up to London, where they spent seven or eight weeks in not very satisfactory lodgings near Manchester Square. They dined with the Miss Thrales ('the party particularly agreeable, and very good *talkers* in it'),[7] visited little Salusbury at Streatham, saw Mrs Siddons as Hermione in *The Winter's Tale*. It would be her last new role; although she was still only forty-seven she was no longer at her best, and at the end of the season, unwilling any longer to endure Sheridan's financial ineptitude, she would resign from Drury Lane.

Hester was enjoying herself – it was almost like old times. 'Well! I can yet make *new* Conquests,' she told Mrs Pennington:

> *Lord Stanhope* professes himself my admirer and the admirer of *my Books*. Lady Corke called *him* and about 300 People much round her last Night – on the Spur of a Moment, because Mr. Piozzi who had met her in Cumberland Street, had promised to sing at a *very private* party for her Ladyships amusement: and there was H: L: P caressed by all the *Liberty Lovers* ...[8]

She told Lady Williams about the excitement that summer over the exploits of the French army officer André-Jacques Garnerin:

> People in London are all talking of the Air Balloon, which I saw flying over Portland Place in the highest Wind possible, and losing itself in the Clouds at an astonishing altitude indeed.
>
> Monsieur Garnerin goes up again tomorrow with an Umbrella Thing to hinder his Fall, he calls it for that Reason a Parachûte. We shall see how it answers – taking so much Money at such a Risk of breaking all his Bones.[9]

In mid-July the Piozzis embarked on a circuitous return to Brynbella. They stopped for a time in Oxford and Cheltenham, and then made for Tenby in South Wales, where Hester was able to indulge her passion for sea-bathing: 'I have begged a Dozen good dips in Cardigan Bay to wash off the London Dust and Dirt and Smoke.'[10]

Their visit to Bath for the winter months was a low-key affair – 'Bath is scarce Bath this year somehow,' Hester wrote to Mrs Pennington, 'were it not for Laura Chapel and Pump I should regret leaving Solitude and Brynbella.'[11] Hannah More, plagued by ill-health, had decided to stay at home in Barley Wood. Hester's hopes of seeing Sarah Siddons were also dashed; yielding to pressure from her husband, who looked after her finances, she had gone to Dublin where she was assured of a lucrative season. A plan for Davies to bring down Piozzi's nephew – Hester now referred to him as 'my *Son Salusbury*' – was abandoned.

Towards the end of their stay, Piozzi became quite seriously ill: 'Dear Mr. Piozzi has I think had la Grippe; and the treacherous Gout always lieing in wait to do one a Mischief, was ready to leap upon the weakened Parts – Throat, Lungs, Larynx – every dangerous Situation. It is a fortnight since he was seized, *exactly*; and he is *now* pronounced out of all Danger – but greatly weakened ...'[12]

In the intervals of nursing her husband, Hester devoured Madame de Staël's *Delphine* which had appeared the previous year and would earn its author exile from Napoleon's Paris. '*Delphine* is delightfully written,' she told Queeney:

> Her combating the Christian Precept Love your Enemies, has been done with such insidious neatness, such artful ingenuity; I think it must obtain her ever lasting Renown as Lucifer's most useful Agent ... I could not keep Delphine out of my head sleeping or waking for many days, nor could avoid admiring at her much misused Powers of agitating the Human Mind. Buonaparte and I are both angry with this great Author, and tis *one* of the odd Things that we should so well agree.[13]

Hester herself then went down with influenza, and was extremely unwell for several weeks. Plans for the 'Musical Party' which the Piozzis usually gave while they were in Bath were abandoned. 'We long to see home again and our kind Neighbours,' she wrote to Lady Williams, 'and my pale lean face will plump up with Country Living on my native Soil.'[14]

Country living would not do a great deal for Piozzi. His health now went into steady decline: 'Mr Piozzi's Gout grows upon him, & as one Mountain of Chalk liquefies & runs off, – others generate; so as to cripple him in a melancholy Manner. He is now confined to Bed & Room, and has been out only in a Bath rolling Chair since we return'd from that Place this Spring after the Influenza.'

During the summer she read of the death of Thelwell Salusbury – 'my Cousin, my Pretendant – & my Enemy', she wrote: 'Poor, *Poor* fellow! He was I verily do believe, the Cause of my losing the Offley Estate, on which *I* counted; as I do on – *nothing* now I'm wiser. But 'tis no Matter, we shall never meet to make our Quarrels up & shake hands heartily – as I would give – Oh, what would I *not* give? to *do*.'

This willingness to wipe the slate clean is one of Hester's most attractive qualities; and within twelve months *Thraliana* affords a further instance of it:

> Well! as King Richard Richard says – '*Let's talk of Graves, & Worms, & Epitaphs.*' They are the Subjects which best fit the Times, on this Day, 7. July 1804 – put I on Mourning for my Uncle's Widow – Poor Lady Salusbury! once my feigned Friend, & long my serious Enemy – yet I am sorry – Ay that I am; & truly so … Fellow-Sinners, Fellow-Fools – quarreling in the Anthill where enough is provided for all, if all would but believe so.

For some years now Hester had had almost no contact with Cecilia and her husband. 'There is Talk of Mr. and Mrs. Mostyn having Sown their Wild Oats, and intending to return home here,' she wrote to Mrs Pennington, 'but perhaps *this* is too good News to be true.'[15] Mostyn had been drinking and eating more than was good for him, and treating his wife badly; he was also heavily in debt, a situation aggravated by his appointment as High Sheriff for Denbighshire – those honoured in this way met the substantial expenses of their year in office from their own pocket.

In October Cecilia again gave birth to a stillborn child – this time a girl. 'But she has a Strength a toutes Epreuves,' Hester wrote to Queeney, '& says 'tis no Loss &c. – was on Horseback the third day and galloping about as usual.' She spent three days at Brynbella shortly afterwards – '& made herself as it appeared to me, *studiously agreeable*', Hester wrote.

The Mostyns' marriage was in serious disrepair: 'Cecy complains of her Husband grievously, accuses him of gross Avarice and rough

Behaviour – scruples not to confess her dislike of the Man & her Resolution to live with him only till The Boys go to School.'

She did not have all that long to wait, although matters would not fall out entirely as she envisaged.

~ ~

Hester had not written anything of substance since completing *Retrospection*. She had made a start in the summer of 1803 on an abridged version of Dumouriez's *Tableau spéculatif de l'Europe*, which had appeared five years previously. But then she discovered from Chappelow that it had been translated almost as soon as it had appeared. 'I live out of the World,' she wrote ruefully, '& resemble the Recluse who asked if *Jealousy* would not be a *new* & admirable Subject for Dramatic Composition?'[16]

She resumed her old habit of dashing off occasional verse – lines to Piozzi on their wedding day; some doggerel verses about Prestatyn, where they spent two months sea-bathing in the autumn of 1804. She also composed some verses in imitation of Percy's *Ballads*, and made a not entirely tactful offering of them on her second wedding anniversary to young Lady Kirkwall, who had fallen out with her husband:

Nae Daunce in my Lordis' Ha',
   Nae Light in My Lady's Bowre,
Nae Cannon pointed o'er the Wa',
   To tell the Gladsome Howre …

Having produced eleven stanzas in this vein, Hester then, rather curiously, added a footnote in *Thraliana* in which she poured scorn on the genre. 'It is curious to see how the old Stuff of w[ch] this is an Imitation obtains favour in the *Reading* Circles,' she wrote: 'You see nothing on a lady's Toilette by way of Literary amusement, but these Delirious Dreams of Faeries & Phantasms, & roasting Babies alive, and Wax Images supposed to be used by Enchanters &c&c&c – fine Times!'

Changing times, certainly, and changing tastes in literature. Her scorn here is directed at works like Southey's *Thalaba* and Scott's *Minstrelsy of the Scottish Border*, which had recently appeared. But she would come in time to think rather better of the Wizard of the North.

As Piozzi's health declined, books became even more important to her. She had been 'most exceedingly entertained' by Dugald Stewart's Life of the Scottish historian William Robertson – 'The letters written to him from *his* own, & *my* own Contemporaries all Characteristic of the Men – Hume, Gibbon, Walpole, Strahan, Garrick and Lord Lyttelton make the Book to *Me* a gallery of Portraits.' In Bath, in the spring of 1805, she read the three volumes of William Godwin's *Fleetwood; or, The New Man of Feeling*. 'Have you read Godwin's new Novel?' she asked Queeney: 'It is a very neat key to the human heart, every dirty Corner and Sluts' Hole of which, he seems to have great delight in opening. – The *Wedding Supper* however is a scene of horrible Sublimity, and kept me awake all Night.'[17]

Returning to Brynbella in what she described as 'a backward melancholy Spring', Hester formed a new resolve – 'I'll study Hebrew to divert Ennui & pass the Summer Months away.' She enlisted the help of the vicar of Tremeirchion, John Roberts. She would not, she told Queeney, have embarked so late on an undertaking of such magnitude 'had I not found out that the Illiterate and Itinerant Preachers of Methodism up and down, *all* study Hebrew, to torment the Clergy'.[18]

She was distressed in the summer by the death of Murphy: 'Oh Melancholy! & by me heart-felt Occurrence! so pass the Companions of one's Youth away.' Her distress did not inhibit Piozzi from submitting a claim against Murphy's estate for £40, which had been lent to him on his note of hand. Murphy, however, had always spent freely, and his assets were not sufficient to pay creditors sixpence in the pound. The Piozzis were reminded that Murphy had rendered them much legal service without payment; they eventually received £12.

The pages of *Thraliana* now increasingly resemble an extended obituary column. 'Here I am then once more,' she wrote at Brynbella in May 1806; '*ripatriata* as the Italians express it – after our excursion to England: Piozzi & his Wife alive after so many Deaths dropping on every side us.' Cator and Crutchley had both recently died, and later in the year Piozzi lost a brother. 'Everyone going, going, going,' Hester wrote: '& I have just got a new Bed Chamber *Clock* – how foolish!'

Taxing as it was, the study of Hebrew was not enough to keep her restless mind fully occupied: 'The Harvest is in, & the Swallows gone,

and the Rain arrived & silly Mrs Piozzi planning a new Book.' She had
in mind a study of the derivation of Christian names, and proposed to
call it 'Lyford Redivivus' – an indication of the extraordinary range
of her reading: Edward Lyford's *True Interpretation and Etymology of
Christian Names* had appeared in 1655. She was still working on it nine
years later.

In the spring of 1807, at the age of thirty, Cecilia found herself a
widow. Mostyn died at Bath of tuberculosis, and was taken home to
Wales to be buried. He died intestate, leaving Cecilia to untangle his
affairs, deal with his debts and bring up her three young sons as best
she could.

It proved an eventful for year for Hester's other daughters: Sophy,
now thirty-six, became engaged to Henry Merrick Hoare, a partner in
the family bank. 'I have every reason to think myself highly fortunate
in having gained the Affections of so amiable a Man,' she wrote rather
stiltedly to her mother.[19] They were married in August and began their
married life in a fine house in York Place close to Regent's Park. The
Piozzis were not invited to the wedding. 'I have a beautiful Picture here
which Mr. Piozzi and I mean As a Nuptial Present to Sophia,' Hester
wrote to Queeney. It was a Gainsborough she had bought at auction
twenty years previously –'the Subject Cattle driven down to drink, and
the first Cow expresses something of a surprize as if an Otter lurked
under the Bank'.[20]

Within a matter of months Hester acquired a second son-in-law: 'I
am delighted beyond all power of Expression that my dearest Girl will
be so richly rewarded for all her numerous and various Virtues. I am
delighted too that a *British Admiral* is to be made happy by accepting
her pretty little White Hand …'[21]

The little white hand in question was the forty-three-year-old
Queeney's; the Admiral was George Keith Elphinstone, the sixty-two-
year-old son of a Scottish peer. Ten years previously he had been created
Baron Keith of Stonehaven Marischal in the peerage of Ireland for his
part in the capture of Cape Colony; he was currently Commander-in-
Chief of the North Sea. A widower for twenty years, Keith, who had
known Queeney since 1791, knew what etiquette required of him:

Madam,

By a letter from your Daughter I am informed she has communicated to you our intended Connexion. Therefore no reason exists from
my withholding a duty any longer and to assure you, Madam, that
the approbation of a parent is a matter of essential consequence to the
General comfort of such a Union, and that I shall be happy to know
it meet's with your's ... Altho' I am well provided for as a Cadet of a
Noble Family and an Industrious officer of the Country, yet I am not
rich for the Rank to which I have been Raised but have enough for all
the Reasonable Comforts of Life ...[22]

This would have raised eyebrows in the wardrooms of the fleet. His
long years as a commander-in-chief entitled him to a healthy slice of
the prize money for ships captured within his command. His service in
India and South Africa had brought him £64,000, and between 1803 and
1806 he received £177,000. In the course of his long career – he had
joined the Navy three years before Queeney was born – he is believed
to have accumulated a greater fortune from prize money than any other
officer.[23]

Susan, now thirty-seven, followed a less conventional path. For some
years she had shared a house with Sophy. Two months before the Hoares'
wedding she went to live with William Wells, a well-known watercolour painter, at his house near Knockholt in Kent. Wells, a friend of
Turner's, was a fashionable drawing master – his pupils included two of
the daughters of the Duke of Clarence, the future William IV. He himself
was the father of nine children, of whom two had died in infancy; his
wife Mary had died only four months before Susan moved in with him.
They did not marry; in the tax roll for the following year, they appear as
'joint occupants' of Wells's house, which was called Ashgrove Cottage.
Hester heard of all this only from her maid and Piozzi's valet. What
she thought of the liaison is fairly plain from the controlled but bitter
irony of what she wrote to Queeney: 'Suzette leaves Town tomorrow
if I am right, and consummates her marriage With Mr *Ashgrove*: If like
Many Modern Couples they should be soon tired of the binding words
to have and to hold, She may get a Divorce any Day.'[24]

꙰

Piozzi was now a hopeless invalid, but he and Hester clung doggedly to their annual routine. Their visit to Bath in 1807 turned into a nightmare: '– on my Birthday 27th day of the new Year, Dr Parry was fetched at 2 or 3 o'Clock in the Morn^g, & between then & the first of May, my wretched Husband swallowed no fewer than 300 medical Draughts'.

Early in March, believing he was close to death, Hester asked whether he wished to see a priest. He declined with some vehemence, but when she suggested a Protestant clergyman he readily assented:

> Dear Mr Leman of the Crescent came at our Call, and my Piozzi is now a Member of our own Communion. He rec^d the Sacrament again according to *L'Eglise Anglicane* on Easter day; and his odd Dream at Milan is verified; how he took me by the Arm & walked out of their Church – resolving to walk in no more. See then what may be done by the old Method, suaviter in Modo, fortiter in re.

They would not visit Bath together again. Hester noted early in 1808 that very few pages remained to her in the last of the six volumes Thrale had given to her all those years ago: 'The *Thraliana* is coming fast to an End.'[25] It now became increasingly plain that Piozzi's life was also drawing to a close:

> Another long cruel Fit of Gout with immense Cretaceous Abscesses in Foot & Fingers began upon my wretched Husband Sunday Night 7: Feb: 1808. & sent him to Bed whence he is not yet risen – and whence God only knows when he will be able to rise … Sickness within – & *a blockading* Snow without, which precludes all Power of calling Physicians. What shall we do?

'Gout' was of course a catch-all term for the many ills afflicting Piozzi. A modern diagnosis would extend far beyond the acute attacks he suffered in his feet and hands and the build-up of deposits of uric acid – the chalkstones so frequently mentioned in Hester's accounts of his illness. Dr Ernest Sadler, who gave James Clifford the benefit of his assessment of Piozzi's symptoms, identified fibroid disease of the heart, bronchitis and diseased blood vessels, which together would account for his low pulse, occasional violent cough and difficulty in breathing except when sitting upright. The abscesses on his feet, which developed into ulcers, were due to phlebitis. Sadler concluded that the inflammation and thickening of those abscesses would have seriously impaired the circulation, and that this carried with it the ever-growing threat of gangrene.

The company of old friends brought little comfort: 'Mr Whalley has been here on a visit – but Mr Piozzi's miserable state of Health poyson'd all Pleasure in Conversation … We have a Mind to go to Chester, & meet the *Child*; & consult Dr Thackeray again for these Violent Spasms – frightful seizures on the Stomach & Breast.'

The 'Child' – Piozzi's nephew – was now a youth of fifteen, and had been moved from Streatham to Enborne, in Berkshire, where he was being tutored by a clergyman called Thomas Shephard. There had been some talk of his going to Eton, but he was not up to it academically. Hester was philosophical, although it is not clear why she had wanted to send him there in the first place: 'Much Vice and Folly will certainly be escaped by your not going to Eton,' she told him; 'I hope you will gain Virtue and Knowledge where you are, and such a Love of both as will keep you out of Mischief when you enter into the World.'[26]

She found his letters a great comfort – 'Write to me soon Dear Love, for I want a Letter sadly.'[27] In return she bombarded him with snippets of Brynbella gossip ('We had a Ewe lambed under the Snow the dreadful drifting Night'),[28] medical bulletins on Piozzi, moral precepts and reminders that he was now a young Englishman: 'I *do* wish that you would be pleased to *Anglify* your Style a little, and not write as the Foreigners do that You arrived *to* Enborne instead of *at* Enborne.'[29] She appears occasionally to have overestimated his sense of humour: 'Dear Salusbury,' she exclaimed in one letter, 'will you never be able to take a Silly Joke?'[30]

She was flattered during the summer by a request to write an epilogue. The play, *The Mysterious Bride*, was by a foppish young man called Lumley St George Skeffington, the son of a baronet and a member of the Carlton House circle.[31] The Prince Regent regularly consulted him on questions of fashion; he was the subject of wide ridicule among his contemporaries and more than once attracted the satirical attention of Gillray. That was all one to Hester – 'Strange that I'm not forgotten at this Distance from Wits and Beaux & all that makes an Epilogue *piquant*.'

She dashed off forty-six lines and got them off to him by return. The play was acted at Drury Lane, but never printed.

As Piozzi sank towards death, the combination of brandy and opium induced delirium. 'Our Bulletin of Health here goes on very Ill,' Hester wrote to Salusbury early in March: 'Poor Uncle has been delirious now a whole Week ... complaining of no Pain at all, rather making odd Preparations for a Journey *in Italy*, for I understand he considered himself as now at *Milan*.'[32]

'I continue according to promise my melancholy Narrative,' she wrote two weeks later:

> The Delirium *gone*, so far as one could perceive; but he said himself that his Head was *not at home*. The Back was dreadful. An open Sore below the lowest of the Vertebræ ... You might have buried a Small Phial Bottle in the Place, and the Discharge nearly insupportable to us all ... We have had him in his Dressing-Room this Morning to shave and change Linen, because there was now not only Fœtor, but Danger; from the Number of putrid Ulcers – *all going*; and we have burned Camphor and Cascarilla Bark, and flung the Aromatic Vinegar about most liberally; and instead of any Fainting or Rigor – soon as he was put to bed – he *stormed* away with anger, directed chiefly against *me* who he said had always used him very ill, and worse now than Ever ...[33]

Piozzi died on 26 March and Hester made her final entry in *Thraliana*: 'Every thing most dreaded has ensued, – all is over; & my second Husband's Death is the last Thing recorded in my first Husband's present! Cruel Death!'

32

Widow Piozzi

TWO WEEKS after the funeral, still dazed with grief, Hester set out for London. 'Perhaps the Noise of Coaches in the Street will make me Sleep,' she wrote to Queeney. 'This death-like *Stillness* hinders my resting somehow; nor can I here close my poor Eyes till Morning's Dawn sets all the Birds o'Singing.'[1] She had hoped to stay at Warren's, but could find only some dingy rooms at a hotel run by a Frenchman in Duke Street. She was still in a very fragile state. 'My Nerves did certainly use me ill enough upon *the Road*,' she wrote to Lady Williams:

> ... and the first time I went to Church here at London, feeling myself one solitary Soul among a *Thousand* human creatures assembled for Service at St. Martin's large spacious Temple – The loud Organ pealing in my Ears, who have not heard a Musical Note or seen 25 People together for 25 Months; affected me too strongly: and I was very near fainting away.
>
> These delicate Feelings will however wear down by Degrees, and leave my Mind dull and *blunted* as an old Woman's *ought to be* ...[2]

Dull and blunted her mind would never be. She wore nothing but black after Piozzi's death (although sometimes permitting herself the frivolity of a white hat in summer), but she was extraordinarily resilient, and her spirits soon began to revive. She was fond of quoting her old enemy Baretti: 'When the Throws went badly with poor Baretti as we played together at BackGammon – or when Matters went ill with his Game by his own fault: These would he say are cursed Dice, but we must play them as they are.'[3]

It was in this spirit that she now faced her new situation. The first matter of business which claimed her attention was the proving of Piozzi's will, and in this she had the assistance of Charles Shephard, the son of Salusbury's tutor, who had acted as her lawyer on a number of occasions. Piozzi had left her everything, apart from £4,000, which he wished to have divided among his relatives in Italy. Shephard also pressed ahead with the process of having Salusbury naturalized. 'The lawyers throw a Thousand Rubs in the Way of this Denizenation Business,' Hester wrote.[4]

She was anxious to get home: 'I am very tired of Town, and if this Affair was once over, and my Carriage ready for Travelling, I would soon slip away from The Heat and Dust and Bugs – and monstrous Expence of a London Hotêl.'[5] She and Salusbury travelled north together in the middle of June. Her health was slowly mending, and it is clear from a letter to Queeney that her old zest for life was beginning to return:

> Oh if I get to London next Year, I will be acquainted with Miss Joanna Baillie, Shee the Painter, and Walter Scott; and when I have Spent an Evening or Two in *their* Company – (but not before;) I will compare these Times with past Times, and if those were really better – for Chat I mean – how highly! and with what encreased Reverence shall I regard them![6]

She was excited to learn in the autumn that Queeney was expecting a child, although excitement was laced with anxiety. 'This unexpected Pregnancy of Lady Keith throws a momentary Gloom over my Prospects of a chearful Winter,' she told Salusbury:

> She *may* find her Life endangered; and She *may* (possibly) feel her Tenderness rekindled towards a Mother who so long adored her: and She *may* request my Presence at her Delivery – If She *does* – Imperious Duty will bear down every Consideration, and I shall quit Friends, Pleasures, – Social Comforts, and my *dearest Salusbury*; for a Sick Room: and Shrieks that will shatter my newly restored Nerves to Death –[7]

The call to duty did not come. Hester was rather deflated. 'Lady Keith goes to London *on* her Business the week after next,' she told Lady Williams. 'I suppose the Admiral is in a hurry to be giving Orders to his little *Cabin-Boy* and they begin expecting before the Time.'[8] The child – a cabin girl as it turned out – was born in December. She had as her sponsors two future Kings of England – the Prince of Wales (Keith had been his secretary) and the Duke of Clarence, who had served under him. 'Lady Keith has never so much as said She would be glad to see me, and shew her Child to me,' Hester grumbled to Salusbury when the infant was three months old.[9] To Queeney herself she was more circumspect: 'A kiss to *la jolie Georgette*, who is a beauty to *my own Taste* I am confident; because everybody says She is so like her dear pretty Mama ...'[10]

She was careful when writing to her daughters always to refer to Salusbury as 'my Nephew' but that was no longer how she herself thought of him. Sometimes he is 'my Dear Child' or 'my darling Boy'; writing to him in the spring of 1810 she signs herself 'Your Affectionate Parent and Friend'; a long letter later in the year begins with the remarkable words 'If my dearest Boy had been the Child of my Body, instead of the *Son of my Soul* ...'[11]

If he fails to answer by return she is overwhelmed by anxiety – 'Oh Salusbury! Have you no Pity? Write only two words – *Alive* and *Well.*'[12] 'Dear Love!' she writes, as she counts the days to his arrival at Brynbella for Christmas, 'when will you come home? I am very tired of sitting *alone.*'[13] He had become the centre of her life – the child she had not been able to give Piozzi; the companion she had lost with his death; the son who would take the place of her two dead boys; the paragon whose affection would cancel out the cold indifference of her daughters; the guarantee that the name of Salusbury would live on. There are passages in her correspondence that read like the effusions of a lover.

She had taken the closest interest in his schooling, both at Streatham and at Enborne, her letters peppered with Johnsonian precept and exhortation: 'Let me beg of you not to give yourself the Future Pain and Disgrace of being out of Countenance for want of knowing the History of Greece, Rome, and England; – They are *Indispensable* to a Gentleman's appearance in proper Company ... A Lad who has not these Old Stories in His head – may as well have no *Head* ...'[14]

Now she was intent on getting him into Oxford. She received conflicting advice: 'Oh now for Pity do not put that fine-pure hearted Boy to Christ Church,' one friend implored her; 'it is the wickedest College in Oxford.'[15] Christ Church, however, Hester was determined it should be – her antennae were finely attuned to social distinctions.

She lobbied influential friends, sent Salusbury to visit the Ladies of Llangollen, stopped at Oxford on her way home to pull what strings she could.

Finally, the Dean of Christ Church agreed to accept Salusbury as a Gentleman Commoner. Hester was jubilant. 'And so your Fortune is fixed, and my Child must be launched into Life,' she wrote to him: '– I feel all over Goose-Skin at the Thought on't – knowing as I do, how sharp Folks are looking to see whether You make Slips or no, – That they may be ready to push You quite down.'[16]

❧ ❦

February of 1811 found Hester in Cheltenham. 'This Place really appears to me to have been well chosen this Year,' she wrote to Lady Williams, 'when a London Jaunt would have been poysoned by the Plagues concerning Streatham Park.'[17] The management of the property was becoming an increasing burden, and when her friend Thomas Whalley suggested she should offer to sell her life interest to her daughters, she jumped at the idea.

The 'Ladies', to Hester's irritation, showed no interest. 'The fair Principals – my amiable Reversionaries are Silent,' she wrote to Chappelow: 'and I have done being amused with *Dumb-Show* Transactions: a *Pantomime* of such Importance would only leave me the Character of *Mother Goose*: though my heart applauds the Project as likely to profit all Parties –'[18]

To her further annoyance, her daughters now asserted she had no right to sell any of the contents of the house. 'I have heard by a Side-Wind,' she wrote indignantly to Salusbury, 'that our Ladies mean to contest my Power over the Plate, Furniture, &c. their Father left – which they aver was only for My Life – a fine Affair!'[19] Impatient with lawyers and their slow ways, she unwisely travelled up to London herself to try to move things forward. The result was predictable: 'Lord Keith and Mrs. Hoare were both very bitter to me about these Matters, and I wish from my heart The Place was sold,' she told Whalley. The root of her anxiety was that 'poor dear Salusbury may have no Incumbrances or dormant Claims fall upon him after my Death'.[20] To that end, she told Salusbury, she proposed to rewrite her will, 'designating you by the name of John Salusbury Piozzi ... and now my own dear and adopted Child'.[21]

Salusbury's Oxford career was short and undistinguished. Hester's bankers raised a discreet eyebrow when she made him an allowance of £125 a quarter,[22] but he was soon overspending it and having tradesmen send his bills to Hester. She scolded him constantly for his failure to write: 'I see neither Common Sense nor Knowledge of the World in persisting to think it a heavy Tax on Life to spend 3 Minutes in writing every Week 3 Words — *safe*, *well*, and *happy*. Those Words are all I want —'[23]

She fretted about his health, and even more about his moral well-being:

Dearest, — Dearest Boy! keep out of these worthless People's Company as much — as You can. — The Word *Boy* puts me in mind of poor Uncle: if he saw this Letter, and heard of the Wine Bill, and the Plate Bill — and *my* Complaints that you never write — and *Your* Humour of forbearing hitherto to accept any profession; I think he *would* say '*Charming Boy*! I am very glad; He is spoiled *enough* now.'[24]

If she was disappointed when he announced towards the end of his first year that Oxford was not for him, she concealed it remarkably well: 'You are the best of all wise Boys, and the wisest of all good ones, in wishing to leave Oxford, and come home with poor Aunt — to take Care of her.'[25] That, however, was not what the indulged and indolent Salusbury had in mind; he spent most of the next year visiting friends, going to balls and attending hunt and race meetings.

Hester meanwhile was engaged in a new round of hostilities over Streatham. Peter Giles, the corn merchant with whom she had been so taken, had not remained for the period stipulated by his lease, and the Piozzis had eventually sued him. A new seven-year lease had been signed with a merchant called Abraham Atkins, but three years later he went bankrupt.

Now, in 1812, Queeney and her sisters had discovered a new *casus belli*. 'I fear I have now sinned against them without hope of reinstate-ment to favour,' Hester wrote to Dr Whalley:

Mrs Mostyn having menaced little Salusbury pretty sharply last summer, what they would do to *him* if I was to die; and how they would
pinch him for dilapidations of their Seat in Surrey; Charles Shephard
counselled me to repair and reside in it next Spring – to show them
it was habitable. I therefore recommended Mead, a Surveyor whom I
have long known; and he selected such Trees as were overshadowing,
and ruining the house, and has *cut them down*. Down came the Ladies
though, in high Wrath; and terrified the man, and wrote most insulting
Letters to Shephard – *cruel* and *bitter* ones to poor me, who will have
little less than 1000£ to lay out, and Reproaches alone for my Reward.[26]

Whalley was sympathetic:

Your adopted son, I trust, and verily believe, will recompence you, for
all the wrong you have suffered from your *legitimate* Daughters. I am
glad that you have, at last, determined to put Streatham in thorough
repair ... You will live long enough, I doubt not, to fetch up, more
much more, than the cost of these Repairs, and then a Fig! for the fine
Ladies, your fashionable daughters.[27]

The renovations were put in hand. Hester appealed to Mead to keep
costs down: 'Do not drive me to unnecessary Expences to please any
ladies living by the Mortification and Ruin of Your old Friend ...'[28] It
would be two years before the work was completed and a new long-term
tenant installed.

~❧ ❧~

Hester was highly alarmed in the spring of 1813 to hear that the 'Ladies'
were claiming rights of reversionary ownership in her Welsh estates
and travelled to London to take legal advice. She was reassured to
have confirmation that although she had signed a deed in 1783 settling
everything on Queeney, she had retained the power of revocation; the
deed itself had in any event been revoked by her marriage settlement
with Piozzi.

Relieved, but very angry, Hester immediately had Shephard draw up
a new will bequeathing to Salusbury '*every* Thing I *possess*, and every
Thing I *claim*: or am, or shall be intitled to'. That was not particularly

surprising. But she also decided to do something extremely foolish. She announced that when Salusbury came of age the following year, she wished to make him a gift of Brynbella and all her Welsh property. Shephard tried to reason with her – reminded her of the unfortunate precedent of King Lear. Streatham remained a liability; she had only a small amount of capital, a few investments and a modest income from Crowmarsh; by making such a large gift to Salusbury she might well be condemning herself to an impoverished old age.

Hester was not open to argument. Indeed she had made her intentions plain to Salusbury while he was still at Oxford, and that regardless of whether, as she would have preferred, he buckled down to a profession:

> If you can perswade Some good Girl to marry you this Time *Three Years* – I will *give* you all I *can* leave You, and you may go abroad together and save Money, if you will not stay at Home and get Money – which would be a likelier Plan for Happiness, and Law the proper Profession. Whatever befalls – except *your* Illbehaviour – or Choice of what I call a Mop-squeezer, or flanting Miss from a Gaming House …[29]

'The estate is *mine*, and if mine *Yours*,' she now wrote: 'the Lady of your Choice will not be *very ill off* –'[30] Another two months passed, however, before Hester learned that Salusbury had already made his choice. An undeclared reason for wishing to leave Oxford was that he had fallen in love with the sister of his best friend, Edward Pemberton. 'The family he connects with are, in all appearance, much respected by their neighbours,' Hester told Whalley; 'very honourable, and very ancient; proud Salopians! *plus noble que riche*; but individually well bred and agreeable.'[31]

She did not meet Harriet Pemberton for several months, but they were soon writing to each other: 'My charming Correspondent has drawn herself into a nice Snare by writing to *me* so kindly,' Hester warned, 'she will be quite *pelted* with Letters.'[32] Harriet, who was a talented watercolourist, sent her a drawing, and Hester in return presented her with a specimen of her needlework – a reticule on which she had embroidered a fly copied from Linnaeus and a Sphinx Moth of Malta. 'But 'tis no small Undertaking,' she wrote modestly, 'to present *Work* of *any* Sort before such a painter and Colourist as our lovely H: M: P.'[33]

Friendship for Hester could never be anything less than wholehearted, and she was soon writing to her prospective daughter-in-law with the same intensity and warmth that years before had characterized her friendship with Fanny Burney and Sarah Siddons:

> Let me never lose that obliging Partiality you are pleased to express towards *me*; for I have had Disappointments *enough* in my long Passage thro' a Thorny World; and could not bear to be Scratched with Briars at the End of the Avenue. From Dear Salusbury I expect a kind hand to conduct me *Safe home*; and a Promise of Endeavouring to obtain the best Apartments for *himself* in our *Father's House*.[34]

She grumbled occasionally (though never to Harriet) about Salusbury's total lack of interest in politics or literature or things of the mind: 'Shall we praise or blame Dear Salusbury's utter want of all Curiosity concerning any one Thing but the pretty Girl he is attached to?' she wrote to a young friend who was doing well at Cambridge.[35] But she pressed on with the formalities required to establish him in the Salusbury line of succession, and by the end of 1813 these were complete. 'My Name and Arms are his *own* now,' she wrote to Harriet: 'and in no one's Power to wash off his Carriage when he keeps one; a trick which Malice *might* have plaid to give *me* – more than *him* – Mortification – but he *is* my Son at last – in true Earnest; my Son by Adoption, inserted into the pedigree of my Descent, and registered in the Herald's College –'[36]

The wedding took place in in November 1814 at Condover Park, the Pemberton's rather grand property in Shropshire; Salusbury had come of age two months previously. 'The happy Younglings jumped into their carriage and away to *their own Brynbella*,' Hester wrote to Dr Whalley: 'from that Magnificent Dwelling I drove hither in a few Days –

> From Apartments of eighteen Feet high where they dine
> To a Chair-lumber'd closet just Twelve Feet by Nine ...'[37]

The days when she could afford a fine house in Bath's Pulteney Street were long past. She settled into cheap lodgings in New King Street.

33

Going, Going, Gone

LIVING in a nutshell was how she described it, and it was not at all what she had been accustomed to: 'One of these half-out-of-Town houses was the foolishest thing in the World. My next-door neighbour is making a Hothouse to poyson me with the Smoke and Choke ... and if one *was* to be ill – The nearest Doctor is too far off.'[1] The cost of the repairs at Streatham ('always a gilded Millstone round my Neck') had been a ruinous £6,500 – upwards of £330,000 at present-day prices – and she still had £2,500 of that to find. There was a silver lining, however – or a silver lining of sorts: the Russian ambassador had taken the house for three years at an annual rent of £600: 'Count Lieven is my tenant, and pays me liberally but so he should; for his dependants smoke their tobacco in my nice new beds, and play a thousand tricks that keep my steward, who I have left there, in perpetual agony.'[2]

She lived in hopes that her study of Christian names would do something to replenish her coffers. *Lyford Redivivus or a Grandame's Garrulity* as it was now called had already been rejected by Hatchard and was currently with Longman, the publisher of Johnson's *Dictionary*. Longman turned it down, however – 'Kind Words but no Money'.[3] Hester was dejected, but not inclined to give up. 'My Book is still a Resource,' she told Salusbury.[4]

Her reduced circumstances did nothing to impair her genius for forming new friendships with people of all ages. Early in her new life in Bath she made the acquaintance of Edward Mangin, a clergyman in the Church of Ireland whose Huguenot ancestors had fled France in the reign of Louis XIV. Mangin, a widower of forty-three with a young daughter, had been a contemporary at Balliol of Southey's; he had a substantial private income, and devoted himself to writing and translation. Poems, essays, a three-decker novel, the nineteen-volume *Works of Samuel Richardson, with a Sketch of his Life* – he was hugely prolific.

To Hester's delight he took an interest in *Lyford Redivivus*: 'Mr. Mangin has undertaken to dispose of my Book ... and says he will *Threaten* to publish [by] Subscription if the Man he applies to, does not propose giving a handsome Price.'[5] Mangin was unsuccessful, however, and an entry in Hester's Pocket Book two months later reads, 'I committed my luckless Book to its new Patron Sir James Fellowes.'[6] Fellowes, who was much the same age as Mangin, was a cultivated physician who had recently retired on half-pay after a distinguished career in the medical departments of the army and the navy – he had been at Santo Domingo with Admiral Christian's fleet and had rendered conspicuous service at Gibraltar during the fever epidemic of 1804–05. He knew Spanish well and was a witty conversationalist; their correspondence indicates that he and Hester were soon on terms of easy familiarity: 'Why Dear Sir James Fellowes! Peter the Cruel was surely *Your* Ancestor instead of *mine*. After the Thousand Kindnesses You and your charming Family – Hombres y Hembras had heaped on your ever obliged H:L:P; – to run out of the Town so, and never call to say Farewell.'[7]

He was a man of considerable charm:

Dear Sir James Fellowes who has this Moment walked home with me says – why Mrs. Piozzi you will live to be a hundred. Why so? because you are so careful of your Health – come now do tell me what is Your Dinner to day? A Calves Foot. – Nothing else! *Nothing*. And what yesterday? A Bason of good Veal Broth – But what do you drink? Why Two, or sometimes *Three* Glasses of the best Wine Money can buy; – Madeira or old Hock ... Oh! *You'll* not want Physick – or Physicians; and when you do – *Here am I*.[8]

Hester discussed with him everything under the sun – from the writings of Cobbett to her relations with Salusbury, from her financial difficulties to her memories of Hogarth, from the state of her bowels to the propensity of the Jews to deal in old clothes. She presented him with her portrait by the talented miniaturist Sampson Towgood Roche and was anxious that he should have annotated copies of her books: 'If you do Retrospection the honour to buy it when in London, send it hitherto me, and I will correct it neatly and put Manuscript Notes to it in Twenty Places.'[9]

Fellowes, for his part, could never hear too much from her about her childhood and her parents and her blighted expectations; about Collier and Johnson and Goldsmith and the great days at Streatham; about the affairs of the brewery and her early married life and Thrale's time in politics. She wrote for him an extended autobiographical note. It ends revealingly: 'But you make me an egotist, and force me to remember scenes and ideas I never dreamed of communicating ... and my heart prepared to shut itself quite up, convinced there existed not a human creature who cared one atom for poor H.L.P. now she had no longer money to be robbed of ...'[10]

There were still bills to be paid, however, most of them relating to Streatham, and money began to be a source of tension between Hester and Salusbury, who had the impertinence to send Brynbella tax bills to her while at the same time profiting from the felling of some of the trees she and Piozzi had planted to improve the property.[11] She did not remonstrate directly with him, but there is occasionally now in her letters a sharpness of tone she had not previously permitted herself: 'I received Dear Salusbury's Letter with the more Delight as I began to think it long in coming, for altho' surrounded like yourself with Attentions and Compliments – My heart will turn more than it ought to do, – more at least than I wish it to turn to those for whom I am leading this out-of-the-way-Life ...'[12]

She was determined to keep her distance. When Harriet proposed a visit, the invitation was turned down with some firmness: 'My Mind is not very changeable, nor does my declining the Pleasure of such a Journey – depend upon Caprice. Surrounding Circumstances, and Dear Salusbury's own Preference of this Place for me – have combined to send me hither, – *and here I fix.*'[13]

Hester's calculation was that by living carefully and making do without servants the debts incurred at Streatham could be cleared in two years: 'But while I am saying so ... comes a Letter from cruel Count Lieven the Russian Ambassador, to say that such is the Pressure of these dreadful Times, he shall never be able to Enjoy my beautiful Place again; and as he does not like (of Course) to pay for what he has not, begs to be *off* &c.'[14]

The Streatham saga continued for another fourteen months, and

Hester made heavy weather of it. This was partly because she listened to so much conflicting advice, but also because she changed her mind several times about what she actually wanted to do. Although she believed that Lieven was '*a privileged Man*' and that there was little chance of extracting any money from him, she nevertheless composed – in French – what she described to Salusbury as 'a sort of gay Supplication'.

There was no reply, although Hester noted in her Pocket Book two days later that she had received Lieven's 'Quarterage £150' and that he had established in his place as subtenant a 'showy' character called Anderdon.

She then asked Salusbury what she should do – only to reject his advice with heavy sarcasm: 'I thank you for your Letter Dearest Salusbury and have the Pleasure to say that Your Opinion is everybody's Opinion – *I must let Streatham Park.*'[15] That was not so, as it happened. One friend, Dr Myddelton, advised her to offer her life-interest in the property, together with the contents, to each of her daughters in turn. If this was rejected, she should dispose of the pictures, apart from the portrait of Thrale, and advertise the furniture and her life-interest for sale.[16]

Although she had strong reservations, she none the less put it to Salusbury. He thought it an excellent idea – and that she should give the proceeds to him. Hester responded with a mixture of controlled outrage and raw emotion: 'I *will not give* the Place; and I *cannot* bear to sell the Place … poor dear old Streatham Park – The Residence of my Youth, The pride of my Age. You are welcome to *all I have* – except my Honour and Conscience; The Loss of *them* would deservedly shorten my Life …'[17]

In July, in one last effort to interest the Hoares or the Keiths, she travelled up to London. Merrick Hoare received her 'with cold civility'. He said her offer was very liberal; he did not himself have the money, but undertook to write to Lord Keith, who as Commander-in-Chief of the Channel Fleet was at Plymouth. Keith, who had recently been made a viscount, certainly had the money, but he also had large estates in Hampshire and Scotland to which he was about to retire.

It was in any case not the best of moments to capture his attention. After his defeat at Waterloo, Napoleon had fled to Rochefort. From there he had sent envoys to the captain of the *Bellerophon*, one of the Channel Fleet's blockading men-of-war. He requested passage to the United States, or, alternatively, to England – he had already drafted a theatrical message to the Prince Regent seeking asylum from 'the most powerful, the most constant, and the most generous of my enemies'. He was taken to Plymouth, and it was to Keith that it fell to inform him that the government rejected his demands to be treated as an emperor and that he was to be exiled to St Helena.

Unsurprisingly, Keith showed no interest in adding to his already extensive property portfolio. 'Nothing more did I ever see or hear of any of the family,' Hester told Whalley, 'except a cold dry note, saying Mrs. Piozzi was at full liberty concerning Streatham Park, with which Lord Keith would have nothing to do.'[18]

There was now nothing for it but to auction the contents and sell her life-interest in the property. Lady Williams tried to interest her in a cottage in Caernarvonshire, but she was not to be persuaded. 'My Intentions are to die at Bath if it so pleases God,' she wrote:

> I *may* too get out of Debt next July, and then I might be tempted (with a freed Income) to take a comfortable House *here* and end my Days – an old *Bath Cat* – Snappish at the Card Table, sullen at the Conversation Parties – and passionate With the Maids at home – following them up and down Stairs with a Cambrick Handkerchief in hope of finding dust on the Mahogony Bannisters.[19]

Hester did not make things easy for those who were exerting themselves to conclude the 'Streatham business'. When the advertisement which Leak, her steward, had drawn up appeared in February 1816 she wrote an intemperate letter to his wife: 'What! expose a Summer Residence to Sale while Frost and Snow is on the Ground! ... Stop the further Advertisments Dear Leak for Pity ...'[20]

Leak did as he was bidden, although he did not conceal his disagreement, but there was another matter on which he expressed his disapproval even more strongly. Sir James Fellowes had become engaged, and Hester had made a suggestion: 'We talked of passing the Honey Moon at Streatham Park,' she noted in her Pocket Book, '– paying me 100£ for the same. It would be a nice Thing after all.' It is clear, however, from a letter to Mrs Leak a few days later, that it was not the only thing she had in mind: 'Had it pleased God to give me *one* more Taste of Happiness in this Side the Grave, he would have inspired Sir James and Lady Fellowes with a Fancy to *purchase* or *take* the Place: where I should then have visited them from Time to Time ...'[21]

She canvassed the notion quite openly with Fellowes himself: 'Whenever I come to Streatham Park (and never will I see it more unless I see *You* sitting there at Bottom of your own table;) The Room where my Mother's Portrait hangs – *must* be *yours*. The Dressing Room will be for your use you know, and Lady Fellowes will keep her Possession of Her own Apartment.'[22]

Leak, who was noted for his bluntness, told her that it was a thoroughly bad idea to have people living in the house so close to the time of the sale, but Hester was adamant. 'Make my House as comfortable as ever you can for my *Friends*,' she wrote to Mrs Leak: 'Had it not been for Sir James Fellowes and his Father, I question whether I should now have been here ... the Doctor attends me now as if I *was his Sister*.'[23]

To Leak himself, with characteristic honesty, she confessed she had a further reason: 'Perhaps; – (but I hope not,) a little Vanity and Folly may mingle with my Gratitude; and I might have a Wish that his Family and Servants should see I had a Place better than the pityful Lodging they found me living in.'[24]

Sir James and his bride did in the event honeymoon at Streatham, their servants and Leak at daggers drawn for much of the time. Hester spent a week there, and she and the newly-weds worked together on the sale catalogue. She returned to Bath before the viewing days; it was reported to her that Sophy and Merrick turned up every day, and that the Keiths also put in an occasional appearance. The sale began on 8 May and lasted until the 13th. Hester was particularly interested in the fate of the Reynolds portraits: 'Johnson sold magnificently,' she wrote; 'I expected more for Garrick and more for Reynolds.'[25] Apart from the portrait of Thrale, she refused to sell only one other: 'I kept dear Murphy for myself – he was the Playfellow of my first Husband, The true and partial Friend of my second; he loved my *Mother*, – and poor as I am, Murphy remains with *me*.'[26]

The sale raised just under £4,000 – a good deal less than Hester had laid out on doing up the house only two years previously. Her life-interest in the house and grounds was acquired by one Robert Elliott, a rope, hemp and flax merchant in Wapping. He was to be responsible for repairs, tithes and taxes and pay Hester £260 a year. He also bought books, china and furniture, and was the largest single buyer at the sale. 'Wish me joy that I have shaken off this Load of Splendid Misery,' she wrote to Whalley, 'that I have by these means set my Income free, and enabled myself to live in a decent Style, such as neither of my Husbands would be shocked to witness.'[27]

❦

A summer visit to Brynbella was now in prospect, and she appealed to Fellowes for guidance: 'May I not dip in my own native Sea some of the hottest Mornings of this tardy Summer? – and would it not help to wash away what is left of Care?'[28] The strain of recent months had been heavier than she knew, however, and she now suffered a severe reaction. 'I have still a little nasty low nervous *Feverette* upon me, with a Pain round my Neck,' she told Fellowes's mother. 'A good stroke of the Guillotine would bring me instant Relief.'[29]

She had been eagerly awaiting a visit from Leak, but within days of his arrival he fell ill and died. Several friends offered to put her up for a few days, but she declined. 'What should I run away for?' she asked Fellowes. 'Poor Leak never injured me, nor I him – We sleep quietly enough under the same Roof.'[30] To Fellowes's mother, she expressed herself more sardonically: 'I have had many kind Offers of the same sort,' she wrote, '– but I am at *Rehearsal* when standing by the Thing I must so soon resemble.'[31]

She finally set off for Brynbella early in August. Salusbury's promise to come and fetch her had come to nothing. Their relationship was no longer what it had been. At the time of the sale Leak had not wanted Salusbury to have a catalogue. Hester had overruled him – 'Not a *Priced* one tho',' she added, 'for I don't want him to see every 20£ I possess, or dispose of: Those days of Confidence are wholly over between *us*.'[32]

She was warmly received, for all that, by Brynbella's 'truly amiable inhabitants'. The Salusburys now had two children. Hester Maria – 'Missey' as she was called – was one year old, and Harriet had given birth to a second daughter, Angelina, shortly before Hester's arrival. She did not see many old friends: 'The Changes in the Neighbourhood by Deaths and Desertions were quite melancholy to review,' she told Fellowes.[33] The weather, what's more, was appalling and there was not a great deal to do – '*No* Newspapers, & *no* Company; *no* Books and no Conversation,' she wrote plaintively in her diary. She stayed for a month, but was glad to get back to Bath: 'Well! now I am returned to the living world again,' she wrote to a friend: 'I have got a pretty neat house and decent establishment for a widowed lady, and shall exist a true Bath Cat for the short remainder of my life, hearing from Salusbury of his increasing family, and learning from the libraries in this town all the popular topics – Turks, Jews, and Ex-Emperor Buonaparte ...'[34]

34

'Old Bath Cat'

HESTER had taken on a new lease of life. The nightmare of Piozzi's last years, her own indifferent health and the endless dramas over Streatham had drained her of much of her vitality. Now, comfortably installed in Gay Street, her income secure, she was able once more to entertain as she had not done in the eight years of her widowhood. Her intellectual curiosity, her keen interest in the world around her, had never been extinguished, but they now once again shone more brightly. Buoyed up by new friendships, she rediscovered something of the serenity and happiness she had known in the early years of her second marriage.

Her correspondence now shows a quickening of interest in the domestic political scene. Britain had emerged from twenty years of war the most powerful country in the world, but peace abroad did not bring tranquillity at home. Discontent had grown steadily since the trade crisis of 1811. New methods of industrial production held no appeal for skilled tradesmen; fear of loss of livelihood led to organized machine breaking, and the word Luddite entered the language.

A post-war slump, and the flooding of the labour market by several hundred thousand soldiers and sailors had led to widespread unemployment; the disastrous harvest of 1816 had brought hunger and distress to the countryside. William Cobbett had launched a mass-circulation edition of his *Political Register*. He exhorted the workers not to riot, but to pursue parliamentary reform: more jobs, higher wages and lower taxation could best be achieved, he maintained, by the return of radical candidates to the Commons. 'Orator' Hunt, the larger-than-life gentleman farmer from Wiltshire, was addressing mass meetings around the country calling for universal manhood suffrage, annual elections and the introduction of the ballot.

After the Spa Field Riots at the end of 1816, Salusbury had suggested that Hester might be safer at Brynbella than in Bath. 'The Time is yet far distant I hope, when poor Aunt shall stand in need of an Asylum,' was the stout reply: 'The blundering Rebellion is completely stifled – smothered like a Man bit by a Mad Dog in Ireland, between Two Featherbeds.'[1]

Early in January, Hunt addressed a public meeting in Bath. There was a strong military presence; several hundred of the principal citizens and all the town's chairmen were sworn in as special constables; the magistrates asked employers to forbid their workers to attend and tavern keepers to allow no drinking. In his memoirs Hunt described the petition gathered in Bath as 'the most momentous ... ever presented to the House of Commons'. Hester was unimpressed: 'Mr. Hunt has tried his Oratory quite in vain; being hissed as much as he was applauded for ought I understand. The People at the White Lyon refused him Admittance – and when he wished to order Dinner, said they had nothing left; because everything was bespoke by the Officers, which his noise and Bustle had called into the Town.'[2]

Very occasionally, she heard from Cecilia, who the previous year had gone off abroad: 'Mrs. Mostyn's Account of Geneva is, that every thing there is at 3 Times the Price it used to be; that no Theatre is open, and no Parties are given but by English, who find it cheaper than Home ...'[3]

Hester, in Bath, could have no such complaints. She was invited everywhere, and attracted a constant stream of visitors. 'I have had a nice Dish of Flattery dressed to my Taste this Morning,' she wrote to Fellowes: 'That grave Mr. Lucas brought his Son here, that he might see the *first Woman in England* – forsooth – So I am now grown one of the Curiosities of Bath it seems and one of the *Antiquities*.'[4]

Her friend Edward Mangin was full of admiration for her skill as a raconteuse: 'She told a story incomparably well; omitting every thing frivolous or irrelevant, accumulating all the important circumstances ... To render all this more fascinating, she would throw into her narrative a gentle imitation – not *mimicry*, of the parties concerned, at which they might themselves have been present without feeling offended.'[5]

The poet Thomas Moore was captivated. 'A wonderful old lady,' he wrote in his memoirs: 'faces of other times seemed to crowd over her as she sat, – the Johnsons, Reynoldses, &c. &c ... she has all the quickness and intelligence of a gay young woman.'[6]

She was diverted by any form of spectacle. A travelling menagerie,

'Ballards' Grand Assemblage of Rare and Living Animals' visited Bath early in 1817. One of its main attractions was a lioness, which had escaped some months previously and attacked one of the lead horses on the Exeter to London mail-coach. 'We have the saucy Lioness here that seized the hapless horse,' Hester wrote to a friend. 'The Creature appears to me as tame as a Lap Dog.'[7]

She remained a tireless and discerning theatre-goer. She saw Edmund Kean as Sir Giles Overreach in Massinger's *A New Way to Pay Old Debts*. He played 'very finely indeed', she told Fellowes: 'A clear Voice and dignified Manner are not necessary to the Character, and personal Beauty would take off too much from one's Aversion.'[8] She also saw Kemble, now much reduced by gout and asthma, who was making his farewell appearance in Bath, and who called on her. 'I was shocked at the Alteration in his Face and Person,' she wrote: 'Poor Fellow! But the Public were, or rather *was* very contented, and huzzaed his Coriolanus gallantly. I was glad for twenty reasons; Brutus and Sicinius being precisely the Hunt and Cobbett of 2,000 years ago, it was delightful to hear how they were hissed.'[9]

'I wish Salusbury would say now and then how they are at Brynbella,' she wrote plaintively early in 1817, 'but 'tis so difficult to *wring* a Word from him ...'[10] A letter from him arrived within a matter of days, as it happened, and with news that thrilled and delighted her. Salusbury had been appointed High Sheriff of Flintshire the previous year; the question of his presenting a loyal address to the Prince Regent had now arisen, and with it the prospect of a knighthood. 'My dearest Creature,' she wrote, 'It were pity not to treat yourself with such a Distinction, as it would certainly give You Consequence in the Country, and be an Advantage to Your Children.'[11]

Salusbury, perennially strapped for cash, had originally been minded to decline the honour – 'from motives of Prudence' as he put it – but Hester's enthusiasm suggested to him that he might have his cake and eat it: 'Your expressions in your letter were so strong that I was induced to comply with your wishes fearing that by refusing I might incur your displeasure – You must be aware that as I have done so, it will lead me into a very great expense – I fear more than we have at present any idea of.'[12]

The ploy worked, and he lost no time in setting out for Bath. Hester's Pocket Book indicates that he did not find it necessary to stay long: 'I gave Salusbury an order on my Banker for 200£ – and he is gone … he went away directly.'[13]

He was knighted by the Prince Regent at a levee on 21 April. Hester was as pleased as Punch. 'My Money melts away now like Butter in the Sun,' she wrote to Reynold Davies: 'I feel gratified however, foolishly perhaps; at entertaining Dear Sir John Salusbury of Bachygraig, (the old Title in my old Family;) and his pretty lady with every amusement I can find for them.'[14]

The local gossip mill also churned out the word foolish. Fanny Burney – Madame d'Arblaye now – had settled in Bath on her return from France. She still corresponded with Queeney, and her account of the Salusburys' visit was tinged with malice: 'Mrs. Holroyd told me, the other day, that Mrs. P came to introduce to her *Lady Salusbury* – & that, when they were departing, she stood formally & respectfully, back, to make way for that Lady to precede her! but Mrs Holroyd, taking her by the arm, said: "For God's sake, Mrs P keep your own place; Why don't you?" Upon this, confused no doubt, she darted forward. "But who could think" added Mrs H to me, "of Mrs Thrale's being so proud of this poor city Knighthood!"'[15]

But Hester's sights were soon set on something rather grander than a 'poor city knighthood'. In the early summer she heard from James Cathrow, Somerset Herald, that a certain nobleman had the nomination of a baronetcy, and that for a consideration, he could become Salusbury's patron. The consideration was a substantial one – 5,000 guineas for the duke and his agent, and a further £350 'for the Patent of Creation under the Great Seal'. That was far beyond anything Hester could afford,[16] but Cathrow returned a little later in the year, this time in a letter to Salusbury, with a more tempting offer – 3,000 guineas, and 'on the condition of no success no pay'.

By August, Hester was writing to Salusbury about 'our own grand Affair':

If you purchased the honour for Yourself, you would be blamed, perhaps laughed at; but if I procure it for you – tho' with the same

Money – the Censure will fall only on me as an old fond Fool … As yet I have not (I *think* I have not) the money they require: and my Journey to London is to ascertain the Quantum, and get it as cheap as I can.[17]

She had two meetings with Cathrow in London. 'Saw the S: H' she noted in her Pocket Book, 'quite Mr Lofty I think; but believe we shall agree: I wrote directly to Brynbella and told all.' She found London 'most embellished' since her last visit. 'When the new Street is finished,' she wrote to Chappelow, 'running from the Regents Park to his Palace, We need not regret la Strada di Toledo at Naples.'[18] She also approved of the improved street lighting in the capital: 'Gas Lights are charming Things, and illuminate London beautifully and more cheaply too than oyl … But they have performed one wholly unexpected Wonder, they have cleared the Strand of Night-walking Females whom Constables had charge to drive away in vain.'[19]

Boswell would have been less appreciative.

❦

Hester was badly upset shortly after her return to Bath by a book called *The Sexagenarian; or, the Recollections of a Literary Life*. The author, who had recently died, was a clergyman called William Beloe, who had made a living as an essayist and translator. He concedes, in three and a half pages of sustained abuse, that 'Mrs. P*****' was 'acute, ingenious and variously informed'. But she was also vain and affected – and 'there was a pert levity about her which introduced a perpetual suspicion of her accuracy'. Beloe goes on to note that Hester had 'several children and many grandchildren', and that she owned a considerable amount of landed property:

> What does the reader expect? Why in course that this property was bequeathed in just and reasonable proportions to the above-mentioned children and grandchildren. No such thing … A young Italian moun-taineer turned up, calling himself the nephew to the never enough to be lamented musician man. He was accordingly imported to this northern region … and upon him, and his heirs … are the estates and honours of one of the oldest families of Cambrian origin, irrevocably vested and settled.[20]

'You know me too well not to believe me completely callous to *Literary* Abuse,' Hester wrote to Fellowes, but to have her beloved Piozzi traduced in this way was deeply hurtful: 'Can you tell me what's good for the Bite of a *dead Viper's* Tooth? Oyl I trust, and emollients: yet 'tis a slow Remedy – I feel ashamed to think how much the Posthumous Poyson has disturbed me. Write a word of Consolation ...'[21]

There was great excitement in Bath in the autumn when it was learned that Queen Charlotte and her granddaughter were to pay an extended visit to 'make a trial of the salutary waters'; Princess Charlotte, the daughter of the estranged Prince and Princess of Wales, had been married the previous year to Prince Leopold of Saxe-Coburg-Saalfeld, and was now pregnant. 'A grand Illumination will welcome her Majesty to Bath,' Hester told Salusbury: '– and a monstrous Plague that will be. You never saw how busy the Painters are, and beautifiers of Shops &c. The People are all so intent on shining beyond their Neighbours, it is quite ridiculous and the Weather giving me Permission to walk abroad, I see all the Sport.'[22]

The sport was short-lived. A day after her arrival, Princess Charlotte went into labour, and after fifty hours gave birth to a stillborn male child. She herself died the following day. Shortly after the funeral, Hester heard from Cathrow that her death had implications for the quest for a baronetcy: 'I am sorry to say that Some unavoidable Changes which have taken Place in Consequence of what has happened, – appear so unfavourable to our Cause; that I cannot – *at this present Time* flatter myself or you with *much* Hope.'

She forwarded the letter to Salusbury. 'The Thing will be done *some-time* – tis plain,' she told him. '*My* sole Difficulty is to keep myself alive ...'[23] There was little sign, as she entered her seventy-eighth year, that she was experiencing any such difficulty or that anybody else thought she was. 'The managers of this Theatre have got a new Tragedy, for which they torment me to write an Epilogue,' she announced to Salusbury, 'but I told the Dimonds that it would better suit me to compose myself to finish the last act of my own Life.'[24]

Her frequent, and sometimes theatrical, references to the imminence of her own demise can be tedious – 'Your absence,' she writes to Mangin, 'has made a long and ugly Parenthesis in the last Page of my long, flat

Folio Life.'[25] But even when talking about her health she contrives to remain sprightly, occasionally coquettish: 'I have been a *Mute in Society* these last days,' she writes to Lady Williams, 'with sore Throat and Hoarseness, and after 70 Years old your Ladyship knows, a Female makes fewer Conquests with her Eyes than her Tongue.'[26]

Her letters for these years, peppered with gossip and assorted pieces of nonsense – 'flimflams' as she calls them – give a marvellously vivid account of the social life of Bath in the second decade of the nineteenth century. 'Apropòs Lord Chancellor's own Daughter is eloped,' she informs Salusbury: '– run away to Gretna Green with a son of Mr. Repton the clever Man who lays out People's Grounds for them: telling how to twist the River, and where to plant the Tree … His Boy, not yet of age; carries off a Lady who was 36 last year, and her Family are enraged …'[27]

There is an entertaining cameo on every page: 'Doctor Gibbes keeps his little Wife in a large Cage – I know not when she will begin to sing; but perhaps when other Birds do. She occupies Two very fine Rooms – the Air kept constantly in an equal Degree of heat – and sees Three People – no more, – at a Time.'[28]

However busy her social life, she still made time to devour whatever the bookshops had to offer. 'Rob Roy is the fashionable reading,' she told Lady Williams, 'but I don't think it equal to Guy Mannering or the Tales of my Landlord … There is a wicked Book in Circulation which is much to be abhorred – and I think *avoided*. The Title Frankenstein.'[29] Hester was writing on 20 January 1818. Scott's latest offering and Mary Shelley's Gothic tale, each in three volumes, had both been published since the beginning of the year.

Fiction still took second place to what went on in the real world or the world of the mind, however. 'The reading Ladies here are all delighted with Captain Basil Hall's Account of the Lootchoo People,' she told a friend. And later in the same letter: 'The Brahmin Ram Mohun Roy's Metaphysical account of the *Veds* entertained me very much: his Mystic Morality so resembles the Quietism of Madame Guyon in Days of Louis 14ze.'[30]

The actor William Charles Macready, then in his twenties, was a guest at Dr Gibbes's house during these years, and recalled the occasion half a century later:

The party was select and very agreeable, but rendered especially interesting by the announcement in the evening of 'Mrs. Piozzi'. It seemed
almost as if a portrait by Sir Joshua had stepped out of its frame, when
the little old lady, dressed *point de vice* in black satin, with dark glossy
ringlets under her neat black hat, highly rouged, not the end of a ribbon
or lace out of its place, with an unfaltering step entered the room ...
She was instantly the centre on which every eye was fixed, engrossing
the attention of all. I had the satisfaction of a particular introduction
to her, and was surprised and delighted with her vivacity and good
humour. The request that she would read to us from Milton was very
readily complied with, and I was given to understand that she piqued
herself on her superiority in giving effect to the great poet's verse ...
The finger on the dial-plate of the *pendule* was just approaching the
hour of ten, when with a kind of Cinderella-like abruptness she rose
and took her leave ...[31]

Sir James Fellowes now lived mainly in Hampshire; Mangin – he
had remarried two years previously – was on an extended visit to Ireland. Correspondence with these two friends who had come to mean
so much to her was no substitute for their company. 'Living among
mere Acquaintance is indeed truly tedious,' she wrote to Mangin: 'My
Heart grows marvellous sick of it, and I shall like a Journey to Wales
for Twenty Reasons. – One good one, is the constant Sight of the blue
Sea that parts us – for no Land lies betwixt.'[32]
    She set off in July – 'my *last* long Frolic' – and found North Wales
sweltering in a heat wave. 'My Ink gets so thick with this hot Weather,
'tis like writing with a Dip in Black Pudden,' she told Mrs. Mangin: 'Our
large Rivers Severn and Dee creep dully and languidly along, whilst the
little Trout-Streams once so sharp and saucy, scarcely cover their slow
Eels that keep close to the Bottom hiding their heads in Mud.'[33]
    She was greatly taken with Salusbury's children – particularly with
young John Owen, who had been named after her maternal ancestor Sir
John Salusbury, 'the Strong', who had been the Member of Parliament
for Denbighshire in the early seventeenth century, a major patron of
Welsh poetry and himself a poet: 'He will be Owen swift and Owen
strong sure enough, if the Mind keeps Pace with the Body: bold and

active rather than Gay and Tricksy – a true Mountaineer.'[34] She had not lost her eye for landscape, and some new farming practices did not meet with her approval. 'We are spoiling the Sublimity of this Vale of Llwydd,' she wrote '– cultivating the fine healthy Hills – lately so brown and solemn; like dressing old Black-robed Judges up in Green Coats and White Waste coats.'[35]

Hester returned home well pleased with her 'frolic'. 'Did I tell you of the Conquest I made in Wales of the Bishop of St. Asaph?' she wrote to Fellowes: 'Luxmore? he says now – What is become of that little Mrs. Piozzi who shone here among us like a Meteor for a Month or two – and then away: when will She return – do you know? We are very dull without her ...'[36]

During the autumn Dr Gibbes gave what Hester described as 'a Dinner of Tip-Tops' for two young Persians who had been sent to England to study scientific advances. She was flattered to be the only lady to be invited, and sent Fellowes a lively account of the occasion:

> It is truly astonishing to see how they have mastered our Language and caught up our European Manners: Men who have Sate on Carpets for 30 Years, and eat with Chopsticks; are really a little better bred than the rest of the Company – manage Knives, Forks, and Chairs with Grace and Propriety – and what they ought *not* to do, – (for they are Musselmen,) take their Glass like an English Country Squire, and flirt with the Girls – famously ...'[37]

Autumn brought its usual crop of ailments:

> Indeed my dearest Salusbury, I am so tired of Mrs. Piozzi and her Health and her Cough, and her Toothach, that I made Doctor Gibbes laugh by protesting this Minute, I would have no more to do with her, but go to the Play: – and if I choked there, get Colossal Conway to squeeze my Throat as he passes the Stage box with his large long Fingers and finish all at once –[38]

He could have squeezed to some effect. William Augustus Conway was six foot four inches tall and muscular with it. When the Theatre Royal's season had opened the previous week, he had played Don Felix in Susannah Centlivre's *The Wonder: A Woman Keeps a Secret*.

For the next two years he would be the most important person in Hester's life. Among her contemporaries and long after her death, it was a relationship that generated almost as much salacious gossip as her marriage to Piozzi.

Conway

WHO EXACTLY was William Augustus Conway? His mother, Susannah Belcher, was a farmer's daughter and in November 1787, in the church of St Mary, Marylebone, she was married to one William Rudd. It was not, however, his child who was baptized in the same church six months later. The father was Lord William Conway, a twenty-nine-year-old bachelor who was the sixth son of the Marquess of Hertford. Of Rudd nothing further is heard. The child was sent off to Barbados; his education was attended to by the chaplain to the House of Assembly. The climate did not agree with him, and he returned to England in 1807. His mother was by then living in Clifton, where she owned several large houses; in the Bristol and Clifton Guide she was listed as a lodging-house keeper. It is not known when he learned the truth about his parentage or when he assumed his father's family name.

In spite of his commanding height and somewhat feminine good looks, Conway was not in the first flight as an actor. Now approaching thirty, he had made his debut eleven years previously in Chester. After two seasons in Dublin, he was offered an engagement at Covent Garden. He made his first appearance in the title role of *Alexander the Great*; the *Annals of Covent Garden* noted the arrival of the 'tall, earnest, handsome, but ungainly Conway from Ireland'.

It was Conway's bad luck that his debut at Covent Garden coincided closely with the legendary debut of Edmund Kean at Drury Lane. Public and critics alike were swept off their feet by his reading of Shylock and Richard III. 'We wish we had never seen Mr. Kean,' wrote William Hazlitt. 'He has destroyed the Kemble religion and it is the religion in which we were brought up.' He himself appeared intent on destroying Conway:

> The tolerating of such a performance in principal parts is a disgrace
> to the national character. We saw several foreigners laughing with

mischievous delight at this monstrous burlesque of the character of Romeo. He bestrides the stage like a Colossus, throws his arms into the air like the sails of a windmill, and his motion is as unwieldy as that of a young elephant ...[1]

Hester thought otherwise. She had first seen him three years previously on the opening night of the Bath Theatre Royal's season. Conway had played the lead in *Alexander the Great*. 'He speaks like Mrs. Siddons a little,' she noted in her diary. More recently, in the spring of 1818, she had been present at his benefit night when he played the title role in Sheridan's *Pizarro*: 'Mr. Conway has had a flaming Night of it,' she wrote to Mangin. 'I dared not venture the Croud, but he must have gained as much as Barry or Mrs. Cibber used to do in my young days.'[2]

Conway now became a regular guest at Gay Street. He was present on Hester's birthday, which she celebrated with 'a sweet Concert & a gay assemblage of Company. Too great a Crowd was the only fault. *Conway* staid them *all* out.' And she began to sing his praises to her friends: 'Conway the Man of high Polish, general Knowlege, and best natural Abilities', she wrote to Fellowes. She also told Fellowes that she had received a tempting offer for the Reynolds portrait of Murphy:

> I should take a good wide Step towards buying the six Thousand
> Pounds which dear Piozzi left to his Relations in Italy, and which I have
> always promised Salusbury to make up for *him* in the Consols 3 per
> Cent – after which Transaction my Money is my *own*, and whatever I
> may feel disposed to give or spend; it shall be without Self-reproach –
> there are 5000£ in *now* You know.[3]

Conway was occasionally troubled by an inflamed throat, and Hester's mothering instincts were aroused:

> Mr. Conway is really at a loss to express in adequate terms his sense
> of Mrs. Piozzi's very kind and flattering attentions to him ... he is
> happy to inform Mrs. Piozzi that notwithstanding the exertions of the
> scene last evening, his throat has not become worse, owing chiefly
> to the frequent application of the Gargle she was good enough to
> prescribe ...[4]

She was not concerned solely with his physical well-being – she now began to present him with annotated copies of her books. Her first offering was of *Retrospection* – 'The Facts selected and compiled par son Ami Octogenaire Hester Lynch Piozzi, Bath April 11ᵗʰ 1819'. Some of her marginal notes might well have brought a blush to the cheek of her young protégé; beside a reference to Edward III's great-grandson, 'the once-wild Prince of Wales', she had written, '*so* designated by immortal Shakespeare – *so* represented by incomparable Conway'.[5]

Some of the entries in her diary at this time might have been written by a young woman infatuated by a matinée idol:

Friday 16 April ... I walked out and met mon bel Ami – Saw him at Night in Don Giovanni; admirable is not praise enough: *Incomparable Conway* ...

Saturday 17 April ... In the evening Young as Henry IV, and Transcendant Conway in his Falconbridge.

Friday 23 April I went to Mrs. Dimond, saw her and her Son, & canvassed for Conway in my flighty way; feel full of *Hope*.

Mrs Dimond and her son were the managers of the Theatre Royal, and Hester's hope was that they would make Conway an offer that would persuade him to stay in Bath for a further season. He had told her that the new manager of the Theatre Royal in Birmingham, a young man called Alfred Bunn, had invited him to join the company as stage manager and leading man, and that his answer would require 'much deliberation'. Her hopes were soon dashed:

Monday 26 April Conway came to Breakfast. We sate late to it, & had much Talk. But I fear all will end in parting.

Conway went to London before taking up his Birmingham appointment, and Hester charged him to call on Mrs Siddons with an invitation – plans for celebrating what she persisted in regarding as her eightieth birthday were already in hand: 'I have asked People from all Parts of the World,' she told Fellowes, 'and some have promised from the farthest *Thule*.'[6]

As soon as he had gone, she was impatient for news of his safe arrival

— 'It is very unkind of Conway not to write.' She set about preparing an annotated copy of her *Letters to and from the Late Samuel Johnson* for him, and she also sat to Charles Jagger, a local miniaturist, so that he might have her picture. The longed-for letter finally arrived — together with a copy of the *Birmingham Gazette*. 'Oh thank you for it, thank you a Thousand times,' she wrote:

> And how is the beautiful Throat ... I used to make dear Piozzi swallow a raw new-laid Egg early in the Morning — against the Treacle Posset he rebelled — yet 'tis the best Thing to prevent or cure a Hoarseness — except Asses Milk. Pray be careful. Now I have read your Name in this darling Paper, it does seem as if the Space between us was swallow'd up ...[7]

'My justly admired Conway drives all before him at Birmingham,' she announced proudly to Fellowes. She also informed him that the bank had lent her money to buy the last few hundred Consols, allowing her to reach the magic figure of £6,000. Salusbury had been characteristically ungrateful: 'I have given that dear Fellow my Plate, Pictures, Furniture, &c. have settled my Estate on His Sons, joyntured his Wife, and laid up 6000£ for him, and now he is so *low spirited* his Lady laments the Alteration of Person and Manner she observes in him. Low spirited!'[8]

She did not reprove Salusbury directly, but she did write to Harriet: 'But what ails our Inestimable to be pale and thin, and sick and Sullen? He must put on a smiling Countenance for very Shame; if I live till next January and you honour My Anniversary with your Appearance. Why Lord bless me! The People here consider Sir John Salusbury as among the most fortunate of Mortals ...'[9]

Conway now found himself subjected to a rolling barrage of correspondence. It was an almost comically one-sided affair. 'I am either by nature or habit so averse from letter writing,' he once told a friend, 'that except when called upon by the necessities of business or the established usages of society I never think of putting pen to paper.' When he did so, the style was painfully formal and stilted. That was of no concern to Hester, who kept them all, tied up in ribbon, till the day she died.

She began one letter to him on 15 June and added to it in bumper instalments over six days. He had sent her his picture, and she was delighted. 'As for me and my Portrait,' she wrote, 'The little *Michaelmas* Daisy beat by a Hundred Storms still holds her head up; and Salutes the towering Tulip with true and disinterested Friendship.'[10] It is possible that some of Hester's more recondite allusions went over Conway's head. She is referring here to the so-called tulip mania which swept the Netherlands in the seventeenth century. A single bulb of the most famous specimen is said to have changed hands for 3,000 florins; it was called Semper Augustus.

Hester knew that Conway fancied himself to be in love with a girl called Charlotte Stratton, the granddaughter of one of her friends; he had received some encouragement, and she had been exerting all her old match-making skills on his behalf. Dining with the family one day, however, she learned that it was all over: 'Charlotte seems resolved to jilt poor Conway after all. I feel quite shocked at her Behaviour,' she wrote in her Pocket Book. She had clearly spoken her mind. ''Twas odd enough to see how much they love, and *fear me*,' she told Conway. 'Oh I was *very* angry, *Very* like a Welshwoman ...'[11]

She told him that whenever she became agitated about not hearing from him, her servant Bessy would say, 'Why Madam! You will not live to see Mr. Conway again, if you go on *so*': 'Well then was my Reply – go see him yourself; and bring word how he looks; what he says, what hopes of his Return – and tell him *truly* that I will come to him in Autumn to his Benefit ... no need for People to stare, and make a Wonder of *that* I suppose.'[12]

A first sign there that in the Pump Room and elsewhere, tongues were beginning to wag – and that she knew it.

Six pages one day, five pages the next – snippets of theatre gossip – a didactic paragraph about the derivation of the word 'calends' – an intriguing account of her first meeting with Piozzi:

> We were both of us past 35 Years old when we first met in *Society* at Doctor Burney's ... where I coldly confessed his uncommon Beauty and Talents – but my Heart was not at home; Mr. Thrale's broken Health and complicated *Affairs* demanded and possessed all my Attention; and vainly did my future Husband endeavour to attract that notice from *me* which he slighted from far more charming Mrs. Crewe.[13]

Finally, after six days, she drew to a close, signing herself 'a Second Mother, who is most truly and faithfully Your attached Friend' and Bessy was packed off in the chaise to Birmingham. The box she carried also contained Hester's miniature, a bloodstone seal with the inscription 'Semper Augustus' which she had commissioned from the London jeweller Hamlet, a supply of lozenges and honey for Conway's throat and an annotated copy of Wraxall's *Historical Memoirs of his Time*.[14]

Early in July, Hester took herself off to Weston-super-Mare. 'I shall gain Strength – recruit my Spirits and save my Money for Winter,' she told Salusbury.[15] She broke her journey at Clifton, and made the acquaintance of Mrs Rudd – 'asked her to supper, talked of dear Conway for 3 hours'. Fry's Hotel at Weston proved both noisy and expensive, and after a few days she moved her small household – 'a Man, 3 Maids & Self & Baby' – into a rented cottage. The sea-bathing was expensive – '4 shillings a Time' – but that was a pleasure she would not deny herself. 'Fine Savage Bathing it is, clambering among rough Rocks,' she wrote to Salusbury.[16]

She embarked on writing what she called 'The Abridgment' – a potted autobiography for Conway's benefit. She also made a start on annotating a copy of her travel book for him. One poignant note explained why she had reacted with seeming coldness when he had performed in *Comus* earlier in the year:

> I dared not trust my Eyes, my Hands, or my Heart with Liberty to express those Feelings at the Recital of Lines I used to read Day & Night when no Words of my own would express the Passion of my Soul which Piozzi's Voice excited & called forth. When in the Summer's Gloom at Streatham Park he used to sing to me under the Trees at Evening how sweetly did his Notes – how cruelly did they float upon the Wind – so that ten Years after I could not sit Comus out, it was as if new to me; Your Manner, your Voice affected me so strongly ... and next Time you acted it I pretended Engagement after the Play and – ran. I was but lately waked from my Torpor succeeding the Torture of losing Piozzi![17]

When no letter came from Birmingham, she quickly worked herself into a state of near frenzy: 'If Conway is very ill I shall rave' – 'Oh

Lord! Oh Lord! no News of Conway' – 'If no letter comes Monday I will send James – that I will … My heart half broke about Conway. What can be the matter?' James returned after three days to report that Conway had been ill, but promised to write. When he failed to do so, James was sent off a second time, this time bearing a 'fine Salmon', a letter 'full of tender reproaches' – and the two annotated volumes of *Observations and Reflections*.

Her infatuation with Conway was not all-consuming. ''Tis the Fashion,' she had written to Salusbury earlier in the year, 'to say my Letters of the Years 1817, 18, and 19 – are better than those of 1768 or 70.'[18] They certainly reflect the continuing breadth and liveliness of her interest in the world around her – the assassination of the duc de Berri, famine in Italy, the fate of Captain's Cook's ship all command her attention; so too, nearer home, do slack-rope performers, the Peterloo Massacre, female cricketers, and the price of fish.

Towards the end of August, Hester 'waked with Spontaneous Diarrhoea'. She was so ill (it was probably a case of food poisoning) that she thought she was going to die. She dashed off a farewell message to Conway: 'Having been vouchsafed a Sort of warning that my temporal Existence is at *length* coming rapidly to a Close; – I write these Lines to my best loved, my latest-found Friend; whose Talents and Kindness have so contributed to Sweeten the last Eight Months of it. They accompany an excellent Gold repeating Watch destined as my *last* Present.'[19]

She survived. The watch, however, seems not to have been sent, because two weeks later she sent him another brief note:

My Dearest Friend–

I am going on the Sea – a party of Pleasure: but lest the Vessel should upset, and I should be lost; I leave Your Money – 50£ and your Watch – a Gold Repeater; safe in this Box …[20]

The party of pleasure was cancelled. Conway was obliged to wait a little longer for his gold repeater.

Hester stayed on for another month at Weston. 'Mrs Pennington is here, and sedulous to renew our *Friendship*,' she told Miss Williams; adding, somewhat ungraciously, 'I would rather it was mere *Acquaintance*, but think She may be useful to Conway.'[21] She continued, as she put it, to 'pelt' him with letters. In one she told him she wished he had a son – 'You promised me to keep my Portrait for him, and I think you will never part with the *Repeater*, till *he* takes it with him to the University.'[22]

What Hester did not know was that Conway already had a son. Frederick Bartlett Conway had been born earlier that year in Bristol. Who the mother was is unknown; Conway's biographer, John Tearle, speculates that she might have been a servant of his mother's. The child was brought up by his grandmother and like his father became an actor. In 1850 he emigrated to the United States, where he continued to act and was briefly manager of the Metropolitan Theatre in New York. There is no indication that Hester ever learned of his existence.

~ ~

At the end of September the *Birmingham Gazette* announced that because of 'an alarming and increasing indisposition' Conway had gone to London to seek treatment. There he consulted Astley Cooper, a pre-eminent surgeon of the day whose patients included Lord Liverpool, the Duke of Wellington and the Prince Regent. 'You have the best medical Advice which I suppose *Europe* affords,' Hester wrote: 'and you are not alone and desolate, as my distracted Imagination had depicted you – dying at an Inn upon the Road … If you grow worse instead of better, – I *will* come. Mine is not a make-believe Attachment; nor is Friendship other than a Sacred Duty.'[23]

She sent him £30 – the equivalent today of some £1,700 – and instructed her London wine merchant to deliver half a dozen bottles of wine. Unconvinced that she was being told the whole truth about his condition, she decided that James must be sent to London to bring her a first-hand report; off he went taking with him 'a Cheddar Cheese & a Pint of Tokay and a Panic stricken short Letter'. A note from Astley Cooper finally convinced her that all danger was past, but the pitch to which her nerves had been strung by his illness remains apparent in her letters. 'That too delicate Trinket inclosing your fine hair has vexed my heart,' she wrote:

One day I *saw* the *Platt oddly displaced*; ('twas when Your health was at its worst,) and into my female foolish Mind, a Thousand silly Superstitions crowded. It shall be laid by for the *Wife* we talk of, and I will court your Mother to get me a *genuine Bit*, which She and I will put ourselves into a plain Chrystal Locket, that I can wear as you do Miss Jagger, about my Neck tyed by a Black Ribbon.[24]

Although it was now October, she had not given up sea-bathing: 'In order to strengthen my Spirits I rushed into the Sea last Monday, but the Waves were too strong, and I was awkward – "Not what I was 40 Summers ago" – and as I came out a large Billow flung me down and bruised me – but to be a little frighted *did me good* …'

Before Conway's illness she had hoped that he would join her at Weston, but that was no longer in prospect. 'Feel some Ill Feels,' she wrote in her Pocket Book, 'wish myself Home.' Back in Gay Street, she addressed Conway in verse:

No more examining the Postman's Hand,
Nor fond Initials traced upon the Sand,
Nor Empty Projects idly plann'd
At Weston super Mare;
But *Resignation Hope* and Joy
By Turns possess, by Turns employ
L'Amie Octogenaire …

Joy because Conway had renewed his engagement in Bath. 'When will you come home dear Mr. Conway?' she continued: 'when will your Medical Adviser trust you to Female Management and Governance? – a Horse for your Doctor, an Ass for Your Apothecary; an Old Woman for your Companion when you prefer Chat to Reading …'[25]

When Conway did finally turn up, the excitement was almost too much for her:

Sunday 5 December No Church – too sick – but Conway came, just 22 weeks since we parted – I had feared many times our meeting was put off – but, God be praised we have met and dined together, neither dead, tho' often both in danger, I choked with my first glass of wine –[26]

He made his first appearance the following week. 'The Coriolanus electrified us all,' Hester told Mrs Pennington, 'and my amiable Friend gets Admirers and Invitations every day.' She herself, however, was now increasingly preoccupied with preparations for her birthday celebrations. News came that Harriet had miscarried, which meant that the Salusburys' arrival would be delayed: 'I suppose they will just come time enough for my Foolery,' she wrote '– which plagues me to Death already.'

'The Thaw loosens my Nerves and Joints a little, but indeed I never was so weary of a Winter in my Life as of this the *Eightieth* …'[27] She could be frank with Mrs Pennington, but with Salusbury she must keep up appearances:

> You will probably find some alterations for the worse, though my Friends here – and Flatterers – not a few; – say that your H:L:P is still a Wonder of Nature – a Mirror of Fashion &c. I was at a large Party last Night, where there was Music and Beauty and Talents and every Thing – Yet was your old Aunt a first Rate Lyon in the Show, and highly contented with the Applause she gained –[28]

The birthday celebrations came close to being postponed. On 23 January, Edward, Duke of Kent, died of pneumonia while on holiday at Sidmouth; his eight-month-old daughter, Alexandrina Victoria, would one day be queen. Hester, a stickler for protocol, immediately had cards printed:

> *Mrs PIOZZI takes this Method*
> *of apprizing her Friends, that the Event,*
> *which afflicts every one, will prevent all*
> *Appearance of rejoicing on her part; so*
> *that the Concert, Ball, and Supper, pro-*
> *posed for the 27th, will not* NOW *take*
> *place. –* Jan. *24, 1820.*[29]

In the event the evening went ahead as planned. More than six hundred guests crowded into the Lower Assembly Rooms. The concert began at ten, and at midnight the company sat down to what Mangin described as 'a costly and superbly arranged banquet'. Flanked at the top table by two admirals, Hester wore an elaborate white dress, with a plumed headdress; it was the first time since Piozzi's death that she had not worn black. At two in the morning she opened the ball with Salusbury. 'Her flow of disciplined animation seemed inexhaustible,' Mangin wrote; she danced 'with astonishing elasticity'.[30] Quadrilles and country dances continued till five, but by ten o'clock Hester was up and about, receiving callers at breakfast.

It was as well that she had decided against postponement. Two days later, the death of George III signalled the start of a period of national mourning.

Land's End

THE SALUSBURYS stayed on for some days after the birthday celebrations. 'Sir John Salusbury is at the Concert,' Hester told Conway: 'My Lady – o'Bed; where She passes most of her time – for though he does not like to see me surrounded with new Friends as he calls them; he does not supply their Place by any *Flattery* of apparent delight in being with me himself'.[1]

For 'new Friends' read 'Conway'. Salusbury, predictably, had not taken to him. Indeed he viewed Hester's interest in this particular new friend with some hostility. He himself had more than once been the beneficiary of her impetuous generosity; the suspicion formed in his small mind that the impecunious actor posed a potential threat to his inheritance.

More than twenty years after Hester's death, there appeared an anonymous pamphlet entitled *Love Letters of Mrs. Piozzi Written When She was Eighty, to William Augustus Conway.* A furious Edward Mangin, then in his seventies, wrote that its 'rascal Editor' was interested only in appealing to 'the reading rabble'. That was clearly so, although the extravagance of language which Hester permitted herself in writing to Conway undoubtedly made his task easier:

> begun at Night 29 January 1820
> all dirtied with pale Ink, and Tears of Tenderness
> My precious, my every day more and more precious friend, Conway le *vrai unique*! ...[2]

Prised from their context, some of her more unrestrained passages could indeed be taken for the effusions of a lover – just as some of those addressed to Salusbury might have been a decade or more earlier: 'Good Night, God bless, and *Fellow*-Angels guard you, They will recognize my Conway, 'spite of the nearly-Invisible Scar upon the Ivory Neck. Once more Good Night ...'[3]

With her birthday behind her, Hester was once more able to give her full attention to his interests. It had become plain on his return to Bath that he was still in love with Charlotte Stratton, and Hester and Mrs Pennington had been exerting themselves – unsuccessfully – to advance the suit of their Chevalier, as they had taken to calling him. Charlotte was not prepared to become the wife of an actor; Mrs Pennington, who had fallen almost as completely under his spell as Hester, was indignant on his behalf: 'It seems as if that Girl alone was exempt from the power of the magic he bears about him. Well, let her go! – sit down at ease with a Country Squire, "suckle fools, and chronicle small Beer".'[4]

Conway was in a bad way in those early weeks of 1820. Miserable about his rejection by Charlotte, his health was once more giving cause for concern; it also seems possible that he had made an attempt to secure recognition by his father's family and was depressed by his failure to do so. On the day after the birthday celebrations he took to his bed and refused to see callers. Hester thought that some fresh reading matter might help: 'Accept dearest Creature of these Books,' she wrote. 'I am not used to make such shabby Presents, but I will bind them for You beautifully if you will read them.' Whether he did is not known.[5]

She was also concerned for his moral well-being:

Accept my best Acknowledgement for having promised me so sweetly that you would try to rise superior to all low Desires ... the Gratification of mere Appetite, among coarse Females, is a Pitfall covered with Weeds ... Shun all such mad Companions, dearest Conway ... Keep your fine Intellects clear, and use them rightly; Improve the talents committed to your trust; and love your anxious trembling, tender parent; your *more* than Mother, as you kindly call your affectionate H:L:P.[6]

Hester realized that for both personal and professional reasons, Conway was unlikely to stay much longer in Bath and would probably return to Birmingham. The period of mourning for the King's death meant that the theatres were closed until 18 February. She learned that Conway's benefit was to be on 11 March; by 4 March she had disposed of 100 tickets and applied for more. 'I think we shall have a Splendid Show of Boxes,' she told Harriet:

Salusbury would have been very angry had he known I went last Night to the grand Ball given by the York House Club upon the King's Accession, and Escape of his Ministers – but who would have refused? When 20 Guineas were vainly offered for *one* Lady's Ticket, and I had *Three presented me*; when many a pretty Girl was pining at home …[7]

Shortly afterwards she received what she described as 'a whimpering Letter' from Salusbury in which he complained yet again about being hard up. Clearly exasperated, she did not mince her words:

Your Estate was a pretty one when I left Brynbella … had you embraced a Profession (as I earnestly wished you would have done;) more Money might have been at your Command … When I have taken the Liberty to tell you so, the Reply was always – 'I *would rather starve*:' adding the names of some Two or Three gentlemen of whom I never heard but from yourself – who were *So* happy upon *So* small an Income …[8]

None of which prevented her from sending him a draft for £100 – for him 'to throw away on Sight of the Coronation', as she put it to Sir James Fellowes.[9]

Her birthday party had made a serious hole in her finances, and she felt obliged once again to economize. She let No. 8 Gay Street for £250 a year. 'Feel low-Spirited at leaving my House,' she wrote. 'Turned out again at 81 Years old!'[10] She was not leaving Bath for purely financial reasons, however: 'I am sick and weary to Death of our over-grown Society *here*,' she told Daniel Lysons, 'and sigh for nothing so sincerely as Retirement.'[11] The plan was to spend six weeks at Clifton and then to travel down to Penzance. 'Old Ocean,' she wrote to Mrs Pennington, '– Can ought else compleatly wash away all Recollection of Bath *Parties*? that fair Assemblage of glaring Lights, empty Heads, aking Hearts and false Faces.'[12]

The undeclared reason for this second self-imposed exile was her mounting anger and frustration at gossip about her relations with Conway: 'Mr Mangin said when I complained slightly of slight Insults – Oh surely Mrs. Piozzi has not an Enemy in the World – *Only* sharp-shooters replied I; So I will *only* take away the Target: and then their Dexterity is useless.'[13]

The sharpshooters did not confine themselves to sniggering behind their hands in the Pump Room; some of them, without signing their names, wrote suggesting she should leave Bath. 'Anonymous Correspondents are best neglected I suppose,' Hester wrote to Fellowes, '– though I do *not* neglect their Advice and rough Admonitions, for I *do* retire from the World, well convinced of its worthlessness and Deceit.'[14]

Nor was the gossip confined to Bath. Earlier in the year James Winston, then the acting manager of Drury Lane, had written in his diary, 'Conway ... was expected about this time to be married to Mrs. Piozzi, whose income exceeded £7,000 a year, and whose age is upwards of 80.'[15] Conway's biographer speculates that this particular tale was carried back to London by Kean, who had appeared in Bath over the New Year and had been a guest at Hester's house.[16]

Forty years after Hester's death, Abraham Hayward published his *Autobiography Letters and Literary Remains of Mrs. Piozzi (Thrale)*. A lengthy review in the *New Monthly Magazine* contained the following passage:

> We ourselves heard the late Charles Mathews say – and no one who knew him will question his veracity – that Conway himself had shown him Mrs. Piozzi's offer of marriage ... Mathews told him at once that he could not honourably take advantage of it. 'That,' said Conway, 'is what I myself felt; but in a matter so important to one so poor as I am, I also felt that my own decision should be confirmed by the opinion of a friend. I now know what to do.'

Charles Mathews was a well-known comic actor of the day. The identity of the reviewer is unknown; Hayward, in the second edition of his book, described him as 'a distinguished man of letters' – possibly it was the novelist Harrison Ainsworth, who was the editor of the magazine at the time. When could such a proposal have been made? John Tearle, in his biography of Conway, draws attention to a reference in Hester's diary during her stay in Penzance to a letter she had written to Conway: 'Come here or meet me in Exeter,' she wrote. The letter has not been traced, but Tearle observes that the business referred to must have been of some importance if she was prepared to drive a hundred miles to discuss it. He also points to an earlier occasion when Conway asked Hester to burn two of his letters.

That adds up to very little by way of confirmation. Marriage to Conway would have annulled the provisions in her will leaving everything to Salusbury (although there was by now not all that much to leave him); it would also accord oddly with her passionate feelings of pride as a member of the Salusbury family. It is plain that Hester had come to think her adopted nephew grasping and ungrateful; equally plain that Conway was of immense emotional importance to her. Just how important – and just how bitterly she had come to look on Salusbury – emerges with startling clarity from the remarkable concluding passage of the account of her life inserted in the copy of *Observations and Reflections* presented to Conway. She has carried the story up to the point where she has made over Brynbella to Salusbury, and records a conversation with Thomas Shephard, Salusbury's headmaster at Enborne:

> Retirement to Bath with my broken heart & Fortune was all I could wish or expect ... Well! no matter – one Day before I left, there was talk how Love had always *Interest* annex'd to it; Nay then Said I – What is *my* Love for Salusbury? Oh replied Shephard, there is *Interest* there. Mrs Piozzi ... *could* not I am *sure exist* without *some* one, upon whom to energize her Affections. his Uncle is gone; and She is *much obliged* to Young Salusbury for being ready to her hand to pet & spoil – her children will not suffer her to love Them, and with a coarse Laugh – what must She do when This Fellow throws her off – as *he soon will?*
>
> Shephard was right enough; I sunk into a Stupor, worse far than all the Torments I had endur'd ... & such was *My* Case when *Your* Talents *roused – Your* offer'd Friendship *opened* my heart to Enjoyment. Without *You* Dulness, Darkness, Stagnation of every Faculty would have enveloped & extinguished all the Powers of hapless H:L:P.

It could pass for a description of the awakening of her feelings for Piozzi all those years before. Whether those feelings prompted her in her ninth decade to offer herself in marriage to someone young enough to be her grandson cannot now be known.

⤙ ⤚

Just before Hester's departure for Clifton, a letter arrived from Cathrow at the College of Arms. 'A most advantageous opportunity now offers for obtaining the Object we have so long had in view,' he wrote.[17] The purchase of a baronetcy for Salusbury was back on the *tapis*. 'If he likes Honours better than *6000£,*' Hester wrote to Fellowes, '– *I will sell mine out* – curtail my Income, and live retired in a cheap Country throwing up my fine House here entirely: *for his Sake* – who is ready at every Turn to Suspect me of unkindness – I guess not why –'[18]

Salusbury lost no time in posting down to Clifton. 'We had a long Business Talk, unpleasant of Course,' Hester wrote in her Pocket Book. It did not take long for Salusbury to get what he wanted, and he took off for London to discuss the details with Cathrow. 'My poor 6000£ gone – Addio!' Hester wrote.[19] In the end the negotiations fizzled out; Salusbury never secured his baronetcy – but retained the money that had been intended to buy it.

Before setting out for Cornwall, Hester made an important decision. 'If my Passion for Clifton keeps warm through next Winter,' she told Harriet ... 'it is odd but I shall prefer this Place to Bath – *for a Residence*: – and *this* House to No. 8 Gay Street.'[20] (She had been staying in a house belonging to Mrs Rudd in Royal York Crescent.)

Hester referred variously to the time she was to spend in Penzance as 'my runaway Frolic'[21] and 'these Ten Months of Banishment'. She adapted, as always, with extraordinary speed to the new and unfamiliar. 'One is out of the Way here – where not even enraged Creditors would follow one,' she wrote to Salusbury:

> We have here a public Library well furnished with Volumes of Science: a Geological School where Lectures are read by Professors; and where I purpose to study with the Assistance of a Gentleman highly qualified, and of Doctor Forbes, – The Medical Man of the Place ...
>
> Here are no Machines – or Appearance of Convenience for Bathing, but I am a good Waterspaniel, and shall be happy to plunge into this blue Sea tomorrow.[22]

She retained all her capacity to live for the moment and to extract enjoyment from the most unlikely situations. 'Now for Penzance and its Parties,' she wrote to Mrs Pennington:

> Mrs. Hill made a splendid one for *me* I rather think, and my Black
> Satten Gown (for no other is yet arrived,) was my best Garment —Bessy
> lent me a Cap of hers — and my youthful Looks were duly appreciated
> — My Whist-playing *applauded* — *We had Two Tables, one for Shillings,*
> *one for Six Pences: a Profusion of exquisite* Refreshments, and Music in
> another Room ... The People know not how to be civil enough, and
> if my Stomach will reconcile itself to the clouted cream — I shall come
> home as fat as the Pigs of the Country —[23]

Conway, heavily engaged once more in the theatre at Birmingham, continued to occupy her thoughts, although she affected to be more relaxed now about his shortcomings as a correspondent. Salusbury, she wrote, had 'half Threatened' her with a visit and asked if she would be glad to see him: 'The Truth is I should be very *Sorry* he came 400 Miles on so mad an Errand — but if he does come he *must* be welcome; and I *must not* say how much I should rejoyce should the same Fancy take our Tall Beau by the Brain pan.'[24]

It is clear from the last letter she wrote to her Tall Beau before leaving Bath that she fully expected him to come to see her in Cornwall: 'My Mind will soon recover its Tranquillity, and I shall spring to welcome my Dearest Friend when he performs his voluntary not-extorted Promise, of visiting me and my *Castle*, changed somewhat in the Plan and Elevation, — but solid and brilliant ... *Shall* I live to finish, and put you in quiet Possession? Such Happiness would surely be too great ...'[25]

There are many references to this mysterious castle in Hester's diaries and correspondence. 'Agreed with the Builder about my Castle,' she wrote shortly after Conway had left Bath, 'to be inhabited 27: Jan: 1821,' and it crops up again in one of her first letters to him from Penzance: 'I wonder if you recollect a certain Friend of mine, named Augustus; who said in Camden Place A.D *1818*; — I could be happy in a Prison, with dear Mrs. Piozzi and her Anecdotes ... Come here in winter and *Try* —*1821* — Imprisonment with H: L: P. and *Her Castle* by the Seaside.'[26]

While travelling down to Cornwall she spent some time one day calculating her income and expenditure for the rest of the year; she would have £574, she reckoned – 'to last 23 weeks and pay the Castle'. No mere construct of her imagination, then, this castle. She might play with the idea of being locked away together with Conway by the seaside, but she had also dreamt up a way of giving concrete expression to the fantasy. The castle was a casket, which she had commissioned from Riviere & Son, a Bath firm of jewellers and goldsmiths. It was to hold a Bible, which she was annotating for Conway's benefit. When she heard from her bankers in October that there was £720 in her account, she decided she could now write for the 'castle' to be delivered. Hester wrote to its 'Governor' to say she was well pleased with it. It appears from her accounts to have cost her between £300 and £400 – perhaps as much as £25,000 at present-day values. Nothing speaks more eloquently or poignantly than this precious castle of the depth and complexity of her feelings for Conway.

Hester had been acquainted for some years in Bath with Harriet Willoughby, a natural daughter of Charles James Fox. She did not share her political views, but found her an agreeable theatre companion because, she told Mangin, 'no flirtations hindered one's minding what passed on the stage'.[27] There had been a coolness between them for a time when Miss Willoughby championed the actor James Warde, Conway's rival for public favour, but when she turned up unannounced in Penzance in the middle of October, Hester was extremely glad to see her: 'A face one is *familiar* with, in so strange and so distant a Region must always be a *handsome* one – and she is driven into Mount's Bay by Stress of Weather like myself – too much in Debt to face Bath – too much in Awe of her rich Relations to intrude long upon *them*.'[28]

Early in November Hester became seriously unwell. There was an outbreak of typhus in the town, and several friends wrote to express their concern. Mrs Pennington urged her either to return to Clifton or to move to Torquay, but Hester was briskly philosophical: 'We are surely in the hands of the Same God at Penzance as at Torquay – and when *he* calls – go we must … I cannot leave my habitation which I have taken for a Term … My Establishment is not a little Clokebag to put on my Shoulder, and carry away from one Place to another.'[29]

She greatly appreciated Harriet Willoughby's company during the winter months, and scoffed at Mrs Pennington's fears that she would be corrupted politically: 'You are a comical Lady in Your Fears lest Miss Willoughby should make me a Radical,' she wrote: 'Poor Miss Willoughby! were it not for her I should not have known Milton from Shakespear by this Time – for to no other Creature here, are those Names familiar.' And she took some satisfaction in informing Mrs Pennington that she was not alone in her uneasiness at Miss Willoughby's presence in Penzance: 'Salusbury seems by his Letters to have Fears lest She should be hovering over my Deathbed to his Disadvantage,' she wrote. 'Sir John is very illnatured in detesting every Body who contributes to my Comfort.'[30]

The weather on the Cornish coast as the new year opened was appalling: 'Fogs and Snow thickening all round – and when any one is able to stand the Storm, and call at the House; – Tales of shipwreck in every Mouth. I will come to Penzance no more.'[31]

She had heard that the house belonging to Mrs Rudd in Royal York Crescent would be ready for her early in March, and she was excited at the prospect of seeing Conway. In spite of past disappointments he had renewed his engagement at the Theatre Royal, Bath; she wrote a long, rambling letter to him on the day he was due to open in *Coriolanus*:

> Your precious Portrait is my only true and comfortable Companion at every Meal, and I shall drink Your Health to the Darling Creature by and by; and success to Coriolanus – 'Well Madam, I'm going, going to the Capitol' Incomparable Conway! how present is that Scene to my Eyes!! – but I want to *hear* the Welcoming Shout of Rapture once more to greet your long sighed for return to their Boards …
>
> Your Bible is in great forwardness, Castle locked fast: – when shall I put it in the Governor's Hand … We may begin to count Weeks now.[32]

She began to plan the details of her new life:

> *Do*, Dear Mrs. Pennington get me a *Foot*man – not a Fellow to wear *his own Clothes*: I must have a *Livery* Servant who will walk before the Chair and ride behind the Coach, and be an oldfashioned – tho' not ill-looking Servant – my little Plate – so small in Quantity – is easily

cleaned, but clean it must be, for I will not live in a State of Disgust when I have a decent Mansion over my Head —[33]

In her last few days in Cornwall Hester attacked the three volumes of the newly published *Kenilworth* and fulfilled a long-held ambition to visit Land's End:

> – and we did stand up on The last English Stone – jutting out from the Cliffs – 300 Feet high – into the Atlantick Ocean – which lay in wild Expanse before us, tempting our Eyes towards the land Columbus first explored – Hispaniola. – Dinner at a mean House affording only Eggs and Bacon, gave us Spirits to go – not *forward* for we could go no further; but *Sideways* to a Tin and Copper Mine under the Sea – ay! one Hundred and Twelve Fathom from the strange Spot of Earth we stood on – In a direct Line *downwards*: where no fewer than Threescore human Beings toil for my Lord Falmouth in a Sub Marine Dungeon ...[34]

Back in Clifton, she took lodgings with Mrs Rudd until the house in Royal York Crescent was ready. It is clear from a letter that she dashed off to Harriet that she was in high spirits:

> I think my dear Lady Salusbury will be glad to hear that I am *returned from Transportation*; and I hope Sir John as a good Magistrate will not *hang* me for coming home *before my Time*.
>
> The Journey from Penzance to Exeter was bad: the Roads rocky, and the Cornish Fog such, we ran foul of every Carriage We met; so mine was broke to Pieces, and I had a pretty Coachmaker's Bill to pay at Exeter.[35]

Something rather more serious had happened at Exeter, which she did not immediately choose to mention to Harriet, but Miss Willoughby received a full account:

> The Bed was very high, and getting into it I set my Foot on a light Chair which flew from the Pressure, and revenged it on my leg in a terrible Manner. The Wonder is, no Bones were broken – only a cruel bruise – and slight *Tear* – and we trotted on hither after Cathedral Service, at which I hardly *could* kneel to thank God for my Escape.[36]

She did eventually tell Harriet about her accident, but made light of it: 'See the Advantage a lean Woman has over a fat one – and 82 over 28. I was always a *blue* Lady – I was 3 Weeks ago a *black and blue* Lady – and That was all.'[37]

For his benefit on 26 March Conway had chosen to take the title role in *Mirandola*, a new tragedy by Bryan Waller Procter.[38] Hester 'wrung Dr. Dickson's consent to go to the play' and thought Conway 'more inimitable than ever'.[39] She enthused to Harriet about how warmly she had been received by the Fellowes family:

> Sir James was kind and charming, – his old Father, (my Valentine) as we call him, did the Honours divinely: and a most magnificent Party was made at Night where Conway and your Ladyship's *old* and affectionate Servant were the Idols of the Evening ...
>
> So you see Clifton will agree with me excellently – as *Mutton*; and I can take Bath as *Pickles* whenever I please.

Providence, however, had other plans. Hester had seen Bath for the last time.

'No Epilogue, I Pray You; for Your Play Needs No Excuse.'

SHORTLY after her return from Bath Hester received what she described as 'a saucy letter from Salusbury'. He grumbled about the price of corn; he was 'very much distress'd in circumstances, as well as depressed in spirits', he told her: 'I feel persuaded (unless times change suddenly for the better) of the necessity of breaking up my establishment at this dear Place; & retiring to some other residence where I can live upon a reduced income.'[1]

Hester was mightily unimpressed, and told him so. She also vented her feelings in a letter to Miss Williams. 'Here is beautiful Weather,' she wrote. 'I suppose,' she continued acidly, 'that will increase the *national Misfortune* of having Bread too cheap. It is a shame to hear Country Gentlemen lament such a Situation of Things – as a Calamity: we who pay Baker's bills on a Monday Morning are glad of it – and thankful.'[2]

She was also still paying doctor's bills: 'Dr. Dickson 1£ of course every Visit,' she wrote in her diary. 'He bids me take Caster Oyl' – a first indication that there was concern about something other than her leg. The castor oil appears to have been ineffective, and a surgeon was called in – possibly to administer an enema. Hester, who had never spared her friends the details of what passed in the sickroom, was now reticent to the point of obscurity. 'Our kind and skilful Dickson is just gone,' she told Mrs Pennington: 'He only waited till things were in the state they should be, I perceive; and today he brought the tall man again, who performed the *operation* and praised my courageous endurance … All that was done yesterday and today (rough usage on the whole) has raised, not lowered, the spirits of your ever obliged and faithful H:L:P.'[3]

The vicar of Tremeirchion had written to ask whether she would make the gift of a bier to carry the parish poor. Hester was still well enough by the middle of April to send him a brisk reply: 'I am happy dear Mr Roberts being able to comply with your request – and much too near the grave to hesitate a moment in facilitating the Carriage of my poor countrymen. Be pleased to procure a proper thing to bear them on, and let me know the amount.'[4]

Later in the month Salusbury wrote again: 'I have now … resolved to make immediate arrangements for letting this beautiful residence as soon as possible and must look out for an eligible tenant who will do as little injury to the place as he can help – in the meantime I must contrive to find a house in Chester.'[5]

It was a bitter blow. This time Hester made no reply; but in her diary, across the space for two days, she scrawled in large letters 'Sickness & Sorrow'.

Those diary entries became progressively briefer and less legible: 'Thursday April 26 More Doctors – less Health, every day'. One of those doctors was her old friend George Gibbes: Sir George now – he had been knighted by George IV the previous year. 'I almost dread your professional efforts in my favour,' she told him, 'for I *would* not recover, and long to flit away.' She suffered internal bleeding, and was heavily drugged. Towards the end she largely lost the power of speech, though not that of effective communication; seeing Gibbes by her bedside, she traced in the air with her hands the outline of a coffin.

Queeney hurried down from Scotland, and was joined by Sophia and Susanna; Cecy was still in Italy, too far away to be reached. 'She knew us,' Queeney wrote to her husband, '& appeared pleased at our being by her Bed side, & whenever she is awake puts out a Hand to each of us – but the Medicines they give her, keep her in a dozing state.'

She died on the evening of 2 May. Conway and Mrs Pennington had both written to Salusbury, but he did not arrive until two days later. The body was taken home to Wales and Hester was buried, as she had wished, beside her beloved Piozzi in the church at Tremeirchion.

❧ ❦

The reading of the will had fallen to Sir James Fellowes. It contained no surprises. After a number of small bequests, Hester's entire real and personal property passed to Salusbury. Fellowes prepared a short memorandum: 'After I had read the Will, Lady Keith and her two sisters present, said they had long been prepared for the contents and for such a disposition of the property, and they acknowledged the validity of the Will.'

Mrs Pennington, at the request of the daughters, penned a eulogy for the Bath newspaper. She also sent a letter to Salusbury telling him that she had loved him as a boy and that she had been promised Hester's silver tea-kettle. 'I think it right to acknowledge receipt of your letter,' he wrote in reply; 'but refrain from entering into particulars, lest any observations I might be induced to make should give you offence.'

A letter he received from Conway a matter of days after Hester's death called for a less boorish response:

> As [you are] one of the Executors of my late revered Friend Mrs. Piozzi I take the liberty of placing in your hands the accompanying Draft, which was presented to me by that lady only two days before her death. I am very ready to acknowledge the acceptance of many acts of kind-ness during her *Life*, but must decline appropriating to myself what I consider a *posthumous* benefaction, which more properly belongs to her Heirs.

The draft had been for £100.

Streatham Park now passed to the Thrale daughters, but they showed little interest in the property. It was sold four years after Hester's death and demolished in 1863. An article in *Punch* recalled the parson who had cut down Shakespeare's mulberry tree for fuel: 'The timbers of the walls which used to reverberate with Johnsonian thunder,' it suggested, 'will now be cut up into no end of snuff-boxes, relics of the immortal Sam.'[6]

Queeney was widowed two years after her mother's death. She lived to be ninety-two, dividing her time between the vast Gothic pile Keith had built on his Tullyallan estate in Scotland and a house in Piccadilly. Sophy survived her mother by only three years, dying in 1824 at the age of fifty-three. Hoare commissioned a memorial from Flaxman, who had executed Thrale's wall tablet. Hoare and Thrale both figured in the epitaph, as did Hester's mother ('WHOM IN HER RECORDED VIRTUES SHE EQUALLED'); of Hester herself there was no mention.

Cecilia returned from abroad in 1827 and eventually settled in Brighton. She bought a large, high-ceilinged house in Sillwood Terrace, close to the sea. She had become a compulsive if indiscriminate collector, and she filled the house with her acquisitions – books, paintings, furniture, sculpture, family memorabilia. In old age she became something of a celebrity in the town, much as Hester had been in Bath; in 1857, the *Brighton Herald* said that her house contained 'our best collection of literary and artistic knicknackeries'. In that year, three months after Queeney's death, she went up to London by train, although her doctors had forbidden her to do so. She collapsed and died at Brighton railway station on her return.

Susanna survived her sisters by only a year. Her liaison with William Wells had long since ended, but she stayed at Ashgrove Cottage for more than fifty years. Someone who saw her there late in life described her as 'a stout easy comfortable old lady, full of good works and alms, and one who, as she has no love for books, or very little, does not care to talk about Dr. Johnson and still less about her mother'.[7] Maybe not, but when Streatham Park was sold, it was she who bought the summer-house in which Johnson had spent so many happy hours.[8] Johnson was the only one who had maintained that the sickly child would survive. She died in November 1858 at the age of eighty-eight.

Salusbury died a month later at Cheltenham. He was sixty-five. Harriet had died many years earlier, shortly after giving birth to their eleventh child. In the event they had managed to stay on at Brynbella for six years after Hester's death, but they then moved permanently to Chester. Salusbury was strapped for cash for the rest of his life. Two years after Hester's death, in a sale at Manchester, he disposed of a large part of her library, together with assorted pictures, prints and plate. In 1836, this time in Liverpool, a further quantity of paintings, prints and household effects went under the hammer.

Hester knew before her death that Conway had decided to try his luck once more on the London stage. He made his first appearance at the Haymarket in Vanbrugh's *The Provok'd Husband*. 'He treads the stage with far more ease and self-possession than he formerly did,' wrote the *British Stage*. 'We hope he will not again quit the metropolis.' But he also attracted the attention of Theodore Hook, editor of the *John Bull*, a scurrilous journal established the previous year to counteract the popular enthusiasm for Queen Caroline. Hook savaged him week after week: 'MR CONWAY (as they call him) was by no means successful in JAFIER, but the contortions of his face were highly entertaining.' After four months of this sort of treatment, Conway's confidence was destroyed; he was never seen on the English stage again.

In September 1823 he sailed for New York, and for several years enjoyed some success there and in other American cities. Four years later, however, he abandoned the theatre and gave himself over to the study of religion, possibly with a view to taking holy orders. Then, in January 1828 he boarded the coastal packet *Niagara*, bound for Savannah. As the boat approached Charleston Harbour he threw himself overboard and was drowned.

Neither Hester's daughters nor Salusbury, the adopted 'son of her heart', thought it necessary to raise any sort of memorial to her. The omission was repaired many years after her death by Orlando Fellowes, Sir James's grandson, who in 1909 organized a subscription and had a simple white marble tablet put up in Tremeirchion Church:

NEAR THIS PLACE ARE INTERRED THE REMAINS OF
HESTER LYNCH PIOZZI,
'DOCTOR JOHNSON'S MRS. THRALE.'
BORN 1741, DIED 1821.
WITTY, VIVACIOUS AND CHARMING, IN AN AGE OF GENIUS
SHE EVER HELD A FOREMOST PLACE.

Johnson, one feels, would have nodded – and growled his disapproval of its not being in Latin.

Notes

To avoid cluttering the text unduly, the numerous quotations from Thraliana have not been individually referenced with note marks. They are however all identified here by a brief italicized tag in the order in which they appear in the narrative.

1. Daughter of Wales

'*an Eleve of the famous Doctor Halley the Astronomer*' Thraliana, 276

1. Their younger brother, Henry, suffered an accident which impaired his mental faculties and remained at home in Wales with his mother until his death in the late 1750s. A fourth child, William, had died in infancy.

'*She was a Young Person ...*' Thraliana, 277

'*an attachment to a French marquise*' James Clifford judged Hester's account to be fanciful. Hester maintained that a gold-headed cane, which she later gave to Henry Thrale, had been a gift to her father from the marquise (*Thraliana*, I, 279, fn 3). She could presumably know this only from him. Odd as he was in many ways, he does not appear to have been a fantasist.

'*Philadelphia Lynch*' Hester, in writing about her grandmother's speedy remarriage, describes her rather oddly as being 'warm with West Indian Blood' (*Thraliana*, 277). Philadelphia's mother, however, was Vere, a daughter of Sir George Herbert. The blood in her veins, whatever its temperature, was purely English.

'*untaught Gawkee Girl*' ibid., 278
'*introduced her into gay Life*' ibid., 279

'*her flashy Cousin John*' ibid.
'*Mad Attachment*' ibid., 280

2. *Doctors' Commons* – a body similar to the Inns of Court whose members concerned themselves with canon and civil law.

3. The marriage settlement is preserved in the Rylands Library (*Ry. Charter* 1008).

4. Rylands *Eng. MS.* 530, 60

5. Both appointments were made in February 1734/5 (*Ry. Charter*, 1231, 1232).
'*he would never see either of them more*' Thraliana, 279

6. Curiously, in her own writings, Hester's year of birth is something of a moveable feast; at different times she gives it as 1741, 1742, 1743 and 1744. Perhaps she was confused by the change from old to new style reckoning in 1752. In later life she celebrated her birthday on 27 January.

'*People of strong Parts ...*' Thraliana, 281

'*Now for a Woman ...*' ibid.
'*to play a thousand pretty Tricks ...*' ibid.
'*Rakish men ...*' ibid.
'*From Lord to Duke ...*' ibid., 280
'*The Mortgage laid by fraud ...*' ibid., 315. Thomas discharged the mortgage seven years later, having by that time acquired a judgeship, a knighthood and a rich wife.

'*My Uncle returned to his Quality Friends ...*' ibid., 282
'*one new gown ...*' ibid., n.1

7. '*I was their Joynt Play Thing ...*' Hayward, A., *Autobiography Letters and Literary Remains of Mrs. Piozzi (Thrale)*, 2 vols, 2nd edn, 1861, ii, 10

8. His wife, Betty, had been twelve years his senior.

'*My* Father *was received* civilly ...' *Thraliana*, 283

'*Sir Robert, after mentioning my Superiority* ...' ibid.

'*I always was in his Sight* ...' ibid., 284

9. Mangin, E. *Pio͡ȝiana; or, Recollections of the Late Mrs. Pio͡ȝȝi, with Remarks*, London, 1833, 8–9

'*a Man of quick Parts* ...' *Thraliana*, 127

'*Great as you think yourself Sir Robert* ...' ibid., 283

'*This degree of odly exerted Spirit struck Sir Robert of a Heap* ...' ibid.

'*She herself would have an annuity* ...' ibid., 284

'*and as Sir Robert dressed both her & me* ...' ibid., 285

10. Hayward, II, 13. James Quin (1693–1766), rumbustious and Falstaffian, was by this time approaching retirement. Cato, in Addison's play of that name, was one of his most celebrated roles. Hester's recollection of what happened when is not always accurate. The display of fireworks to celebrate the peace of Aix-la-Chapelle did not take place until November 1748. Garrick was then thirty-one. He had embarked on his dazzling career as actor-manager at Drury Lane the previous year. Cates is an old word for dainties or delicacies. Shakespeare makes it the subject of an elaborate play on words in one of Petruccio's speeches in *The Taming of the Shrew*: 'But Kate, the prettiest Kate in Christendom, /Kate of Kate Hall, my super-dainty Kate – /For dainties are all cates, and therefore "Kate" – /Take this of me, Kate of my consolation' (II, 1, 187).

'*I was as familiar at Grosvenor Square* ...' *Thraliana*, 286. Hester was writing in 1778.

11. He was, among other things, commissary of the Dean and Chapter of St Paul's.

'*My Father, like other Men of desperate Fortunes* ...' Salusbury seems to have been easily gulled by the mining promoters with their rosy prospectuses. He had been involved in a project to sink a mine for lead and copper on his land as far back as 1731 (*Ry. Charter*, 1190, 1191 and letters from Bridge, Rylands *Eng. MS.* 531, 532).

12. It had been called this briefly in the 1620s under a charter granted by James I to Sir William Alexander.

13. 'Nova Scotia. A New Ballad. To the Tune of King John and the Abbot of Canterbury', *Gentleman's Maga͡ȝine* 20 (1750): 84

14. Cornwallis was then in his mid-thirties. A former royal page, he had fought at Fontenoy and Culloden. When he gave up his command of the 20th Foot to go to Nova Scotia his place was taken by a young major called James Wolfe. Cornwallis's identical twin, Frederick, became Archbishop of Canterbury.

'*My Father now was happy* ...' *Thraliana*, 289

2. Great Expectations

1. Rylands *Eng. MS.* 530, 37

'*leaving my Mother & myself to scrattle on* ...' *Thraliana*, 289

2. Hayward, ii, 15–16

3. Rompkey, Ronald (ed.), *Expeditions of Honour: The Journal of John Salusbury in Halifax, Nova Scotia, 1749–53*, 1982, 140

4. Cornwallis to Board of Trade, 24 July 1749

5. *London Maga͡ȝine* 18 (1749): 471

6. Rompkey, 68. Hugh Davidson, a Scot, occupied the dual position of Secretary and Treasurer. Salusbury refers to him sarcastically elsewhere as 'Our oracle'. He was later sent home for illegal trading practices.

7. Ibid., 78

'*half of which she laid out in finery* ...' *Thraliana*, 292

8. The farms, Tŷ-coch in the parish of Henllan, and Tŷ-mawr in the parish of Llanrhaiadr, had been mortgaged for £600. The Thrales would attempt to recover them in 1772.

9. The *Gentleman's Magazine* xxii (1752), 385 reported that Sir Henry's estate was worth £150,000.

'*I fancy Sir Tho' coaxed his Lady ...*' *Thraliana*, 294.

'*and might have been very happy ...*' ibid., 294–5

'*She was extremely kind ...*' ibid., 295

'*I never did* much love her' ibid., fn 4

10. Letter dated 22 July 1756 (Rylands *Eng. MS.* 616)

'*I had not the sense ...*' *Thraliana*, 3. The translation survives in the John Rylands Collection, together with her version of a complete chapter of the novel itself (Rylands *Eng. MS.* 626; 625).

11. Rylands *Eng. MS.* 628

12. Bloom, Edward A. and Lillian D., *The Piozzi Letters, Correspondence of Hester Lynch Piozzi, 1784–1821 (formerly Mrs. Thrale)*, 6 vols, 1989–2002, v, 421

13. Paulson, Ronald, *Hogarth: Volume 3, Art and Politics, 1750–1764*, 1993, 218

14. When the picture was finished, Charlemont, pleading poverty, sent Hogarth a note for £100. 'Imagine that you have made me a Present of the Picture,' he wrote, 'and that I have beg'd your Acceptance of the inclosed Trifle.' Hogarth held on to the picture for another year, meaning to engrave it, but abandoned the idea. It remained in the Charlemont family until 1874. It is now in the Albright-Kent Art Gallery, Buffalo, New York. The version Hester saw at Fonthill, the home of William Beckford, the eccentric and reclusive author of *Vathek*, was presumably that of his father, the former Lord Mayor of London, much of whose extensive Hogarth collection had been destroyed in a fire at Fonthill in 1755.

15. Bloom, iv, 283

16. Arthur Collier senior had the family living of Langford Magna in Wiltshire, and published his *Clavis Universalis, or a New Inquiry after Truth, being a Demonstration of the NonExistence or Impossibility of an External World* in 1713. There are similarities between his views and those of Berkeley.

17. Coote, C., *Sketches of the Lives of English Civilians*, 1804

'*to many, nay to most people ...*' *Thraliana*, 16

'*To perplex and disappoint ...*' ibid.

18. She was notorious not only for the complexity of her marital arrangements. A former maid of honour to Augusta, Princess of Wales, she had caused a stir at a masquerade in Ranelagh Gardens in 1749 by the scantiness of her attire. 'She was Iphigenia for the sacrifice,' wrote Elizabeth Montagu, 'but so naked, the High Priest might easily inspect the entrails of the victim.' (Climenson, E. J., (ed.), *Elizabeth Montagu, her Correspondence from 1720 to 1761*, 2 vols, 1906, i, 265).

19. There were intimate friendships between the Fielding and Collier families, although that between Henry Fielding and Collier himself came to an end over a legal dispute which cost Fielding £400, a loss for which he held Collier responsible. One of Collier's sisters had collaborated with Sarah Fielding in *The Cry, a Dramatic Fable*, published in Dublin in 1754.

20. Rylands *Eng. MS.* 534, 104

'*a Man who engrossed my whole Heart ...*' *Thraliana*, 297

21. Hayward, ii, 44

'*My Friend D'. Collier ...*' *Thraliana*, 301

'*Doctor Collier used to caution me ...*' ibid., 12

'*Doctor Collier used to say ...*' ibid., 25

22. Hayward, ii, 29

23. Rylands *Eng. MS.* 536, 23

'*Doctor Parker has some pleasant Stories ...*' *Thraliana*, 20

'*my very earliest Friends, Admirers &
Sweethearts.*' ibid., 807

24. Rylands *Eng. MS.* 624, f3

25. Hayward, ii, 28. Hester's memory
played her false here. The *St James's
Chronicle* did not begin publication until
1761.

'*It is an Ode ...*' *Thraliana*, 63
'*After Seven Years Marriage ...*' ibid., 295

26. Hayward, ii, 18
'*where We were no longer Visitors ...*'
Thraliana, 295
'*I used to be my Father's Favourite ...*'
ibid., 296–7
'*Every week we killed an Ox ...*' ibid.,
297
'*This trifling Performance ...*' ibid., 76–7
'*whenever a proper Match might be
offer'd.*' ibid., 296

27. Hayward ii, 18
'*As his Ill humour ...*' *Thraliana*, 296
'*to which no Objection ...*' ibid.
'*Dr. Marriott wrote the prettiest verses in
French ...*' ibid., 32

28. Broadley, A. M., *Doctor Johnson
and Mrs Thrale*, 1910, 105
'*another old* Loveyer true.' *Thraliana*,
806
'*my Cousin, my Pretendant ...*' ibid., 1041
'*a Welch Wench ...*' ibid., 288–9
'*No Civilities could conquer ...*' ibid., 302

3. The Bartered Bride

'*a young & blooming Widow ...*'
Thraliana, 303
'*She cast her Eyes ...*' ibid. Dates and
people's ages were not Hester's strongest
point. Her uncle was still only fifty-three.

1. Hayward, ii, 19
'*a very handsome and well accomplished
Gentleman*' *Thraliana*, 300

2. Hayward, ii, 19–20
'*She had no Notion ...*' *Thraliana*, 299
'*because the poor young Fellow had
married a Wench ...*' ibid., 300. Hester
is a shade malicious. Halsey had been

widowed shortly after Ralph's arrival and
had been thinking of making the girl his
second wife. Thrale's mother remains a
shadowy figure. Her Christian name was
Mary; her surname was possibly Dabbins,
Dobbins or Dobbinson. (See Hyde, 1977,
8, n.3.)

3. The following year Lade broke a
leg while out hunting and died of blood
poisoning.
'*was bred up at Stowe and Stoke ...*'
Thraliana, 300. Cobham stood at the head
of a small group of independent Whigs
which he had formed in association with
George Lyttelton and George Grenville
in 1733. Variously known as 'the boy
patriots' or 'Cobham's cubs', they opposed the Walpole ministry on what they
saw as its over-eagerness to compromise
on foreign affairs. Their number included
Pitt the Elder.

4. Lyttelton was later Governor of
South Carolina and of Jamaica. He also
served as ambassador to Portugal and a
commissioner of the Treasury. Westcote
was an Irish title; he was subsequently
created Baron Lyttelton of Frankley in the
peerage of Great Britain.

5. G. B. Hill (ed.), L. F. Powell (rev.)
*Boswell's Life of Johnson, Together with
Boswell's Journal of a Tour to the Hebrides
and Johnson's Diary of a Journey into North
Wales*, 6 vols, 1934–50, i, 491

6. A contemporary MS records that
he was defeated 'notwithstanding y^e
superfluity of his money' (Hill, G. B.,
Johnsonian Miscellanies, 2 vols, 1897, I,
292–3, n.6).
'*Besides he was of late grown so Jealous ...*' *Thraliana*, 300–1
'*He artfully represented ...*' ibid., 302.
In another account, written many years
later for the actor William Augustus
Conway, Hester describes how her father
railed against Thrale for 'wearing Hart's
Portrait *out*side his Snuffbox; boasting
of Gallantrie'. Quoted in Tearle, John,

Mrs. Piozzi's Tall Young Beau, William Augustus Conway, 1991, 39.

'*With this promise he grew more content ...*' *Thraliana*, 303

'*My Uncle grown weary of our Company ...*' ibid.

7. Rylands *Eng. MS.* 534, 17

8. Hayward, ii, 21

'*My Father charged me violently ...*' *Thraliana*, 303–4

9. Hayward, ii, 21–2. In an earlier account (*Thraliana* 304) Hester wrote that it was her father's friend Colonel Thomas D'Avenant that he had gone to see, hoping he would accompany him to Offley.

'*His Affections and Aversions ...*' *Thraliana*, 127

10. A settlement of £10,000 would be worth in the region of £1.3 million today.

11. Collier's letters to Hester at this time, all in English, mostly undated, are to be found in Rylands *Eng. MS.* 534

'*Well! She knew her power ...*' *Thraliana*, 305–6

12. Rylands *Eng. MS.* 534

'*Ill used by everyone ...*' *Thraliana*, 17

13. Clifford, James L., *Hester Lynch Piozzi (Mrs. Thrale)*, 2nd edn, 1987, 44

'*Mr Thrale ... said he knew.*' *Thraliana*, 306

14. Something like £1.6 million today.

15. Rylands *Eng. MS.* 533, 1

'*pretended to rejoyce ...*' *Thraliana*, 306

'*And what a House it was then!*' ibid., 782

4. *Mistress of Streatham*

'*Except for one five minutes ...*' *Thraliana*, 306

1. Harvard *Piozziana*, 'Poems and Little Characters, Anecdotes &c. Introductory to the Poems', 5 MS vols, 1810–14, written for John Salusbury Piozzi Salusbury, I, 50, 51

2. Hayward, ii, 24

'*Mean Time my Husband ...*' *Thraliana*, 307

'*M.' Thrale grew passionately fond of her ...*' ibid. The girl had a sister who had run away to Scotland with a butler. Hester was concerned that flightiness might run in the family.

'*My Mother perfectly agreed with him ...*' ibid., 306

'*It is a Mind in which nothing has grown up ...*' ibid., 169

'*like a Man who had been drown'd ...*' ibid., 225

'*I liked none of 'em but Murphy ...*' ibid., 307 n.1

3. Hayward, ii, 24

4. Ibid. This was later confirmed to her by Humphrey Jackson, a well-known chemist and inventor, whose influence over her husband she came to distrust.

5. *St James's Chronicle*, 3–5 May 1763. His assailant, one Samuel Beaton, was hanged at Kennington Common three months later (*Gentleman's Magazine* 33:411).

6. Harvard *Piozziana*, I, 55

7. Hayward, ii, 441

8. 'My pen is in such a sublime humour,' Walpole wrote to George Montagu, 'that it can scarce condescend to tell you that Sir Edward Deering is going to marry Polly Hart, Danvers' old mistress, and three more baronets, whose name nobody knows ... are treading in the same steps' (*Walpole Correspondence*, 10, 40, letter dated 10 August 1762).

9. Hayward, ii, 23

'*& then most probably went again ...*' *Thraliana*, 308, n.1

'*My Mother charged me ...*' ibid., 307

'*As for poor me ...*' ibid., 308

'*It was now Time ...*' ibid.

10. *Johns. Misc.*, i, 240

11. Later pupils at the school included Cecil Rhodes. Johnson's *ménage* expanded with the years. 'He has *now* in his house,' Hester wrote in 1777, 'whole Nests of

People who would if he did not support them be starving I suppose: – A Blind woman & her Maid, a Blackamoor and his Wife, a Scotch Wench who has her Case as a Pauper depending in some of the Law Courts; a Woman whose Father once lived at Lichfield & whose Son is a Strolling Player, – and a superannuated Surgeon to have Care of the whole *Ship's Company*' (*Thraliana*, 184–5).

12. *The Ghosts*, III, 801–2

13. *Johns. Misc.*, i, 28

14. Ibid., 31

'*his figure, dress or behaviour*' ibid., 233

'*We liked each other so well ...*' *Thraliana*, 159

'*a good one says he – for a* Lady.' ibid., 55

15. Hector Boece (Boethius) (c.1465–1536), Scottish historian, studied at the University of Paris, where he struck up a friendship with Erasmus. He later became the first principal of the newly founded King's College, Aberdeen.

16. Harvard *Piozziana*, I, 57

17. Redford, Bruce (ed.), *The Letters of Samuel Johnson*, 5 vols, 1992–94, I, 250

18. Hyde, 1977, 22

19. Hayward, ii, 25

20. Redford, III, 218

21. *Johns. Misc.*, i, 234

5.   Enter James Boswell

'*My Mother and he did not like one another ...*' *Thraliana*, 182

1. Hayward, ii, 25

2. 'This Dog,' Johnson declared on another occasion, when the animal was begging for food when they were at table, 'would have been a fit member of the Society established by Lycurgus. She condemns one to a State of perpetual Vigilance' (*Thraliana*, 181–2).

3. Hyde, 1977, 21

4. Ibid., 24. When Hester Maria was twenty months old, her parents commis-

sioned Zoffany to paint her portrait. She so astonished the painter, Hester wrote, 'that he told the King of her odd performances' (*Thraliana*, 308, n.3).

5. Ibid., 24–5

6. Bate, W. Jackson, *Samuel Johnson*, 1978, 434

7. Redford, III, 369

8. Ibid., 1801

'*One Day that I mentioned ...*' *Thraliana*, 309

'*I had my Children to nurse ...*' ibid., 309–10

9. Redford, I, 284

10. Harvard *Piozziana*, I, 56

11. *Life*, I, 494

12. *Johns. Misc.*, i, 339

13. Ibid., 307

14. Redford, I, 293. Chambers, a member of the Club, had succeeded Blackstone as Vinerian Professor of Law two years previously at the early age of twenty-nine. He later became Chief Justice of Bengal.

'*He is supposed by those that knew ...*' *Thraliana*, 497

15. Ibid., n.1

16. Hyde, 1977, 27

'*If I offered to think ...*' *Thraliana*, 307

17. Tinker, Chauncey B., *The Letters of James Boswell*, 2 vols, 1924, i, 173

18. *Johns. Misc.*, i, 47

'*Such however is his nobleness ...*' *Thraliana*, 384–5

'*Poor Johnson!*' ibid., 625

'*In return I observed to him ...*' ibid., 169–70

'*Doctor Goldsmith ...*' ibid., 83

19. Broadley, 8

20. *Johns. Misc.*, ii, 169

21. *Life*, I, 494

22. Hyde, 1977, 30

23. Ibid.

24. Redford, I, 324–5

25. *Johns. Misc.*, i, 324

26. Ibid., 224

27. Hayward, ii, 444

28. Hyde, Mary, *The Impossible Friendship*, 1972, 14

29. *Life*, II, 77–8

6. *Thrale's Annus Horribilis*

1. Hyde, 1977, 33

2. Ibid., 33

3. Ibid., 34–5

4. Ibid., 35

5. Ibid., 38

'*miserably lean and feeble indeed ...*' *Thraliana*, 37

'*It had now been nine Years ...*' ibid., 310

'*My Mother try'd all* her *Power ...*' ibid.

'*sate like one Thunderstruck ...*' ibid.

'*Well! I returned to Streatham ...*' ibid., 311

6. Greene, Donald J. (ed.), *The Yale Edition of the Works of Samuel Johnson, Volume X, Political Writings*, 1977, 313–45

7. Rylands *Eng. MS.* 629, I

8. Hyde, 1977, 39–40

9. In 1767 Thomas Dimsdale (1712–1800) had introduced a procedure that was considered less intrusive and safer. The following year he was invited to St Petersburg by Catherine the Great to inoculate herself and her son. He was richly rewarded, and created a councillor of state, with the hereditary title of baron.

10. *Johns. Misc.*, i, 196

11. Hester's version and Johnson's original are reproduced in *Johns. Misc.*, i, 197–8.

12. Redford, I, 371

13. Ibid., 376

14. *Johns. Misc.*, i, 307

15. Johnson is alluding to the speech in *3 Henry VI* in which the King taunts the future Richard III over his monstrous birth.

16. Chapman, R. W. (ed.), *The Letters of Samuel Johnson with Mrs. Thrale's Genuine Letters to Him*, 3 vols, 1952, I, 269

17. Redford, I, 378

18. Hyde 1977, 49

19. Ibid., 50

'*My Mother's Disorder ...*' *Thraliana*, 311

20. Redford, I, 378

21. Ibid., 362

'*M*ʳ *Thrale had for some Time ...*' *Thraliana*, 311

'*& begged for Counsel and Comfort.*' ibid., 312

22. Hayward, ii, 25

23. Ibid.

24. Ibid., 25–6

'*that wicked* Haman!' *Thraliana*, 312

25. *Book of Esther*, Chapters 3–7

26. See in particular Appleby, John H., 'Humphrey Jackson, F.R.S., 1717–1801: A Pioneering Chemist', which appeared in *Notes and Records of the Royal Society*, 1986 May; 40(2), pp. 147–68.

'*My Mother said She had 2 or 3 Thousand Pounds ...*' *Thraliana*, 312

'*I now tried first ...*' ibid.

27. The record of the conversation was made the following year in a notebook which Hester entitled 'A Book in which was written within and without, Lamentation & Mourning & Woe', Rylands *Eng. MS.* 616, 2.

28. *Oxford Magazine*, 228/2

29. Hayward, ii, 26

'*seem'd* first *affected with that horrible Stupor ...*' *Thraliana*, 805

'*Women have a manifest Advantage ...*' ibid., 313

30. Hyde 1977, 55

7. *Siberian Winter*

1. Chapman, I, 283

2. Redford, I, 401

3. Chapman, I, 283

4. Ibid., 284

5. Redford, I, 410

6. Rylands *Eng. MS.* 616. She had started keeping a notebook devoted to brewery affairs.

7. Chapman, I, 310

8. Redford, II, 17. Some years later Johnson spoke of James to Boswell as 'a physician who for twenty years was not sober' (*Life*, III, 389).

9. Chapman, I, 300

10. Redford, II, 19

11. Ibid., 20–1

12. Chapman, I, 314

13. Hyde 1977, 60

14. *The Westminster Magazine or, The Pantheon of Taste*, i, 1773, 178

15. Wimsatt, William K. Jr and Pottle, Frederick A. (eds), *Boswell for the Defence*, 1769–74, 1959, 174–5

16. *Life*, II, 211

17. Hyde 1977, 62–3

18. Redford, II, 37

19. Hyde 1977, 63

20. Masochism first appeared, as did the term sadism, in Krafft-Ebbing's *Psychopathia Sexualis*, published in 1886.

21. Chapman, I, 331–2

22. Hyde 1977, 66–8

23. Ibid., 65, 69

24. *Westminster Magazine* (1773), 374–5

25. Chapman, I, 335

26. Hyde 1977, 74. She had had a severe attack of measles in 1752, shortly before her twelfth birthday – 'leaving at their Departure a small red swelling on my Cheek, which my Mother called the Measle-Mark, and it remained there till the *Change of Life* took it quite away' (*Thraliana*, 801).

'*Here is much ado about nothing ...*' *Thraliana*, 82

27. Beattie's persistence was rewarded, in August, by the award of a royal pension of £200.

28. *Life*, II, 148

29. Forbes, W., *An Account of the Life and Writings of James Beattie*, 1806, I, 436

8. *Travelling Hopefully*

1. Redford, II, 53

2. Ibid., 56–7

3. Ibid., 62

4. Ibid., 70

5. *Life*, V, 211

6. Redford, II, 71. The island in question was Isa, in Loch Dunvegan. Macleod offered it to Johnson on condition that he live there at least one month in the year.

7. Chapman, I, 384

8. Redford, II, 117–18

9. Hyde, 1977, 86

'*dictated by his Wife ...*' *Thraliana*, 313

'*Doctor Goldsmith said here one Day ...*' ibid., 84–5

10. Collison-Morley, Lacy, *Giuseppe Baretti and His Friends*, 1909, 217–19

11. Hyde, 1977, 76

'*Will: Burke was tart upon Mr Baretti ...*' *Thraliana*, 47

'*A man made up of Contradictions ...*' *Thraliana*, 84

12. Broadley, 159

13. Ibid., 159–60

14. *Johns. Misc.*, i, 337

15. Broadley, 160–3

16. Ibid., 164

17. Ibid., 166

18. Ibid., 171–2

19. Ibid., 173. Cotquean – a contemptuous term for a man who busied himself unduly with woman's work.

20. *Life*, V, 431

21. Broadley, 174

22. Ibid., 183

23. *Life*, V, 436

24. Broadley, 184–5

25. Ibid., 193–4

26. Redford, II, 151

27. Barrett, Charlotte (ed.), *Burney Diary: Diary and Letters of Madame D'Arblay*, with Preface and Notes by Austin Dobson, 6 vols, 1904–05, I, 130

28. Broadley, 203

29. Ibid., 206

'*My good Steward Mr Bridge ...*' *Thraliana*, 315

30. *Life*, V, 456

31. Broadley, 210

32. Ibid., 213

33. Ibid., 217. The 'old Mr Lowndes' was Charles Lowndes, of Chesham, Secretary to the Treasury. He was then seventy-five.

'*Tis now Time ...*' *Thraliana*, 475. Later she added a footnote: 'Irish Roman Catholics are always like the Foreigners somehow: dirty & dressy, with their Clothes hanging as if upon a Peg.'

34. Broadley, 219

'*I had been tied to my eldest Girl ...*' *Thraliana*, 316

9. '*Sure We are Made of Iron*'

1. Hyde, 1977, 106–7

2. Chapman, I, 360

3. *The Patriot, Addressed to the Electors of Great Britain*, 1774, Greene, 387–400

'*were run mad with Republican Frenzy.*' *Thraliana*, 317

'*Madam says the Man ...*' ibid., 115

4. Hyde, 1977, 108

5. Ibid.

'*My Master's Behaviour ...*' *Thraliana*, 317

6. Hyde, 1977, 110

7. Ibid.

8. Redford, II, 159

9. Ibid., 166

10. It also challenged the arguments advanced the previous year by Burke in his *Speech on American Taxation*.

'*M^s Montagu made many polite advances ...*' *Thraliana*, 135

11. *Life*, II, 88

12. *D'Arblay Diary*, I, 352

13. *Johns. Misc.*, ii, 58. The words occur in *Memoirs of the Life of Mrs. Elizabeth Carter* by the Rev. Montagu Pennington, London, 1807.

14. Ibid., 40, 43. Massy – an old word meaning weighty and solid.

15. Ryskamp, Charles, and Pottle, Frederick A. (eds), *Boswell: The Ominous*

Years 1774–1776, 104–5, entry for 28 March 1775

16. Ibid., 136, entry for 8 April 1775

17. Redford, II, 193–4.

18. Chapman, II, 21

19. Hyde, 1977, 115

20. Ibid., 116–17

21. Ibid., 118

22. Hyde, 1972, 30

23. Chapman, II, 30

24. Redford, II, 218

25. Chapman, II, 54

26. *Walpole Correspondence*, 32, 237

27. Redford, II, 231

28. Ibid., 234

29. Chapman, II, 59

30. Hyde, 1977, 124

31. Chapman, II, 69–70

'*This supposition ...*' *Thraliana*, 318

32. Rylands *Eng. MS.* 600, 26

'*a purseproud Tradesman ...*' *Thraliana*, 220

33. Redford, II, 243

34. The reference is to Swift's *A Tale of a Tub*. Swift relates in his preface that it is the practice of seamen when they encounter a whale to throw out an empty tub to divert his attention from the ship.

35. Chapman, II, 66

36. Hyde, 1977, 128

37. Tyson, Moses, and Guppy, Henry, *The French Journals of Mrs. Thrale and Doctor Johnson*, 1932, 69

10. *Fair Stood the Wind for France*

1. Tyson and Guppy, 70–1

2. The others were New Year's Day, Good Friday, Easter Day and 28 March, the anniversary of the death of his wife.

3. *Johns. Misc.*, i, 74

4. Tyson & Guppy, 70

'*he bustled for us ...*' *Thraliana*, 48

5. Tyson and Guppy, 69

6. Ibid., 72–3

7. Ibid., 73. This was the old cathedral church of St Vaast, built between 1030

and 1396. It was destroyed during the Revolution.

8. Ibid., 75
9. Ibid., 74–5
10. Collison-Morley, 282. He was commenting on the selection of her correspondence with Johnson which Hester published four years after his death.
11. Tyson and Guppy, 79
12. Ibid., 79–80
13. Ibid., 81–2
14. *Johns. Misc.*, i, 215–16
15. Tyson and Guppy, 84
16. Ibid., 88–9
17. Ibid., 95
18. Ibid., 93
19. Ibid., 92
20. Ibid., 98
21. Ibid., 99
22. Ibid., 100
23. Ibid., 103
24. Ibid., 102. Baretti later told Joshua Reynolds's sister Frances that when they went to drink tea with Madame du Boccage on another occasion she produced an old china teapot which would not pour: 'She came over to the table, caught up the tea-pot, and blew into the spout with all her might, then finding it pour, she held it up in tryumph, and repeatedly exclaim'd, "V*oila, voila, j'ai regagné l'honneur de ma Théière*"' (*John. Misc.* ii, 291).
25. Ibid., 108
26. Ibid., 170
27. Ibid., 109
28. Redford, II, 272
29. Tyson and Guppy, 138–9
30. Ibid., 124
31. Ibid., 125
32. Ibid., 177
33. Ibid., 178–80
34. *Johns. Misc.*, i, 216. Samuel Foote's comedy *The Englishman in Paris*, first performed at Covent Garden in 1753, was still frequently revived.
35. Tyson and Guppy, 147–8. The

painting is now in the National Gallery, London.

36. Ibid., 146–7
37. Ibid., 143
38. Ibid., 150
39. Ibid., 156–7
40. Ibid., 165
41. Ibid., 164
42. Ibid., 165

11. 'An Unforeseen and Heavy Calamity'

1. Hyde, 1977, 145
2. Ibid.
3. Ibid., 143–4
4. Collison-Morley, 285–90
5. *Life*, II, 468
6. 'His behaviour,' Hester later wrote, 'shut my heart against him suddenly, and I could never open it to him more' (*Thraliana*, 130).
7. Hyde, 1977, 151–2
8. It was invented by the Reverend Thomas Daffy, a seventeenth-century Leicestershire clergyman.
9. William Heberden, Cambridge-trained, a Fellow of the Royal College of Physicians. Johnson, whom he would attend in his last illness, described him as '*ultimus Romanorum*, the last of the learned physicians' (*Life*, IV, 399, n.4).
10. Hyde, 1977, 152
11. *European Magazine*, May 1788, p. 314. Count Manucci was a young Florentine nobleman whom they had met in France at Madame du Boccage's house.
12. Hyde, 1977, 153
13. Redford, II, 311
14. *European Magazine*, May 1788, 315
15. Redford, II, 313
16. Chapman, II, 121
17. *Life*, II, 470
18. Ibid., 468–9
'*In one of the Chapels …*' *Thraliana*, 338–9

'*Mad notwithstanding all this Folly I am
not ...*' ibid.

'*unforeseen and heavy Calamity*' ibid., 44

'*I was too proud of him ...*' ibid., 319

19. Redford, II, 318–19
20. Chapman, II, 123–4
21. Hyde, 1977, 164
22. *Life*, III, 46, 49
23. Chapman, II, 128
24. Hyde, 1977, 159
25. Chapman, II, 138
26. Redford, II, 341
27. Hyde, 1977, 160
28. Redford, II, 340
29. Collison-Morley, 289

'*very odd and very Cross ...*' *Thraliana*, 45

'*Not a Servant ...*' ibid., 43–4

30. *European Magazine*, June 1788

12. The Book with the Foolish Name

1. Hyde, 1977, 165–6
2. Ibid., 167. Jacques Daran (1701–84)
was the author of a celebrated study of
diseases of the urethra and numbered
Louis XV and Rousseau among his
patients. Hester, however, is mistaken in
believing that he practised in London.
The likelihood is that Thrale was treated
by a surgeon called Thomas Tomkyns,
who had studied under Daran and claimed
to be the only person familiar with his
secret remedies.

'*I do think it is only a Consequence ...*'
ibid.

'*It is many years ...*' *Thraliana*, 1

3. Hyde, 1977, 168
4. Ibid., 172, 173
5. Ibid., 172

'*Such was the fertility of his Mind ...*'
Thraliana, 137

6. *Life*, II, 407
7. Clifford, 149
8. Redford, II, 361
9. Ibid., 365
10. Hyde, 1977, 175
11. Ibid., 176

12. Redford, III, 14
13. Troide, Lars E. (ed.), *The Early
Letters and Journals of Fanny Burney*,
vol. 2, *1774–1777*, 224–7
14. Terrified at the initial success of the
Jacobite rising in 1745, the banker Thomas
Snow wrote to Gideon demanding the
immediate return of a £20,000 loan.
Gideon sent him a bottle of smelling salts
– wrapped in twenty £1,000 banknotes.

15. Rylands *Eng. MS.* 539, 12
16. Chapman, II, 167
17. Redford, III, 16
18. Ibid., 19
19. Hyde, 1977, 178

'*The Account of poor Doctor Collier's
Death ...*' *Thraliana*, 25

20. Chapman, II, 172
21. Redford, III, 25–6
22. Chapman, II, 175

'*but M' Garrick was sick ...*' *Thraliana*,
108–9

23. Hyde, 1977, 189–90

'*Dear Mr Thrale ...*' *Thraliana*, 517

24. Redford, III, 88
25. Ibid., 69
26. Chapman, II, 209
27. Redford, III, 66
28. Chapman, II, 209

'*Writing as I do ...*' *Thraliana*, 158

'*All my Friends reproach me ...*' ibid.

29. Redford, III, 61
30. Chapman, II, 202
31. Ibid., 218–19

'*M' Thrale twitted her ...*' *Thraliana*, 272

32. *Walpole Correspondence*, 33, 136
33. Chapman, II, 224
34. Ibid., 232
35. Redford, III, 99
36. Hyde, 1977, 198

'*and her eldest Daughter ...*' *Thraliana*, 17

'*Her Face is eminently pretty ...*' ibid., 323

13. Enter Little Burney

1. Hyde, 1977, 198
2. Chapman, II, 244

3. Greville had taken Burney into his service as a musical companion in the 1740s, eventually paying Arne £300 to release him from the remainder of his apprenticeship.

4. *Memoirs of Doctor Burney, arranged from his own manuscripts, from family papers and from personal recollections by his daughter, Madame D'Arblay*, 3 vols, 1932, II, 101–13

5. Hyde, 1977, 201

6. Ibid.

7. Ibid.

8. Chapman, II, 247–8

9. Hyde, 1977, 203

10. Chapman, II, 249

11. Johnson conveyed the news to Boswell, who had returned to Scotland: 'Mrs. Thrale, poor thing, has a daughter' (Redford, III, 119).

12. Hyde, 1977, 204. Aphelion – that point of the orbit of a planet or a comet at which it is furthest from the sun.

13. Ibid.

14. Ibid., 205–6
'*And so the Wings of* Speculation ...' *Thraliana*, 333
'*Was I to make a scale* ...' ibid., 328–9

15. Ibid., 329–31. She awarded herself 17 for 'Worth of Heart' and 'Conversation Powers'; a more modest 10 for 'Ornamental Knowledge' and 'person Mien and Manner'.

16. Troide, Lars E. and Cooke, Stewart J. (eds), *The Early Journals and Letters of Fanny Burney, vol. 3, The Streatham Years, Part I, 1778–1779*, 66

17. Ibid., 83

18. Ibid., 90. Lade later became racing manager to the Prince of Wales and married Laetitia Derby, the former mistress of the Duke of York and of John Rann, the dandy highwayman hanged at Tyburn in 1774. Laetitia's foul mouth gave rise to the expression 'to swear like lady Lade'. The Prince of Wales was besotted by her; it was he who commissioned from George Stubbs the equestrian portrait of her now in the Royal Collection at Windsor.

19. Ibid., 94
'*Our Miss Burney* ...' *Thraliana*, 368

20. Sabor, Peter, Cooke, Stewart J. *et al.* (eds), The *Complete Plays of Frances Burney*, 2 vols, 1995, I, 12–13n
'*I like it very well* ...' *Thraliana*, 381

21. Troide and Cooke, 349–50

22. Ibid., 105

23. Ibid., 104

24. Chapman, II, 258

25. Ibid., 261
'*than any* professed *Virgin* ...' *Thraliana*, 363

26. Chapman, II, 259
'*an absurd old Fellow* ...' *Thraliana*, 450

27. Redford, III, 133

28. Ibid., 144

29. Hyde, 1977, 213

30. Troide and Cooke, 205–6
'*Mr Thrale is fallen in Love* ...' *Thraliana*, 356

31 Hyde, 1977, 217–18

14. The Flight of Time

'*my Thorn as I call it* ...' *Thraliana*, 365
'*I knew him only just well enough* ...' ibid., 364
'*The Flight of Time* ...' ibid., 363
'*He sees Thrale's Love* ...' ibid., 357, n3
'*Tho' he loves Sophy Streatfield* ...' ibid., 367. 'I am very fond of bathing,' she wrote: 'tis such a Friend to Beauty & to Love! Smoothing the Skin, illuminating the Complexion, exciting Ideas of such perfect Cleanliness, bracing up everything that frequent Pregnancy relaxes –'

1. Hayward, II, 36
'*The Bishop of Llandaff's Bill* ...' *Thraliana*, 379
'*Costollo an Irish Counsellor* ...' ibid., 388. An action for damages for criminal conversation may be brought by a man against a person who has had sexual relations with his wife.

'*I have this Moment …*' ibid., 375

2. Chapman, II, 287

'*I made a good fortnight's work …*'
Thraliana, 387. John Hinchcliffe, a liberal
churchman, was also Master of Trinity
College Cambridge. Hester thought well
of his wife, too – 'She is quite a woman of
Fashion and three parts a Beauty.' She was
the sister-in-law of Mrs Crewe.

3. Hayward, II, 37

'*I'm confident he will recover …*'
Thraliana, 389

4. Hester missed him. 'Johnson is
away,' she wrote tetchily, '– down at
Lichfield or Derby, or God knows where,
something always happens when *he is
away*' (*Thraliana*, 390).

5. Redford, III, 168

6. Ibid., 169

'*One Evening at the Borough …*'
Thraliana, 845

'*Even the Opposition People …*' ibid.,
391

'*Here is my mad Master …*' ibid.

'*Few People live in such a State of
Preparation …*' ibid.

'*If ten Men can be found …*' ibid.

'*Abortions and Profluvia . …*' ibid., 399

'*I beg'd him to make haste home …*'
ibid., 401

'*Now tho'M*r *Thrale's heart …*' ibid.

'*Perkin's expression …*' ibid., n.2. The
OED defines the phrase as 'stricken by the
supposed malign influence of an adverse
planet; blasted; sometimes said in reference to paralytic or other sudden physical
affections'.

7. Chapman, II, 301–2

8. The text of the dialogues was published in 1932 in the *Bulletin of the John
Rylands Library*, vol. 16, pp. 97–111.

'*I have got a strange Fit of the horrors …*'
Thraliana, 408–9

'*M*r *Thrale longs to see his S: S: …*'
ibid., 409

9. Redford, III, 187–8

'*Now this was rather a Testimony …*'

Thraliana, 418. She also named their
friend William Weller Pepys, master in
chancery, whom she had hoped would
look after her daughters if she were to die,
but he declined. Jeremiah Crutchley and
Thrale's cousin Henry Smith were later
added.

10. Redford, III, 214

11. Ibid., 212. Johnson was right – the
island did not fall. Spain had ruled
Jamaica between 1509 and 1655. During
that time the native population was wiped
out and slaves were imported from Africa.
The English took possession in 1670, but
were harassed for more than a century by
black insurgents who had taken refuge in
the mountains.

12. Troide and Cooke, 451

'*The Thraliana will be full of nothing …*'
Thraliana, 410

'*'Tis a dreadful Thing …*' ibid., 409

'*I had a Grave coloured Gown …*' ibid.,
410

13. Redford, III, 217, 219

'*5: January 1780. Here is another New
Year begun …*' *Thraliana*, 416

15. '*Like a Cock at Shrove Tide*'

'*Sophy Streatfeild is come to town …*'
Thraliana, 422

'*She shewed me a Letter from him …*'
ibid., 461

'*Every body's Admiration …*' ibid., 493

1. Hayward, i, 118–19

2. Troide and Cooke, 374

3. Ibid., 316

4. Mangin, 22–3

'*M*r *Thrale is very unkind …*' *Thraliana*,
424

'*I wish the King …*' ibid., 423

'*Miss Streatfield was one …*' ibid., 432

'*His Sisters …*' ibid.

5. Rizzo, Betty (ed.), *The Early
Journals and Letters of Fanny Burney,
Volume IV, The Streatham Years: Part II,
1780–1781*, 2003, 25. Mrs Lawrence was

the daughter of a Worcestershire vicar,
a member of the Read family of Brocket
Hall in Hertfordshire.

6. Redford, III, 236–7. Johnson would
not finish the last of the Lives, that of
Pope, until early the following year.

7. Rizzo, 62, 66

8. Ibid., 32

9. In 1772 the Bishop of Ely had
presented Whalley to the rectory of
Hagworthingham in Lincolnshire,
stipulating, because of its unhealthy
situation, that he should never take up
residence. Whalley happily complied
with this unusual condition for more than
fifty years, arranging for his duties to be
carried out by a curate.

'*of all the Voices ...*' *Thraliana*, 439. She
recognized, however, that not everyone
agreed, and added a footnote: 'Johnson
says tis the Voice of a Carpenter in a
Work Shop.'

10. Chapman, II, 360

11. Ibid., 352

12. Rizzo, 58

13. Ibid., 156

14. Redford, III, 248

15. Chapman, II, 352

16. Ibid., 353

17. Redford, III, 252

18. Rizzo, 109

19. Redford, III, 256

20. Rizzo, 177

21. Ibid., 173

22. Perkins's conduct was described
in the obituary published of him in the
Gentleman's Magazine in 1812 (lxxxii, 2,
592).

23. Rizzo, 174

'*dawdling Journey cross the Country ...*'
Thraliana, 437

'*We have now got Arms ...*' ibid.

'*Of Reynolds ...*' ibid., 473

'*We never lived asunder ...*' ibid., 445

24. Hayward, II, 449

'*He is so intelligent a creature ...*'
Thraliana, 452

'*He is amazingly like my Father ...*'
ibid., 448, n.7

'*I dread the General Election ...*'
ibid., 449

'*I worked at Solicitation ...*' ibid.,
459, n.1

'*On Sunday Morning ...*' ibid., 453–4

25. She was writing to Mrs Lambart,
sister of Sir Philip Jennings Clerke.

'*& we stole hither unobserved ...*'
Thraliana, 454

26. Chapman, II, 403–4

16. A Farewell to Trade

'*This last Election ...*' *Thraliana*, 459

1. Rylands *Eng. MS.* 550. Letter dated
5 October 1780

'*Here is Sophy Streatfield again ...*'
Thraliana, 460–1

'*He wants to have a part ...*' ibid., 461–2

'*Mʳ Thrale has been ill again ...*' ibid.,
464

2. Clifford, 193

3. Rizzo, 286

'*A Dutch War ...*' *Thraliana*, 468

4. Lord George Gordon was about to
stand trial for high treason. In the event
he was acquitted.

'*So now we are to spend ...*' *Thraliana*,
478. The Shelburnes lived in a large house
in Berkeley Square, bought half-finished
from Bute.

'*It was violently admired ...*' ibid., 481

5. Rizzo, 292–3

'*Lord John is tame & gentle ...*' *Thraliana*, 480

'*I am so afraid ...*' ibid., 483

'*I have set up Piozzi's Concert ...*'
ibid., 485

'*Well! now I have experienced ...*'
ibid., 486

'*how shall we drag him thither? ...*'
ibid., 487

6. Reed, Joseph W. and Pottle, Frederick A. (eds), *Boswell, Laird of Auchinleck,
1778–82*, 1977, 304

7. *Life*, IV, 73

8. Ibid., 81–2

9. Ibid., 72

'*I checked him rather severely ...*'
Thraliana, 488

'*I read the letter to Piozzi ...*' ibid., 489

'*I suppose that you* Know ...' ibid.

'*with Strong Beer in such Quantities! ...*'
ibid.

'*What's the meaning of this? ...*' ibid.

'*seeing Death certain ...*' ibid., 490

10. *Johns. Misc.*, i, 96

'*I ran forward to Brighthelmston ...*'
Thraliana, 490

11. *Johns. Misc.*, i, 96

12. Redford, III, 332

13. This would give her close to
£190,000 a year at today's prices, and the
best part of £3 million if the brewery were
sold.

'*my being entangled with the Trade ...*'
Thraliana, 491

14. Redford, III, 340

15. Hayward, ii, 47

'*If an angel from heaven ...*' *Thraliana*,
492

'*Miss Owen & Miss Burney ...*' ibid.

'*David Barclay the rich Quaker ...*'
ibid., 494

16. Barclay was a partner in the oldest
surviving Quaker bank in London. A
close friend of Benjamin Franklin's, he
had made an unsuccessful attempt some
years previously to mediate between
Franklin and the North government to
avoid a break with the American colonies.

17. Rizzo, 350

'*Well! Here have I with the Grace of
God ...*' *Thraliana*, 499

17. *Hoarded Folly*

1. Reed and Pottle, 316–21

2. Martin, Peter, *A Life of James
Boswell*, 1999, 437

3. Wain, John, *Samuel Johnson*, 1974,
355

4. Rizzo, 364

5. *John. Misc.*, i, 99

'*My Italian is going to his own country ...*' *Thraliana*, 497

'*What a Blockhead ...*' ibid., 502

6. Pine (1730–88), had been a
well-known portrait painter since the
1760s. His strong republican views led
him to support the cause of American
independence, and in 1784 he settled in
Philadelphia.

7. Rizzo, 451. Hester presented the
picture to Perkins and his wife; it belongs
today to Scottish Courage Ltd, the direct
corporate descendant of the Thrale
brewery.

'*I verily think that my Health ...*'
Thraliana, 503

8. Chapman, II, 439

'*I am growing excessively uneasy ...*'
Thraliana, 515

'*Concealed Fire burns very fatally ...*'
Thraliana, 517. Hester goes on to draw
a comparison with 'the unnatural Vice
among the Men (now so modish)', and adds
somewhat comically, 'The Scotch seem
strangely addicted to this Enormity, & 'tis a
cold Country too:– I can think of no reason
but one – their wearing Fillibegs.–'

9. Rizzo, 499–500

10. Ibid., 504

11. Ibid., 507–9

'*As My Peace ...*' *Thraliana*, 197

12. Redford, III, 375

13. Ibid., 379

'*I have got my Piozzi home ...*' *Thraliana*,
519–20

'*I am beginning a new Year ...*' ibid., 523

'*They say Pacchierotti ...*' ibid., 525

'*She has begun the new Year ...*' ibid.,
523. The end, as it happens, was un-
remarkable. Sophy died, unmarried, at the
age of eighty in 1835.

'*The World will watch me at first ...*'
Thraliana, 526

'*My face is all over Pimples ...*' ibid.,
524–5

'if *neither I should marry* ...' ibid., 525

'*Travelling with Mr Johnson* ...'
ibid., n.2

'*Here is Mr Johnson very ill* ...' ibid., 528

14. Redford, IV, 7–8

'*when I took off my Mourning* ...'
Thraliana, 531

'*Here's a proposal of Marriage* ...'
ibid., 535

'*'Tis now Sir Philip Jennings Clerke's
Turn* ...' ibid., 538

'*The establishment of Expence* ...'
ibid., 540

15. Shelburne, who had succeeded North as Prime Minister earlier
in the year, felt that his country house
at Bowood, near Bath, was too far from
London.

'*I fancied Mr Johnson* ...' *Thraliana*, 540

'*He* loved *Mr Thrale* ...' ibid., 541, n.1

'*In Italy we shall live* ...' ibid.

16. *Life*, IV, 157–8

17. Sherbo, Arthur (ed.), *Anecdotes of
the late Samuel Johnson, LL.D. during the
Last Twenty Years of His Life*, 1974, 293

18. *Johns. Misc.*, i, 108–9

19. Ibid., 109

18. No Mercy in This Island

'*He is so amiable, so honourable* ...'
Thraliana, 544–6

1. Redford, IV, 90

2. *Burney Diary*, II, 122

'*One day the paper rings* ...' *Thraliana*,
547. The allusion is to *The Merry Wives of
Windsor*.

3. Chapman, II, 482–3

'*He will get me to be sure!!* ...' *Thraliana*, 548

'*I called her into my Room* ...' ibid.,
548–50

'*Ah what a triumph* ...' ibid., 551

'*'Tis Time to be in earnest* ...' ibid., n.3

'*I am all the Mode* ...' ibid., 553–4

'*Why, this is a leaden goddess* ...'
ibid., 554.

'*My Lover is jealous of me* ...' ibid., 555

'*I called him gently to Account* ...'
ibid., 557

'*While My Heart* ...' ibid., 556

'*with frigid Indifference* ...' ibid., 558–9

'*Adieu to all that's dear* ...' ibid., 557

'*I may in six or seven Years* ...' ibid., 560

4. *Johns. Misc.*, i, 111

'*I perswaded him* ...' *Thraliana*, 561

'*Here I am settled* ...' ibid.

5. Chapman, III, 14

'*Mr Thrale had not much Heart* ...'
Thraliana, 564

'*in Consequence of his Agitation* ...'
ibid., 563

'*Not a person to speak to* ...' ibid., 565

'*Here blows a dreadful Wind* ...' ibid.

'*Come friendly Muse!* ...' ibid.

'*Plays out of Number* ...' ibid., 591

6. Hayward, II, 54

7. Redford, IV, 151

8. Ibid., 157

'*Dreadful Event!* ...' *Thraliana*, 568

9. Redford, IV, 150

10. Ibid., 154

11. Ibid., 205

'*I am come here chiefly on my own
Account* ...' *Thraliana*, 569–70

'*but no such Testimony* ...' ibid., 572

'*What is become of him* ...' ibid., 574

'*Mr Chanou told Daniel* ...' ibid., n.4

'*My dearest Piozzi's Miss Chanou* ...'
ibid., 583

'*I saved her in the first attack* ...'
ibid., 580

'all *our Tenderness* ...' ibid.

'*Call the man home* ...' ibid., 584

'*who loves him* ...' ibid., 582

'*I am sometimes ready to think her
treacherous* ...' ibid., 581

12. Lansdowne, The Marquis of (ed.),
The Queeney Letters, 1934, 86–7

'*Here is the most sudden and beautiful
Spring* ...' *Thraliana*, 593

'*who loves my Piozzi* ...' ibid.

13. Bloom, I, 62. Some years later Miss
Nicolson acted as companion to Charlotte

Charpentier, the future wife of Sir Walter Scott.

'*My Daughters parted with me ...*' *Thraliana*, 598–9

14. Bloom, I, 77
'*2: July 1784. The happiest Day of my whole Life I think ...*' *Thraliana.*, 599–600

15. Bloom, I, 72
16. Ibid., 74
17. Ibid.
18. Redford, IV, 338
19. Bloom I, 81–2
20. Redford, IV, 343
21. Bloom, I, 93–4
22. Barrett, II, 271
23. Bloom, I, 98
24. Ibid., 96
25. Lansdowne, 171.
26. Bloom, I, 99
27. Ibid., 101
28. Ibid.
29. Hayward, II, 63
30. Bloom, I, 107
31. Ibid., V, 194
'*we part in Peace, and Love, and Harmony ...*' *Thraliana*, 611
'*we parted coldly, not unkindly ...*' ibid., 612

19. Second Marriage, First Honeymoon

1. Tyson and Guppy, 191
2. When she got to Paris she thought it worth petitioning the Controller-General of Finances, Charles Alexandre de Calonne, for their return – 'My Republican Spirit boyl'd a little,' she wrote. It is not known whether she was successful.
3. Tyson and Guppy, 197
4. Ibid., 206
5. Ibid.
'*The Italians talk a great deal ...*' *Thraliana*, 614
'*No letters from Miss Thrale tho' ...*' ibid.
6. *Observations and Reflections Made in the Course of a Journey Through France,*

Italy and Germany, 18–19 (quotations taken from the edition edited by Herbert Barrows published in 1967)
7. Ibid., 20.
8. Ibid., 21. Hester's servants, on the other hand, thought he resembled John the Baptist.
9. Bloom, I, 116.
10. Lysons is described in the *Oxford Dictionary of National Biography* as 'an excitable, vigorous, and ambitious man, with a loud voice and a penetrating eye'. He later acquired a reputation as an antiquarian and became a favourite of the Royal Family. In 1803 he was made Keeper of the Records in the Tower of London.
11. Bloom, I, 119
12. *Observations*, I, 45
13. Bloom, I, 116
'*I took Voltaire's Works out of her Closet ...*' *Thraliana*, 615
'*Yesterday I received a Letter from M*r* Baretti ...*' ibid., 615–6
'*I have got D*r* Johnson's Picture here ...*' *Thraliana*, 617. Queeney had sat to the portrait painter George James in Bath.
14. Bloom, I, 120
15. *Life*, IV, 411
16. Blunt, M., *Mrs. Montagu*, '*Queen of the Blues*', 2 vols, 1925, II, 165
17. Ibid.
18. *Morning Post*, 4 March 1785
19. Kippis had written a life of Captain Cook and was the editor of *Biographia Britannica*, the *DNB* of its day, a publication capable of rousing strong feelings. 'Shall I beg you to transcribe the passage in which Dr Kippis abuses my father and me,' Horace Walpole wrote to his friend Cole in 1778, 'for I shall not buy the new edition, only to purchase abuse on me and mine' (*Walpole Correspondence*, 2, 90).
'*I think my Anecdotes too few ...*' *Thraliana*, 625
20. Bloom, I, 125
'*Here am I! ...*' *Thraliana*, 628

'Mʳ Boswell, (who I plainly see is the Authour) ...' ibid., 629–30

21. St James's Chronicle, 8 January 1785

22. Bloom, I, 125. Johnson had also thought highly of Lort. He had proposed him for membership of the Club three years previously, but he had been blackballed.

23. Ibid., 131–2
'The Country People hereabouts ...' Thraliana, 631

24. Lansdowne, 194

25. Bloom, I, 131
'I asked a very pretty Woman ...' Thraliana 636. The confessor, that is to say, was used to it.
'No Footman here is unmarried ...' ibid., 636–7
'the Intercalations of these People ...' ibid., 637
'I have always been partial to Peter ...' ibid., 638

26. Harvard Piozziana, II, 40–1

27. Bloom, I, 134

28. In the event London had to wait three years. Marchesi accepted an offer from Catherine the Great of a three-year contract at 1,500 guineas a year, together with a house and carriage; appalled by the climate of St Petersburg, he remained only for a year. In 1796 he was acclaimed as a national hero when he refused to sing for Napoleon on his entry into Milan.

29. Bloom, 140

30. Ibid., 141

31. Observations, 103

32. Ibid., 129

33. Ibid., 130

34. Ibid., 132

35. Ibid., 136

36. Harvard Piozziana, II, 55–6

37. Bloom, I, 148

38. Ibid., 155

39. Ibid., 156

40. Lansdowne, 207

41. Bloom, I, 143

42. Ibid., 146

43. Ibid., 156–7. Hester confessed to being put 'a little out of countenance' by the Cardinal's opening gambit when they were introduced: 'Well, madam! You never saw one of us red-legged partridges before I believe; but you are going to Rome I hear, where you will find such fellows as me no rarities' (ibid., 144).

44. Ibid., 160

45. When Horace Walpole saw a copy of the Miscellany the following spring he dismissed the contributors as 'a 'constellation of ignes-fatui [who] have flattered one another as if they were real stars'. But he had words of praise for 'a short and sensible and genteel preface by La Piozza' (Walpole Correspondence, 25, 633–5).

46. Observations, 162

47. Smith, Orianne, 'British Women Writers and Eighteenth-Century Representations of the Improvvisatrice', CW3 Journal, Issue 2 (Winter 2004).

20. The Day War Broke Out

1. She blamed her illness on the sirocco, the strong south to south-easterly wind that blows from Africa. 'One of the Scirocco Winds seized me Suddenly when I had often laughed at those that talked of its Effects,' she told Lysons (Bloom, I, 167).

2. Ibid., 165

3. Ibid., 164

4. Ibid., 165, 166

5. Observations, 170

6. Ibid., 171

7. Ibid.

8. Bloom, 165

9. Ibid., 168

10. Ibid.

11. Lansdowne, 215
'It was very delightful ...' Thraliana, 642–3

12. Observations, 184

13. Thonius Phillips van Leeuwenhoek (1632–1732), a tradesman and scientist

from Delft, known for his work on the improvement of the microscope and his contributions to the establishment of microbiology.

14. *Observations*, 190

15. Bloom, I, 171–2

16. Ibid., 171. Hester sanitized her quotation from *The Tempest* for Lyson's benefit. What Shakespeare actually wrote was 'Monster, I do smell all horse-piss, at which my nose is in great indignation.'

17. *Observations*, 223

18. Bloom, I, 170

19. The editor's taste had not improved significantly by 3 February: 'Signora *Piozzi*, finding the air of Italy by no means so prolific as she expected, proposes with her *cara sposa* to *people a Roman colony*, somewhere in Britain; – Bath, or near it, is the elected spot.'

20. Bloom, I, 180–1

21. *Walpole Correspondence*, 13, 337

22. Lustig, Irma S. and Pottle, Frederick A. (eds), *Boswell: The English Experiment, 1785–9*, 1986, 1323

23. Although Hester returned Boswell's Journal to him without comment, Johnson later reported to him what she had thought of it: 'Mrs. Thrale was so entertained by your "Journal", that she almost read herself blind,' he wrote. And he added, 'She has a great regard for you' (Redford, II, 266).

24. Bloom, I, 176

25. Tyson and Guppy, 43

26. Hyde, 1972, 105

27. The lines occur in Act V Scene 1.

28. Bloom, I, 191

29. *Johns. Misc.*, i, 351

30. Waingrow, Marshall (ed.), *The Correspondence and Other Papers of James Boswell Relating to the Making of the Life of Johnson*, 1970, 140–3

21. 'Our Magic Lanthorn'

1. *English Review*, vii (1786)

2. *Gentleman's Magazine*, lvi (1786)

3. *Monthly Review*, lxxiv (1986)

4. Roberts, William, *Memoirs of the Life and Correspondence of Mrs. Hannah More*, 4 vols, 1834, ii, 16

5. *Walpole Correspondence*, 25, 636

6. Ibid., 640–1

7. James Macpherson was the supposed translator of the Gaelic poem 'Ossian' which Johnson had pronounced an imposture. When Macpherson threatened him with physical violence, Johnson returned a robust reply: 'I will not desist from detecting what I think a cheat, from any fear of the menaces of a Ruffian.' He also equipped himself with a stout oak stick, with a knob on the end the size of an orange.

8. McCarthy, William, *Hester Thrale Piozzi: Portrait of a Literary Woman*, 1985, 98. McCarthy elaborates this point later in his analysis: 'As a writer, Boswell had no natural quarrel with Johnson; therefore he never comes to grips with Johnson's writings. He merely admires them sentimentally. Piozzi, never a sentimentalist of Johnson or of anything else (she is much too fierce for that), resembles Johnson both in temperament and in her acquired literary behavior. Like Johnson, she is a literary fighter, and she wins her fights by many of the same means' (ibid., 126).

9. *Thraliana*, xxiv

10. *The London Chronicle*, 18–20 April 1786. Boswell also churned out a further eight largely obscene verses, supposedly composed by Hester, in which she describes her present state of married bliss. These remain unpublished in the decent obscurity of the Yale University Library.

11. *Observations*, 278–9

12. Ibid., 274–5. The handsome and vain Giovan Angelo Braschi had been elected Pope in 1775. An ostentatious patron of the arts and a notorious nepotist, his papacy was something of an economic disaster, largely because of the

heavy debts incurred by attempts to drain
the Pontine marshes. He was forced into
exile in 1798 after Rome fell to the French
and died the following year.

    13. Bloom, I, 198, n.1

    14. Ibid., 194

    15. Ibid., 196, n.5

    16. Ibid., 196, n.1. Two years earlier
Hester had described James in *Thraliana*
as 'an Ignorant Man, and I have heard – a
vicious one – but exquisitely skilled in
Mimickry, and Arch Imitation'. Some
years later, he made another appearance:
'Mrs Greatheed & I call those Fellows
Finger-twirlers; – meaning a decent word
for Sodomites: old Sir Horace Mann & Mr
James the Painter had such an odd way of
twirling their Fingers in Discourse; – & I
see Suetonius tells the same thing of one
of the Roman Emperors' (*Thraliana*, 584,
875, n.1).

    17. Lansdowne, 223

    18. Bloom, I, 199
'*Oh if one could live alone in Italy ...*'
Thraliana, 645, n.2

    19. Bloom, I, 201. Lysons, writing at
the end of July, passed on Cadell's view
that publication of the Letters should
be delayed until after the appearance of
Hawkins's edition of Johnson's *Works* –
'unless you wish them to be serviceable
to the Knight, in his compilations'. He
added, 'By the way, no great matters are
expected from this promised piece of
Biography' (ibid., 208).

    20. Lansdowne, 228

    21. Ibid., 228–9
'*What a glorious Country is ours! ...*'
Thraliana, 662

    22. Bloom, I, 203

    23. Ibid., 204

    24. Claude Fleury (1640–1723), French
ecclesiastical historian. His *Cathéchisme
historique*, published in 1679, was judged
to be tainted with Jansenism, and placed
on the Index.
'*Well! I am now about to close my*

Residence in Italy ...' *Thraliana*, 676–7

    25. Lansdowne, 235

    26. *Observations*, 359

    27. Lansdowne, 235
'*Saltsburg was pleasant to me ...*'
Thraliana, 678

    28. Bloom, I, 218

    29. *Reminiscences of Michael Kelly of
the King's Theatre and Theatre Royal Drury
Lane*, 2 vols, 1826, I, 249–50

    30. Lansdowne, 239

    31. Ibid., 237

    32. Bloom, I, 222–3

    33. *Observations*, 386

    34. Ibid. Lobositz, or Lowositz
as Hester called it, is the present-day
Lovosice in the Czech Republic.

    35. Lansdowne, 242
'*Was I sixty Years old ...*' *Thraliana*,
678–9

    36. Bloom, I, 224, letter to William
Parsons, 8 December 1786

    37. Rylands *Eng. MS.* 536. The source
of this canard is unknown. It was given
currency by the *European Magazine* in a
biographical sketch of Hester published
that autumn: 'Public report hints, that Mrs.
Piozzi will return to England in the course
of next winter, and that her husband will
then be naturalized, and assume the name
of Salisbury' (x, 1786, pp. 5–6).
'*Sir Lucas Pepys ...*' *Thraliana*, 681

    38. Lansdowne, 244. A month later,
however, writing to Lysons from Brussels,
she had changed her mind: 'Potzdam,
Berlin, and Sans Soucy, exceeded all my
Imagination' (Bloom, I, 226).

    39. Lansdowne, 245–6
'*Brunswick, Hanover, & Osnaburgh ...*'
Thraliana, 679
'*Ay Brussells was something like
indeed ...*' ibid. The Princesse Gou-
vernante, as Hester calls her, was the
Archduchess Christina, daughter of the
Empress Maria Theresa. She was the wife
of Prince Albert of Saxony, the Governor
of the Austrian Netherlands.

40. Bloom, I, 230

41. Lansdowne, 248. Queeney's companion was a Mrs Cochran, a widow of about forty who had been recommended to her by Lady Yates.

22. *Pen and Ink Conversation*

1. *Morning Herald*, 17 March, 1787

2. Hyde, 1972, 116, n.1

3. The house was pulled down only after the Second World War. It stood on the site of the present Vogue House.

4. Hayward, I, 299
'*We had a very fine Assembly ...*' *Thraliana*, 681

5. Michele Mortellari, a native of Sicily, was a composer and singing master who had recently settled in London.
'*As for seeing our Daughters ...*' *Thraliana*, 679

6. The fees were over 100 guineas. Boswell would later send his daughter Veronica there.
'*I find M*^r *Smith ...*' *Thraliana*, 681. 'Staring' is used here in a now obsolete sense to mean sensational.
'*while she is at School ...*' ibid., 680
'*This is a pretty House ...*' *Thraliana*, 681. Mrs Montagu and her circle also kept their distance, something which Hester noted with no more than a mild shrug: 'The old Blue Stocking Society as the folks call them, appear to be shy of me this Spring' (ibid.).
'*perhaps she keeps them for some professed enemy of mine ...*' ibid., 680. Hawkins had published part of a letter he had received from Johnson when he was in Ashbourne in the summer of 1784: 'Poor Thrale! I thought that either her virtue or her vice would have restrained her from such a marriage. She is now become a subject for her enemies to exult over, and for her friends, if she has any left, to forget or pity' (Redford, IV, 351).

7. Bloom, I, 235

8. Twenty years earlier, when the question of publishing a letter of his had arisen, Johnson himself had entreated his correspondent to have it revised – 'there may perhaps be some negligent lines written' (Redford, I, 281).

9. Redford, II, 228

10. Bloom, I, 234
'*Foreigners have a much stronger Manner ...*' *Thraliana*, 685
'*thanking me for my* polite Attentions ...' ibid.

11. Bloom, I, 237
'*I have got the Child home ...*' *Thraliana*, 686
'*The Harrass of these Letters ...*' ibid.

12. Bloom, I, 239

13. Her relationship with Johnson had been uneasy. This was partly because she was a close friend of Lucy Porter, and did not take kindly to Johnson's marriage to Lucy's mother, Tetty. She was also the granddaughter of John Hunter, the former headmaster of the town's grammar school, and was not amused when Johnson declared that because of the strong family resemblance, he trembled at the very sight of her.

14. *Letters of Anna Seward*, 6 vols, 1811, I, 339–40

15. 'I propose to try on Monday to seek a new wife,' he wrote in his diary on 22 April 1753, 'without derogation from dear Tetty's memory.' Baretti told Hester that when Miss Boothby died three years later, Johnson 'was almost distracted with his grief' (*Johns. Misc.*, i, 257).

16. Bloom, 242, n.5
'*He was a cheating fellow ...*' *Thraliana*, 690
'*Chester Wall ...*' ibid.

17. Bloom, I, 245
'*The Inns ...*' *Thraliana*, 691

18. Bloom, I, 244–5
'*Ours was a Match of mere Prudence ...*' *Thraliana*, 692
'*My Health is going very fast ...*' ibid.

19. Bloom, I 244
'*who is likewise a Conspirator in forming this new Play ...*' *Thraliana*, 693
20. Her salary was £10 a year.
'*I know of only six professed Enemies ...*' *Thraliana*, 694
21. Bloom, I, 248
'*The Books written by that Lady ...*' *Thraliana*, 695
'*How little I thought ...*' ibid., 703
'*I did not miscarry then ...*' ibid., 704
22 Harvard *Piozziana*, II, 100
'*The Care and Attention ...*' *Thraliana*, 704
'There *was a Man ...*' ibid., 705
'*Here comes Mr Cator ...*' ibid.
'*Hastings's Tryal ...*' ibid., 709
'*The Letters are out ...*' ibid., 711

23. *God Save the King!*

1. Hyde, 1972, 126, fn. 45
2. *Morning Post*, 12 March 1788
3. *World*, 11 March 1788
4. *Monthly Review*, 78:324–31
5. *Memoirs*, ii, 101. She also recorded an acerbic remark by Burke: 'How many maggots have crawled out of that great body!'
6. Blunt, ii, 278
'*My letter to Jack Rice ...*' *Thraliana*, 711
7. McCarthy, 143
8. Wollstonecraft, Mary, *A Vindication of the Rights of Woman*, 1792, 102–3
9. McCarthy, 61
10. 7 March 1788, *The English Experiment*, 194
11. Waingrow, 272–3
12. *European Magazine* 13:313–17, 393–9; 14:89–99
13. Hayward, i, 315
14. Bloom, I, 275
15. Charles James Fox said that when his 1783 India Bill was being debated Sayers's caricatures had done him more mischief than the debates in Parliament or the works of the press.

16. Harvard *Piozziana*, II, 123–4
'*Miss Hamilton who is* Italian Mad ...' *Thraliana*, 712–3
'*There was some hesitation in the Public ...*' ibid., 713
'*They have shelfed it*' ibid., 715
'*The inflexible Sisters ...*' ibid., 717
'*with the Water quite washing ye Wall ...*' ibid., 718
'*I will write my Travels ...*' ibid., 717
'*Here is very little Society ...*' ibid., 718
17. Bloom, I, 265
18. Ibid., 275. A notably ugly man, Francis Hastings, tenth Earl of Huntingdon was now close to sixty. He had served as bearer of the sword of state at the coronation of George III and had been Lord Lieutenant of the West Riding of Yorkshire.
19. Ibid., 267
'*it is the 5th we have passed together ...*' *Thraliana*, 718
20. Bloom, I, 263
21. Ibid., 267
22. Ibid., 270
23. Ibid., 269
'*I am strangely lowspirited ...*' *Thraliana*, 720
24. Bloom, I, 281
25. Ibid., 278
26. Ibid., 283
27. Ibid., 284
28. Ibid., 285
29. Ibid., 286
30. Ibid., 289, n.17. It was only in 1966, in an article in the *British Medical Journal,* that Ida Macalpine and Richard Hunter convincingly identified the king's illness as porphyria, a rare hereditary condition that can cause severe neurological damage.
'*Fox, Burke, Sheridan ...*' *Thraliana*, 722. 'We are turning Democrates here wholly from love of the King,' she added in a footnote; ''tis very odd to see a Spirit of *Loyalty* operating to make us all *Republicans*.'

'*Among ten Thousand ...*' ibid., 725. Mrs
Siddons had taken the play to Windsor in
the autumn to read it to the Royal Family,
but her visit had coincided with one of the
King's first paroxysms.

'*Our King ...*' ibid., 731

31. *The World*, 11 March 1789

'*So may God of his mercy ...*' *Thraliana*,
732–3. The ode appeared in the *World* on
11 March, the 10–12 March issue of the *St
James's Chronicle* and the *Public Advertiser*
on 12 March.

'*I have a great deal more Prudence ...*'
ibid., 726

'*She says Piozzi and I ...*' ibid., 735

'*Mrs Siddons dined in a Coterie ...*'
ibid., 729

'*We hardly looked at each other ...*' ibid.,
728–9

'*I met Sophy Streatfield ...*' ibid., 738

'*Mʳˢ Garrick ...*' ibid., 729

'*I love Dr More ...*', ibid., 748

32. James Duff (1729–1809), Earl
Fife in the peerage of Ireland, sat in
the Commons as the MP for Elgin. His
agricultural improvements twice earned
him the gold medal of the Society for the
Encouragement of Arts, Manufactures,
and Commerce.

33. Hayward, II, 70

24. *Land of the Mountain ...*

'*if I go with him ...*' *Thraliana*, 721

'*I long to see Green Fields ...*' ibid., 749

1. Bloom, I., 299

2. Ibid., 303

3. Ibid., 306

4. Rogers was offered the poet
laureateship on the death of Wordsworth,
but declined the honour in deference to
Tennyson.

5. Bloom I, 326, n.7

'*My Book is budding ...*' *Thraliana*, 749

6. Bloom, I, 299

7. *Morning Post*, 15 June 1789

8. *European Magazine* 16 (1789): 332

9. *Walpole Correspondence*, 42, 244–5,
letter dated 13 June 1789.

10. Bloom, I, 300

11. *Observations*, 2

12. Ibid.

13. Ibid., 93

14. Ibid., 92

15. Bloom, I, 307

16. The cathedral, begun in the twelfth
century, had suffered the attentions of
Scottish parliamentarians in the mid-
seventeenth century, when much of the
nave was destroyed.

17. Bloom, I, 306–7

18. Kemble, who had taken over the
management of Drury Lane the previous
year, had also recently negotiated a seven-
year lease on the Liverpool Theatre.

19. Bloom, I, 314–15

20. Ibid., 321

21. Ibid., 317, 316

22. Ibid., 320

23. Ibid., 332, 331. George Augustus
Polgreen Bridgetower, to give him his full
name, subsequently secured the patronage
of the Prince of Wales, and was for a time
one of the first violinists in the Prince's
private band at the Brighton Pavilion.
Later, in Vienna, he was introduced to
Beethoven, and together they gave the
first performance of what would become
the 'Kreutzer' sonata.

24. Ibid.

25. Ibid., 332

'*Poor Bridgetower! ...*' *Thraliana*, 757

'*'Tis now productive of Sensations ...*'
ibid., 759

'*Mʳ Piozzi talked* half an hour ...'
ibid., 761

'*I met Miss Burney at an Assembly ...*'
ibid., 760–1

'*They say it to ensnare me ...*' ibid., 751

26. Bloom, I, 304

'*I am writing for the Stage ...*' *Thraliana*, 752–3

'*I hear Baretti's Enmity towards me ...*'
ibid., 752

27. The piece was not without its admirers. Frederick Augustus Hervey, fourth Earl of Bristol and eccentric absentee Bishop of Derry, confessed to being convulsed with fits of laughter, and declared it to be *'de la main d'un maître'* (Childe-Pemberton, W., *The Earl Bishop*, 2 vols, 1924, ii, 440).

'We are going to Streatham ...' *Thraliana*, 767

28. Her daughters, that is to say – to whom, under Thrale's will, the property would pass on her death.

25. Streatham Regained

'Well! We have lived more merrily than wisely ...' *Thraliana*, 771

'If I go first ...' ibid., 768

'the Plate so fine too ...' ibid., 775

'Surely to doubt one Word ...' ibid., 776

'I do myself verily think ...' ibid.

'She speculated ...' ibid., 780

'With Regard to Identity of Body ...' ibid., 781

'I think mighty well of her Virtue ...' ibid., 769

1. *The Hothams: being the Chronicles of the Hothams of Scarborough and South Dalton from their hitherto Unpublished Family Papers*, 2 vols, London, 1918, 2, 250. Siddons was writing to Sir Charles Hotham, 8th Baronet, who had retired from the army as a major-general in 1775 and had many friends in the theatrical profession.

'My last Set of Friends ...' *Thraliana*, 771–2

'The thermometer stood this day ...' ibid., 771

'Mr Piozzi gave his Haymakers ...' ibid., 772

'Poor Piozzi ...' ibid., 782–3. 'If I could have got Floretta on the Boards of old Drury,' she mused elsewhere, 'She would have paid the Mason's Bill perhaps' (ibid., 772).

2. Bloom, I, 338–41. Jonathan Sterns, attorney at law, was a Harvard graduate who in 1797 was appointed solicitor-general of Nova Scotia. He died the following year after being severely beaten in a street fight with the province's attorney-general, an Irish emigré called Richard John Uniacke.

3. A note of who had been present at her marriage was also required.

'Dr Parker, Mr Hale of Kings Walden ...' *Thraliana*, 807–8

'My Property in America ...' ibid., 789

'I am not sorry ...' ibid., 783

4. The thirty-three-year-old Vancouver had sailed with Cook on both his second and third voyages.

'the most pious among them ...' *Thraliana*, 784

'Poor dear dead Mrs. Byron! ...' ibid., 787

'I loved Dr Lort ...' ibid., 787. Delap lived at Lewes, in Sussex.

5. Bloom, I, 346

6. Ibid., 348

'I believe my oldest Friend ...' *Thraliana*, 801

7. It was in fact shortly before her twelfth birthday.

8. Rather more than £30 million today.

'Thus have his poor Girls ...' *Thraliana*, 804

'Our fears of a War with Russia ...' ibid., 805. Hester held in her memory a huge store of not always perfectly remembered prose and verse. It is not 'sleeping Justice' that Milton endows with a 'red right hand' in Book II of *Paradise Lost* but 'intermitted vengeance'.

'may she dear Soul! ...' ibid.

'our Establishment here is too magnificent ...' ibid., 797

'Now I have had two Husbands ...' ibid., 808

9. Count Gasparo Gozzi (1713–86), Venetian critic and dramatist much admired for his elegant style.

10. William Beckford (1760–1844), who had inherited the greatest sugar fortune in the West Indies at the age of ten, was obliged to go abroad in 1785 because of a homosexual relationship with the son of Viscount Courtenay. Sodomy at the time was a capital offence.

'*The Wits expect me to tremble ...*' *Thraliana*, 807

11. *Morning Post*, 22 February 1790
'*That poor Man ...*' *Thraliana*, 809–10

26. *Bozzy's Revenge*

'*The Death of my Son ...*' *Thraliana*, 811
'*We drank her Health ...*' ibid.

1. Clifford, 356
'*I have written a pamphlet ...*' *Thraliana*, 812–13
'*Piozzi likes the Money ...*' ibid., 813
'*The View from our Cottage ...*' ibid., 814–15
'*Very astonishing ...*' ibid., 820

2. Bloom, I, 368

3. Ibid., 369, n.3
'*This Man is a Hero of Rascality ...*' *Thraliana*, 820
'*You have catered here ...*' ibid., 836
'*Mr Kemble has sent for my little Drama ...*' *Thraliana*, 820–1. The actress Elizabeth Farren was, like Sarah Siddons, the daughter of touring players. Charles James Fox had been an early suitor; she was now the constant companion of the Earl of Derby. She did not, however, marry him until the death of his first wife in 1797.
'*who is God be praised ...*' ibid., 822
'*Yet my Duty teaches ...*' ibid., 824

4. Bloom, I, 375
'*Mr Piozzi is angry ...*' *Thraliana*, 829
'*Pretty News! ...*' ibid., 833

5. Henry Drummond was one of the thirteen children of the fourth viscount of Strathallan, an officer in the army of the Young Pretender, who played a key role in the 1745 rising and was killed at Culloden.

6. Bloom, II, 46–7

7. Ibid., 47, n.5
'*The sight of our Family ...*' *Thraliana*, 834
'*My darling Mother ...*' ibid., 835, n.1

8. Hester enlisted the help of Lysons to have the banns erased.
'*he is now empowered ...*' *Thraliana*, 834, n.1
'*dismal enough ...*' ibid., 836
'*Let us be careful of our health ...*' ibid., 835
'*a two Volume Book ...*' ibid., 837–8
'*We sent for Haygarth ...*' *Thraliana*, 847. John Haygarth (1740–1827), had been physician to Chester Infirmary since 1766. A Fellow of the Royal Society, he was known for his pioneering work in the treatment of fever and the prevention of smallpox.

9. Bloom, II, 90–1

10. Ibid., 70

11. Ibid., 96. The Piozzis had been so indignant at what they considered the inadequate response of Henry Drummond that they had closed their account at the bank.

12. Bloom, II, 98
'*'Tis now expected ...*' *Thraliana*, 851–2

13. Bloom, II, 98

14. Ibid., 101–2
'*A new & strange Event ...*' *Thraliana*, 856

15. Bloom, II, 109
'*spoke of no Business ...*' *Thraliana*, 856
'Dinner Concert Supper *and* Ball ...' ibid., 857–8

16 Bloom, II, 549–52
'*Miss Thrale has been here ...*' *Thraliana*, 859
'*I wonder whether God Almighty ...*' ibid., 859–60

27. *Land of Her Fathers*

1. Bloom, II, 144

2. Ibid., 154

3. Ibid., 164–5

4. Alvise Zenobio, an immensely wealthy Venetian nobleman of radical views, had been in Britain since 1784. He managed to thwart the attempts of the government to deport him by getting himself arrested for debt and sent to prison.

5. *Walpole Correspondence*, 12, ii, 92–3

6. Lord Peter's brown loaf, in Swift's *A Tale of a Tub*, contained 'the quintessence of beef, mutton, veal, venison, partridge, plum-pudding, and custard'.

7. Several sections were also reprinted on poorer-quality paper and without engravings for use in schools.

8. Hayward, II, 317

9. Scolar Press, Menston, Yorkshire, 1968

'*I see my Neighbours* ...' *Thraliana*, 883

'*When Mr Pio{{z}}{{i}} rides to Brynbella* ...' ibid., 886–7

10. Bloom, II, 185

11. Ibid., 190

12. Ibid., 208

13. Mrs Radcliffe's Gothic novel had been published earlier in the year.

14. Bloom, II, 194

'*Mr. Yorke of D'Affrenalli* ...' *Thraliana*, 917

'*Yet tho' I have had my Share* ...' ibid., 907. Lloyd was a bencher of Middle Temple and a Fellow of the Royal Society.

'*153 Persons guillotined* ...' ibid., 885

'*Cecy vexes me* ...' ibid., 891

15. William Makepeace Thackeray (1769–1849), a Cambridge graduate, was the son of an old friend of Chappelow's. One of his cousins would become the father of the novelist.

'*Well! Cecilia Thrale has given her Word* ...' *Thraliana*, 918–19

16. Bloom, II, 256

'*One is not oneself quite Young enough* ...' *Thraliana*, 920–1. Nor was she best pleased to hear that Susan had

been invited to the wedding festivities at Carlton House.

'*if they wait till he is of Age* ...' *Thraliana*, 929–30

'*throws out threatenings* ...' ibid., 930

'*Oh Lord! Oh Lord!* ...' ibid., 931

17. Bloom, II, 264–5

18. *Oracle and Public Advertiser*, 18 June 1795

19. *True Briton*, 24 July 1795

'*This House is too expensive* ...' *Thraliana*, 932–3

'*I have been happier* ...' ibid., 934

'*Drummond is Married I hear* ...' ibid., 934, n.3. Drummond's bride was the daughter of a London banker. Like the Mostyns, they eloped, and were married at Gretna Green.

'*On this happy Morn^g* ...' ibid., 941

28. '*Justice! The Law!*'

1. He would have presented them today with a bill for some £1.5 million.

2. Clifford, 383

'*They have behaved very well* ...' *Thraliana*, 946–7

'*Lord Madam! said he* ...' ibid., 956

'*It was often at my Tongue's end* ...' ibid., 946, n.4

'*Good God!* ...' ibid., 944–5

'*they have threatened* ...' ibid., 943

3. Bloom, II, 505

4. Ibid., 294

5. Clifford, 385

6. Bloom, II, 335. She was writing to the Reverend Daniel Lysons, Samuel Lysons's elder brother.

7. Ibid., 316–17

8. Ibid., 317, n.2

'*This Day I determined on a Project* ...' *Thraliana*, 951–2

'*I should like to begin* ...' ibid., 952, n.2

'*Mostyn's Grandfather was a famous Fellow* ...' *Thraliana*, 962, n.1

'*Cecilia's Maid says her Mistress* ...' ibid.

'The Maids think there is something ...'
ibid., 955

9. Bloom, II, 339

10. Ibid., 344–5

11. Ibid., 347

'Such Proceedings ...' Thraliana, 954,
959–60

12. Bloom, II, 365

'The Boy has proved his Manhood ...'
Thraliana, 967, n.3

13. Bloom, II, 392

'We are going to Streatham Park ...'
Thraliana, 971

14. Bloom, II, 404–5

15. Nine years later Hester makes
one last brief mention of him in *Thraliana* – along with Crutchley, who had
also recently died: 'Cator & Critchley
likewise, once my Copartners – Coexecu-
tors; Friends, Enemies, Indifferents – but
gone!! no longer Friends *or* Enemies.'

16. Bloom, II, 436, n.6

'M Murphy plagued me ...' Thraliana,
973, n.3

'They will not let me go to Her *...'*
ibid., 974

'I hate these Country Accoucheurs ...'
ibid. The crochet, much like a forceps in
design, had a sharp tooth at the end of
each slim blade. This could pierce and
be embedded in the head of a foetus for
removal. They were often used when the
foetus was already dead and the condition
of the mother critical.

'M Piozzi asked me Yesterday ...' ibid.,
975–6

17. Bloom, II, 467

18. Ibid., 422

'I liked M Piozzi's Brother ...' Thraliana, 639, n.1

'Oh what a Melancholy New year ...'
Thraliana, 983–4

19. She had been plagued for some
time with rheumatic pains in her right
arm.

'Italy is ruined, *& England* threatened ...' *Thraliana,* 984

29. Piccolino

'I am ill myself ...' Thraliana, 985

1. Bloom, II, 478

2. Ibid., 323, n.2

3. Ibid., 478

4. *Thraliana,* 957, n.2

5. Bloom, II, 478

6. *The Times,* 21 March 1798

'He pays 550 pr ann ...' Thraliana, 985

7. Bloom, II, 319

8. Ibid., 329

'he said we would not Quarrel *...'*
Thraliana, 986. Sir Francis Wronghead,
a credulous Tory squire, is a character
in Vanbrugh and Cibber's *The Provok'd
Husband.*

9. Bloom, 482

10. Ibid., 491

11. *True Briton,* 18–28 April, 1798

12. Bloom, II, 495

13. Ibid., 507

14. *Retrospection: or a Review of the
Most Striking and Important Events, Characters, Situations, and Their Consequences,
which the Last Eighteen Hundred Years
Have Presented to the View of Mankind,* 2
vols, 1801, ii, 437

'Strange Conduct ...' Thraliana, 990, n.2

15. Bloom, II, 534

16. Ibid., 547

17. Ibid., 541

18. Ibid., III, 49

19. Ibid., 55

20. Ibid., 49. Count Luigi Fenarole
was the boy's godfather.

21. Ibid.

'Mrs Wynne & Miss Mostyn ...'
Thraliana, 995

22. Bloom, III, 59

23. Ibid., 62

24. Genest, John, *Some Account of the
English Stage from the Restoration in 1660
to 1830,* 10 vols, 1832, vii, 459

25. Bloom, II, 529

26. Ibid., III, 55–6

27. Rodger, N. A. M., 'Nelson,
Horatio, Viscount Nelson (1758–1805)',

Oxford Dictionary of National Biography, Oxford University Press, online edn, May 2006

28. Bloom, III, 89

'*Since I left Wales* ...' *Thraliana*, 993

29. Bloom, III, 78. She was scornful of her son-in-law: 'I hear *He* is so full of the Notice he received from the Prince of Wales, that no *other* Company can please him:– They are hasting to London *now* 'tis said, that the Acquaintance may not be lost for want of due Cultivation.'

30. Ibid., 70

31. Ibid., 72

32. Ibid., 75

'& I *danced* in the *old Hall* ...' *Thraliana*, 1000

33. Bloom, III, 102

34. Ibid., 106

35. Ibid., 79

36. Ibid., 100

'*Can such Things* be?' *Thraliana*, 1002

37. Bloom, III, 143–4

'*The Plague is come* ...' *Thraliana*, 1002, n.3

38. Bloom, III, 154

39. Ibid., 158

30. Buzzers and Stingers

1. Bloom, III, 177–8

2. Ibid., 180

3. Ibid., 197

4. Hayward, I, 346

5. Bloom, III, 216. Hester is quoting from the opening air of a musical farce called *The Deserter* by Charles Dibdin, which had been popular on the London stage since the early 1770s.

6. Ibid., 216. The main hall was demolished in 1817. The gatehouse and farm buildings still stand today.

7. Ibid., 429

8. Russell, J., *Memoirs, Journal and Correspondence of Thomas Moore*, 8 vols, 1853–56, iv, 329

9. Bloom, III, 201

'*an Indurated Gland in the* Mammelle droite ...' *Thraliana*, 1007–8

10. Bloom, III, 235

'*The Garden gains surprisingly* ...' *Thraliana*, 1012–13

11. A Rowlandson caricature shows him hammering out a book on an anvil. 'The Bookselling Blacksmith', says the caption, 'one of the King's New Friends'.

12. Bloom, III, 243

'*remit all past Malice* ...' *Thraliana*, 1014

13. Bloom, III, 263

14. Ibid., 269

15. *The Gentleman's Magazine*, pt 2 (1801): 603

16. *The Anti-Jacobin Review and Magazine*, March 1801, 241–6

17. *Critical Review* 32 (1801), 28–35

18. Bloom, III, 290

19. *British Critic*, April 1802 (19:355–8)

20. Hester wrote the mock review in 'Minced Meat for Pyes', a notebook she began in the 1790s when she was at work on *Retrospection*. Quoted in Merritt, P., *Piozzi Marginalia*, 1925, 77–9.

21. Clifford, 2nd edition, 1987, xliv

22. Preface to *Retrospection*, vol. i, viii–xi

23. *Oracle*, 22 April 1799

31. 'Cruel Death'

1. Wickham, H. (ed.), *Journals and Correspondence of Thomas Whalley, D.D.*, 2 vols, 1863, ii:188

'*I had more Pleasure* ...' *Thraliana*, 1015

'*I suppose he will add the Order of the Elephant* ...' ibid., 1020–1

2. A paper which Edward Jenner, a doctor in Gloucestershire, had submitted to the Royal Society in 1797 had been rejected as too revolutionary. He conducted further experiments and published his results the following year, coining the word vaccine from the Latin '*vacca*' for cow. His ideas were at first ridiculed, but vaccination soon became widely accepted.

'Here is a pretty Book concerning the Prolongation of Life ...' Thraliana, 1024. The Art of Prolonging Life was a translation of Die Kunst das menschliche Leben ʒu verlängern by the eminent German physician Christoph Wilhelm von Hufeland, which had been published in Vienna and Prague four years previously.

'Mr Dobbs of Ireland must be quite a Lunatic ...' ibid., 1019

3. Bloom, III, 238
4. Ibid., 322
5. Ibid.
6. Ibid., 329–30
7. Ibid., 353
8. Liberty Lovers – Hester is scoffing at those members of the Opposition who had long favoured peace with France.
9. Bloom, III, 365
10. Ibid., 367
11. Ibid., 390
12. Ibid., 397
13. Ibid., 400
14. Ibid., 409

'Mʳ Pioʒʒi's Gout grows upon him ...' Thraliana, 1036

'Poor, Poor fellow! ...' ibid., 1041

'Well! as King Richard Richard says ...' ibid., 1055

15. Bloom, III, 415

'But she has a Strength a toutes Epreuves ...' Thraliana, 1062, n.1

'Cecy complains of her Husband grievously ...' ibid.

16. Charles Dumouriez had served in the French army for more than thirty years before the outbreak of the Revolution. In 1793 he was appointed lieutenant general and given command of the Army of the North, but the following year he defected to the Austrians. He eventually came to England, received a pension and became a valuable adviser to the War Office.

'You see nothing on a lady's Toilette ...' Thraliana, 1056

'The letters written to him ...' ibid., 1064

17. Bloom, IV, 60

'I'll study Hebrew ...' Thraliana, 1065. She heard from Cecilia that Queeney had set herself to study Hebrew six or seven years previously.

18. Bloom, IV, 80, n.8

'Oh Melancholy! ...' Thraliana, 1067

'Here I am then once more ...' ibid., 1071

'Everyone going, going, going ...' ibid., 1080

'The Harvest is in ...' ibid.

19. Bloom, IV, 146

20. Ibid., 153. The painting had originally belonged to the musician C. F. Abel, who was a close friend of the artist's – Gainsborough is said to have given it to him in exchange for a viola da gamba he particularly admired. It is now in the Earl of Shelburne's collection at Bowood.

21. Ibid., 159

22. Ibid., 163

23. Owen, C. H. H., 'Elphinstone, George Keith, Viscount Keith (1746–1823)', Oxford Dictionary of National Biography, Oxford University Press, 2004

24. Bloom, IV, 140

'on my Birthday ...' Thraliana, 1081

'Dear Mr Leman of the Crescent ...' ibid.

25. Clifford, 424, n.1

'Another long cruel Fit of Gout ...' Thraliana, 1087

'Mʳ Whalley has been here on a visit ...' ibid., 1092

26. Bloom, IV, 202

27. Ibid., 174

28. Ibid.

29. Ibid., 196

30. Ibid., 211

31. 'Skeffington is a Character as We say,' Hester wrote in Thraliana, '– a man wearing Rouge, and making it his Point to appear the very Prince of Petits Maitres in Society ... I wonder how he will end, most probably by marrying a Dairy Maid when Threescore, & retiring into the

Country to try for Heirs to the Estate'
(*Thraliana*, 1094).
    '*Strange that I'm not forgotten ...*'
Thraliana, 1092
    32. Bloom, IV, 215
    33. Ibid., 220–1
    '*Every thing most dreaded has ensued ...*'
Thraliana, 1099

32. *Widow Piozzi*

1. Bloom, IV, 227
2. Ibid., 232
3. Ibid., III, 414
4. Ibid., IV, 234
5. Ibid., 240
6. Ibid., 242. Joanna Baillie, the daughter of a Church of Scotland minister, was a poet and playwright. At their house in Hampstead she and her sister Agnes entertained many of the eminent writers and painters and scientists of the day. The Dublin-born Martin Archer Shee was a fashionable portrait painter; he would eventually succeed Lawrence as President of the Royal Academy.
7. Ibid., 246
8. Ibid., 249
9. Ibid., 273
10. Ibid., 283
11. Ibid., 296
12. Ibid., 271
13. Ibid., 319
14. Ibid., 152
15. Ibid., 270. The friend was Joseph Townsend, rector of Pewsey in Wiltshire, well known for his writings on geology.
16. Ibid., 309
17. Ibid., V, 71
18. Ibid., 83
19. Ibid., 85
20. Ibid., 90–1
21. Ibid., 101
22. His allowance of £500 a year would today be worth some £24,000.
23. Bloom, V, 114
24. Ibid.

25. Ibid., 149
26. Ibid., 152
27. Ibid., 154
28. Ibid., 162
29. Ibid., 144
30. Ibid., 182
31. Ibid., 207
32. Ibid., 226
33. Ibid., 225
34. Ibid., 232
35. Ibid., 285. She was writing to the son of her neighbours Sir John and Lady Williams.
36. Ibid., 227
37. Ibid., 306. Hester is quoting from a poem of Goldsmith's called *The Haunch of Venison*, a Poetical Epistle to Lord Clare.

33. *Going, Going, Gone*

1. Bloom, V, 310
2. Ibid., 308
3. Ibid., 311
4. Ibid., 315
5. Ibid., 330
6. Who would have no greater success than Mangin.
7. Bloom, V, 405
8. Ibid., 334
9. Ibid., 366
10. Hayward, ii, 30
11. Bloom, V, 337
12. Ibid., 314
13. Ibid., 322
14. Ibid., 340
15. Ibid., 347
16. Ibid., 355–6. Myddelton also mentioned in passing that Louis-Philippe, the Duke of Orleans, was looking for a house – he had taken refuge in England during Napoleon's Hundred Days. Nothing came of it.
17. Ibid., 359
18. Ibid., 393
19. Ibid., 396–7
20. Ibid., 449

21. Ibid., 451
22. Ibid., 452
23. Sir James's father, who was much the same age as Hester, was also a doctor.
24. Bloom, V, 460
25. The Johnson fetched £378 – something in excess of £20,000 at present-day prices. The Garrick, which went for £183 15s, was bought by Dr Burney's son Charles. The Reynolds self-portrait went for £128 2s.
26. Perhaps she also remembered that it was Murphy who had introduced her to Johnson.
27. Bloom, V, 483
28. Ibid., 487
29. Ibid., 495
30. Ibid., 501
31. Ibid., 498
32. Ibid., 486
33. Ibid., 514
34. Ibid., 516

34. 'Old Bath Cat'

1. The meetings at Spa Fields in Islington were organized by members of the Society of Spencean Philanthropists, who met in small groups all over London, mainly in public houses, and advocated revolution. If it is true that they hoped to overthrow the government by seizing the Tower of London and the Bank of England, they made a very poor fist of it. They succeeded only in looting a gunsmith's shop and killing one onlooker. By nightfall order had been restored.
2. Bloom, VI, 61
3. Ibid., 67
4. Ibid., V, 416
5. Mangin, 19–20
6. *Moore Memoirs*, ii, 299
7. Bloom, VI, 76
8. Tearle, 60
9. Ibid., 61
10. Bloom, VI, 75
11. Ibid., 79–80

12. Ibid., 78, n.2
13. Ibid., 79, n.10
14. Ibid., 87
15. Hemlow, Joyce, et al. (eds), *The Journals and Letters of Fanny Burney (Madame d'Arblay)*, 1791–1840, 12 vols, 1972–84, ix, 390. Although the two women encountered each other from time to time and exchanged the occasional letter, attempts by various members of the Burney family to effect a reconciliation did not succeed. 'Mrs. D'Arblaye's Visits and caresses produced no Renewal of Acquaintance,' Hester wrote coldly to Salusbury (Bloom, V, 194).
16. It would represent some £315,000 today.
17. Bloom, VI, 104
18. Ibid., 118
19. Ibid., 116, n.16
20. *The Sexagenarian; or the Recollections of a Literary Life*, 2 vols, 1817, i, 385–8
21. Bloom, VI, 117
22. Ibid., 128
23. Ibid., 141
24. Ibid., 142
25. Ibid., 146
26. Ibid., 155
27. Flimflams were sometimes improved in the telling. In fact they were married by special licence at St George's, Hanover Square.
28. Elizabeth Gibbes would die five years later 'after a severe and lingering illness'.
29. Bloom, VI, 155
30. Hall, Basil, *Account of a Voyage of Discovery to the West Coast of Corea, and the Great Loo-Choo Island*; London, 1818; Rammohoun Roy: *Translation of an Abridgement Of The Vedant, Or Resolution of all the Veds; The Most Celebrated and Revered Work of Brahminical Theology*; one of a number of pamphlets brought to England from Calcutta in 1816 and 1817.
31. Pollock, Sir Frederick, Bart (ed.),

*Macready's Reminiscences, and Selections
from his Diaries and Letters*, 2 vols, 1875,
i, 109–10

32. Bloom, VI, 189
33. Ibid., 207
34. Ibid., 208–9
35. Ibid., 208
36. Ibid., 226
37. Ibid., 233
38. Ibid., 231

35. Conway

1. *The Examiner*, 27 October 1816
2. Tearle, 33
3. Bloom, VI, 161
4. Ibid., 251
5. Tearle, 79
6. Ibid., 81
7. Bloom, VI, 266. Mrs Siddons rarely
put pen to paper, but Conway's visit
earned Hester a warm note which gave her
much pleasure: 'I saw Mr Conway only for
a few minutes, and those in company with
many talkers,' she wrote, 'but long enough
to satisfy me that you are as young and
gay both in mind and person as in those
never-to-be-forgotten days of felicity at
dear, dear Streatham Park' (quoted in the
Athenæum, 9 August 1861).
8. Tearle, 91
9. Bloom, VI, 273
10. Ibid., 274
11. Ibid., 277–8
12. Ibid., 279
13. Ibid., 307
14. Ibid., 281
15. Ibid., 280
16. Ibid., 298
17. Ibid., 303
18. Tearle, 109
19. Bloom, VI, 270
20. Ibid., 316
21. Ibid., 323
22. Ibid., 326
23. Ibid., 324
24. Ibid., 331

25. Ibid., 333–4. Miss Jagger, possibly an actress, had presumably taken
Charlotte Stratton's place in Conway's
affections.
26. Ibid., 337
27. Tearle, 127
28. Bloom, VI, 355
29. Ibid., 356
30. Mangin, 160

36. Land's End

1. Bloom, VI, 362
2. Ibid., 360
3. Ibid., 362
4. Mrs Pennington shared Hester's
fondness for literary allusion. She is
quoting here a line of Iago's from the
second act of *Othello*.
5. Bloom, VI, 360. Hester sent him
*The Truth of Christianity Demonstrated
In A Dialogue Between a Christian And A
Deist* which had appeared more than fifty
years previously and the newly published
*Anecdotes, Observations, and Characters of
Books and men. Collected from the conversations of Mr. Pope, and other eminent persons
of his time.*
6. Tearle, 142
7. Bloom, VI, 371. Hester was writing
days after the uncovering of the Cato
Street Conspiracy. Those arrested,
members of a group of Spencean Philanthropists, had plotted to murder the entire
Cabinet, seize the Bank of England and
establish a provisional government.
8. Ibid., 383
9. Ibid., 374
10. Ibid., 390, n.8
11. Ibid., 392
12. Ibid., 385
13. Ibid., 394
14. Ibid., 395–6
15. Nelson, Alfred L., and Cross,
Gilbert B. (eds), *Drury Lane Journal:
Selections from James Winston's Diaries,
1819–1827*, 1974, 5

16. Tearle, 134
17. Bloom, VI, 397, n.3
18. Ibid., 395
19. Her £6,000 would be worth upwards of £370,000 today. Its loss meant that her income was reduced by the equivalent of some £12,000 a year.
20. Bloom, VI, 406
21. Ibid., 419
22. Ibid., 418–19
23. Ibid., 420
24. Ibid., 425–6
25. Ibid., 393. Conway's birthday was close to Hester's on January 27.
26. Ibid., 416
27. Tearle, 64
28. Bloom, VI, 452. Miss Willoughby was not, in fact, remotely handsome. She bore a strong resemblance to her father, who was an extremely ugly man; she also had a squint.
29. Ibid., 462
30. Ibid., 490, 495
31. Ibid., 477
32. Ibid., 483–4
33. Ibid., 497
34. Ibid., 498
35. Ibid., 504
36. Ibid., 507

37. Ibid., 512–13
38. Procter (1787–1874) wrote under the pseudonym of Barry Cornwall. A contemporary at Harrow of Byron's, he had originally been a solicitor. The friend of Lamb, Leigh Hunt, Browning and Dickens, he eventually returned to the law and in 1832 was appointed metropolitan commissioner in lunacy.
39. 'He scarce cleared 30£ when all Expences were paid, I hear,' Hester told Miss Williams – £2,000 or so at present-day prices.

37. 'No Epilogue'

1. Bloom, VI, 515, n.2
2. Ibid., 514.
3. Tearle, 202
4. Bloom, VI, 515
5. Tearle, 203
6. *Punch*, 20 June 1863
7. Lansdowne, xxiii
8. The summerhouse remained at Ashgrove until the 1960s. It was later moved to the grounds of Kenwood House in Hampstead, the home in the Thrales' day of Lord Mansfield. It was destroyed in an arson attack in 1991.

Suggestions for Further Reading

Hester's Principal Published Works

Anecdotes of the Late Samuel Johnson, LL.D during the Last Twenty Years of His Life, 1786 (Edition edited by Arthur Sherbo, 1974, Oxford University Press, London)

Letters to and from the Late Samuel Johnson, LL.D to which are added some Poems never before printed, 2 vols, 1788 (Strahan and Cadell, London)

Observations and Reflections made in the Course of a Journey through France, Italy, and Germany, 1787–89 (Edition edited by Herbert Barrow, 1967, University of Michigan Press, Ann Arbor)

British Synonymy; or, an Attempt at Regulating the Choice of Words in Familiar Conversation, 2 vols, 1794 (Facsimile edition, 1968, Scolar Press, Menston)

Retrospection: or a Review of the most striking and important Events, Characters, Situations, and their Consequences, which the last eighteen hundred Years have presented to the View of Mankind, 2 vols, 1801 (Stockdale, London)

Thraliana: The Diary of Mrs. Hester Lynch Thrale (Later Mrs. Piozzi) 1776–1809, ed. Katharine C. Balderston, 2 vols, 1942, 2nd edn, 1951 (Clarendon Press, Oxford)

The Piozzi Letters, Correspondence of Hester Lynch Piozzi (formerly Mrs. Thrale), 1784–1821, ed. Edward A. Bloom and Lillian D. Bloom, 6 vols, 1989–2002 (University of Delaware Press, Newark; Associated University Presses, London and Toronto)

Select Bibliography

Barrett, Charlotte (ed.), Diary and Letters of Madame D'Arblay, with Preface and Notes by Austin Dobson, 6 vols, 1904–05 (Macmillan, London)

Bate, W. Jackson, Samuel Johnson, 1978 (Chatto & Windus, London)

Blunt, R., Mrs. Montagu, 'Queen of the Blues', 2 vols, 1925 (Constable, London)

Brewer, John, The Pleasures of the Imagination: English Culture in the Eighteenth Century, 1997 (Allen Lane, Penguin Press, London)

Broadley, A. M., Doctor Johnson and Mrs Thrale, 1910 (John Lane, Bodley Head, London)

Chapman, R. W. (ed.), The Letters of Samuel Johnson with Mrs. Thrale's Genuine Letters to Him, 3 vols, 1952 (Clarendon Press, Oxford)

Clifford, James L., Hester Lynch Piozzi (Mrs. Thrale), 2nd edn, 1987 (Columbia University Press, New York)

Climenson, E. J. (ed.), Elizabeth Montagu, her Correspondence from 1720 to 1761, 2 vols, 1906 (John Murray, London)

Collison-Morley, Lacy, Giuseppe Baretti and his Friends, 1909 (John Murray, London)

Coote, C., Sketches of the Lives of English Civilians, 1804 (publisher unknown, London)

D'Arblay, Madame, Memoirs of Doctor Burney, arranged from his own manuscripts, from family papers and from personal recollections by his daughter, Madame D'Arblay, 3 vols, 1932 (Edward Moxon, London)

Forbes, W., *An Account of the Life and Writings of James Beattie*, 1806 (Constable, Edinburgh)

Fowler, E. G., *John Salusbury Piozzi Salusbury: The Italian Welshman*, 1993 (Coelion Trust, Ruthin)

Furet, François, *Revolutionary France 1770–1880*, 1992 (Blackwell, Oxford)

Genest, John, *Some Account of the English Stage from the Restoration in 1660 to 1830*, 10 vols, 1832 (H. E. Carrington, Bath)

Greene, Donald J. (ed.), *The Yale Edition of the Works of Samuel Johnson, Volume X, Political Writings*, 1977 (Yale University Press, New Haven, CT)

Hayward, A., *Autobiography Letters and Literary Remains of Mrs. Piozzi (Thrale)*, 2 vols, 2nd edn, 1861 (Longman, Green, Longman and Roberts, London)

Hemlow, Joyce, et al. (eds), *The Journals and Letters of Fanny Burney (Madame d'Arblay)*, 1791–1840, 12 vols, 1972–84 (Clarendon Press, Oxford)

Hill, G. B., *Johnsonian Miscellanies*, 2 vols, 1897 (Constable, London)

Hill, G. B. (ed.), Powell, L. F. (rev.), *Boswell's Life of Johnson, Together with Boswell's Journal of a Tour to the Hebrides and Johnson's Diary of a Journey into North Wales*, 6 vols, 1934–50 (Clarendon Press, Oxford)

Hyde, Mary, *The Impossible Friendship*, 1972 (Harvard University Press, Cambridge, MA)

Hyde Mary, *The Thrales of Streatham Park*, 1977 (Harvard University Press, Cambridge, MA)

Kelly, Michael, *Reminiscences of Michael Kelly of the King's Theatre and Theatre Royal Drury Lane*, 2 vols, 1826 (unknown publisher, London)

Langford, Paul, *A Polite and Commercial People: England 1727–1783*, 1989 (Oxford University Press, Oxford and New York)

Lansdowne, Marquis of (ed.), *The Queeney Letters*, 1934 (Cassell, London)

Lewis. W. S., et al. (eds), *The Yale Edition of Horace Walpole's Correspondence*, 48 vols, 1937–83 (Yale University Press, New Haven, CT)

Lustig, Irma S. and Pottle, Frederick A. (eds), *Boswell: The English Experiment, 1785–9*, 1986 (Heinemann, London)

McCarthy, William, *Hester Thrale Piozzi: Portrait of a Literary Woman*, 1985 (University of North Carolina Press, Chapel Hill and London)

Mangin, E., *Piozziana; or, Recollections of the Late Mrs. Piozzi*, 1833 (Edward Moxon, London)

Morgan, Lee, *Dr. Johnson's 'Own Dear Master': The Life of Henry Thrale*, 1998 (University Press of America, Lanham, MD)

Nelson, Alfred L., and Cross, Gilbert B. (eds), *Drury Lane Journal: Selections from James Winston's Diaries, 1819–1827*, 1974 (Society for Theatre Research, London)

Paulson, Ronald, *Hogarth: Volume 3, Art and Politics, 1750–1764*, 1993 (Rutgers University Press, New Brunswick, NJ)

Pennington, Rev. Montagu (ed.), *Memoirs of the Life of Mrs. Elizabeth Carter*, 1807 (Rivington, London)

Pollock, Sir Frederick, Bart (ed.), *Macready's Reminiscences, and Selections from his Diaries and Letters*, 2 vols, 1875 (Harper, New York)

Porter, Roy, *Enlightenment: Britain and the Creation of the Modern World*, 2000 (Allen Lane, Penguin Press, London)

Redford, Bruce (ed.), *The Letters of Samuel Johnson*, 5 vols, 1992–94 (Princeton University Press, Princeton, NJ)

Reed, Joseph W. and Pottle, Frederick A. (ed.), *Boswell, Laird of Auchinleck, 1778–82*, 1977 (McGraw-Hill, London and New York)

Rizzo, Betty (ed.), *The Early Journals and Letters of Fanny Burney, Volume IV, The Streatham Years: Part II, 1780–1781*, 2003 (McGill-Queen's University Press, Montreal and Kingston, London, Ithaca)

Roberts, William, *Memoirs of the Life and Correspondence of Mrs. Hannah More*, 4 vols, 1834 (R. B. Seeley and W. Burnside, London)

Rompkey, Ronald (ed.), *Expeditions of Honour: The Journal of John Salusbury in Halifax, Nova Scotia, 1749–53*, 1982 (University of Delaware Press, Newark; Associated University Presses, London)

Russell, J., *Memoirs, Journal and Correspondence of Thomas Moore*, 8 vols, 1853–56 (Longman, Brown, Green and Longmans, London)

Ryskamp, Charles, and Pottle, Frederick A. (eds), *Boswell: The Ominous Years 1774–1776*, 1963 (William Heinemann, London)

Sabor, Peter, Cooke, Stewart J. et al. (eds), The *Complete Plays of Frances Burney*, 2 vols, 1995 (William Pickering, London)

Seward, Anna, *Letters of Anna Seward*, 6 vols, 1811 (Constable, Edinburgh)

Tearle, John, *Mrs. Piozzi's Tall Young Beau, William Augustus Conway*, 1991 (Fairleigh Dickinson University Press, Rutherford, Madison, Teaneck; Associated University Presses, London and Toronto)

Tinker, Chauncey B., *The Letters of James Boswell*, 2 vols, 1924 (Clarendon Press, Oxford)

Troide, Lars E. (ed.), *The Early Letters and Journals of Fanny Burney, vol. 2, 1774–1777*, 1991 (Clarendon Press, Oxford)

Troide, Lars E. and Cooke, Stewart J. (eds), *The Early Journals and Letters of Fanny Burney, vol. 3, The Streatham Years, Part I, 1778–1779*, 1994 (Clarendon Press, Oxford)

Tyson, Moses, and Guppy, Henry, *The French Journals of Mrs. Thrale and Doctor Johnson*, 1932 (Manchester University Press and the Librarian, John Rylands Library, Manchester)

Waingrow, Marshall (ed.), *The Correspondence and Other Papers of James Boswell Relating to the Making of the Life of Johnson*, 1970 (Heinemann, London)

Wickham, H. (ed.), *Journals and Correspondence of Thomas Whalley, D.D.*, 2 vols, 1863 (Richard Bentley, London)

Wimsatt, William K. Jr and Pottle, Frederick A. (eds), *Boswell for the Defence, 1769–74*, 1959 (William Heinemann, London)

Wollstonecraft, Mary, *A Vindication of the Rights of Woman*, 1792 (J. Johnson, London)

Index